Jonathan Dickinson

and the formative years of

American Presbyterianism

JONATHAN DICKINSON

AND THE FORMATIVE YEARS OF

AMERICAN PRESBYTERIANISM

Bryan F. Le Beau

THE UNIVERSITY PRESS OF KENTUCKY

Publication of this volume was made possible in part
by a grant from the National Endowment for the Humanities.

Scholarly publisher for the Commonwealth,
serving Bellarmine College, Berea College, Centre
College of Kentucky, Eastern Kentucky University,
The Filson Club Historical Society, Georgetown College,
Kentucky Historical Society, Kentucky State University,
Morehead State University, Murray State University,
Northern Kentucky University, Transylvania University,
University of Kentucky, University of Louisville,
and Western Kentucky University.
All rights reserved

Editorial and Sales Offices: The University Press of Kentucky
663 South Limestone Street, Lexington, Kentucky 40508-4008

Library of Congress Cataloging-in-Publication Data

Le Beau, Bryan F.
    Jonathan Dickinson and the formative years of American
Presbyterianism / Bryan F. Le Beau.
        p.   cm.
    Includes bibliographical references and index.
    ISBN 0–8131–2026–8 (cloth : alk. paper)
    1. Dickinson, Jonathan, 1688–1747.   2. Presbyterian Church—United
States—Clergy—Biography.   I. Title.
BX9225.D465L43   1997
285'.1'092—dc21
[B]   97–1321

This book is printed on acid-free recycled paper
meeting the requirements of the American National Standard
for Permanence of Paper for Printed Library Materials.

Manufactured in the United States of America

For Chris

CONTENTS

ACKNOWLEDGMENTS

THE SUBJECT OF THIS BOOK has been with me for a long time. It was first suggested to me over twenty-five years ago when I was a master's student, and I have returned to it on several occasions. It was the subject of my first published article, and it has finally, I think, been put to rest with this book. At each stage of my work I have relied on the expertise and generosity of others, of whom there are far too many to name. Nevertheless, there are some who deserve special recognition.

For suggesting the subject and for showing me the way, I thank John B. Frantz, associate professor of history at the Pennsylvania State University. For providing access to, and guidance in employing, the facilities necessary to pursue my research, I credit in particular the staffs at the Pennsylvania State University Pattee Library, the Presbyterian Historical Society, Princeton University's Firestone Library, and Creighton University's Reinert Alumni Library. For the financial support necessary to visit these and other sites, I gratefully acknowledge former dean of the Creighton University Graduate School Michael G. Lawler and the New Jersey Historical Commission.

For their excellent critiques and advice at various stages in my research on Dickinson and in the writing of this book, I am grateful to John Frantz; Joyce Goodfriend, professor of history at the University of Denver; Milton Coalter Jr., library director of the Louisville Presbyterian Theological Seminary; Allen C. Guelzo, Grace F. Kea Associate Professor of American History at Eastern College (Pennsylvania); and Wilson H. Kimnach, professor of English at the University of Bridgeport and executive editor of sermons for the Jonathan Edwards Project at Yale University. This is a far better book for all their help than it would have been without it.

For her assistance in the preparation of this book I would like to recognize Maryellen Read, secretary of Creighton University's Center for the Study of Religion and Society. Maryellen's proofreading, many suggestions, and continuous reworking of the manuscript were invaluable.

And, finally, I must thank Chris Le Beau. Few historians are so fortunate as to have a wife who is not only supportive but also holds a degree in history and is an accomplished reference librarian. Chris has been my partner in all things, and to her goes much of the credit not only for this book but for all that I have accomplished.

INTRODUCTION

DURING THE FIRST HALF of the eighteenth century, Presbyterians of the Middle Colonies were separated by divergent allegiances, mostly associated with groups migrating from New England with an English Puritan background and from northern Ireland with a Scotch-Irish tradition. Such divergent allegiances, Leonard Trinterud has argued, led first to "a fiery ordeal of ecclesiastical controversy" and then to a spiritual awakening and to a blending of that diversity into a new order, American Presbyterianism.[1] Several Presbyterians stand out as having made significant contributions to the new order, but the most important was Jonathan Dickinson.

The list of those who have praised Dickinson is long indeed. Among his contemporaries, on both sides of the Atlantic, Jonathan Edwards described him as "learned and very excellent," and the Scot John Erskine wrote: "The British Isles have produced no such writers on divinity in the eighteenth century as Dickinson and Edwards."[2] Later, to cite just three examples, Ashbel Green referred to Dickinson and Edwards as "among the first men of their times"; Leonard Trinterud concluded that, as a thinker, no one in the Presbyterian Church of the colonial period, if indeed of any period, could be compared to him; and Alan Heimert and Perry Miller called him "the most powerful mind in his generation of American divines."[3]

Nevertheless, Dickinson remains the most underrepresented intellectual and ecclesiastical leader of the eighteenth century. Apart from my own work, only four articles—two by David Harlan, one by Lee Eric Schmidt, and another by Leslie Sloat—have been published on him.[4] The first three focus on his role in the Great Awakening, and the last concerns Dickinson and the subscription controversy. The articles are well done, but Dickinson was concerned with other major issues. Each needs to be explored and a study prepared of the entirety of his work. That is what this book is intended to do.

My primary goal has been to examine and contextualize the writings of Jonathan Dickinson within the history of early American Presbyterianism. I show that, although he acted as a moderate rather than as a radical, perhaps accounting for his lack of appeal to other historians, Dickinson was nevertheless a driving force in the formation of the Presbyterian Church in the Middle Colonies. His leadership in the earliest stages of that formative period led Presbyterians to accommodate the diversity of traditions within their ranks, to reconcile their Old World ideas and New World experiences, and to resolve the classic dilemma of American religious history, the simultaneous longing for freedom of conscience and need for order. In the process of defending the rights of Presbyterians to dissent from the established Church of England, Dickinson gave voice as well to a theoretical position that served the yet nascent cause of denominationalism and even religious liberty.

Dickinson was a moderate New Sider whose acceptance of enlightened rationalism made him one of the earliest eighteenth-century evangelicals to allow that the two were not necessarily antithetical. His moderate position in the First Great Awakening attracted to him most of the New Side Presbyterians of the Middle Colonies, thereby solidifying the movement, defending it against its Old Side and New Side critics, and preparing the way for the creation of the College of New Jersey (Princeton).

Two problems confront and ultimately shape this study; in the past they may have discouraged scholars from even embarking on such a project. They are the loss of all records from the period during which Dickinson served the First Presbyterian Church of Elizabeth Town (today, Elizabeth), New Jersey, and the disappearance of his diary. On January 25, 1780, the First Church burned to the ground, taking with it all its records. The last reference we have to Dickinson's diary is in a letter written by his brother two years after Jonathan's death. Given such losses, and the survival of only a few personal letters and papers, we have little direct knowledge of Dickinson's personal life. Therefore, convinced that it is nevertheless worth pursuing, this study focuses almost exclusively on his public life and on his more than two dozen published works, which were intended to serve the Presbyterian Church. Put another way, fully realizing the well-established limits of such an approach, this is necessarily an intellectual biography framed by institutional history.[5]

My study opens with an introduction to Dickinson's New England background, his youth in the Connecticut River valley of western Massachusetts, his education at Yale, his ministerial training, his ordination, and his entrance into the Presbytery and Synod of Philadelphia. It discusses the religious links between New England and the Middle Colonies, which Dickinson personified, as well as his rise to prominence among Presbyterians for his defense of church doctrine challenged by English and colonial Baptists.

Chapter 2 introduces the first major area of concern for the Presbyterian Church in the Middle Colonies in which Dickinson played the leading role. The subscription controversy arose over a proposal that the Presbyterian Synod of Philadelphia formally require subscription to the Westminster Confession as a prerequisite for ministerial ordination. At stake, however, were the fates of the two contending traditions within the infant church, that of the Scots and Scotch-Irish and that of the New Englanders, and the struggle therein to find a mutually acceptable response to the demands of the former for creeds of human creation, devised for the better governing of the church, and of the latter for freedom from such institutional constraints on individual conscience.[6]

Chapter 3 examines the first major test of the compromise reached in the subscription controversy, the case of Samuel Hemphill. Hemphill fulfilled Dickinson's prediction that required ministerial subscription to the Westminster Confession would not keep out those of unorthodox beliefs. Nevertheless, Dickinson took up his pen in support of the Synod of Philadelphia's right to discipline those members whose views on essential matters differed substantially from its own. In doing so, he made clear the limits to which he believed freedom of conscience could be pursued. He also defended the church against public attack by Benjamin Franklin, who chose to champion Hemphill's Deism against Presbyterian Calvinism.

Chapter 4 takes up the first phase of Dickinson's twenty-year battle with leading spokesmen for colonial Anglicanism. During the 1720s and 1730s, in an exchange of treatises with John Checkley, Samuel Johnson, James Wetmore, Arthur Browne, and John Beach, Dickinson addressed conflicting interpretations of the origins, nature, and validity of Presbyterian versus Anglican ordination and of Anglican episcopacy versus Presbyterian polity. He also considered their differing views on church establishment and the rights of religious dissenters. In his opposition to Anglican establishment and its suppression of religious dissent, Dickinson anticipated later arguments for the separation of church and state and American denominationalism.

Chapter 5 considers Dickinson's response to some of the major issues raised by the Enlightenment. In two major works, published some thirteen years apart, during which time the Great Awakening occurred, Dickinson took up the challenge posed by the new empirical psychology to traditional Calvinist doctrines on free will and moral autonomy and on free and irresistible grace. While defending the Calvinist doctrines to which he had always adhered, Dickinson became one of the first of that persuasion to offer a tacit endorsement of enlightened rationalism.

Jonathan Dickinson symbolized the moderate New Side position of the First Great Awakening. Chapters 6 and 7 explain how he came to define that position, to be among the first to occupy it, and to assume its leadership among Presbyterians in the Middle Colonies. Dickinson, an early proponent of the Awakening, welcomed George Whitefield into his Elizabeth Town pulpit, rejoiced in the flowering of the Awakening, and defended the Awakening against those who opposed it. At the same time, however, Dickinson warned against the Awakening's enthusiastic excesses and divisive tendencies, often at the hands of its most ardent supporters.

Chapter 7 continues the story of Dickinson's travail in 1741 and 1742—years which witnessed, in both the Middle Colonies and New England, a polarization of radical New Siders/New Lights and Old Siders/Old Lights. During those years, Dickinson became the undisputed leader of the moderate New Side, attracting to him retreating radicals such as Gilbert Tennent, who had come to regret and to reject the divisiveness they had provoked.

Chapter 8 takes Dickinson through the final years of the Great Awakening. Dickinson tried to heal the breach that had occurred between New and Old Siders in the Synod of Philadelphia, but when that failed he left the synod to join forces with those the synod had expelled and to form the New Side Synod of New York. Dickinson also defended the moderate New Side position against a variety of other critics including his old nemeses, the Anglicans and Baptists; those he considered Antinomians, such as Andrew Croswell; and even his fellow moderate evangelical, Experience Mayhew, who challenged Dickinson on his limited allowance for free will.

The final chapter considers Dickinson's leading role in the founding of the College of New Jersey (Princeton) and his brief tenure as the college's first president. Included therein is some discussion of how the college grew out of a long-standing concern for ministerial education in the Middle Colonies as well as out of the Great Awakening. Also discussed, as they relate to the founding of the College of New Jersey, are Dickinson's response to the expulsion of New Light David Brainerd from Yale and his participation in New Jersey's Quit Rent Controversy and the land riots of 1745 and 1746.

Finally, the epilogue provides excerpts from the responses of Dickinson's contemporaries to his death. It reviews Dickinson's contributions to the formation of the Presbyterian Church in the Middle Colonies. It reminds the reader that he or she cannot understand Dickinson's words and deeds without reference to the history of his church. It also suggests that as the leader of the British colonies' second largest church, engaged in the major religious issues of the day, knowledge of Jonathan Dickinson provides significant insights into the entirety of the early American religious experience.

Two final notes are necessary, and both deal with language. First, not surprisingly, Dickinson was not concerned with inclusive language. Thus, except where he intended to single women out, he used masculine terminology. As in many instances I have allowed Dickinson to speak for himself, for the sake of continuity but without prejudice to women, I have assumed the same voice. Second, because I often quote Dickinson at length and with due regard for the reader, I have taken the liberty of modernizing certain spellings. This has been done where there is any chance that a word might be mistaken and Dickinson's meaning misunderstood. Otherwise direct quotations appear in the original.

1

BECOMING
ESTABLISHED

IT HAS BEEN TOLD THAT on a certain Sabbath in 1708 the Elizabeth Town,
New Jersey, church choir led the congregation in a voluntary, or hymn of
its own choosing. At the conclusion of the hymn, the story reads, Samuel
Melyen, minister for only four years, offended by what he believed had
been designed to reprove him, descended from the pulpit, took his wife by
the arm and left the church, never to officiate again and departing for parts
unknown. Little evidence has survived to confirm this story of the concluding event in the career of this unpopular minister. Such voluntaries, or
even church choirs, were rare at the time and place, and Samuel Melyen
was not married. Nevertheless, the story's suggestion of congregational dis-
sension is substantially in accord with what is known of the Reverend Melyen.
As one historian has put it, "His ministry was short, his sun going behind a
very dark cloud."

Samuel Melyen was ordained at the Elizabeth Town church in May
1704. He was the son of Jacob Melyen, one of the founders of the town,
and the grandson of the Dutch patroon Cornelius Melyen. He graduated
from Harvard in 1696, but he was at the bottom of his class, having been
demoted for disciplinary reasons from a ranking of seventh of nine. Nevertheless, after teaching briefly in Hadley, Massachusetts, Samuel Melyen was
installed as pastor of the Elizabeth Town church. He left the post amidst
undefined charges of immorality, probably intemperance, but he continued to reside in Elizabeth Town until his death in 1711.[1]

His sister, Joanna, with whom Samuel lived nearly his entire life, married his successor, Jonathan Dickinson, whose career stands in stark contrast to that of Samuel Melyen. Dickinson's pastorship would be beyond
reproach, and it would be the longest in the history of that church, lasting
some thirty-nine years.

Jonathan Dickinson was born on April 22, 1688, in the Connecticut River
Valley town of Hatfield, Massachusetts. He was the second of six children
and the eldest son born to Hezekiah Dickinson, merchant, and Abigail

Blackman Dickinson. Hezekiah, born in Wethersfield, Connecticut, in 1645, was the son of Nathaniel Dickinson, one of the wealthiest of that community's first settlers. Nathaniel, born in Ely, England, in 1600, came to Massachusetts as part of the Great Migration of 1630 but moved to Wethersfield no later than 1637, three years after it was settled. Thereafter he served terms as Wethersfield town clerk and as the town's representative in the General Court.

As was common at the time, the Dickinsons were mobile, moving frequently among various Connecticut River towns. In 1659 Nathaniel Dickinson migrated from Wethersfield to Hadley, Massachusetts, where he continued to be a man of distinction in the community, serving as town assessor and magistrate. He died in Hadley in 1676.[2]

Given the prominent role his grandson would play in the church, it is ironic to note that Nathaniel Dickinson quite likely moved to Hadley in protest against Wethersfield's adoption of ideas on doctrine and discipline associated with what would become the Half-way Covenant and the Presbyterian scheme of church polity. That protest prompted some twenty-two families to move from Wethersfield to Hadley, where they joined an even larger group who had left Hartford, Connecticut, for the same reason. From Hadley, Hezekiah Dickinson moved to Hatfield, back to Hadley, and down the river to Springfield, Massachusetts. Abigail, whom Hezekiah Dickinson married on December 4, 1679, was the daughter of Samuel Blackman of Stratford, Connecticut, and the granddaughter of the Reverend Adam Blackman, Stratford's first minister.[3]

Little is known of Jonathan Dickinson's early years. Quite likely, he entered school in 1694 at the age of six, as Hadley law provided, and remained there for one year.[4] At the age of seven, however, Jonathan moved to Springfield, where he likely finished his primary education and grammar school. Springfield, being older and larger than either Hadley or Hatfield, had what could be termed a public primary school, as well as other private primary schools in the homes of both men and women, the latter often called Dame Schools. Dickinson could have attended any of these and then moved on to grammar school in the tower of the town's meeting house.[5]

As a young man, Dickinson spent time in Stratford, Connecticut, with his maternal grandparents, where he probably came into contact with the Reverend Israel Chauncy, one of the founders of Yale College. In 1702, one year after its founding, Jonathan was enrolled in the college, then known as the School of the Church or as the Collegiate School. (It was renamed in 1718 for Eli Yale, a London benefactor.) He took up residence with the Reverend Abraham Pierson, the Collegiate School's first president, or rector, in whose Killingworth (later Clinton) home the college then existed.[6]

Dickinson's tutor for his first year at the Collegiate School was Daniel Hooker, Harvard graduate and grandson of the noted Puritan divine Thomas Hooker. Hooker was succeeded by John Hart, later minister of the Congregational church in East Guilford, Connecticut. Though lasting some three years, it seems that Hart did not please those entrusted to him, and students did not hesitate to express their unhappiness. College trustees cautioned the students against taking any actions that might tend to discourage "so great and happy an undertaking" as that upon which the college had recently embarked, but during the winter of 1705/06 Hart resigned. Samuel Whittelsey, class of 1705, filled in until Phineas Fiske was appointed tutor, but by then Dickinson had graduated. It is not known what part, if any, Dickinson played in the Hart affair.[7]

When Dickinson graduated in 1706 there were at least fifteen students at the Collegiate School. His classmates were Jared Eliot, who would succeed Rector Pierson, and Timothy Woodbridge, later minister of Simsbury, Connecticut. That all three of the class of 1706 and the majority of those graduates soon to follow became ministers reflects the purpose of higher education in Puritan New England. Erected by a general synod of the consociated churches of Connecticut and chartered by the Connecticut General Assembly in 1701, the Collegiate School's founders and benefactors were committed to "the grand errand" of propagating "the blessed reformed Protestant religion in th[e] wilderness." They confessed that, as the posterity of the founders of the colony, they had been negligent in carrying out that errand but that the anticipated "religious and liberal education of suitable youth" would be "the most probable expedient" in its renewal. According to the laws of the college, each student would consider "the main end of his study . . . to know God in Jesus Christ and answerably to lead a Godly sober life."[8]

For some of its founders, the Collegiate School was established in response to Harvard's defection from orthodoxy, caused by the rise of the so-called liberal forces of latitudinarianism under the leadership of Thomas Brattle and John Leverett. The more conservative Increase and Cotton Mather had succeeded in forcing their dismissal from the Harvard Corporation, but the mood had changed sufficiently at the college to lead the younger Mather to join the already existing movement for a more orthodox college in Connecticut. As noted in his "Proposals for Erecting an University," which Mather sent to the Collegiate School's trustees in 1701, such a college would be a "preserver of religious orthodoxy" in New England.[9] Dickinson, one of the college's first graduates, would qualify only as a moderate preserver of that orthodoxy and would eventually challenge its more conservative actions.

The Collegiate School provided students with an education in literature, the arts, and sciences, such that "by the blessing of Almighty God they may be better fitted for public employment both in church and in civil state." In November 1701 the college trustees—all but one of whom were Harvard graduates—formulated a course of study largely in accordance with the example set by Harvard and by European colleges and universities.

Students were to be grounded solidly in theoretical divinity, but a classical education was also required. The curriculum would include mathematics, grammar (notably Latin, Greek, and Hebrew), rhetoric, logic, natural philosophy (including astronomy, biology, and physics), geography, metaphysics, and ethics. Ethics was in the process of being separated from theology, the line of demarcation being drawn so as to define theology as dealing with inner affections and ethics with outward manner. Lectures were in Latin, and students were to converse in Latin while in class or in their rooms, but, understandably, enforcement of that regulation was difficult.

Although no specific record of texts has survived, in Latin grammar Dickinson probably explored the works of Tully or Cicero and Virgil, whereas in Greek and Hebrew he would have studied the Old and New Testaments. Aristotle was central to the young scholar's introduction to logic, but instruction in Locke and Hobbes was yet to come. Natural philosophy continued to be defined as "the art of seeking out the imprints of nature," but there was no formal instruction as yet on Newton. Metaphysics consisted mostly of what would be termed natural theology, philosophical anthropology, and mental philosophy or psychology.[10]

It should be noted in reference to natural philosophy that instruction in biology proved particularly useful to those who became ministers as several of them would care for the bodies as well as the souls of their parishioners. Throughout the seventeenth century, and even into the early years of the eighteenth century in many rural areas, the clergy were the only people sufficiently well educated to perform the role of community physician. Therefore, although the Collegiate School was not established to prepare students to practice medicine, natural philosophy did provide the foundation for further independent study. Of the 225 graduates of the college in its first twenty-eight years, fourteen practiced medicine. Five of the fourteen practitioners, including Dickinson, were ministers. In 1740, Dickinson published *Observations on that Terrible Disease Vulgarly Called the Throat Distemper,* in which he described the diphtheria epidemic that had swept the Elizabeth Town area in 1735. It has been characterized as "the first printed notice of the true character" of that disease in America.[11]

Dickinson's pulpit oratorical style was undoubtedly molded by his college training in rhetoric, which emphasized what would be known as the "plain style," its central tenets being that "style ought to be regulated by subject" and that to otherwise embellish a sermon would be "to do violence to the purpose of rhetoric." In theology, the all-important subject, in addition to the Westminster Assembly's Confession of Faith and Catechisms, Dickinson studied William Ames and William Perkins. Ames, in *Medulla Theologiae* (1622), and Perkins, in *Cases of Conscience* (1632), wrote in response to the Catholic Counter Reformation and from a decidedly anti-Arminian perspective, especially in response to Jacobus Arminius's teachings on conditional, resistible grace. Nevertheless, it is important to note, in terms of the development of Reformed theology in Puritan New England and in view of our later discussion of Dickinson's Calvinism, that in their attempts to reassert Calvinist tenets of divine sovereignty and irresistible grace, neither Ames nor Perkins placed predestination in the forefront of consideration.[12]

Briefly stated, Ames and Perkins focused on the concept of the covenant. They did not deny the basic Calvinistic precepts of God's omnipotence, the depravity of man, and predestination, but they did suggest that God, after the Fall, in his infinite mercy freely consented to bind himself to a covenant with man, offering salvation to those who entered into and abided by it. They argued that God established a covenant of grace with Abraham, in which salvation was promised in return for faith in the coming Christ, the mediator between God and man. Sealed by Christ's coming, his death and resurrection, man was thus redeemed from his sin and preordained for salvation through the work of the Holy Spirit. Without denying predestination, Ames and Perkins asserted that the Holy Spirit would come to those who entered a covenant with God and led a sanctified life, thereby providing an incentive for introspection and personal spiritual testing. This was seized upon by the Puritans of New England, including Dickinson, when the demands of the older and more rigorous doctrines of predestination had all but been rejected.[13]

From its inception, its trustees stipulated that the Collegiate School would offer not only the bachelor's degree but also the master of arts in divinity, generally after an additional three years of study. Earning both degrees was appropriate preparation for the ministry, but it was also the hallmark of a complete education. Of the first 386 graduates of the Collegiate School, 341 earned their master's. Of the 56 men of the classes of 1702 through 1716, 41 became ministers. Dickinson was included in both groups.[14]

Few of the master's candidates remained at the college; most opted instead to continue their studies elsewhere. Occasionally, they were licensed, if not ordained, before the end of three years. Such was the case with

Dickinson. It is not known where Dickinson pursued his studies upon graduating in 1706. There is no evidence that he remained in Killingworth. Given common practices he probably studied divinity with an ordained minister, but he also may have served as a local schoolmaster. In either case, he could have taken up residence in any number of Massachusetts or Connecticut communities.[15]

Jonathan Dickinson's father died on June 14, 1707. As the eldest son in a family that still had four children under the age of eighteen, he might have felt compelled to return to Springfield, if he had not already done so. By the time of his father's death, however, Dickinson would already have been established in his studies. If not near home, he would not likely have returned unless he were needed, which was probably not the case. The Dickinsons were financially secure, and his mother remarried in January 1708.[16]

In general, the Collegiate School required candidates for the master's degree to return to campus for examination, which consisted of a written treatise, or thesis, on a topic in logic, natural philosophy, or metaphysics and "the solution of two or three problems" proposed by the rector. Once again, there is no record to suggest that Dickinson did not return to the college (by then in Saybrook, Connecticut) for his degree in 1709, as would be the case when degrees were awarded in absentia, so it may be assumed that he did.[17]

While Jonathan Dickinson was pursuing his bachelor's degree in Killingworth, Joanna Melyen occasionally visited her cousins, the Hubbards and the Fowles, at nearby Guilford. Joanna may have met Dickinson during one such visit. She may have drawn the young scholar's attention to Elizabeth Town, and later she may have attracted the ministerial aspirant to the vacancy that had occurred upon her brother's resignation. It is also likely, however, that Dickinson had at least a passing knowledge of the Puritan settlements in northern New Jersey from his acquaintance with Rector Pierson, who had been pastor of the Newark parish for over twenty years before moving to Killingworth.[18]

In 1708 Jonathan Dickinson began officiating in Elizabeth Town. Within months of his arrival he married Joanna, and on September 29, 1709, at age twenty-one, he was ordained and installed by the newly consociated ministers of Fairfield County, Connecticut, as minister of that church with which he would be associated for the rest of his life.[19]

Joseph Morgan delivered the ordination sermon, in which, as was common on such occasions at that time, he focused less on purely theological topics and more on worldly issues such as maintenance of the pulpit and deference due its occupant. Both were becoming problems in colonial America.[20]

Morgan reiterated the standard Reformed version of the Fall and reminded those present that God might justly have left all mankind to perish without hope for deliverance. In his infinite mercy, however, God chose to send his Son with the message that faith had become the way of salvation. Faith was to be acquired through the revelations of the gospel, Morgan explained, and God had appointed ministers to instruct mankind in those revelations.

Perhaps recalling the circumstances surrounding Samuel Melyen's departure from the Elizabeth Town pulpit, Morgan reminded the congregation that although it ought to remove "wicked men" from the pulpit, it should not reject those otherwise honest ministers whose only flaw was their comparatively "weak means." God does not necessarily tie his blessing to the "strength of the means," Morgan insisted; in fact, he sometimes encourages "humble diligent endeavors" or even "chastises or punishes . . . carnal confidence, by denying a blessing upon strong means."

Morgan told the ministers in attendance that if the preaching of the gospel and its ordinances involves nothing less than men's salvation or damnation, then only "the choicest, the ablest and wisest of men" should be employed in it. "He that has not an awful sense of this," Morgan noted, "is not fit for so sacred a work." And finally, he instructed that if a preacher were to be effectively employed, he must be free of all other cares and encumbrances. A minister's work employs "the head and heart and all the strength," he explained, and it is displeasing to God, as well as a disservice to the congregation, if, for whatever reason, a minister is prevented from making the work of the ministry his sole employment. To go so far as to hinder him in that work, Morgan warned, would make that individual "a murderer of souls, a fighter against God, and a helper of the devil."[21] Although its immediate past might have caused him some concern, Dickinson's lengthy and apparently warm relationship with the Elizabeth Town congregation made Morgan's directives unnecessary.

Upon his ordination, Dickinson's congregation included not only Elizabeth Town, with a population of some three hundred families, but also Rahway, Westfield, Connecticut Farms, Springfield, and part of Chatham. For many years, the congregation covered all of present-day Union County, the southern part of Morris County, and sections of Somerset, Middlesex, Hunterdon, and Warren Counties. As it was a difficult journey from the outlying villages to Elizabeth Town, Dickinson continued his predecessors' practice of visiting distant farms and villages where he conducted private services. As of 1716, he was probably paid about eighty pounds per year plus "house, glebe and perquisites of marriages," a comfortable but hardly munificent wage, not out of line with that received by his ministerial colleagues.[22] On a more personal note, the first of Dickinson's children, a son named Melyen, was born on December 7, 1709, but he died one month later. In the course of the next sixteen years, seven more children would be born to Jonathan and Joanna, all of whom survived their infancy.[23]

Like Dickinson, Elizabeth Town had a New England heritage. In 1664, soon after seizing it from the Dutch, Charles II granted to his brother, the duke of York, all lands lying between the Connecticut and Delaware Rivers. The duke, in turn, gave what would become New Jersey to proprietors George Carteret and John Berkeley. They and the colony's first governor enticed New Englanders to settle there with comparatively large measures of religious and civil freedom. The colony of New Jersey became known for providing "the utmost freedom of conscience, consistent with the preservation of the public peace and order." Beginning with Governor Richard Nicolls, towns were required to have one corporately supported minister, chosen by its freeholders, but this only added to the appeal for New Englanders. There was no mention of providing for additional ministers, and if Puritan New Englanders could maintain a majority of the freeholders in the towns they created they could erect "New Zions in the New Jersey wilderness." New Englanders arrived in large numbers, organized into groups known as associates, and founded the towns of Elizabeth (named after the wife of George Berkeley), Newark, Middletown, Shrewsbury, Woodbridge, and Piscataway.[24]

The New England settlers of northern New Jersey were mostly middle-class artisans, tradesmen, and small farmers. Except for a handful of Anglicans, Quakers, and Baptists, they were mostly Independents, or Congregationalists, as they would be more commonly known. Most sought to take advantage of the New Jersey proprietors' generous land policy. Some left New England rather than submit to the growing laxity promised by the Half-way Covenant, and others sought to escape the social, political, and ecclesiastical rigidity of Puritan New England. In January 1684, John Barclay, a resident of Elizabeth Town, wrote of northern New Jersey: "There be people here of several sorts of religion, but very zealous. The people being mostly New England men, do mostly incline to their way; and in every town there is a meeting-house where they worship publicly every week."

The first church in Elizabeth Town was of the New England "way." Organized within the first year of settlement, in 1666 or 1667, it now claims to be the state's oldest congregation organized for the worship of God in the English language. The original church structure was built soon after organization of the congregation on grounds provided for that purpose by the first purchasers, or associates. In 1724, it was replaced by a larger building, which was later destroyed, having been "fired by the torch" of a Tory refugee or by British soldiers on January 25, 1780.[25]

Like the congregation itself, the first ministers to serve the Elizabeth Town church were of New England extraction. The first pastor on record was Jeremiah Peck, who was born in England but raised in New Haven, Connecticut, and educated at Harvard. Peck served as pastor to parishes in Guilford and Saybrook, Connecticut, as well as in Newark, New Jersey, before assuming the Elizabeth Town post in 1668. He returned to Greenwich, Connecticut, in 1678 and was succeeded in 1680 by Seth Fletcher. Fletcher was born in Massachusetts, and, like Peck, he was a Harvard graduate. He served congregations in Hampton, New Hampshire; Wells, Maine; and Southampton, Long Island, before arriving at Elizabeth Town.[26]

In 1687, some five years after Fletcher's death, John Harriman filled the Elizabeth Town pulpit. He, too, was a Harvard graduate, but he is said to have been "brought up [in New Haven] under the eyes of Mr. [John] Davenport." When, in 1662, New Haven was joined to Connecticut Colony (Hartford), many members of Davenport's congregation, fearing the impact that would have on the civil and religious order of their community, began migrating to Long Island and New Jersey. In time, some established what they then called New-Ark-of-the-Covenant, later Newark. Harriman ended up in Elizabeth Town, where he remained until his death in 1705.[27]

Leonard Trinterud has argued that the history of the Presbyterian Church in the United States has been shaped by that which its founding fathers thought and did during the church's first half century, 1706–1758. Those founding fathers represented the two dominant sources of the population that came to constitute the Presbyterian Church in the Middle Colonies: New Englanders and Scots and Scotch-Irish, or Ulster Scots. From New Englanders, concentrated in northern New Jersey and among whom Jonathan Dickinson would be prominent, came the tenets of English Puritanism, modified by the New England experience. From the Scots and Ulster Scots came the influence of Scottish Presbyterianism, modified in part by their experience in both the poverty and persecution of northern Ireland.

The New England settlers of northern New Jersey were descendants of those Puritans whose migration from Old to New England in the seventeenth century began before any formal division into Congregationalist and Presbyterian ranks. Therefore, at least nominally, nearly all who participated in that "errand into the wilderness" were gathered under the titles Dissenter or Independent and later shared the work of the Westminster Assembly of Divines. By the end of the seventeenth century, however, what has been referred to as the "bifurcation of New England" had begun.[28]

The division of Independents into Congregational and Presbyterian persuasions in New England was tied, in part, to conflicting concepts of church membership. During the first half of the seventeenth century, New England Congregationalists insisted that applicants for church membership and for admission to the sacraments be judged by their having received "God's renewing graces." As theirs was a visible church of the elect, their sacraments served as sealing ordinances or signs of divine grace already received. Others, though equally convinced of the necessity of individual conversion as the only means of salvation, believed that the elect were known only to God. Therefore, although ministers and elders would still examine applicants as to their faith and deportment, generally only flagrant transgressors of God's law merited exclusion. To them, sacraments were tools through which the Holy Spirit worked to effect salvation. Disagreement concerning this policy was exacerbated by the practice common to both groups of baptizing only the children of church members, which in turn was made more complex by adoption of the Half-way Covenant in 1662.[29]

The division of Independents was more directly tied, however, to conflicting interpretations of ecclesiastical polity. To one group the true church existed only in its individual congregations, and the universal church was but the totality of those congregations. To the other the universal church transcended the totality of its individual congregations. It was the "one body of Christ," and its preference for ministerial associations and, later, presbyteries and synods reflected that perspective. Whereas lay lines of authority in the first case were drawn through elders who were chosen to exercise the prerogatives of the congregation, in the second case elders shared that power with various levels of the consociational and Presbyterian polity.

Tendencies toward Presbyterianism existed throughout New England, but they were particularly strong in the Connecticut River valley, in which Jonathan Dickinson was raised, and in the colony of Connecticut. They were incorporated into the Saybrook Platform at about the time Dickinson was preparing for the ministry. The Saybrook Platform adopted the Savoy Confession, which in turn was nearly an identical restatement of the Westminster Confession. It added another fifteen articles, however, which provided Connecticut with what Leonard Trinterud has called "a sort of halfway house" between Congregationalism and Presbyterianism.[30]

In brief, the Saybrook Platform provided for the establishment of county consociations with the power of oversight over local congregations, county ministerial associations with the responsibility for advising and examining candidates for the ministry, and a general colonial ministerial association with functions at first undefined. Because the Connecticut General

Assembly adopted the platform with the reservation that it was not binding on all churches, not all congregations accepted it or interpreted its provisions in the same manner. The churches of Fairfield County, however,
provided the most radical departure from the Congregational way of any
Connecticut consociation, and it was the Fairfield consociation of ministers that ordained Jonathan Dickinson.[31]

The first presbytery in the British colonies of North America was
formed in Philadelphia in 1706. Its seven charter members were Francis
Makemie, John Hampton, George McNish, and Samuel Davis, all from
Ireland and pastors on the eastern shore of Maryland; Nathaniel Taylor and
John Wilson, both from Scotland and settled in Upper Marlborough and
New Castle, Delaware, respectively; and Jedediah Andrews, the sole New
Englander in the group, who officiated in Philadelphia. The ordination of
John Boyd within months of the presbytery's formation added the "Old
Scot's Church" of Freehold, New Jersey. The New England–based congre-
gations of northern New Jersey were not represented, but that soon
changed.[32]

Over the next decade, Elizabeth Town and the other northern New
Jersey congregations already heavily influenced by the Saybrook Platform
modified their Presbyterianized Congregationalism to the point where they
too could join the Presbytery of Philadelphia without abandoning all aspects of their New England way. In New Jersey, congregations of New England parentage found themselves not only fully disestablished, in contrast
to their previous experience, but on an equal legal footing with several
other denominations, especially the Church of England and the Society of
Friends. In their perceived need for order in this comparatively strange
state of disorder, they strove to maintain close ties with New England—
most directly with the consociations of Connecticut—but they soon found
themselves outside the fold of that ecclesiastical structure.

Distance was one factor in that isolation. So too was the growing
heterogeneity of each congregation, as their doors increasingly swung open
to welcome Scots, Ulster Scots, and others. But any alliance between the
churches of New Jersey and the governmentally sanctioned consociated
congregations of Connecticut would almost certainly not have been tolerated
even by the relatively liberal New Jersey proprietorship and royal colonial
government. Seeking an alternative arrangement, one by one, each of the
northern New Jersey congregations joined the Presbytery of Philadelphia.[33]

By 1716 the number of ministerial members of the Presbytery of
Philadelphia reached twenty-five: eight were Scots, seven were Irish, three
were Welsh, and seven were New Englanders. Moreover, the congregations
they represented were drawn from an area sufficiently large—including

Pennsylvania, Delaware, Maryland, New York, and New Jersey—that the presbytery felt compelled to reconstitute itself the Synod of Philadelphia and to divide its membership into four new presbyteries: Philadelphia, New Castle, Long Island, and Snow Hill. One year later, Jonathan Dickinson joined the Synod and the Presbytery of Philadelphia.[34]

Dickinson was well informed on consociated or Presbyterian polity. He was also conversant with the Presbyterian ministers of the Middle Colonies even before he was officially admitted to their ranks. The records of the Presbytery of Philadelphia, for example, list Dickinson as having assisted in the ordination of Robert Orr in Maidenhead, New Jersey, on October 20, 1715. Three of the members of the presbytery originally appointed to that task were unable to carry out the assignment, necessitating a call to Dickinson. It is possible that Dickinson was already a corresponding member of the presbytery.[35]

On April 29, 1717, Dickinson participated in the ordination of John Pierson at Woodbridge, New Jersey. Once again, as Dickinson was not among those originally chosen by the Presbytery of Philadelphia, he may very well have been called to replace someone unable to attend as appointed. It is also possible, however, that Dickinson had by then joined the Presbytery of Philadelphia. A church history of the Elizabeth Town congregation suggests that he joined in the spring of 1717, and, indeed, although Dickinson's name does not appear in the records of the Presbytery of Philadelphia through 1716, his name is included on the rolls of the first meeting of the newly constituted Synod of Philadelphia on September 17, 1717. It is reasonable to assume, as it would have been common practice, that Dickinson joined the Presbytery of Philadelphia prior to his admission to the synod. If so, this might well have occurred in the spring of 1717. Unfortunately, records for the Presbytery of Philadelphia during that period have been lost.

The records of the Synod of Philadelphia note that on September 19, 1718, Dickinson delivered 1 pound 12 shillings from his congregation for the synod's fund "for pious uses." The fund had been established at the synod meeting of 1717, at which time the body proposed that members "use their interest with their friends, on proper occasions" to contribute something to be disposed of at the discretion of the synod. Dickinson's contribution suggests that the Elizabeth Town congregation was in accord with his decision to join the Presbyterians. Once again, church history suggests that the congregation joined soon after Dickinson's entrance to the presbytery in the spring of 1717. It also notes, however, that Dickinson moved slowly in establishing such ties in deference to his formerly Independent/Congregational parishioners. Another source notes that the Elizabeth Town congregation initially did not share its pastor's attraction to

Presbyterian polity and that it took until 1717 for Dickinson to persuade his congregation to join, the implication being that he would have joined earlier with their support.[36]

Whatever the exact dates, in 1717 Jonathan Dickinson was the youngest member of the Presbytery and Synod of Philadelphia, but his rise to prominence within both was rapid. In 1719 he assumed the first of his many terms as clerk of the presbytery. In 1720 he was chosen clerk of the synod and was appointed to his first term on the synod's commission, which was empowered, when the synod was not in session, to act on its behalf. In 1721 he published the first of his several major publications. With *Remarks upon Mr. Gale's Reflections on Mr. Wall's History of Infant Baptism,* Dickinson took an important step forward in establishing himself as a trusted and authoritative spokesman for the church.[37]

In "To the Reader," Thomas Wood, the publisher of *Remarks upon Mr. Gale's Reflections,* explained that he had been so impressed by the ingenuity, learning, and plausibility of John Gale's attack on infant baptism that he had asked Jonathan Dickinson, who was a friend and "a well-wisher to truth," not only for his remarks on the most material of Mr. Gale's passages but also for a "vindication" of infant baptism. Dickinson's response, which was prepared in 1716, Wood noted, was made without any intention of its being published, but as it was subsequently approved in manuscript form by persons of "considerable character," and as Wood came to believe that it might serve "to promote the truth," he decided to publish it, presumably with Dickinson's permission.[38]

At the beginning of the eighteenth century there were few Baptists in the colonial America. They had been present from the earliest years of settlement, but their growth was slow. As a small minority, and with an antipaedobaptist disposition, they were considered a schismatic sect by the larger British paedobaptist dissenting groups and established churches in England and in the colonies.[39]

Although Baptist congregations and associations had come into existence in Great Britain in the first half of the seventeenth century, colonial Baptists in the same period, for the most part, did not gather into separate churches. They learned to accommodate their heretical views to established doctrine. According to one account, for example, when the children of Baptists were christened in paedobaptist churches, the parents would simply look the other way in deference to their belief in adult believer's baptism through total immersion.[40]

William McLoughlin has suggested that the Baptist movement in New England, wherein we find the first Baptist churches in the British colonies of North America, was essentially "an indigenous, parallel movement" to that in England rather than an offshoot or extension of it. That movement, he has explained, "stemmed from a common source in the theological and ecclesiological principles of the general Puritan movement," needing no other source or stimulus than the ideas that the Nonseparatist Congregationalists brought to New England. As such, McLoughlin has argued, Baptists accepted not only much of Puritan theology but also the philosophical and social framework of the community in which they lived. Nevertheless, Baptists posed a challenge to Puritan theology in four areas: the right or efficacy of the baptism of infants, the right of separatism or schism, pietism and zeal in the face of increasing formalism, and the doctrine of preparation for grace. Such theological challenges may not have been sufficient to deny Baptists a place in the more tolerant Rhode Island, but they would ensure a less than congenial welcome elsewhere in Puritan New England. They struck at the very core of the Bible Commonwealths of Massachusetts and Connecticut by questioning the continuity of the Abrahamic covenant, challenging the concept of uniformity of belief and practice, criticizing the drift away from the concept of a voluntary church of visible believers, and urging a greater reliance on God's grace than on institutionalized continuity.[41]

Harassment and prosecution, legal and otherwise, followed in Massachusetts and Connecticut, until both colonies were forced to implement provisions of England's Act of Toleration of 1689. A new age of accommodation began, but it was only gradually realized, and for decades deep-seated popular prejudices remained against what were believed to be the Baptists' heretical principles, as well as fears that Baptists were out to subvert all religion.[42]

Thus, with their comparatively high degree of religious toleration, it is not surprising that so many Baptists came to settle in the colonies of Pennsylvania and New Jersey. Indeed, those colonies, with good reason, came to be the center of Baptist growth. By the time Dickinson took up his pen in response to John Gale in 1716, Baptist churches had been established in New Jersey at Middletown, Piscataway (originally part of the Elizabeth Town tract), Cohansey, Cape May, and Hopewell. In contrast to the course of their relations with New England Congregationalists, however, there is little evidence of any significant hostility between the Baptists and their Presbyterian neighbors.

As early as 1688, following the example of their British brethren, Baptist leaders in the Middle Colonies initiated a series of regular meetings, leading, in 1707, one year after the Presbytery of Philadelphia was created, to establishment of what was to be known as the Philadelphia Baptist Association. Although participants in the 1707 meeting were drawn from only five churches, their numbers grew as the association created a church polity, adopted a confession, settled church disputes, involved itself in matters of discipline, sent out missionaries, and issued advisory positions on, and gradually played an increasingly larger role in, ministerial ordination.[43]

Before the mid-eighteenth century, most Baptists were of British stock, the most significant division among them occurring along Arminian versus Calvinist, or General versus Particular, lines. In brief, Arminian or General Baptists believed in general atonement, or that Christ died to make salvation available to all people. Calvinist or Particular Baptists insisted upon particular atonement, or that Christ died only for the elect. Until the mid-eighteenth century, General Baptists outnumbered their Particular Baptist brethren. This was especially true in New England and in the Southern Colonies, but the picture was not so clear in the Middle Colonies. In fact, it is possible, although by no means certain, that Particular Baptists were in the majority in and around Philadelphia and in southern New Jersey, thereby providing a Calvinistic flavor to the Philadelphia Baptist Association of 1707.[44]

Such was the colonial setting into which the works of William Wall and John Gale were introduced. William Wall, an Anglican divine and biblical scholar, published *The History of Infant Baptism* in London in 1705. He wrote it in response to what he saw as the growing challenge of antipaedobaptists to the practice of infant baptism and to what he believed was the insufficiency of the arguments put forth by Baptists in defense of adult baptism. As such, it was well received by his fellow Anglicans, and it was reprinted several times in the course of the next century. In 1706 Wall published an abridgement of his *History* for the general reader in the form of a dialogue between a supporter and an opponent of infant baptism. *A Conference between two Men that had Doubts about Infant Baptism* went through some nine editions over the next 103 years.[45]

Wall was not without his critics, however, and chief among them was the General Baptist minister John Gale. Between 1705 and 1707, Gale wrote a series of letters critical of Wall's *History of Infant Baptism,* which were gathered and published in one volume in 1711. In 1719, Wall met with Gale and other Baptists, whereupon he "obtained more full and correct information concerning the present state and opinions of the English baptists" (1:x), and in 1720 he issued his reply, *A Defense of the History of Infant Baptism, Against the Reflections of Mr. Gale and Others.*[46]

Wall's *History of Infant Baptism* was a massive undertaking (the 1836 Oxford edition ran two volumes of over 500 pages each) in which the author set out to do nothing less than to "sift the whole question [of infant baptism] from the beginning; to search in ancient authors, how the first

Christians did practice in this matter; and to give the result of his researches to the world." In his introduction to volume one, Wall noted that he well understood how the untrained who look to Scripture, as they should, for an understanding of what Christ would have them do in the matter of baptism would be confused. He noted, by way of example, that in the New Testament's account of the period immediately following the death of Jesus Christ, there is no record of infants being baptized by the apostles. But, then, neither is there any instance of Christian children having their baptism postponed until they became adults. The record is more complete, Wall argued, for those Christians who lived in the first few centuries after the apostles (1:vii, xxix, xxx, xxxii).

Wall dealt with the effect of baptism in different contexts throughout his *History of Infant Baptism.* In one instance, in the midst of his observations on the ritual of baptism among the ancient Jews, he wrote of the ceremony as one's new birth, regeneration, or being born again, all of which suggest that baptism put one into a new state, putting off all former relations (1:30–32). Elsewhere, he argued that all people, save the Virgin Mary, are "sprung from the concupiscence of that one man [Adam]" and are liable to the same original sin and condemnation and in need of the grace of Christ to be delivered from it (1:393, 404). Therefore, baptism is "no more than what is necessary, that they, who by their generation are subject to that condemnation, may by regeneration be freed from it. And as there is not a person in the world who is carnally generated but from Adam, so neither is any spiritually regenerated but by Christ (1:394)."

Though responding to the Baptists, Wall included Presbyterians in his commentary. In his discussion of the proper administration, he denounced the Presbyterian practice of baptizing only those infants born of "godly and religious" parents. At somewhat greater length he criticized their ritual as well. Early in his account, Wall had allowed that, with the exception of "sick, weakly persons," the first Christians baptized people, whether infants or adults, by standing them in water and submerging their entire bodies three times—thus, trine immersion. Such a ceremony, Wall argued, was likely based on custom, and Christ chose not to alter it. The customary mode of administration was altered over the centuries, however, and baptism by immersion had given way to baptism by affusion. It was a justifiable development, both in terms of its historical origins and practicality of administration within the confines of the church structure, Wall wrote, and it was the ritual adopted by the Church of England (1:38, 304, 2:227–30).

Wall charged the English Presbyterians with making a far more conspicuous change. Until the time of Elizabeth, he explained, Presbyterians had objected to that section of the English Book of Common Prayer which made any allowance, regardless of the seriousness of the situation, for baptism—or, for that matter, for the ministration of any of the sacraments—by a minister in a private house, rather than the church. "And yet how strangely have these men since run into the other extreme," he continued, by allowing that very thing. Indeed, they had made "house-baptism" the most common means of administering the sacrament, whether the child be ill or well, contrary not only to the teachings of the Church of England but also to the rules of their own Directory. Presbyterians did this in order to gratify the "humors" of their own people, Wall noted, while they continued to resist the efforts of Anglican clergy to bring them back into the fold (1:304–5).

Finally, for our purposes, Wall criticized those antipaedobaptists who had found it necessary to renounce their communion with all other Christians and to speak of those they had renounced as if they were apostates from the Christian religion. The result was schism, even if the antipaedobaptists did not see their separation as schismatic. They saw the church as one from which they ought to separate, Wall explained, as it held tenets to which they could not assent, administered offices in ways they could not approve, and was based on what they judged to be errors that would overthrow the foundation of Christian faith (2:326, 527).

Although Wall acknowledged that there would always be a variety of opinions in religion, he warned that to have the proliferation of churches keep pace with that number would be a mistake of dreadful consequences. It would make Christ's church, which should be one body, "a rope of sand" and give its enemies the most advantageous weapon by which they might destroy it. Schism had become so common in England, Wall contended, that, at least on the unthinking mind, the burden of guilt had been noticeably lessened. In particular, he once again indicted the Presbyterians, explaining that whereas earlier Puritans had refused to separate over their differences, Presbyterians had made "good Brownism" out of the same teachings, thereby providing an example for antipaedobaptists (2:532–33, 561).

In his thirteen letters "to a friend," John Gale attempted to refute Wall's defense of infant baptism. He argued that although Wall had presented himself as a fair and impartial writer, he had misrepresented many things and inserted innuendos that would "provoke the passion of hasty bigots" against antipaedobaptists. On the specific issues, Gale cited several passages from the writings of major church figures of the first three centuries of the Christian era, whom Wall had ignored and who favored antipaedobaptism. He also reinterpreted some of the passages Wall cited in defense of infant baptism so as to show that either they were really in opposition to it or they did not serve Wall's purpose.[47]

On the matter of how and to whom baptism was to be administered, Gale cited twenty-five instances in the Old Testament and Apocrypha where the word *baptize* was used to suggest baptism by immersion. He also offered several references to the works of early Church fathers, wherein immersion was deemed necessary and indispensable. Writings to the contrary of the early Church fathers, though they be of learned men, are guilty of "loose expositions and misapplications of Scripture," Gale insisted, and they "are not to be endured." Similarly, Gale cited passages from the New Testament, which suggest that those who are to be baptized are likewise to be taught, thereby excluding infants.[48]

Continuing on the latter point, Gale wrote that baptism is intended for the remission of actual, not original, sins. Those who are baptized, he pointed out, continue to be "liable to the same inconveniences established by Adam's sin on his posterity, though not in the same degree." If they were not, or if the baptized were cleansed of the effects of original sin and cleared from the imputation of guilt, then the baptized would be as free from those things as Adam was in innocence. The experience of seventeen hundred years, Gale insisted, would belie that conclusion, thereby leading us to believe either that the ceremony had failed to achieve what God intended of it, which cannot be, or that it was not designed for that purpose.[49]

Finally, Gale took up Wall's criticism of the Baptists' separation from the Church of England. Like Wall, Gale described schismatics as those who unnecessarily cause divisions or who "rashly and unjustly either give or take occasion so to separate." He agreed that schism was a sin. If, however, any church over a lengthy period of time, due to the mismanagement of its governors or even to misguided piety and zeal, degenerates into dangerous corruptions and, despite the petitions of its members, fails to redress those errors, "those few wiser and more conscientious not only lawfully may, but are indispensably bound to renounce" that communion. Such was the case, Gale asserted, with antipaedobaptists when they were members of the Church of England.[50]

When he took up his pen, it is clear that Dickinson was more interested in refuting Gale than he was in defending Wall. In fact, although he was in substantial accord with him, Dickinson composed his *Remarks upon Mr. Gale's Reflections* without having read Wall's *History*. In many respects it did not matter, because the key issues that separated Wall and Gale separated all paedobaptists from antipaedobaptists. Not having read Wall, however, Dickinson was unaware of Wall's criticism of Presbyterians in matters of baptism and schism. Nevertheless, in his *Remarks* Dickinson unintentionally responded to those criticisms by representing the teachings of his Puritan forefathers and his Presbyterian brethren (6).

Dickinson dismissed as unconvincing Gale's nonscriptural evidence on immersion as the sole mode of baptism. First, Dickinson asserted that Gale had relied too heavily on church fathers who were "too late to determine the matter." Second, he insisted that when Gale employed the words of those who do have "primitive antiquity" on their side, he had used questionable translations or quoted apostolic constitutions which had since been deemed spurious or of a later date (30).

Dickinson agreed with Gale that in Scripture the word *baptism* includes dipping in its signification. But, he added, in some cases it is better defined as sprinkling, staining, or washing. Therefore, Dickinson insisted, as depending on its usage the word *baptism* can have more than one meaning, to force a uniform definition out of such diversity of literal translation, especially by applying a metaphorical construction, as Gale had attempted, is unjustified. Such a procedure renders all writings, sacred and profane, "unintelligible, without any constant, steady meaning, and liable to subversion, according to the capricious fancy of every humersome [*sic*] wrangler." Scripture, thereby, becomes but a bone of contention, he asserted, and we provide "enthusiastical sectaries" a means by which to cite Scripture as supporting their sentiments, no matter how extravagant (7–9, 32, 37–39).

To Wall, the question of age in the administration of baptism constituted a nonessential. To New England Puritans, including Presbyterians, it threatened the very basis of their commonwealth, or congregational community. For both, Dickinson continued to argue not only that the denial of baptism to infants was unscriptural and contrary to the teachings of the early church but that it implied that a new covenant had been created by Christ with those who accepted his messiahship, superseding, not succeeding, that established between God and Abraham. He denied the existence of any scriptural evidence to support such a proposition and continued to insist that it was the convenant of Abraham that prescribed not only infant baptism and grace for salvation but also laws for the Bible Commonwealth and the covenantial basis of their congregations. Infant baptism, by which newborns entered the visible, if not the invisible, church, provided a cohesive force within each community, and any threat to one was perceived as a threat to the other.[51]

Dickinson asserted that those who are in the covenant of grace, whether adult or child, have the right to have the covenant sealed to them by baptism. He also recalled God's blessing on Abraham, which included the covenant and the seal of circumcision, and pointed out that it was not limited to one individual, one generation, or even the land of Canaan, but that it passed to the Gentiles and is everlasting through Christ. God pledged to take the seed of Abraham into the covenant with him, Dickinson explained, and he used circumcision as the seal of that covenant. Christ established a covenant with the same terms for Christians, and baptism was to be its seal. If Baptists insist that infants are not to be included in the covenant as Abraham's spiritual seed, Dickinson argued, then they must show how, why, and when they had been cut off from it.[52]

Dickinson continued in substantial agreement with Puritan divines such as William Ames and Thomas Shepherd when he wrote that none should be baptized but those who are of "the seed of Abraham" and have "a visible covenant [or federal] right [or holiness] to be baptized." Those "visible children of God," Dickinson insisted, are the children of believers, and to deny baptism to them would be to deny Christ's order to provide "God's visible household" their just rewards, to deny their children their place within the Abrahamic covenant and under the care of the church in the way of salvation (58–60, 62–63).

Where Gale had argued from Scripture that those who are to be baptized must first be taught, thereby excluding infants, Dickinson countered that this prerequisite did not apply to infants, except insofar as by being baptized infants are obligated to learn both the doctrines and practices of Christianity. Through the administration of the ordinance of baptism, he continued, parents dedicate their children to Christ and oblige themselves to bring them up according to Christ's teachings, thereby satisfying the demands of Scripture (69).

It is interesting to note that in *Remarks upon Mr. Gale's Reflections,* though Gale had written on both, Dickinson spent relatively little time on the effects of baptism and even less on original sin. Clearly, he preferred to limit his comments to the two previously identified issues and to speak only in general terms of baptism's cleansing of the soul of its natural corruption. He explained that baptism savingly cleansed man of the "pollution and defilement of sin," but it did so "not as a removal of dirt from the body but as an appeal to God for a clear conscience, through the resurrection of Jesus Christ" (27, 33–34).

Dickinson concluded his *Remarks* by citing several early church writers as evidence of the existence of infant baptism and pointing to the absence of any record of its having been introduced thereafter, contrary to some other earlier practices. Such an innovation, he insisted, would not have gone undetected and the record thereof been so totally obliterated. Errors had crept into the church over the centuries, he pointed out, but they had been met with opposition, of which there are many accounts. Finally, Dickinson argued, if Gale were correct, if infant baptism had been adopted contrary to Christ's institution, then the church, thereafter, would have been built on a false foundation and all its members effectively "unchurched." Dickinson could not bring himself to even entertain that possibility (84–85).

Dickinson returned to the subject of infant baptism in 1746, the year before he died, but by then much had changed. Both groups, Baptists and Presbyterians, had grown considerably, and both were immersed in the turmoil created by the First Great Awakening. Baptism would remain the subject, but the precipitating issue would be quite different, and Dickinson, at a time when he would be called upon to assume the role of reconciler within the church, would have to defend it without as well.

In 1721, however, as his editor suggested, major figures within the Presbyterian Church looked with favor on *Remarks upon Mr. Gale's Reflections*. For his first published effort, Dickinson had chosen wisely and done well. He had selected a topic about which there was little quarrel within Reformed circles and, in his response, he did not stray from the teachings of the most prominent and trusted Puritan divines. Thus, although it can hardly be called groundbreaking or even original, it readily attracted the approbation of the young Dickinson's brethren within the Synod of Philadelphia and, in 1722, they elected him their moderator. As moderator, however, as we shall see, Dickinson faced his first crisis within his newly adopted church.

2

ACCOMMODATING FREEDOM OF CONSCIENCE

On SEPTEMBER 27, 1721, the Reverend George Gillespie entered the following overture at the Synod of Philadelphia: "As we have been for many years in the exercise of Presbyterian government and church discipline, as exercised by the Presbyterians in the best Reformed churches, as far as the nature and constitution of this country will allow, our opinion is, that if any brother have any overture to offer to be formed into an act by the synod, for the better carrying on in the matter of our government and discipline, that he may bring it in against the next synod."

The overture was adopted by a majority vote, but following its adoption Jonathan Dickinson, Malachi Jones, Joseph Morgan, John Pierson, David Evans, and Joseph Webb entered a protest. The subscription controversy had begun.[1]

The Westminster Confession has been central to the church since its adoption by Parliament in 1648, but the history of its influence on the Presbyterians in British America begins with its adoption by the Presbyterian Synod of Philadelphia in 1729. Thereafter, "through two and one-half centuries," Edward A. Dowey has written, "marked by migrations of people, shifts in theology, regional divisions, schisms, and reunions, it has continued to be the confession of the several American Presbyterian churches."[2]

The subscription controversy arose when, in response to its failure to attract confessionally orthodox clergy, the Synod of Philadelphia proposed to make subscription to the Westminster Confession a prerequisite for ministerial ordination. It soon gave rise, however, to a crucial encounter between those who sought to impose institutional Old World authority on those with sufficient New World experience to resist such overtures. Dickinson led the resistance, mostly composed of New Englanders. He fought for liberty of conscience and left his mark on American Presbyterianism. But, in doing so, he was confronted by, and forced to

resolve, the classic dilemma of American religious history—the longing for
freedom and the need for limits.

The Westminster Standards, which included the Confession, two
Catechisms, and a Directory, were the product of the seventeenth-century
English Puritan Revolution. A Calvinistic scheme of Christian doctrine,
they placed the Reformed churches of England in a unique position between that of the Thirty-nine Articles and the Synod of Dort. The Standards were created by the Westminster Assembly of Divines and adopted
by Parliament, only to be set aside when episcopacy, the Thirty-nine Articles, and the Book of Common Prayer were restored in 1660.[3]

In England, Puritan groups, including Presbyterians, continued to
accept the principles of the Standards, but they did not insist upon subscription to them for ministerial candidates. As late as March 1719, on the
eve of the subscription controversy in America, English nonconformist
ministers meeting at Salters Hall in London could not agree on a requirement for ministerial subscription. Though called in response to growing
fears of Arianism, Socinianism, and other heresies, suggesting that "such
human words were necessary to insure the purity of the church," two-thirds
of the Presbyterians present remained opposed.

In Scotland and northern Ireland, however, where the Presbyterian
churches were more directly descended from the continental, rather than
the English, Reformation in general and the Knoxian tradition in particular, the Standards were maintained in all respects. Presbyterians had long
considered themselves the Church of Scotland, even when it was not sanctioned by law, and they accepted the trappings of establishment, including
the Westminster Standards, as statements of theology, polity, and discipline. By custom, beginning in 1647, most ministers subscribed to the
confession and the rest were understood to be in agreement with it. In
1690 that custom was written into law by vote of the Scots Parliament and
General Assembly. Similarly, in 1698, the Synod of Ulster ruled "that young
men, when licensed to preach, were to be obliged to subscribe to the Confession of Faith, in all the articles thereof, as the confession of their faith."
In 1705 subscription was extended to ministerial candidates, and in 1716
the Synod of Belfast adopted a similar measure.[4]

Opposition and problems arose almost immediately, whereupon the
Synods of Belfast and Ulster, while not abandoning subscription, nevertheless wavered between nonimposition and complete acceptance, the latter
passing and then rejecting, for example, what were known as the Pacific
Articles. The Pacific Articles, adopted by the Synod of Ulster of 1720, reaf-
firmed ministerial subscription, but they allowed "scruples" provided they
did not alter the fundamental faith of the Westminster Confession. Specifi-

cally, they read that if a ministerial candidate should "scruple" any phrase of the confession, he would "have leave to use his own expression," which the presbytery could accept if it found the person "sound in faith" and the expression "consistent with the substance of doctrine." The Pacific Articles were withdrawn three years later.[5]

Presbyterians from northern Ireland were by far the largest group of immigrants to join the Presbyterian Church in British Colonial America. Their numbers increased dramatically after 1717, and by the late 1740s they were arriving at a rate of 12,000 per year, mostly in the Middle Colonies. They brought with them their tradition of ministerial subscription.[6]

New Englanders accepted the principles of the Westminster Confession. This they stated in the Cambridge and Savoy Platforms of 1649 and 1658 and more explicitly in the Saybrook Platform of 1708. Like their English counterparts, however, they objected to any requirement by which they were to subscribe to the confession, or any part therein, as a doctrinal standard. It may be that New Englanders continued to oppose subscription decades after they moved to the Middle Colonies because they feared that by their advocacy of subscription the recently arrived Scots and Ulster Scots intended to place American Presbyterianism under the ultimate control of either the Synod of Ireland or the General Assembly of Scotland.[7]

Although there is no mention of it, the Presbytery of Philadelphia may have adopted the Westminster Confession as a doctrinal statement at its founding. Some of the minutes of its first meeting have been lost. The records thereafter, however, make it clear that there was no formal consideration of ministerial subscription to the confession by that body or by the Synod of Philadelphia until 1721. By that point, it is clear that some members of the synod were considering calling for subscription as the only means by which they might eliminate the earthly as well as the spiritually unsound from their ranks.[8]

Those who would become subscriptionists could cite a long list of ministerial infractions, and they believed that punishments in such cases given out by the Synod of Philadelphia were insufficient.[9] Many members of the synod also feared the dangers of Arminianism, Antinomianism, and other heresies that they believed were ever present to prey upon their weaknesses. They argued that the examination of ministerial candidates had become a mere formality and that their spiritual status was being taken for granted. They pointed out that the absence of locally trained ministers had led to their dependence on Great Britain for clergy, and that although at first they had been confident of the doctrinal soundness of the new arrivals, as of late their suspicions had been aroused. In 1721, George Gillespie—a Scot, in the largely Ulster Scot Presbytery of Newcastle—with the support of his presbytery save four New Englanders and two Welshman, acted on those suspicions and presented his overture to the Synod of Philadelphia.[10]

On April 30, 1722, the Reverend Jedediah Andrews, formerly of Massachusetts, then pastor of the Presbyterian church in Philadelphia, wrote to the Reverend Benjamin Colman, Presbyterian minister of Boston, apprising him of what had happened at the Philadelphia Synod of 1721. Andrews wrote that in the past year two or three things had happened concerning the Synod of Philadelphia "of no very promising aspect." He referred to the protest made by Dickinson and others at the Synod of 1721, which, he suggested, had caused a wound he was attempting to heal. He added, "I know not but the Pacific Articles have had their good use," suggesting that the articles had by then been considered as a means of compromise. Andrews reported that he believed the quarrel between the two sides to be over "words," for, having considered the matter in several letters he had exchanged with Jonathan Dickinson, he could find no real differences. But he still believed that the "squabble at New York" was at the bottom of it all and that it had had "an evil influence" on their peace.[11]

The "squabble at New York" had arisen from the settling of a church and minister among the Presbyterians of New York City in 1716. The congregation styled itself a church of "Scots from North Britain," and it called to its pulpit the Reverend James Anderson, recently arrived from Scotland. Things did not go well, however, for the Presbyterian Church of New York. Due to Anglican opposition, the New York Council rejected the church's petition for incorporation, and soon thereafter the congregation became divided over title to the church property and use of donated funds to retire the church debt. When the Synod of Philadelphia came to Anderson's support, the opposition separated from the congregation and appealed to the trustees of Yale to send them a minister. When a meeting between the Presbytery of Long Island and college trustees failed to reach any resolution, the trustees, in 1722, sent to the New York Separatists nineteen-year-old Jonathan Edwards.

In less than a year, the separation failed, as the Separatists could not support a minister, and thereafter wounds gradually healed. Conferences between representatives of the Synod of Philadelphia, including Jonathan Dickinson, and of the Yale trustees led to reconciliation of their differences over jurisdiction, but in 1721 Jedediah Andrews was undoubtedly correct in reporting that strains remained not only between the New England ministers and the members of the synod but also between the New England brethren within the synod and those of Scot and Ulster Scot background. On October 31, 1722, Joseph Morgan, a New Englander, informed Cotton Mather that he and other New Englanders had not been satisfied with the actions of the Long Island Presbytery in the matter, but that most had "held their peace as they had been suspected of having had a hand in setting up the separate meeting" in New York.[12]

When the Synod of Philadelphia met in September 1722, Jonathan Dickinson preached the opening sermon and took advantage of the opportunity to attack Gillespie's overture of 1721. Gillespie's overture, as we have seen, was quite general, but Dickinson's sermon clearly identified subscription as the issue before the synod and suggested that it was related to the continuing controversy over subscription in Great Britain, especially in Ireland and Scotland. Dickinson's response would identify him with the cause of British nonsubscriptionists; of individual conscience as opposed to the imposition of human creeds and dogmas; of the primacy of Scripture in relation to unscriptural doctrines, especially of an exclusionary nature; and of evangelism in the midst of the growing tide of formalism.[13]

Dickinson attacked both the practical and theoretical implications of Gillespie's overture in *A Sermon Preached at the Opening of the Synod at Philadelphia, September 19, 1722. Wherein Is Considered the Character of the Man of God, and his Furniture for the Exercise both of Doctrine and Discipline, With the True Boundaries of the Church's Power.* On the one hand, Dickinson argued that the creation of any rules for doctrine, worship, or discipline that go beyond those provided by Scripture, which in themselves constitute a perfect pattern given us by God, constitutes "a bold invasion of Christ's royal power" and "a rude reflection upon his wisdom and faithfulness." No matter how artfully such rules are "painted over, with the fair colors of apostolic tradition, antiquity, order and decency . . . or greater good of the church," he warned, it may be justly asked, "Who has required this at your hands?" Further, Dickinson recalled, such human inventions had been a leading factor in the division of Christianity and the loss of "the true word of Christ" by which "the weak are wounded, infidelity strengthened, and religion itself" becomes a "subject of debate, instead of a rule of faith and life."[14]

Dickinson next reminded his brethren that ministers are chosen by God and that their mission and commission come from him. Ordination may be the instituted means by which the ministry is propagated through succeeding ages of the church, but it is only a mediate act. The office itself comes immediately from Christ. Further, the minister's calling is to preach the gospel, thereby instructing the ignorant, awakening the secure, comforting the mourners, detecting the self-deceivers, and rescuing sinners from destruction and reconciling them to God.

Dickinson agreed that "several circumstantial appendages to the worship of God," such as time and place of worship, are not provided for in

Scripture. They have been left to human institutions. The essential rules on church government, discipline, and worship, however, are not among those areas, Dickinson insisted, as for those Christ has provided all the necessary forms and ordinances. Christ has instituted a system of government in his church by which "offenders may be reduced, rotten members cut off, scandal restrained, and the church edified." He has appointed his own officers, laws, ordinances, and censures, without which the church would quickly become a "Babel without discipline," and the Presbyterians had established, and were operating by, a system of government that as closely approximated Christ's direction as could be expected in this imperfect world.

In his September 19 sermon, Dickinson did not quarrel with the power of the synod to discipline "inconsistent" ministers. He had, in fact, participated in such actions. Neither did he deny that the ministers of Christ have been commissioned to interpret God's laws. Even the ministers of Christ, however, cannot claim infallibility in their interpretations, he insisted. They do not have the authority to impose their interpretations on others, and no man can be obligated to receive them "any further than appear to him just and true," or any further than his conscience might allow.

Dickinson argued, therefore, that the Synod of Philadelphia could censure its members only in cases of scandal and instances of heresy. Disciplining the scandalous involves no violation of conscience, he explained, and though the synod has no right to impose its opinions on others, it does have an undisputed right to reject theirs. Subscription, however, he maintained, fits neither purpose. It only succeeds in eliminating the conscientious and strengthening the hypocritical. The conscientious feel called upon to "scruple," if they disagree with any portion of the required creed, whereas hypocrites agree to it no matter what their personal feelings and thereby gain synodical sanction for their future disruptive actions.

Dickinson concluded his sermon by agreeing that it might be useful to adopt a plain and comprehensive creed or confession of faith by which they might be able to distinguish those who accept from those who reject "the faith once delivered to the saints." It might even be necessary, since "the worst of heresies may take shelter under the express words of Scripture." Such creeds or confessions should not be forced on those of differing sentiments, however, as the church must take pains not to exclude from its communion any such dissenters as it can "charitably hope Christ won't shut out of heaven." Therefore, they should "open the doors of the Church as wide as Christ opens the gates of Heaven; and receive one another, as Christ also receives us, to the glory of God."

On September 27, Dickinson and his protesting brethren presented four articles representing their sentiments on Gillespie's overture to the Synod of Philadelphia. The synod approved the articles, at which point Dickinson and his group withdrew their protest. The articles stated that presbyteries and synods exercise full executive power of church government, including church discipline; that the "mere circumstances" of church discipline, such as the time, place, and "mode of carrying on in the government of the Church," belong to those same judicatories, provided the acts that result are not imposed on any who conscientiously dissent from them; that synods could compose directories addressing all aspects of discipline and recommend them to their members, provided all subordinate judicatories, including presbyteries, could decline when conscientiously opposed; and that appeals could be made on such matters from all inferior to superior judicatories, who had the power to hear them. The minutes record that the synod was so pleased with this that it "unanimously joined together in a thanksgiving prayer and joyful singing [of] the one hundred and thirty-third psalm"—"The Benefits of Brotherly Concord."[15]

It may be argued that the synodical action of 1722 represented a compromise between the forces for and against ministerial subscription. It helped clarify the synod's role in church government and discipline, and it marked Dickinson's and the other New Englanders' more complete acceptance of the Presbyterian form of church government than that of their presbyterianized Congregational roots. The agreement also included, however, the limitations of conscience Dickinson sought, and for the moment at least, the forces of ministerial subscription had been stalled.[16]

During the course of the next five years, it became apparent that those matters which precipitated the Philadelphia Synod's debates of 1721 and 1722 were far from resolved. Disciplinary problems continued, and in 1723 George Gillespie wrote to a friend in Scotland expressing his continued disappointment with the state of religious affairs. "There are not above thirty ministers and probationer preachers in our synod," he reported, "and yet six of the said number have been grossly scandalous." Moreover, "the greatest censure inflicted as yet," he added, was suspension for four Sabbaths.[17]

News arrived from abroad of similar difficulties, and in 1724, possibly as the result of the Synod of Belfast's suspension of its Pacific Articles, the New Castle Presbytery, to which George Gillespie belonged and which had gathered even more Ulster Scots into its ranks in the previous two years, began using subscription as a test of ministerial ordination.[18]

In 1727, John Thomson of Lewes, Delaware, a member of the New Castle Presbytery, asked that the Synod of Philadelphia "publicly and authoritatively adopt the Westminster Confession of Faith, Catechisms, etc. for the public confession of our faith . . . and oblige every presbytery within our bounds, to oblige every candidate for the ministry to subscribe or otherwise acknowledge . . . the said Confession." Debate on the overture was postponed until the synod's meeting of 1728.[19]

At the Synod of 1728, with the unanimous support of his presbytery, John Thomson submitted an explanatory overture, in which he described his proposal of the previous year as "an expedient for preventing the ingress and spreading of errors among either ourselves or the flocks committed to our care."[20] The several general propositions upon which the proposal was based can be briefly summarized.

In *An Overture Presented to the Synod,* Thomson argued that it is the duty of every Christian and each minister of the gospel, organized into one "body politic," or church, "to maintain and defend the truths of the gospel against all opposition" and "to perpetuate and propagate" those truths "unto posterity, pure and uncorrupt." Moreover, it is incumbent on the church to "fortify itself against all assaults and invasions" that may be made on gospel truths, including those made by "secret bosom enemies to the truth," who do not openly oppose the truth but seek to undermine it from within. As an organized body of Christians united by order and government, according to the "Institution of the Word," he offered, the church is invested with sufficient authority to do this.

Thomson explained that the Presbyterian Church in the Middle Colonies was so defined as not to be a part of any other church and therefore it was not accountable to any other ecclesiastical judicature. Consequently, it was the Presbyterian Church's responsibility to exert the inherent authority derived from its being an organized body politic. Thomson argued that the Presbyterian Church was in "a careless defenseless condition, as a city without walls," because it had failed to formally adopt any particular system of doctrine, composed by themselves or others as a confession of faith. Ministers had no confession by which to subscribe or to testify to their "owning," he pointed out, and there was no bar to their entering the church "corrupt in doctrinals." No method was available to discover those who propagated errors, thereby corrupting others at a time when many "pernicious and dangerous corruptions in doctrine" had "grown so much in vogue and fashion," even among the Reformed.

Thomson reminded his brethren that the colonial Presbyterian Church at that time was weakened by infancy and poverty. It had been unable to establish a seminary for ministerial candidates, and it was dependent on other places for men to fill their vacant pulpits. As a result, they were in danger of having their ministry corrupted by those who were "leavened with false doctrine" before they came among them. Nevertheless, he continued, some among their ranks were indifferent, mistakenly charitable or tolerant, dispirited, or afraid to openly contest even the most serious heresies when espoused by men "under the patronage and protection of so many persons of note and figure."

In the explanation that accompanied the 1729 published text of his overture, Thomson wrote that as what he had proposed was new to the colonial Presbyterian Church, it had caused some concern and was being misconstrued, especially as to its intent. He insisted that his goal was to provide a "bond of union" where none existed and by which the several parts of the Presbyterian Church in the Middle Colonies might be joined together and properly denominated one church. Scripture was not sufficient to that end, he explained, as all ministers acknowledged Scripture to be their rule without necessarily determining in what sense they understood it. There were too many divergent theories in the world and no apostles to point to the "true" ways of God, as was the case in the New Testament Church. A common confession of faith was necessary.

At least in part anticipating the major stumbling block to his proposal, Thomson suggested that if some could point to particulars in the Westminster Confession that they believed to be unsound, they would be heard. If they could adequately defend their objections, they would be allowed to maintain them. In all likelihood, there would be some clauses or paragraphs that upon examination would be "judged either unsound or unsafe," but given such instances he saw no reason to refuse the standards in their entirety. The Westminster Confession and Catechisms may have been composed by man and therefore "short of that perfection . . . Scripture justly claims," he explained, but they are nonetheless of divine authority, as they are "contained in the Word of God" and composed of words "agreeable to divine matter."

Finally, though once again insisting that his proposal was not intended to cause division within the Presbyterian Church, Thomson argued that peace and unity were to be prized, but only to the extent that they were joined by "truth and a good conscience." Otherwise, "truth and a good conscience" were preferable, even at the expense of separation. If separation occurred, he added, he hoped both parties would maintain "a Christian brotherly affection, and consequently a neighborly charitable Christian communion" in all things wherein their principles and consciences would allow. In that way, hope would remain for a reuniting "upon the access of greater light and clearer convictions."

Once again, any vote on Thomson's overture was deferred until the synod's next meeting, during which time members were to discuss it with their presbyteries.[21] In the months that followed, however, Dickinson prepared his rebuttal, which was published in 1729.

In *Remarks upon a Discourse Intitled An Overture Presented to the Reverend Synod of Dissenting Ministers Sitting in Philadelphia, in the Month of September, 1728,* Dickinson mostly expanded on what he had said in 1722, with two notable exceptions. First, in response to what Thomson had implied, Dickinson made it clear that he was committed to maintaining the Presbyterian community, or union. He agreed that it was the church's duty to maintain and defend the truths of the Gospel against all opposition, but he disagreed with Thomson's insistence that subscription to the Westminster Confession and Catechisms was the "most reasonable" means to those ends and that the synod should enjoin that subscription upon every member on pain of exclusion for those who refused. Dickinson argued that such an imposition would actually cause confusion among member congregations, be an obstruction to "spiritual edification," and "procure rents and divisions" in the church, as it had in Ireland. Where he had argued that division was preferable to compromising on "truth and a good conscience," Dickinson accused Thomson of provoking contention, schism, and the total subversion of their congregations.[22]

Second, Dickinson proposed alternative safeguards by which to protect the church. He proposed a strict examination of all candidates for the ministry. Such an examination, unlike subscription, would reveal the seriousness, the natural or acquired abilities, and other ministerial qualifications of the candidate as well as his soundness in the faith. This was the way it had been done in the past, he pointed out, and it had been successful. If anything more was needed or, as John Thomson contended, if some "bond of union" was necessary to unite Presbyterians, Scripture required that it be "a joint acknowledgment of our Lord Jesus Christ for our common head, [and] of the sacred Scriptures for our common standard both in faith and practice." Agreement on the essential and necessary articles of Christianity and on the methods of worship and discipline are "a sufficient external bond of union, either for the being or well-being of any church under heaven."

Third, Dickinson cited chapter 20, article 2 of the Westminster Confession: "God alone is the Lord of the conscience, and hath left it free from the doctrines and commandments of men which are in any thing contrary to His Word, or beside it, in matters of faith or worship. So that to believe such doctrines, or betray true liberty of conscience, and the requiring an implicit faith, and an absolute and blind obedience, is to destroy liberty of conscience and reason also." It would be a "glaring contradiction," Dickinson asserted, to impose subscription on this article.

On April 7, 1729, Jedediah Andrews wrote once again to Benjamin Colman, this time more alarmed than he had been in 1722. In this letter, he reported that the Synod of Philadelphia was about "to fall into a great difference" over the matter of subscribing to the Westminster Confession of Faith. The overture for subscription had been offered by "all the Scotch and Irish members present," he noted, and they would "certainly carry it by numbers." The New Englanders, he continued, were willing to adopt the Confession as that of their church, but they would not agree to making it a test of orthodoxy and a term of ministerial communion. "Some say the design of this motion [for subscription] is to spew out our countrymen, in all their disciplinary and legislative notions," Andrews concluded. He did not know how much truth there was to that, but he remained uneasy as to its outcome.[23]

On September 17, 1729, the Synod of Philadelphia met again to consider Thomson's motion for ministerial subscription. This being their third meeting on the subject, and both sides having been heard, a committee consisting of Dickinson, Thomson, Jedediah Andrews, John Pierson, Thomas Craighead, Hugh Conn, James Anderson, and elder John Budd was appointed to compose an overture upon which the synod could act. The members of the committee were carefully selected so as to represent various positions. Thomson and Anderson clearly spoke in favor of subscription, and Dickinson and Andrews opposed it. Conn and Craighead, both of Ireland, preferred the Irish Pacific Articles, and Pierson and Budd sided with them.[24]

The synod committee reported on the morning of September 19. Their overture, likely crafted by Dickinson, began much as Dickinson would have it by noting that members of the synod did not claim any authority to impose their faith on the consciences of other men; instead, they professed their "abhorrence of such imposition." Members of the committee expressed their willingness to receive one another "as Christ has received us to the glory of God" and to "admit to fellowship in sacred ordinances" all those they believed Christ would "at last admit to the kingdom of heaven." Nevertheless, they continued, they felt obliged to take care that their faith be kept pure and uncorrupt for themselves and their posterity. They therefore agreed that all current ministers of the synod, as well as those who might wish to be admitted in the future, "declare their agreement in, and approbation of, the Confession of Faith, with the Larger and Shorter Catechisms of the Assembly of Divines at Westminster, as being in all the essential and necessary articles, good forms of sound words and systems of Christian doctrine."

The synod voted, in what was to be known as the Adopting Act, to formally adopt the Westminster Confession and Catechisms as the confession of their faith and instructed all presbyteries within their bounds not to admit any candidate for the ministry without his having declared his agreement with all the "essential and necessary articles of the confession" either by subscribing to the said Confession of Faith and Catechisms or by "a verbal declaration of his assent thereto, as such ministers and candidates shall think best." Reminiscent of the Irish Pacific Articles, the synod added that in the event that any ministerial candidate had reservations as to any of the articles of the confession or catechisms, he should "at the time of his making said declaration declare his sentiments to his presbytery or the synod." Either body could then admit him to the exercise of the ministry, if it judged his "scruple" to be concerned only with unessential and unnecessary articles in doctrine, worship, or government or not "erroneous in essential and necessary articles of faith." That afternoon, all but one of those present at the Synod of Philadelphia, after proposing whatever scruples they had, declared the Westminster Confession and Catechisms to be the confession of their faith. They excepted only certain clauses in the twentieth and twenty-third chapters, as they did not want subscription to those clauses to suggest that they supposed that civil magistrates had any "controlling power over synods with respect to the exercise of their ministerial authority, or power to persecute any for their religion, or in any sense contrary to the Protestant succession to the throne of Great Britain."[25]

The synod concluded its consideration of ministerial subscription by giving thanks to God for the "unanimity, peace, and unity, which [had] appeared in all their consultations and determinations relating to the affair." On September 22, it unanimously declared that it judged the Westminster Directory "for worship, discipline, and government of the church" to be "agreeable in substance to the word of God, and founded thereupon." It recommended to its members that the Directory be "observed as near as circumstances will allow, and Christian prudence direct," but for reasons noted above it stopped short of formally adopting it, thereby leaving presbyteries a greater measure of autonomy than intended by the original Directory.[26]

The synod's prayer of thanksgiving notwithstanding, "peace and unity" in religious affairs did not follow passage of the Adopting Act of 1729. Some have suggested that matters got worse. Martin Lodge, for example, has written that the 1730s constituted a period of disintegration of organized religion in the Middle Colonies, marked by an institutional breakdown in which churches failed to fulfill the religious needs of the laity. The clergy, which continued to be undermanned, grew increasingly impotent and unable to effectively administer its office, at the same time that the ranks of church members, especially Presbyterians, swelled from immigration. The results, Lodge has argued, were lack of belief, religious slothfulness, and confusion as to what to believe in the face of the multiplicity of religions and religious ideas, all seeking proselytes in an American setting uniquely suitable to such pluralism.[27]

Undoubtedly fortified by this and other similarly unfortunate courses of events, subscriptionist forces began to gather support in an attempt to gradually eliminate any question as to terms of conscience that might be raised from wording of the Adopting Act of 1729. In 1730, the Presbytery of New Castle recorded in its minutes that some members of its congregations were troubled and offended by "some ambiguous words or expressions" included in the synod's letter to them informing them of the Adopting Act. They wished to remove "all causes and occasions of jealousies and offenses" in relation to the Adopting Act and "openly before God and the world" testify that they were of one accord in adhering to the same doctrine. The New Castle Presbytery called for unqualified subscription to the Westminster Confession and Catechisms; in 1732, the Presbytery of Donegal followed suit.[28]

In 1730 the Synod of Philadelphia issued a directive which it hoped would clarify matters by providing its sense of what it did not intend by its actions in 1729. Following receipt of expressions of dissatisfaction as to the wording of clauses in the Adopting Act dealing with the admission of candidates to the ministry, "supposing some expressions not sufficiently obligatory upon intrants," the synod, which Dickinson inexplicably did not attend, unanimously ruled that it did not interpret the Act of 1729 as requiring ministerial candidates "to receive and adopt the Confession and Catechisms at their admission in the same manner and as fully" as members of the synod had on the afternoon of September 19, 1729. The synod failed to elaborate on what it did require. In 1733, in order "to use some proper means to revive the declining power of godliness," the Synod of Philadelphia, once again in Dickinson's absence, recommended to all its members that they "take particular care about ministerial visiting of families, and press family and secret worship, according to the Westminster Directory." It asked every presbytery to inquire into the diligence of each of its members in such particulars. In 1734, finding that their recommendation had not yet been fully implemented, the synod again urged its member presbyteries to "conscientiously and diligently . . . pursue the good designs thereof."[29]

Also to come out of the Synod of 1734 was an overture initiated by Gilbert Tennent, which voiced that body's concern with respect to the trial of candidates for the Lord's Supper as well as for the ministry. The actual overture, which was worded by a committee consisting of the Reverends James Anderson, John Thomson, Robert Cross, and Jonathan Dickinson, a mix of pro and antisubscriptionists, asked that in the matter of candidates for both "due care [be] taken in examining into the evidences of the grace of God," as had been their "principle and practice," and as had been recommended in the Westminster Directory for worship and government. Without further direct comment on candidates for the Lord's Supper, the synod exhorted presbyteries to take special care not to admit to ministerial office "loose, careless, and irreligious persons." They were instructed to "inquire into the conversation, conduct, and behavior" of all candidates as well as to diligently examine them as to their "experiences of a work of sanctifying grace in their hearts," admitting none but those who were "in the eye of charity serious Christians." The synod also admonished all ministers within their bounds to "approve themselves to God, to their own consciences, and to their hearers, serious, faithful stewards of the mysteries of God."[30]

In 1735 members of Dickinson's Presbytery of East Jersey complained to the Synod of Philadelphia that they had been incapable of complying with the "excellent design of the act of the last synod with respect to the examination of candidates for the ministry, because several of their members—John Cross in particular—had not attended meetings of the presbytery and had moved from one congregation to another, apparently without the presbytery's permission. The synod had declared such conduct "disorderly and justly worthy of Presbyterial censure" and admonished Cross "to be no further chargeable with such irregularities for the future." The synod responded to the East Jersey complaint by reminding presbyteries of their charge to be in compliance with the act of 1734 and to examine the methods by which their ministers discharged their "awful trust."[31]

Finally, in 1735, the synod wrote to the General Synod of Ireland expressing their concern with the state of the church in respect to "the great and almost universal deluge of pernicious errors and damnable doctrines that so boldly threaten[ed] to overthrow the Christian world." So many "wolves in sheep's clothing are invading the flocks of Christ everywhere in the world," the letter read, that the Synod of Philadelphia found it necessary to put itself "in a posture of defense" against such happenings. The synod recognized that at least in the near future they would likely receive most of their supply of ministers from northern Ireland, and they feared that they were in danger of being imposed upon by ministers from there who, "though sufficiently furnished with all formalities of Presbyterial credentials," had nevertheless been involved in that deluge of errors. The Synod of Philadelphia therefore proposed:

> That no minister or probationer come in among us from Europe, be allowed to preach in vacant congregations until first

> his credentials and recommendations be seen and approved by
> the presbytery unto which such congregation doth most prop-
> erly belong, and until he preach with approbation before said
> presbytery, and subscribe or adopt the Westminster Confession
> of Faith and Catechisms, before said Presbytery . . . and that no
> minister employ such to preach in his pulpit until he see his
> credentials, and be satisfied, as far as may be, of his firm attach-
> ment to said Confession, etc., in opposition to the new upstart
> doctrines and schemes.

No congregation would thereafter be allowed to call any minister or probationer, regardless of how well certified he may be, until he had preached for
at least six months within the bounds of the Synod of Philadelphia. No
student would be licensed to preach "until he first repair[ed] unto the dwelling or lodgings of at least most of the ministers of the presbytery to which
he [had] offer[ed] himself, and thereby given them an opportunity to take
a view of his parts and behavior."[32]

The final paragraph of the letter of 1735 included a statement in
opposition to the then common practice of some presbyteries in northern
Ireland of ordaining men to the ministry "*sine titulo*" just before they left
for the colonies. This practice, the Synod of Philadelphia asserted, not only
was no longer necessary, presbyteries having been established in the colonies, but it also deprived colonial presbyteries of the right to judge the
qualifications of those who intended to labor among them. The synod let it
be known that they would no longer ordain such ministers until they had
submitted to such trials as their presbyteries might think proper. It further
requested that ministers coming to the colonies bring with them, besides
their presbyterial credentials, private letters of recommendation from Irish
ministers who were well known to their American brethren.

Philadelphia responded to a request from the people of Paxton and
Derry, seeking "an explanation of some expressions and distinctions" in the
Adopting Act of 1729. As the petitioners pointed out, "great stress" had
been laid by the friends of Samuel Hemphill, whose case will be taken up
in the next chapter, on certain general terms in the act, such as "necessary
and essential doctrines." Seeking to remove any offense or misunderstand-
ing concerning its "first or preliminary act," the synod declared, "*nemine
contradicente*," that it had adopted and still adhered to the Westminster
Confession and Catechisms "without the least variation or alteration and
without any regard to said distinctions." It added that its position in 1736
was in agreement with "the meaning and true intent" of that of 1729 and
that it hoped its explication would satisfy members of the church as to its

"firm attachment" to the "good old received doctrines" contained in the confession. The synod explained that after those ministers present in 1729 had declared their scruples, it had unanimously agreed to the solution of those scruples and declared the Confession and Catechisms to be those of their faith, excepting only the above mentioned twentieth and twenty-third chapters.[33]

Although some historians have insisted that the Synod of Philadelphia's Acts of 1736 were merely clarifications of the Adopting Act, most would agree with the preceding narrative, which suggests that, given the course of events between 1729 and 1736, the synod was attempting to preclude any abuse by limiting interpretations of the Adopting Act's liberal provisions without eliminating its terms of conscience.[34] Given his absences from the synod on both occasions and his failure to vote on either measure, the question remains, however, whether Dickinson, who was largely responsible for the Adopting Act of 1729, supported the Acts of 1730 and 1736. Some have suggested that he did not, implying either that those measures were passed in his unintended absence or that, anticipating his defeat on those overtures, Dickinson chose to absent himself from the synod.[35] As he did not comment directly on the matter, however, we must rely on the record of his activity in the period to provide at least a tentative answer to the question.

Dickinson missed four meetings of the Synod of Philadelphia between 1729 and 1736, which is a higher absence rate than he established during any other comparable period. Moreover, though he offered to the synod acceptable, if unrecorded, excuses for his absences in 1731 and 1733, no mention is made of 1730 and 1736. As we have no other explanation to offer, there being no indication of distractions closer to home, for example, this lends some support to the theory that Dickinson did indeed absent himself from the Synods of 1730 and 1736. The rest of the record, however, suggests a different interpretation.[36]

To begin with, if he was protesting the synod's actions, Dickinson's absences did not adversely affect his standing in the synod. The synod continued to appoint him to various committees and to special assignments throughout the period. As only one example, Dickinson was appointed to the synod's administrative commission every year from 1730 to 1736.[37] Second, when Dickinson was present, in 1732, 1734, 1735, and even 1738, he voiced no opposition to, and in fact showed signs of supporting, what the synod had done in his absence. He never protested the synod's actions of 1730 and 1736, a tactic he had taken, and would continue to take, when other votes went against his wishes, and he supported those previously mentioned related overtures of 1734 and 1735, the latter of which he coauthored. Third, and perhaps most significantly, Dickinson publicized his support of the synod's action in the Samuel Hemphill affair.

Before turning to the Hemphill affair, however, it is interesting to note that in the midst of all of the above noted activities Dickinson was considered for a position as assistant to fellow New Englander Jedediah Andrews of Philadelphia. In 1733, Andrews, due to age and infirmity (he was fifty-nine and had served thirty-five years as minister), petitioned the Synod of Philadelphia for an assistant. The synod agreed, and in 1734 application was made by the congregation to the synod for the settlement of Ulster Scot subscriptionist Robert Cross, then at Jamaica, New York. After some debate, at which time representatives from Jamaica spoke in opposition to such a move, the synod decided against the application.[38]

The following year the synod received "supplications" from the different segments of the Philadelphia congregation. Once again, those of Scot and Ulster Scot heritage called for Cross; those of English, Welsh, or New England parentage asked for Dickinson. Those supporting Cross petitioned to be allowed to form a separate congregation, and, though voicing its displeasure with such a prospect, the synod nonetheless agreed to allow the separation, five ministers dissenting, including Dickinson. In 1737, the synod formally settled Cross among the Separatists of Philadelphia, while Andrews remained in charge of the main congregation. Within a year, however, the two factions were reunited with Andrews as pastor and Cross as junior pastor.[39]

There is no record of Dickinson having ever encouraged the call to settle in Philadelphia, though the size, location, and prestige of the congregation might have provided some incentive to do so. Neither is there any indication that he was unhappy with his post at Elizabeth Town. As the synod minutes make no mention of Dickinson in its deliberations over filling the post at Philadelphia after the initial call for him, it can be assumed that his name was withdrawn soon thereafter or that he withdrew it himself, both of which are quite likely in view of the pending division of that body. Of course, if the wishes of that segment of the congregation which called for the settling of Cross among them were to be honored— something the synod tried to accommodate in nearly every instance, and that was reasonable considering its size—Andrews would be left with a much smaller congregation over which he could preside without assistance.

To conclude, the subscription controversy arose over the desirability of ministerial subscription to the Westminster Confession or any other human creed. But it also raised the classic dilemma of American religious history—the simultaneous and seemingly irreconcilable longing for freedom of conscience and the need for order. The dilemma persisted into the twentieth century, but under Dickinson's leadership the Synod of Philadelphia in 1729 arrived at its own solution to the problem. By allowing for freedom of conscience within the confines of its commitment to the Westminster Confession, the synod took one step which, when matched in time by the similar moves of other mainstream Protestant churches, constituted what George Marsden has described as an American corrective to an essentially dogmatic Old World Reformation. Jonathan Dickinson made a substantial contribution to that corrective, but, as we shall see, it was not an untroubled one.[40]

3

Defending the
Need for Limits

The Adopting Act of 1729 restored a large measure of unity to the Synod of Philadelphia, but it did not bring peace. Under Dickinson's leadership, the synod had been able to establish a position that struck a balance between freedom of conscience and the need for order, but it was soon forced to defend that position in a direct challenge to its application. Having been the primary spokesman for freedom of conscience in the debate that led to the Adopting Act, Dickinson stepped forward to define its limits in a quarrel that soon moved outside synod walls to become a public spectacle at the hands of none other than Benjamin Franklin.

The story begins in the Philadelphia parish of the Reverend Jedediah Andrews. It may be recalled that in 1733 Andrews had petitioned the Synod of Philadelphia for an assistant. The synod agreed, but some controversy followed, and the petitions of groups within the congregation for either Robert Cross or Jonathan Dickinson delayed the final decision until 1737. In September 1734, Samuel Hemphill, who had recently presented his credentials to the Presbytery of New Castle and the Synod of Philadelphia, received an interim appointment to the position.[1]

Hemphill, who had studied at the University of Glasgow, was recommended to the Synod of Philadelphia by the Ulster Presbytery of Strabane by whom he had been received in 1729. He brought "ample and satisfactory certificates" of his qualifications for, and ordination to, the ministry and on September 21, 1734, upon subscribing to the Westminster Confession and Catechisms, he was admitted to the synod. Hemphill had already adopted the Confession of Faith in Ireland, and as required by the Adopting Act he did so once again in Philadelphia, without statement of scruple or objection. Within a year, Samuel Hemphill stood accused of preaching sermons of unsound doctrine (e.g., Arian and Deist), of plagiarizing his sermons, and of defying synod orders to desist in such activity. He took his case to the press for public support and attracted the attention of Benjamin Franklin.[2]

Samuel Hemphill had difficulties in Ireland before he relocated to the colonies. According to Hemphill, in an account presented by Franklin, the Reverend Patrick Vance accused Hemphill of heterodoxy. No action was taken against Hemphill, but Vance wrote of the affair in a letter to his brother-in-law, J. Kilpatrick in Pennsylvania. In that letter, Franklin reported, Vance accused Hemphill of heresy, used "all the invidious names that malice could invent," and recommended that he not be allowed to settle in America as a minister. If, in fact, Kilpatrick did circulate the Vance letter indicting Samuel Hemphill, however, the Synod of Philadelphia did not reject him. The Presbytery of Newcastle, of which Hemphill was a member before joining Andrews in Philadelphia, raised questions as to the orthodoxy of two sermons he had delivered in New London, Pennsylvania, but again no action was taken.[3]

Reactions to Hemphill's preaching in Philadelphia were mixed. Franklin, who normally preferred to contemplate the eternal in the privacy of his own home, had been invited by Jedediah Andrews to join the Presbyterian church. Franklin attended for five Sundays in a row. He became a pew holder and a contributor, but he nevertheless ceased to attend weekly services, finding Andrews's sermons "dull, uninteresting, and unedifying" as well as sectarian. As Franklin put it, Andrews's sermons seemed aimed at making good Presbyterians rather than good citizens. Attracted back to the church by news of its new minister, Franklin found merit in Hemphill's sermons and reported that they were "universally applauded." When charges were brought against Hemphill by Andrews, Franklin came to his support.[4]

Others in the congregation objected to Hemphill's sermons, and they boycotted his services. Matters grew worse during the winter of 1734/35, and by spring, Franklin reported, Jedediah Andrews was going "from house to house among his congregation, declaring Hemphill . . . a Deist, Socinian, and the like." On April 7, 1735, at a meeting of the Synod of Philadelphia, Andrews formally charged Hemphill with "erroneous teaching." In a letter to an unnamed Boston minister, dated June 14, Andrews explained that when members of his church decided that he should have an assistant, "some leading men not disaffected to the way of Deism so much as they should be" imposed Hemphill on him and the congregation, and soon thereafter "free thinkers, Deists, and nothings, getting a scent of him, flocked to him." By the letter, of course, Andrews may simply have intended to distance himself from what appears from the synod records to have been his voluntary request for help and his uncontested acceptance of the Reverend Hemphill.[5]

The Samuel Hemphill affair, more often than not, is remembered for Benjamin Franklin's involvement. Still, most Franklin biographers have relegated the subject of Samuel Hemphill to footnotes. Carl Van Doren, in his highly regarded volume, devoted one paragraph to the subject, and it is entirely omitted from the equally influential *Franklin of Philadelphia* by Esmond Wright.[6]

In his *Autobiography,* written a half century later, Franklin devoted only two paragraphs to the Samuel Hemphill affair. He described Hemphill as "a young Presbyterian preacher . . . with a good voice, and apparently extempore, most excellent discourses, which drew together considerable numbers of different persuasions." Hemphill's sermons, Franklin continued, had "little of the dogmatical kind, but inculcated strongly the practice of virtue, or what in the religious style are called good works." When members of the congregation who considered themselves orthodox Presbyterians, along with "most of the old clergy," accused Hemphill of heterodoxy and attempted to silence him, Franklin explained, "I became his zealous partisan, and contributed all I could to raise a party in his favor, and we combated for him a while with some hopes of success." Franklin considered Hemphill an elegant preacher but a poor writer, so he wrote for him "two or three pamphlets, and one piece in the *Gazette* of April 1735." It was those public pieces that drew Dickinson into the fray.[7]

Theological points lay at the heart of his differences with the Synod of Philadelphia, but other perceived attributes of the church moved Franklin to make his criticism public. In a passage from his private correspondence with his more orthodox sister, Jane Mecom, for example, he chastised Presbyterians for their "bigotry and utter lack of charity toward any who disagree with them." As Alfred Owen Aldridge has suggested, Franklin's Hemphill pamphlets were informed by anticlericalism, but his animus was directed at those whom he believed to be narrow sectarians within the denomination.[8]

Merton Christensen, one of the few to investigate the Samuel Hemphill affair to any extent, has argued that it shows Franklin to be less thoroughly secular and more anticlerical—at least in relation to the Presbyterian clergy of Philadelphia—than has sometimes been supposed. Melvin Buxbaum, however, who has provided the most comprehensive account of Franklin's relationship with the Presbyterians, has used stronger language, describing Franklin as a polemicist who "was as guilty of censoriousness and bigotry as he accused Presbyterians of being." That made Dickinson's defense of the Synod all the more difficult.[9]

Franklin's entry into the fray on behalf of Samuel Hemphill followed the Philadelphia Synod's meeting of April 7, 1735, where it formally brought charges against Hemphill and appointed a commission to conduct a hearing. "A Dialogue between Two of the Presbyterians Meeting in this City" appeared in the April 3–10, 1735, issue of Franklin's *Pennsylvania Gazette*.

In his first defense of Samuel Hemphill, Franklin chose not to refute the specific charges brought against Hemphill by the synod's commission. Instead, he provided a Socratic dialogue wherein S, Hemphill's spokesman and "a lover of virtue who considered particular orthodoxies and religious enthusiasm irrelevant and potentially inimical to sound religion and human happiness," had the better of T, who represented the synod. More specifically, T was critical of Hemphill, the "new fangled preacher," as Hemphill talked of nothing but the duties of morality, which T was convinced would "carry no man to heaven" and therefore was not fit to be preached in a Christian congregation.

S argued that morality should be the principal goal of preaching, citing Christ's Sermon on the Mount, by example, as "an excellent moral discourse." Faith, S explained, is merely a means of producing morality, by which man is to be saved. Christ was "a teacher of morality," and he instructed those who were deficient in it that they "ought first to believe in him as an able and faithful teacher." To expect salvation from such faith alone, however, especially where it does not lead to virtue, appeared to S neither a Christian nor a reasonable doctrine. What God requires is that "we should live virtuous, upright, and good-doing lives."

When T asked why, if faith is of use in producing a good life and salvation, Hemphill did not preach faith as well as morality, S responded that perhaps Hemphill's approach was similar to that of the physician who "suits his physic to the disease he finds in the patient." In other words, Hemphill had assumed that those whom he addressed, being baptized Christians educated in their religion, already had faith. That they were deficient in morality, however, he found evidenced by their lack of charity toward each other and their continuous and notorious bickering among themselves.

Where T argued that Hemphill ought to have preached "as Presbyterians use[d] to preach" and abide by the Westminster Confession of Faith, S questioned whether preachers should be confined to that or any other confession. Confessions, he suggested, represent the church's apostasy from the primitive simplicity of the gospel. They are the product of those, reformers or not, who were not, or are not, perfect, the most recent and most directly applicable case being that of the Presbyterians. They were not satisfied with the Church of England's Thirty-nine Articles, S explained, and, "fancying themselves infallible in their interpretations" they tied themselves to the Westminster Confession.

T argued that, if a majority of the synod was against an "innovation," they might justly prevent its preaching. S maintained, however, that that was as much as to say that "if the majority of the preachers be in the wrong, they may justly hinder any man from setting the people right." He cited the case of opponents to the Reformation in its initial stages and reminded T that the reformers had denied the infallibility of the pope and his councils.

S expressed optimism that the commission would find Hemphill innocent of the charges brought against him, thereby delivering "our profession from the satirical reflection" of a few in the congregation that would "persecute, silence, and condemn a good preacher, for exhorting them to be honest and charitable to one another and the rest of mankind." This might imply an initial optimism on Franklin's part as to the outcome of Hemphill's hearing before the synod. Or it may have been a ploy on Franklin's part to make the commission, if it did not find Hemphill innocent, seem ridiculous and hostile to virtue, as well as to the spirit of the Reformation, which taught that man had the right to interpret the gospel in light of his own experience.[10]

The trial began on April 17, 1735, before a commission of the synod that had been expanded for the occasion to include some twenty ministers. Both pro- and antiministerial subscriptionists were represented. Jonathan Dickinson, however, for some unknown reason, did not attend. The trial lasted until Saturday, April 26.[11]

Jedediah Andrews, the plaintive, presented eight articles in which he referred to specific doctrines preached by Samuel Hemphill that he found unsatisfactory. In brief, he accused Hemphill of teaching that "Christianity is nothing else but a revival or new edition of the laws and precepts of nature"; that "the sacrament of the Lord's Supper is only a means to promote a good and pious life"; that "the Doctrine of Christ's Merits and Satisfaction . . . represents God as stern and inexorable, and is only for tyrants to impose and slaves to obey"; that those who preach the Doctrine of Christ's Merits and Satisfaction make it "a charm of the word of Christ in their preaching, thereby working up their hearers to enthusiasm"; and that "saving faith" is nothing more than "an assent to or persuasion of the truth of the doctrines of the gospel on rational grounds." Andrews reported that Hemphill had not preached on original sin or on "prayer or the blood or spirit of Christ"; that he had "run down . . . the Protestant Doctrine of Justification by Faith" by arguing that it "concerned new converted heathens and not us"; and that he had commonly said that "reason is our rule, and was given us for a rule."

Existing accounts of the hearing offer only a few details as to what transpired. Hemphill was free to offer anything in his defense, and he and others spoke on his behalf, but there is no record of what he or they said. A large part of the testimony came from those who had been present when Hemphill preached but who by no means agreed on what they had heard. Some testified to have heard unsound statements, and others denied having heard any such thing. The latter, however, were dismissed by the commission as presenting "negative evidence," in that they were merely stating that they had not heard something which might well have been said without their knowledge.

Hemphill called for the removal from the commission of the Reverends John Thomson and George Gillespie, charging them with not being proper judges, as they had already spoken out against him. According to Franklin, Thomson had condemned Hemphill in letters to "several gentlemen," and Gillespie had referred to him in the company of others as being "a New Light man" and as having used other words "importing that he was guilty of preaching errors." As Hemphill did not produce Thomson's letters, and as the charges were denied by the accused and the subject of contradictory testimony, the commission allowed Thomson and Gillespie to remain.[12]

Hemphill pleaded his case in part by suggesting that when he subscribed to the Westminster Confession he had done so with the understanding that it meant subscription to its essential articles, which, he pointed out, the synod had not identified. The commission responded by noting that as per terms of the Adopting Act Hemphill was to have stated any objections he had to that body of doctrine at the time of his subscribing but that he had not. That the synod had not identified those articles of the confession it considered essential, reserving to itself the liberty to judge each case on its own merits, did not excuse Hemphill's behavior.[13]

On Sunday, April 20, while the commission was in recess, Ebenezer Pemberton and Robert Cross preached sermons to their fellow commissioners on the dangers of being led astray by perverters of the gospel. The substance of both sermons was pointedly in line with charges brought against Hemphill.[14]

Thus, when the commission reconvened, Hemphill charged Pemberton and Cross with having preached sermons that were inflammatory and detrimental to any sense of impartiality on the part of the commission. The commission, however, ruled that the sermons were not necessarily directed against Hemphill, "for it is always the duty of ministers to warn against perversion of doctrine."

The commission asked Hemphill to provide them with the texts of his sermons. At first he refused, but then he produced his notes, whereupon the commission examined them for evidence of the charges Andrews had brought against him. Hemphill protested the commission's use of his notes rather than entire sermons and their not having told him in advance what particular points they had found objectionable, but the commission persisted and found sufficient evidence to condemn him. It unanimously declared his doctrines "unsound and dangerous," as well as "contrary to the Scriptures and our excellent Confession and Catechism," and suspended him from the ministry until the entire synod could take up the matter at its next regular meeting in September.[15]

In July 1735, Benjamin Franklin published his observations on the trial in which he sought to clear Hemphill's character of what Franklin believed to be false aspersions that had been cast upon it and "to convince the world how unjustly some men will act, when they have their own private end in view." *Some Observations on the Proceedings against the Rev. Mr. Hemphill; with a Vindication of His Sermons* was so popular that a second edition was necessary by August.

Franklin's approach, no doubt with Hemphill's assistance, has been described by Merton Christensen as an attempt whereby, if Franklin could not portray Hemphill as orthodox, he would at least make him appear reasonable. Where the commission found that Hemphill had preached that Christianity is "only an illustration and improvement of the law of nature," Franklin responded that such a message was neither subversive of the gospel nor disagreeable to the fundamentals of the Westminster Confession of Faith. What Hemphill meant, Franklin wrote, was that Christ's design in coming into the world was to restore mankind to the state of perfection in which Adam was at first created. Christ's laws, then, have "a natural tendency to our present ease and quiet" and "carry their own reward, though there were nothing to reward our obedience or punish our disobedience in another life." Put another way, what God has created must be "agreeable to our nature, since a desire of happiness is a natural principle which all mankind are endued with."[16]

The commission had condemned Hemphill for denying the necessity of conversion for those who are born in the church and who have not degenerated into "vicious practice." Franklin wrote that, when placed into context, what Hemphill had suggested was that the conversion of which Christians speak whereby people become "new creatures" is "most visible in the first conversion of heathens to Christianity, or of wicked professors . . . to the Gospel of Christ." Those brought up in a "Christian country" and with the benefit of a "virtuous education" and not having engaged in "vicious practices" experience a much more gradual conversion. They "can't so properly be called new creatures," Franklin explained, because "they were always what they are," except for the daily improvement they make in virtue.

In his defense of the light of nature, Hemphill did not deny the necessity of divine revelation, Franklin wrote. Neither in his emphasis on good works did he seek to undermine the doctrine of justification by faith. What Hemphill had preached against, Franklin offered, was Antinomianism, or those who held that Christ's merits and satisfaction will save men without their performing good works. He had spoken out against those who had taught that to believe that good works or a holy life is necessary for men to be accepted by God depreciates the sufferings of Christ, thereby leading men never to look upon God as a lawgiver but only as a savior. This is "the most impious doctrine" ever broached, Franklin added, as it has "a natural tendency to make men act as if Christ came into the world to patronize vice, and allow men to live as they please," thereby doing "dishonor both to the father and the son."

And finally, Franklin supported Hemphill's contention that although he had declared his assent to the Westminster Confession he had done so only in its essentials, as he saw them. As at the time the synod had not indicated to him what they believed the fundamentals were, Hemphill had no reason to believe that he had preached anything contrary to what either held to be essential. That many of those who were "so zealous for the confession" once had agreed that there were articles in the confession of no great moment, no doubt a reference to Dickinson and the other antisubscriptionists, led Franklin to conclude that what they had done was nothing less than an inquisition intended to no other end but to defend the character of Jedediah Andrews.[17]

Melvin Buxbaum has suggested that with publication of *Observations,* Franklin was no longer, if indeed he ever was, appealing to the Synod of Philadelphia for Hemphill's reinstatement. Instead, he was bent on building resentment toward that body, the church, and Calvinism. The synod certainly saw it that way. In its response, which appeared on September 4, 1735, a specially appointed synod commission accused Franklin of engaging in character assassination when he should have attempted to defend Hemphill on the merits of the case. It also defended its position on ministerial subscription to the Westminster Confession. The primary author of that defense was Jonathan Dickinson, who, though he was not one of Hemphill's judges, no doubt felt sufficiently implicated by Franklin to respond. His task, Dickinson recognized, was to define the limits of conscience for which he had provided in the Adopting Act.[18]

At the outset of *A Vindication of the Reverend Commission of the Synod in Answer to Some Observations on Their Proceedings against the Reverend Mr. Hemphill,* Dickinson addressed Franklin's criticism of those members of the commission who, "though zealous for the confession" in the case of Samuel Hemphill, once had been more indifferent to the confession than Hemphill. Dickinson pointed out that the nature of the debate concerning ministerial subscription had changed considerably since 1729. He offered the following observation on that change:

> The prodigious growth of errors and infidelity, has long been a matter of melancholy complaint; and the frequent attempts that have been made in this unhappy age to undermine the great doctrines of the gospel, have justly filled the minds of all serious persons with horror and surprise. Those who have had a tender regard for the common interests of religion and a desire that it might be propagated to posterity pure and uncorrupted, have thought themselves obliged vigorously to appear in its defense, and courageous to resist the torrent of irreligion that seems to threaten the destruction of the Christian world. (1–2)

Dickinson explained that members of the synod had hoped that in their "remote corner of the earth" they would escape the "epidemical corruption of the age" and be spared those destructive errors that had "overspread so great a part of the church," but this had not been the case. Therefore, though he continued to voice his concern for violations of the individual conscience and the imposition of human creeds, he also defended required ministerial subscription to the Westminster Confession, as provided for in the Adopting Act on 1729 (1–3).

In response to Hemphill's defense that he had declared the Westminster Confession only in its fundamental articles, as he had understood them, and that he had remained faithful to those essentials, Dickinson pointed out, as had the commission, that Hemphill had declared his assent to the confession without exception or scruple. Subsequently, however, he had delivered sermons that were not only inconsistent with the principles he had professed but that differed from those principles "in some of the most weighty and fundamental doctrines." It mattered not, contrary to what Hemphill insisted, that the synod had not identified those articles it considered fundamental in the Westminster Confession; by the Adopting Act of 1729, it reserved to itself the right to judge each qualification raised by individuals upon the occasion of their subscribing to it (4, 23–24).

The commission was called to inquire into the accusations made against Samuel Hemphill. Having found those accusations to be justified, Dickinson explained, the commission considered itself obligated "in fidelity to our Great master, and to the people committed to our charge," to declare those doctrines unsound and to exclude Hemphill from their ministerial communion. In their exclusion of Hemphill, Dickinson asserted, the commission, on behalf of the synod, had exercised a right to which it was entitled, the right of all societies to judge the qualifications of their members. Hemphill, Dickinson added, had the same right: he could declare noncommunion from the synod, if he saw reason for it (4–5).

Dickinson reiterated the commission's reasoning in not excluding Cross and Pemberton. He acknowledged that the commission viewed Hemphill's refusal to produce his sermons as "a tacit acknowledgment of his guilt." He defended the commission's denial of "negative evidence," its use of Hemphill's notes to determine heretical statements, and even its refusal to make known to Hemphill in advance that which it deemed heretical. How was that possible, Dickinson asked, when they had not yet arrived at any specific charges (7, 11–12)?

Dickinson addressed the six articles upon which the commission had condemned Samuel Hemphill. Citing the same evidence available to the commission, but elaborating on its reasoning, Dickinson too found Hemphill guilty of promoting "a revival or new edition of the laws and precepts of nature" without reference to the necessity of faith in Jesus Christ. Such preaching, Dickinson argued, would likely lead people to conclude that they have no need of justification by the righteousness of Christ or sanctification under the influences of the Holy Spirit because when they obey the laws of nature they have a righteousness of their own sufficient for their justification (15–16).[19]

Similarly, for much the same reasons, Dickinson condemned Hemphill for denying the necessity of conversion for all people, Christians and non-Christians alike; for "declaim[ing]" against the doctrine of Christ's merits and satisfaction," as representing God as "stern and inexorable"; for having described saving faith as merely "an assent to or persuasion of the gospel upon rational grounds," thereby belittling the necessity of receiving Christ on gospel terms; for having opened the door of the church wide enough to admit all "honest heathen," by suggesting that those with no other knowledge of God and their duty than that which the light of nature teaches them will be accepted; and for subverting the doctrine of justification by faith by encouraging men to build their hopes for salvation solely upon their purity of heart and virtuous life rather than faith in Christ (24–26).

Sometime between the end of the commission's hearing in April and the meeting of the synod in September, however, a new issue had arisen, and Dickinson was the first to address it, if only briefly. Hemphill was charged with plagiarizing Samuel Clarke and other English Deists, and Dickinson used the accusation to effect, no doubt expecting that Hemphill's impropriety would undermine his cause among those who had been defending him. Dickinson noted that Hemphill had boasted of how universally his sermons were applauded, to what large audiences he preached, and how much "they were approved by people of all persuasions for the strain of Christian charity that runs through them." Dickinson responded by being critical of anyone who was forced to "be the trumpeter of his own praises," but he also pointed out that if Hemphill had given credit to those from whom he had "borrowed much of what he delivered," it would have made a considerable difference in his reputation and in the "great part of that glory, which he vainly arrogate[d] to himself."[20]

Dickinson ended *A Vindication* by forgiving Hemphill for the injuries he had inflicted by his false accusations and his "uncivil, abusive, and calumnious" actions. He prayed that God would forgive Hemphill for his heresies and that he might yet "be made sound in that faith, which he has so unhappily endeavored to destroy," and "upon just terms" be restored to the ministry. At the same time, however, referring to the "ridicule and banter" to which Hemphill had subjected the commission, Dickinson called upon his readers to "stand fast in one spirit, with one mind striving together for the faith of the Gospel, in nothing terrified by our adversaries, which is to them an evident token of perdition, but to us of salvation and that of God."[21]

The Synod of Philadelphia met on September 17, 1735. On September 20, it notified Samuel Hemphill that he was to appear before the synod two days later if he had anything further to offer in his defense. On September 22, the synod received a letter from Hemphill, wherein he wrote that he rejected the synod's claim of authority and that, as their dispute had already been made public, whatever he had to say would be contained in an answer then in press. Hemphill's letter concluded with a postscript reading: "I shall think you will do me a deal of honor, if you entirely excommunicate me." The synod branded the letter "disrespectful and contemptuous" but granted Hemphill's request, confirming the commission's action against him. By a unanimous vote, citing "contumacy in his errors" and his disregard of the commission's censure, the synod declared Hemphill "unqualified for any future exercise of his ministry" within its bounds.[22]

Immediately following its vote on Hemphill, the synod ruled that those who had been appointed "to justify the commission against any complaints from Mr. Hemphill . . . having complied with the commission's order in that matter" were, if necessary, to answer any further publications by Hemphill "or his friends in the cause." No names were offered, but the reference is to Dickinson and those members of the commission who had worked with him in preparing *A Vindication*. That the synod implies that Franklin's *Observations* was the work of Samuel Hemphill is consistent with its having been published anonymously and with Dickinson's not having identified its author. Dickinson may not have been aware of Franklin's involvement, but it also may be that he did not want to bring it into the open. In this instance, the synod continued the anonymity of the opposition, but it extended its scope to include Hemphill's "friends."[23]

The synod also resolved that if a member were to prepare "anything for the press upon any controversy in religious matters," it was first to be submitted to one of the two committees appointed for that purpose. Members of the Hemphill commission dominated both committees. Dickinson joined Jedediah Andrews, Robert Cross, Ebenezer Pemberton, and John Pierson in forming the committee for the area north of Philadelphia, and Robert Cathcart and Hugh Stevenson were assigned to cover the southern territory with James Anderson and John Thomson.

Finally, it is important to recall, as noted in the previous chapter, that on the same day that it censured Samuel Hemphill, the Synod of Philadelphia approved more rigorous measures concerning the admission of ministerial candidates from "the north of Ireland." It cited the "almost universal deluge of pernicious and damnable doctrines" that threatened to overthrow the Christian world, often in the form of "wolves in sheep's clothing," and it voiced its fears that the church was "in great danger of being imposed upon" by such ministers from Ireland, though they were arriving "sufficiently furnished with all formalities of Presbyterian credentials." The only person referred to by name by way of example was Samuel Hemphill.[24]

On September 22, the day on which the synod condemned him, Hemphill's promised response to the Synod of Philadelphia appeared as *A Letter to a Friend in the Country . . . Concerning the Terms of Christian and Ministerial Communion.* Although, for our purposes, it will be assumed that Hemphill was responsible for the substance of *A Letter,* its authorship is by no means uncontested. The preface to *A Letter* is titled "The Publisher to his Lay-Readers." The text is signed "H—p—ll." The editors of the Franklin papers suggest, however, that not only did Franklin write the preface but he may also have had a hand in preparing the text. Similarly, Christensen assumes that the text is Hemphill's, but Buxbaum has argued that it is "either entirely or fundamentally and substantially Franklin's work," explaining that Hemphill was not even "a good enough writer to pen his own sermons."[25]

If, indeed, Hemphill was the primary author, he did not consider the theological points raised against him, as he had before the commission and as had dominated the discussion thus far. Instead, he steered the matter even further in Dickinson's direction by focusing on the issues of ministerial examination, subscription, and exclusion. He argued for a minister's right to personally interpret Scripture, and he argued against forced interpretation as tending "to obscure truth and cut off further revelation." He also insisted that as long as a minister believes in Scripture, he should be allowed to preach in any communion he chooses. In sum, Hemphill, no doubt with Franklin's full support, appropriated a major portion of the position on freedom of conscience Dickinson had taken during the debates over ministerial subscription, even citing Dickinson in the process. He ignored, however, the limits Dickinson had imposed on his own liberal sentiments both in his remarks to the synod and in the Adopting Act he largely wrote.

In his preface, Franklin condemned the synod's exclusionary policy, referring to its members as "a smug and tyrannical clergy which denie[d] truth to itself and to others" while pretending to piety and morality. He called upon his "brethren of the laity" to unite in a determined effort to preserve "the glorious cause of Christian liberty" not only in the church but beyond: "Let us then to the utmost of our power endeavor to preserve and maintain truth, common sense, universal charity, and brotherly love, peace and tranquility, as recommended in the Gospel of Jesus, in this our infant and growing nation, by steadily opposing those, whose measures tend to nothing less than utterly to subvert and destroy all."[26]

Franklin thus posed a potentially explosive secular interpretation to the freedom of conscience doctrine he and Dickinson had espoused to varying degrees, but for the moment neither pursued it. At that point, sticking to the case at hand, he argued that the only way to promote such liberty and advance truth was to humble the repressive power of the clergy. That, he insisted, could come about only if the laity joined in asserting their "natural rights and liberties" in opposition to the "unrighteous claims" of the clergy which pretended to be "the directors of men's consciences." Whenever men "blindly submit" to the "impositions of priests, whether Popish, Presbyterian or Episcopal," Franklin wrote, "ignorance and error, bigotry, enthusiasm and superstition" ensue. It had happened before, Franklin continued, pointing out that "all the persecutions, cruelties, mischiefs and disturbances" that have ever occurred in the church had resulted from such usurpation of power and abuse of authority by "her lawless sons." And it would happen again, he warned, if they suffered the clergy "to get upon our backs, and ride us, as they do their horses, where they please." Opposition to repressive clerical authority would likely lead to charges of heresy, but, rather than being a reproach, such a charge might be their "greatest glory and honor."[27]

That Hemphill had nothing new to offer in his defense hardly mattered. Ignoring the particulars, Franklin had turned his defense of Hemphill into an all-out attack on the Synod of Philadelphia, and he continued that attack in October 1735 in *A Defense of the Rev. Mr. Hemphill's Observations, or An Answer to the Vindication of the Reverend Commission.* Once again

Franklin offered little if anything new in substance to the discussion. Nevertheless, *A Defense* has been described as Franklin's "most witty and urbane" contribution to the controversy, offered in a satirical "tone of burlesque and abuse" for the sake of principle without any thought of victory, and as "the most unrestrained attack on a Calvinist establishment" Franklin ever wrote, wherein rather than continue to defend Hemphill, he sought "to overcome Dickinson's cool and superior argument with vituperation" and to render the members of the Philadelphia Synod contemptible and absurd by painting them as enemies to "reason, justice, and liberty."

Franklin challenged the "slavish and arbitrary principles" of the commission, which, he asserted, were inconsistent with virtue, religion, and Christian liberty. He suggested that if the commission had been inclined to speak the truth, it simply should have explained that Jedediah Andrews's "long established character for virtue and integrity" was sufficient evidence to find Hemphill guilty of the charges brought against him. He allowed that the synod had the power to expose and to combat the "evil tendencies" of a member's assertions, but he continued to insist that it had no right to censure its members, thereby preventing them from speaking their minds. And, he went so far, once again, as to suggest that the commission's position was irreconcilable with nascent American liberty. Franklin wrote: "In this free country where the understandings of men are under no civil restraint, and their liberties sound and untouched, there is nothing more easy than to show that a doctrine is false, and of ill consequence, if it readily be so, by peremptorily declaring it unsound or dangerous, without vouchsafing to show how or where, as the commission did at the beginning of this affair, and indeed have yet done no better."

Franklin even defended Hemphill's plagiarism by accusing his accusers of doing much the same. "Are they beholden to no author, ancient or modern, for what they know, or what they preach?" Franklin asked. Had they not told everyone that they "ought to have a good salary because they are at great expense in learning and in purchasing books"? Their problem, Franklin argued, is that they had chosen "the dullest authors to read and study, and retail the dullest parts of those authors to the public." We are thereby "entertained with such dull, such horrid stuff" and such "want of the Bongout [good taste] that spoils all." Hemphill, in contrast, had borrowed from "the best writers of the age." Employing Jonathan Swift's metaphorical model of the spider and the bee, in his essay "A Full and True Account of the Battle . . . Between the Ancient and the Modern Books" (1704), Franklin wrote: "Thus the difference between him and most of his brethren, in this part of the world, is the same with that between the bee and the fly in a garden. The one wanders from flower to flower, and for the use of others collects from the whole the most delightful honey, whereas the other (of a quite different taste) places her happiness entirely in filth, corruption, and ordure." Franklin continued to champion what he titled God's "first revelation," which is that man is obliged to practice the laws of morality, which are discoverable by the light of nature. He continued to espouse what he believed to be the primary end and design of that revelation, namely, "to promote the practice of the great laws of morality and virtue both with respect to God and man." He did so, however, by describing the synod's criticism of Hemphill's preaching on that subject as follows: "Asses are grave and dull animals, Our authors are grave and dull animals; therefore Our authors are grave, dull, or if you will, Rev. Asses."[28]

The Synod of Philadelphia, and Jonathan Dickinson in particular, must have smarted to read Franklin's immoderate attack. Dickinson would respond, first on behalf of the synod and later on his own, though employing a pseudonym. In both cases, he resisted any temptation he might have had to respond in kind. Instead, he continued to offer what has already been described as his characteristic "cool and superior argument." Yet again, he penned a carefully reasoned explanation of what he had written earlier in defense of the Adopting Act, a copy of which he attached to the first publication and its application to Samuel Hemphill.

In *Remarks upon a Pamphlet, Intitled, A Letter to a Friend in the Country,* published in November 1735, Dickinson continued to decry any imposition on freedom of conscience in the matter of religion. He hailed the "age of liberty" to which Franklin had referred and into which he believed the world had entered, wherein the cause of liberty had been defended "by many learned and ingenious persons" against the claims of tyranny and persecution, and wherein people, beginning to consider themselves rational creatures and free agents, were no longer likely to "put their necks under the yoke" of doctrinal imposition. At the same time, however, Dickinson warned, the age of liberty had created difficulties for the church: "As one extreme commonly begets another, there now appears greatest danger that liberty will be abased to licentiousness, and that to escape imposition we shall open a door to infidelity, and instead of charity and mutual forbearance we shall make shipwreck of the faith as well as peace of our churches by the mixed communions of those most opposite to one another in the essential and fundamental articles of their faith."

Hemphill's sermons and the articles written in his defense, Dickinson offered, had had "a direct tendency to this sad effect." He too was committed to "the glorious cause of Christian liberty," but let them [Hemphill and Franklin] "not use their liberty . . . for a cloak of maliciousness." More specifically, as he had thirteen years earlier, Dickinson argued that

Presbyterians should admit to ministerial communion anyone they suppose qualified for the work according to the instructions Christ has provided in the gospel, no matter how different they might be. To refuse entry to such individuals would be to reject those sent by Christ to deprive Christ's people of the advantages he has provided for them and "to tyrannize over our brethren, by rejecting their labors in Christ's vineyard." Nevertheless, as widely as those lines are drawn, Dickinson warned, to admit others would be to "send poison into Christ's household, instead of the portion of meat which he has provided, and to prejudice, instead of advancing, the interest of their precious souls."

It is true, Dickinson allowed, that Christian societies, or churches, are subject to the one lawgiver and that no such society has the power to impose its laws or its interpretations of Christ's laws on others. However, he continued, as he believed had been established by the Reformation, every Christian society, like every Christian, is on an equal level of liberty and has an equal claim to power and authority. As God "has given no charter to any particular church, exclusive of others," each church has an equal assurance of its own orthodoxy. Thus, though each church is equally fallible and though their decrees do not bear the stamp of divine authority, churches are not obliged to admit to their communion anyone with whom they disagree on the essentials of their faith: "For though it be true, that I have no juster pretense than any other person, to determine what is a fundamental article of religion, and on that account to impose my opinion upon others, yet I have an undoubted right to judge for myself, and to reject those opinions which I think fundamentally erroneous, and consequently to enjoy the liberty of my conscience, by refusing communion with those that I think unqualified for it."[29]

Perhaps to counter Franklin's appeal to freedom of conscience as precluding the synod's right to define its own membership, Dickinson concluded his *Remarks* with a contrasting statement by John Locke. Locke was also well known and highly regarded for speaking out against persecution and compulsion of the mind, and he had no particular association with Presbyterians. The passage, which Dickinson believed described his own position, is from Locke's *Letter Concerning Toleration* (1689): "This is the fundamental and immutable right of a spontaneous society, that it has power to remove any of its members, who transgress the rules of its institution. But it cannot by the accession of any new members, acquire any jurisdiction over those, that are not joined with it. And therefore peace, equity, and friendship are always mutually to be observed by particular churches in the same manner as by private persons without any pretence of superiority or jurisdiction over one another."

Remarks upon a Pamphlet was followed by a belated reaction to *A Defense* by one Obadiah Jenkins, entitled *Remarks upon the Defense of the Reverend Mr. Hemphill's Observations: In a Letter to a Friend. Remarks upon the Defense* was signed by "a gentleman in New York who has followed the controversy," but it has been attributed to Jonathan Dickinson. Dated November 24, 1735, but having been published in Bradford's *American Weekly Mercury* on January 6, 1736, nine months after Hemphill's trial, Dickinson's response added little to the debate.[30]

By November 1735, the Reverend Hemphill had disappeared into obscurity, or as Franklin preferred to put it: "He left us in search elsewhere of better fortune." It may be, as Alfred Owen Aldridge has suggested, that Franklin's urging caused Hemphill to remain in the fight longer than he might have otherwise, but by the time Franklin finished defending him, as Melvin Buxbaum has written, he was seen as a scoundrel whom no denomination wanted.[31]

As for Benjamin Franklin, he would later write in his *Autobiography* that upon their defeat he left Philadelphia's Presbyterian church, but for years he continued his subscription for the support of its ministers. He took a pew in Philadelphia's Anglican Christ Church, to which he became a subscriber as well, in this case for the construction of a new church building. Franklin had two of his children baptized at Christ Church, and he and his wife were buried there.[32]

The Reverend Samuel Hemphill was not nearly so important to Benjamin Franklin as the source of his censures, the facts of his dismissal, and the nature of his doctrines. Franklin's involvement in the Hemphill affair stemmed from what he considered "the overweening assumption of power" which the Presbyterian clergy assumed to condemn Hemphill, as well as the doctrines upon which he was expelled. He did not seek to disprove the charges against Hemphill—that Hemphill had preached ideas that contradicted the Westminster Confession—but rather to show that what Hemphill had taught was not wrong, that it was to the greater glory of God and benefit of man, and that he should be free to express himself regardless of how his expressions might run counter to Christian dogma or Presbyterian doctrinal statements. Franklin continued to support Hemphill and to vilify the opposition even after others had abandoned him, as Merton Christensen has suggested, "not because he had any hopes of restoring Hemphill to the pulpit" but because he believed both he and Hemphill were right.[33]

Franklin used the occasion of the Hemphill affair to showcase his ideas on the reasonable and benevolent nature of God and to emphasize Jesus as supreme lawgiver rather than as the incarnate Son of God. He used it as a public forum to espouse the grand design of the sufficiency of nature as a guide to man's obligations to worship God and to love one another and to promote the "commonsensical verities of natural religion," which were the reasonableness of biblical revelation, the moral life, the inherent goodness of man, the responsibility of man for his own actions, the inviolable individual conscience, and faith as predicated on reason and a firm assertion of the mind.[34]

In their consideration of the commission's censure of Samuel Hemphill, both Christensen and Buxbaum point to a rigged trial. In Buxbaum's words, the commission was led by "a predetermination to find the minister guilty by hook or crook" and by judges who were "little more than prosecutors." The commission's reaction is best seen, however, in the context of those events which preceded and surrounded it: the subscription controversy and charges of heresy and scandal among the Presbyterian clergy of the 1720s and 1730s, as well as Hemphill's "public defense." If the commission determined to get rid of Samuel Hemphill rather than reprimand and reinstate him, as they had others guilty of similar or even more serious errors, they did so as representatives of a church under siege, and then only after Hemphill had left them little choice.

As implied by the quote with which Dickinson concluded *A Vindication,* it might have been best if the commission had not responded publicly at all. In view of Dickinson's positive comments on reconciliation in *A Vindication,* one is left to speculate what the synod's response might have been if Hemphill had not gone public with his defense. Once he did, holding the church up to public ridicule, he sealed his fate, but in the end, as Dickinson explained, both Hemphill and the church lost: "The preacher received all the return blows; and the judges, after seeing themselves, their faith, and their institutions defamed, were in the untenable position of perhaps lending credibility to the attacks by their silence, or . . . losing dignity by responding."[35]

Finally, although it may not be terribly surprising that those who had proposed adoption of ministerial subscription to the Westminster Confession before 1729 chose to rally in its defense when challenged by Samuel Hemphill, it is curious to find that he who stepped forward to defend the synod and whom the synod chose as its defender had been the champion of the antisubscriptionist forces. This may have been Dickinson's natural response to having had his earlier remarks used against him by Hemphill and Franklin. But two other points need to be made.

First, contrary to what many pro-subscriptionists may have thought at the time, Hemphill's delinquency was not attributable to any laxity of the Adopting Act, presumably resulting from the position taken by Dickinson and his fellow New Englanders. Indeed, the Hemphill affair might be seen as proof positive of what Dickinson had forewarned, namely, the inadequacy of ministerial subscription as a defense against unorthodoxy.[36]

Second, given the above, Dickinson had no reason not to defend the Adopting Act of 1729. He was forced to defend the act by emphasizing those provisions which authorized the synod to expel Hemphill. But he persisted in confirming its terms of conscience. In doing so, while not relinquishing the position he had taken on the dangers of imposing human institutions and creeds, Dickinson clarified both the limits of his own antisubscriptionist sentiments and the common ground upon which the synod's formerly pro- and antisubscriptionist forces could stand in their defense. If that common ground had been theoretically established by the compromise that led to the Adopting Act, the Samuel Hemphill affair gave it substance.[37]

Finally, in his recent study of religious pluralism and denominationalism in colonial New Jersey, Douglas Jacobson has referred to Jonathan Dickinson as the "theological genius" of that colony's denominational movement. Citing Dickinson's publications in the subscription and Hemphill affairs, he has argued that Dickinson outlined an approach that could be adopted by any religious group that found itself in a similarly pluralistic situation, and that approach was based on the premises that "God has willed religious diversity into the very nature of creation" and that a church should not seek to forcefully eliminate diversity but rather "to embody the virtues of divine love and patience" within the limits necessary to retain its own identity or sense of truth.[38]

Jacobsen's assessment is essentially in accord with the foregoing account of Dickinson's response to the subscription and Hemphill affairs. It is quite possible that the ideas Dickinson expressed in both cases would be useful to those seeking an intellectual or theological framework for their acceptance of religious diversity or in the formulation of a nascent religious pluralism or denominationalism. Given our discussion of the context of his comments or their purpose, however, it is problematic at this point to suggest that Dickinson intended such an interpretation or application of his ideas. A stronger case for Dickinson's growing attraction to religious toleration, if not freedom, will be made in the pages to come.

4

Dissenting on Matters of Church and State

Relations between Presbyterians and Anglicans in the American colonies were never good. To the Anglicans, Presbyterians were a constant reminder of the attraction of nonconformity to large segments of the population, both at home and in the colonies, as well as of past hostility during the Puritan Revolution and in the Solemn League and Covenant. To Presbyterians, Anglicans embodied charges of illegitimacy and memories of persecution in England, Scotland, and Ireland. Invoking the church's name encouraged Presbyterian vigilance lest Anglican establishment in England become a reality in the colonies, as it would in Virginia, Maryland, the Carolinas, Georgia, and four counties of New York.[1]

That there was a connection between church relations and political discontent and even social and cultural development has been pointed out by a long line of historians of whom Arthur Cross, Ruth Bloch, Rhys Isaac, and Jack Greene are among the most recent. According to Cross, that the majority of the colonists professed a religion hostile, or at least alien, to the Anglican establishment "offered good ground for nourishing the seeds of political discontent" that culminated in the movement for independence. To Bloch, the conflict between Calvinists and Anglicans forged a link in the minds of American Calvinists between Great Britain and the Antichrist and between the struggle for independence and the "cosmic battle with Satan." That link, Bloch has pointed out, was spawned, if not indelibly lodged, in the popular consciousness decades before the American Revolution in the debates between Calvinist Dissenters, like Dickinson, and leaders of the Anglican Church.[2]

Isaac and Greene have further weighted the eighteenth-century Anglican-Dissenter debates by arguing that the Dissenters' opposition to an Anglican establishment should not be seen merely as political resistance to further incursions by the British power structure. Such opposition, whether it be in Virginia where an establishment existed or in the Middle Colonies where it did not, they have found, drew its passion from strong reactions against the further importation of British hierarchical and deferential norms into a maturing colonial society distinguished by a sociocultural configuration that emphasized individual freedom and was underscored by a deep and broadly diffused suspicion of established authority.[3]

Jonathan Dickinson was the principal Dissenter in the Presbyterian-Anglican debates for over twenty years. He spoke from the perspective of the Middle Colonies, but as the debates transcended regional boundaries, so did his remarks. Presbyterian-Anglican relations were especially strained in the Middle Colonies, where Presbyterians existed in sufficiently large numbers to pose a threat to the Church of England; where, except for the four counties of New York, no establishment existed but Anglicans never ceased to struggle for it; and where the Church of England was inextricably linked with proprietors and royal governors. A similar struggle, however, occurred in New England, where Anglicans challenged established Congregationalists, and even in parts of the South. The Church of England retained its established status throughout the South, but it was challenged in the colony of Virginia, when in the mid-eighteenth century the Presbyterian minister Samuel Davies obtained from London a ruling that the Act of Toleration gave Presbyterians full toleration.[4]

Anglican efforts to assert authority in the colonies were advanced by establishment of the Society for the Promotion of Christian Knowledge in 1698 and the Society for the Propagation of the Gospel in Foreign Parts in 1701. The SPCK was dedicated to the dissemination of seventeenth-century Anglican thought. The SPG set about to propagate the gospel among the "heathen," but it soon led the Anglican cause in the Middle Colonies and New England. The SPG insisted that it sought only "sufficient independence for the free scope of its missionary activity, and wished to leave all other matters to its civil and ecclesiastical superiors." As it was part of the Anglican organization, which in turn was closely interwoven with the British government, however, and as it favored creation of an American episcopate, Dissenters suspected its motives from the start.[5]

The bishop of London had jurisdiction over the Anglican Church in America, but that did not satisfy the SPG. Without the appointment of a separate bishop for the colonies, it pointed out, ordinations would never be allowed and, they believed, the church in the colonies would continue to lack any effective hierarchy or episcopal authority or even any system of ecclesiastical courts to guide expansion and enforce discipline. Dissenters would continue to freely exercise their influence over the religious lives of the population, it argued, creating "a Sodom of uncleanness and a pest house of iniquity."[6]

Though never successfully implemented, then, calls for the appointment of a bishop or bishops to the American colonies occurred regularly. Arthur Cross has found that nearly all such appeals came from the Middle Colonies, but possibly the most serious proposal as far as Dickinson was concerned occurred in 1715. In June of that year the SPG presented a memorial to King George I proposing that four American bishoprics be established in the colonies—two for the islands and two for the mainland. One of the mainland seats would be in Burlington, New Jersey. No action was taken on the proposal, but the archbishop of Canterbury set aside one thousand pounds for that purpose.[7]

Calls for an Anglican bishop, as well as fears of establishment, of course, reflected the increased number of Anglican churches in particular colonies or regions. Before 1701, there were 111 colonial Anglican churches. There were 79 in Virginia but only 2 in New York and 2 in Pennsylvania. After the founding of the SPG, the tempo picked up and by 1750 there were 289 Anglican churches, 20 in New York, 19 in Pennsylvania, and 18 in New Jersey. Their numbers never equaled those of the Dissenters, but the Middle Colonies had become their fastest growing area.[8]

The effort to spread Anglicanism in the Middle Colonies was given a boost when George Keith, a prominent Pennsylvania Quaker, renounced the Society of Friends, traveled to England to take Anglican orders, and returned as a missionary for the SPG. From 1702 to 1704, he and John Talbot toured the colonies and, in a letter to Thomas Bray of the SPG in London, reported that if Anglican ministers were not sent to the Middle Colonies, Presbyterian ministers from New England would "swarm into these new countries" and prevent any increase among Anglicans.[9]

New York, though a colony in which Anglicans were outnumbered seventeen to one by English Dissenters, French Calvinists, Lutherans, and Dutch Reformed, established the Church of England in New York City and its adjacent counties. That establishment became central to the expansion of the Church of England north of the Potomac.[10] Upon the transferral of government from the proprietors to the crown in 1702, attempts at expansion were begun in New Jersey. The colony's first royal governor, the Anglican Lord Cornbury (Edward Hyde), received the following charge: "You shall take special care that God almighty be devoutly and duly served throughout your government, the Book of Common Prayer as by law established read each Sunday and holy day, and the blessed sacrament administered according to the rites of the Church of England." In 1703, thanks to the governor's influence, St. Mary's Anglican Church was established in Burlington, New Jersey, and in 1705 an assembly of fourteen Anglican clergy meeting in Burlington demanded that in order to qualify for certain civil offices men be required to receive the sacraments in the Anglican church. The Dissenter-dominated legislature blocked the measure, but the struggle had begun.[11]

In 1703 George Keith conducted the first Anglican service in Eliza-beth Town, New Jersey, and in a report to the SPG he noted that he had found many who had formerly been "a sort of Independent . . . well af-fected to the Church of England." They deserved to be provided an Angli-can minister, he wrote, and he recommended that one be sent. That minister, the Reverend John Brooke, arrived in 1705. As we have seen, the only other church in Elizabeth Town in 1705 was that of the original New En-gland settlers, that which was soon to become Jonathan Dickinson's.

It is said that John Brooke began his tenure in Elizabeth Town by conducting Anglican services in a barn. At times he worshiped in the Inde-pendent Church, but he could not use the Book of Common Prayer. He reportedly got around this by reciting passages from memory. Many of the first Anglican services in Elizabeth Town were held in private homes, but by 1706 Brooke had gathered sufficient local support to lay the corner-stone for St. John's Church, which, as Nelson Burr has put it, became "a sort of Cathedral church" in colonial New Jersey.[12]

In 1709 the Reverend Edward Vaughn assumed the St. John's rectorship in 1709 and Dickinson entered the pulpit of the First Church. Both came as young men—Vaughn from England, Dickinson from New England. Both served for thirty-eight years in their respective parishes, and they died during the same week in 1747. Vaughn was neither the intellect nor the man of letters that Dickinson was, but he did well in building his congregation.[13] In 1711 Vaughn wrote to the SPG secretary in London that since his arrival he had baptized seventy-two children and eleven adults, "unfortunately brought up in dark Quakerism and Anabaptism," who were so pleased to be members of the church that they frequented services "with great devotion and seeming delight." In 1721 he counted some 200 church members, and in 1731 he reported that in the last two years he had bap-tized 556 children and 64 adults. As to the larger population of Presbyteri-ans, Vaughn wrote: "They are not so very rigid in that persuasion as altogether to deny their attendance on my ministry."[14]

Vaughn and Dickinson thus became competitors, but their competi-tion was part of a larger Anglican-Presbyterian rivalry in the Middle Colo-nies. They were, after all, on opposite sides not only of religious matters but also of civil matters, as were the churches they represented. Their ri-valry no doubt contributed to Dickinson's zeal as defender of his faith. One historian has written that Dickinson became "fully alive" due to Vaughn's efforts, and another wrote that the Presbyterian-Anglican division in Elizabeth

Town was "the origin of the greatest animosity and alienation between friends, townsmen, Christians, neighbors and relations that the town ever beheld, kindling a flame which was not extinguished until the conclusion of the Revolutionary War." It should be pointed out, however, that despite their serious rivalry, Dickinson and Vaughn were friends and respected each other's work. When Dickinson died, St. John's wardens and vestry reported that Dickinson's "artful insinuations" among the people having been silenced, they faced "the agreeable prospect of a plentiful harvest." Vaughn, however, who himself lay dying, exclaimed, "Oh that I had hold of the skirts of Brother Jonathan."[15]

Thus, the stage was set on the local, colonial, and intercolonial levels for one of the most public and extensive quarrels between Presbyterians and Anglicans in the first half of the eighteenth century—a pamphlet war between Dickinson and an array of SPG missionaries that began just after Dickinson had entered the fray over ministerial subscription but did not end until his death. The pamphlet war began in 1723, while the "Yale conversions" or the "great apostasy" of 1722 was still fresh in everyone's mind. In 1722 "the heavens opened and consternation rained down," Perry Miller has written, when Yale rector Timothy Cutler, tutor Daniel Browne, the Reverends Samuel Johnson and James Wetmore, and other ministers of the New Haven area defected to the Anglican ranks. What the defection offered, John Woolverton later added, was "striking and indisputable evidence that the Church of England posed an intellectual threat to colonial dissent" and an influential challenge to the right of establishment of the Puritan church in Connecticut and Massachusetts.[16]

John Checkley, perhaps the most notorious American Anglican polemicist of his time, fired the first salvo with *A Modest Proof of the Order and Government Settled by Christ and his Apostles . . . in the Church* (1723). Checkley, who had studied at Oxford but not taken a degree, was already well known in the colonies. He had reprinted the works of notable English Anglican divines and published his own tracts critical of the Calvinist doctrines of election and predestation, for which Massachusetts had fined him—twice! The year before he published *A Modest Proof,* Checkley sailed to England hoping to take Anglican Holy Orders, only to have the bishop of London, Edmund Gipson, refuse him as "a violent and unreasoning partisan" among people who were already bitterly hostile to the claims he advanced on behalf of the Church of England.[17]

In *A Modest Proof,* Checkley presented both the structure and substance of the initial stage of the Anglican–Presbyterian/Congregational debate. He raised four questions concerning the order and government settled by Christ and his apostles on the primitive church, as revealed in the New

Testament: What sacred offices were instituted by them? How were those offices distinguished? Were those offices to have perpetual standing in the church? And who succeeded in those offices and rightly executes them to this day? In brief, Checkley answered that the power of ordination was initially vested in the apostles, and from them, through all ages, in a succession of bishops who provided the "true ministers" of the gospel. Checkley wrote that regardless of one's gifts, it constitutes an offense against God to intrude upon the sacred function of the ministry without such ordination, or laying on of hands, by those whom Christ has ordered to preside over the affairs of the church.[18]

That he also appointed seventy others and sent them forth with the same commission as that of the apostles, but only after they were "less solemnly ordained" and called disciples rather than apostles, Checkley continued, shows that Christ intended to provide for two distinct ranks within the government of his church. Those of the first rank, the apostles, were not only to preach the gospel and to administer its ordinances but also to found, build, and govern the church in Christ's name. By his authority they and their successors, bishops, were to "dispose of all affairs for the edification of the church" and to constitute and ordain its ministers. Christ instructed the apostles, and through them his bishops, "in all things pertaining to the Kingdom of God." He opened their minds so that they might understand the Scriptures, and he "endued them with the Holy Ghost, to guide them into all truth" (iv–v, 11, 16, 18).

The second rank in church governance, that of the seventy disciples, became the church's presbyters, or ministers. In the "measure and proportion" of their commission the seventy were essentially the same as the apostles, Checkley wrote, but they were not equal to them. Like the apostles, the seventy were Christ's "messengers and ambassadors." The apostles used them to promote the gospel and to establish churches among those who received it, but they did so as the apostles' "assistants and helpers," and they were subject to the apostles in all matters. Thus, the relationship between bishops and presbyters, or ministers, was to continue, he insisted, until the end of time (19, 21, 24–27, 36).

Checkley suggested that his interpretation of the order and government settled by Christ on his church had been accepted for over fourteen hundred years. At length, he allowed, it was "invaded and suppressed by the usurpation and tyranny of the Roman papacy," whereby not only the church's government but also its doctrine, worship, and discipline were corrupted. Leaders of the Reformation attempted to recover the church's original purity and liberty, but "the adversary scattered his tares among the good seed which sprung up in briars and thorns." Doctrinal disputes and further divisions ensued, thereby disturbing the church even further and giving both hope and pleasure to its enemies. One of those doctrinal disputes, initiated by England's Dissenters, Checkley continued, led to rupture and schism as well as "alienation of minds," "confusions and barbaric cruelties," and "convulsions and revolutions in church and state." They "solemnly combined together to ruin and overthrow that order settled by Christ in his church" (2–4, 63).

Tellingly, in concluding *A Modest Proof,* pointing in the direction in which the debate would move, Checkley wrote that he was convinced that doctrinal differences over the nature of church government were related to political debates of the period. He wrote, if only in one brief reference to the point: "Political interests and state differences have all along been inter-woven with this contest about church government, and have supported and maintained it. And perhaps at bottom 'tis none of the least prejudice against episcopacy, that they of that persuasion have generally asserted the just rights and prerogatives of princes as the surest foundation of a kingdom's happiness and tranquility; and accordingly have maintained the doctrine of non-resistance and passive obedience, etc. whereas its rival government hath been thought by some, more serviceable for checking and curbing the power of princes" (5).

That Thomas Walter, Edward Wigglesworth, and Thomas Foxcroft, all of Massachusetts, as well as Dickinson, responded to Checkley, suggests the intercolonial nature of the quarrel. That Dickinson became the pri-mary respondent in the ongoing debate reflects both the similarity of their response and the high regard in which Dickinson was held in both sections of the colonies. Dickinson entitled his response *A Defense of Presbyterian Ordination.* With it, he was joined in a public debate that did not end until he had gone to press a dozen times. It began on the subjects of Anglican episcopacy and the validity of Presbyterian ordination, but, as Checkley warned, it soon evoked Anglican charges of schism and sedition and Dickinson's defense of religious toleration and the separation of church and state.[19]

In *A Defense of Presbyterian Ordination* Dickinson suggested that the point to be examined was the Anglican doctrine of ministerial purity through apostolic succession. He began by defining the role of the ministry. Its purpose, Dickinson wrote, is to destroy "the strongholds of sin and Satan" in the hearts of men, thereby rescuing those who are "sin's miserable captives" for the advancing Kingdom of Grace. The ministry is to dissipate the darkness of heathenism which, before its existence, had covered the earth. It is to make Christ known to man, the necessary first step in salvation, as by the "ordinary means" of salvation one cannot be saved but by knowing him.[20]

Like Checkley, Dickinson wrote that although ministers are called by God, "whoever entreth not by the door into the sheepfold, but climbeth up some other way . . . is a thief and a robber." God has provided the means by which the church can be protected from the intrusion of such pretenders, Dickinson continued, but the "High Church Party" (that which Checkley represented) had neither employed those means in its attack on Presbyterian ministers nor even been directed toward that end. Checkley and other Anglicans had labeled Presbyterians "a small upstart sect" and accused them of attempting to "unchurch all the Protestant world but themselves" and to nullify all church ordinances but their own. To Dickinson, that was but an act of "bigotry and contempt" founded on oppressive "Jacobite principles of passive obedience and non-resistance" (ii–iii, v, 11).

Dickinson took up the four questions raised in *A Modest Proof* and offered his interpretation of the history of prelacy, as a corrective to what Checkley had offered. Checkley had maintained that diocesan episcopacy had gone largely unchallenged for fourteen hundred years. Dickinson countered that prelacy was unknown in the church for the first three centuries, and where it was suggested, it was opposed by figures of note including Jerome, St. Ambrose, and St. Augustine. The rise of prelatic power and superiority, Dickinson wrote, led to "dreadful convulsions," "tumultuary uproars," and "bloody massacres" all occasioned by the "ambitious pursuit of ecclesiastical dignities" by those who would be deemed "the ambassadors of the Prince of Peace" (3–5).

Checkley had accused the Roman papacy of destroying the peace and order of the church by usurpation and tyranny aimed at erecting a secular power and dominion where none had previously existed or was intended. Dickinson charged the Church of England, as an established church which had questioned the legitimacy of Dissenting bodies, with intending much the same thing. Checkley had asserted that after the Reformation most of those of the Reformed tradition had adopted a polity similar to that of the Church of England. Dickinson countered that the element in its polity with which Anglicans were most closely identified, the doctrine of "the divine right of prelacy," was unknown in any of the Reformed churches outside England. Those churches under the influence of John Calvin, "first founder of the Presbyterian principles," constituted "the greatest and most considerable part of the reformed church," Dickinson wrote, and they replaced prelacy with the Presbyterian order. Lutherans had retained the use of bishops, he allowed, but they had done so in name only, their powers being far less than those of diocesan bishops (6–8).

Turning to Scripture, Dickinson questioned Checkley's inferring from the differences between the apostles and the seventy disciples that Christ intended to create two distinct orders of gospel ministers. As they were sent forth by Christ, Dickinson wrote, the original twelve were called apostles, but the seventy were said to be "apostlelein" as well. If the seventy disciples were not apostles in the gospel sense, he continued, they were nevertheless messengers, and after Christ sent forth the original apostles, he sent them as well. And, if it were granted that the seventy did constitute a distinct order at the time of their initial commission, little could be inferred from it, Dickinson pointed out, as there was no Christian Church at that time. The church was not established until after Christ's death, when the resurrected Christ commissioned the apostles, and only the apostles (9, 12–13). (Dickinson did agree with Checkley that deacons constitute a separate and inferior order in the church.)

Dickinson agreed with Checkley that some things about the apostles were extraordinary and temporary. They had been, after all, witness to Christ's life, doctrine, miracles, suffering, resurrection, and ascension. They had been made "infallible guides" in delivering gospel doctrine, given an unlimited commission and jurisdiction over all churches, and entrusted with the power "to confer miraculous gifts on others, to discern spirits, and to back their censures with corporal punishments." Those extraordinary powers expired with the apostles, however, while their more common functions—preaching, dispensing the sacraments, ordaining others to the work of the ministry, and governing the church—did not. The apostles may have exercised an extraordinary power over others in the church, Dickinson allowed, but that power was temporary and ceased with their passing. All other powers, those with which they were "to serve the edification, good order and government of the constituted church in all succeeding ages," the apostles shared with the seventy disciples, and they remained (14–16, 20–21).

Neither could Dickinson find any substantial evidence in Scripture to support Checkley's assertion that bishops, but not presbyters, succeeded the apostles in that office. The apostles did pick their successors, Dickinson allowed, but they did not confer on them their extraordinary powers. Indeed, Scripture suggests that the offices of bishop and presbyter, which succeeded the apostles, were coordinate, of the same order, and exercised the same key powers, most notably of ordination. If, then, bishops had come to consider themselves superior to presbyters, Dickinson reasoned, they had done so in an unscriptural manner, contrary to Christ's direction and to the example of his apostles (31, 36–37, 41–44).

Dickinson concluded his *Defense of Presbyterian Ordination* by asking why the "High Church Party" was condemning almost all other Protestant Churches for want of a regular ministry when there were many faithful servants among them. Was it not, thereby, giving strength to the papists by "sapping the Reformation at the very root"? Dickinson insisted that such tactics had been rejected by some eminent Anglicans; that they constituted an "egregious reflection" on Parliament, as that legislative body had established a presbyterian order in Scotland; and that they cast "a poor reflection on the fidelity of our blessed savior," in that if they were correct it would follow that Christ had left a major part of his church without either ministry or ordination (43–44).

In 1724, Checkley responded anonymously to Dickinson, as well as to Thomas Walter, Thomas Foxcroft, and Edward Wigglesworth, with *A Defense of a Book Lately Re-Printed at Boston, Entitled, A Modest Proof of the Order and Government, Etc.* (1724). "As I was concluding my letter [a reference to his response to Walter, Foxcroft, and Wigglesworth]," Checkley wrote, "the press was delivered of a misshapen production, sprung from the disordered brain of one J. Dickinson." Dickinson, he offered, "with the same degree of assurance as when canting from his tub," had become an advocate for Presbyterian ordination with all the pretenses to modesty and manners Presbyterians were "equal strangers to."[21]

Checkley accused Dickinson of having too narrow a view of the extent and order of the "mystical body of Christ" through the ages, thereby, in ruling out all innovations, rejecting some of the best, as well as the worst, parts of the church. Checkley also advanced the potentially more dangerous charge that the government would likely find seditious Dickinson's brief but critical reference to "the doctrines of passive obedience and nonresistance" as Jacobite principles that "ought to be exploded." Checkley wrote that it was "daring" of Dickinson to "dive into the political reasons of state" but that he ought to be careful in doing so. The king and the officers of his government were members of the Church of England, he reminded Dickinson, and they were under "the strongest, the most solemn and sacred engagements so to be." Therefore, to insult the Church of England, Checkley reasoned, implying that this is what Dickinson had done, was to insult the king and his officers and "their sentiments of things of the highest consequence" (54, 72).

Dickinson having been forewarned, Checkley addressed a number of matters of church history and scriptural evidence, but at length he cut to what he saw as the heart of the matter: "They are bold and insolent intruders into the enclosure wherewith our Lord has fenced his vineyard, who usurp the ministerial function without being ordained to it by a successor to the apostles, in whom, by the original charter, the powers of ordination and jurisdiction over a plurality of presbyters in churches are annexed, either in fact or right." That, Checkley wrote, he believed he had already shown to be the case for Presbyterians in general and for Jonathan Dickinson in particular: Jonathan Dickinson was never ordained by any "successor." Ergo, "Jonathan Dickinson is a bold and insolent intruder, etc. and no minister of the gospel at Elizabeth Town" (60).

If that were not egregious enough, Checkley continued, the contempt with which Presbyterian intruders had treated those holding episcopal offices had encouraged "libertines" to call into question the credentials of every minister and the truth of all revealed religion. Divisions and separations had resulted, which had weakened the Church of England, "the chieftest bulwark in Christendom against Popery." Where Dickinson had accused the Church of England of "unchurching Protestants," Checkley insisted that the fault lay with the Dissenters. The Anglicans had unchurched no one who had "true pastors and sacraments"; those who did not were not part of the Mystical Body of Christ to begin with (71–73).

Dickinson's second response to Checkley appeared in 1724. In *Remarks upon .. the Defense of . . . A Modest Proof,* Dickinson criticized the particularly venomous nature of Checkley's attack, defended the points he had made in *A Defense of Presbyterian Ordination,* and pointed to what he saw as contradictions in Checkley's response. Dickinson reported that the vile epithets Checkley had used against him had served only to reveal the true spirit of his adversaries, who were obviously neither "followers of the prince of peace" nor men of "meekness and moderation." Further, they had succeeded in making plain "the badness of [their] cause," as it needed to be defended "with swords and staves."

Dickinson admitted that in *A Defense of Presbyterian Ordination* he had referred to the High Church Party as "an upstart sect," thereby identifying Checkley as a Tory. No doubt hoping to deflect Checkley's suggestion that such a statement was a slight of the government, however, Dickinson explained that the High Church Party was but a faction that had not existed until Archbishop William Laud's time, and that it was no more a part of the Established Church "than a wen, or such like excrescence is part of a man." Where Checkley had suggested that Dickinson's condemnation of what he had termed the Jacobite principles of passive obedience and nonresistance might have been labeled seditious, Dickinson pointed out, first, that such principles were associated with defenders of the Stuart kings, those truly Jacobites and from among whom the High Church Party had arisen; and, second, that the Prince of Orange and the "present most happy establishment" had been founded on principles quite the opposite and more attuned to those Dickinson espoused.[22]

In closing, Dickinson took up Checkley's barb that he had never been ordained by any successor to the apostles and that, therefore, he was a usurper, a "bold and insolent intruder into the enclosure wherewith our Lord Jesus has fenced his vineyard." Dickinson simply responded that, as he had already shown, all ministers of the gospel have the same commission; they have the same office and authority, including the power to ordain, whereby he became a gospel minister. If that were not the case, he added, all Protestants but those of the Church of England would be cut off from the Mystical Body of Christ. As that is not true, all remain "within the pale of the true church."[23]

In 1725 Checkley responded to *Remarks upon . . . the Defense of . . . A Modest Proof* with *A Letter to Jonathan Dickinson*. The letter ran only some fourteen pages, and though intended to "expose the defects" of Dickinson's presentation, it added little to the discussion of matters theological. Checkley did take the opportunity to insist that Dickinson's differentiating between a High and Low Anglican Church was but a "fiction of the church's spiteful enemies" and that the Church of England remained one in doctrine and discipline. Where Dickinson had referred to his party as Tories, Checkley responded that, because the Whigs had been "stigmatized with such an ignominious brand," to be called a Tory was a mark of honor to which "all that love the Church of England and the Constitution will doubtless consent."[24]

Checkley also added to the political charges he had made against Dickinson. He responded to Dickinson's charge that the "wrathful and furious" Anglicans had defended their cause "with swords and staves," by laying at the feet of the Dissenters the "effusion of blood" spilled from 1641 to 1660 in the English Civil War, the "murder" of Charles I, and the persecution of the Episcopal Church in Scotland by Presbyterians since the Revolution of 1688. And he took issue with Dickinson's implying that Britain's postrevolutionary government had been founded on the principle of resistance. Instead, Checkley insisted, the Prince of Orange had come to the throne through abdication. Resistance, with which Checkley had charged Dickinson, was "a principle abhorred by the English nation and only entertained by the seditious and worst sort of dissenters." If "every English breast" were inspired by the principle of obedience, Checkley wrote, there would not be a rebel in the nation and no plots or conspiracies against the king, to wit he mentioned the Jacobite Rebellion of 1715 (2–4).

Checkley concluded his letter by referring to Dickinson as "a trifler," whose judgment on the subject at hand should not be taken seriously. He wrote that Dickinson's "party" should disown him, as what he had written had only betrayed their cause. Moreover, if Dickinson insisted on writing again, with nothing more to offer than he had thus far, he would not further jeopardize his reputation by responding. Checkley urged Dickinson "to be quiet . . . [and] to mind [his] own business," but if he did not, truth would "bear the test." It would "stand alone against all the assaults . . . made upon it by impotent malice, venom, disordered brains, petulance and ignorance, empty skulls, profane ribaldry, [and] saucy puny scribblers" (10–12).

Dickinson's "party" did not disown him. He did not respond to Checkley, but neither did he heed Checkley's advice and be quiet. Instead, eight years later, Dickinson again engaged leaders of the Church of England. What provoked Dickinson to reenter the fray in 1732 is unclear, but it might well have been Samuel Johnson's renewed efforts to secure an American episcopacy. Johnson was among the Yale converts of 1722. Later that year, he left for England where he received Holy Orders and was appointed a missionary of the SPG. In 1724, Johnson established the first Anglican church in Connecticut, at Stratford, from which he made continual efforts to expand the Church of England throughout the colonies, and on April 5, 1732, after a conference involving a group of New England ministers, Johnson appealed directly to the bishop of London, Edmund Gibson, for a bishop. He wrote that in the opinion of New England's governmental leaders the Anglican establishment did not extend to America. As so many New Englanders were destitute of pastoral care, however, they would "submit even to a Church of England establishment" to get it. Therefore, Johnson urged the bishop to support an Anglican establishment in the colonies, but he also noted that any bishop so assigned should insist only on essentials and exercise "the greatest leniency" in the matter of nonessentials.

Two other points on this exchange are of interest to us here. First, in his response to Samuel Johnson, Bishop Gibson wrote that until such time as a bishop was appointed, "it would be much happier for the church" if the colonial charters were revoked, something he thought the people might accept as it was under those charters that they had found themselves in such a "wretched, mobbish way of management." This likely caused some considerable alarm in New England. Second, Johnson seems to have found it necessary to repeatedly assure his diocesan that attempts to secure bishops for America did not proceed from a desire to be independent. No doubt responding to some concern voiced by the bishop of London or to some idea then current in English circles, Johnson insisted that the reverse was true, as "it has always been a fact, and is obvious in the nature of the thing, that anti-episcopal are . . . anti-monarchical principles." Any idea of seeking independence, he explained, rather than arising from a colonial episcopacy would more likely flow from the want of it—"from that turbulent outrageous spirit which enthusiasm is apt to inspire men with."[25]

In *The Scripture Bishop* Dickinson reviewed much of what he had already written on the scriptural and historical basis of Presbyterian polity, but he focused primarily on the nature and effects of Anglican establishment and the origins and justification of Presbyterian dissent. In its first dialogue, for example, Eleutherius, a recent convert to Presbyterianism from the Church of England, spoke of the martyrs who, "rather than wound their consciences by a compliance with what they thought sinful," had been driven from the more pleasant environs of England to live "among the wild pagans in an American desert, choosing to forsake their dear country and dearest friends to undergo the perils of the sea and the greater perils of barbarous savages in a howling wilderness." He spoke of the persecution of nonconformists that followed the Restoration, including the silencing in one day of over two thousand "of the most learned and pious ministers in England," denying them their ministry, stripping them of their estates, and sending them to prison, where they "languished and died."

Praelaticus, the Anglican, explained that what had happened was the fault "of particular persons then at the helm, not of the Constitution" and that the Anglican Church sought only an ecclesiastical, not a secular, supremacy. But that only prompted Eleutherius to question the purpose of what followed, namely, of having bishops sit as members of Parliament and on various governing councils, as well as presiding over "Bishops Courts." In the latter instance, he pointed out, alleged offenders had been subject to heavy fines, exorbitant fees, and imprisonment without any attempt being made to bring them to sincere repentance.[26]

The Anglicans were duly enraged by Dickinson's *Scripture Bishop,* and they issued two responses. One, anonymously published but attributed to Samuel Johnson and James Wetmore, was *Eleutherius Enervatus* (1733). Wetmore was also among the Yale converts of 1722. Like Samuel Johnson he was ordained in England and became a member of the SPG. He returned to the colonies and served, first, in 1723 as assistant rector of Trinity Church in New York City and, beginning in 1726, as rector of the Anglican church at Rye, New York.[27]

Eleutherius Enervatus was also written in the form of a dialogue between Eusebius and Eleutherius, to which was appended two letters on the subject "some time ago sent to the supposed author of that pamphlet" *Scripture Bishop.* (Jonathan Dickinson was not identified by name.) The dialogue has been attributed to James Wetmore; the letters are believed to have been written by Samuel Johnson. Wetmore offered that the letters had been written by a layman some time ago and sent to Dickinson. In private correspondence, however, Timothy Cutler noted that they were authored by Samuel Johnson, "at the desire of a layman whom Dickinson challenged."[28]

Eusebius's role in the dialogue, of course, was to enervate what

Eleutherius, or Dickinson, had offered in *The Scripture Bishop*. As one would expect, Eusebius charged Eleutherius with failing to prove either that presbyters have the power to ordain or that bishops and presbyters are of one order. His primary thrust, however, was to counter Dickinson's charges against the Anglican establishment by accusing Presbyterians, or the "English Separatists," of an unlawful separation from the Church of England and therefore of bearing "the horrid guilt of setting up altar against altar" for no good reason.[29]

Eusebius explained that the "old nonconformists" in their zeal to bring "the Geneva discipline into England" had been especially critical of the English constitution. When the Act of Uniformity (1559) was adopted, they not only objected to the hierarchy and ritual imposed thereby but refused to submit to the act, resigned their cures, and separated from the church. There were others who agreed with the Separatists in principle, Eusebius added, but who nonetheless condemned them for separating.

When Eleutherius interjected, as Dickinson had, that the Separatists had been persecuted for their actions, Eusebius quickly retorted that it was warranted as nonconformists tended to "destroy all peace, order, and love" and to "bring the nation into the greatest confusion." In the most scathing attack yet, Eusebius, or Wetmore, accused the Separatists of subverting all civil and ecclesiastical government, demolishing churches, persecuting the clergy of the church "in the most cruel manner," "robbing and butchering all honest loyal subjects to the king and sons of the church they could lay hands on," and murdering the king and "the best in the nation." The government had to act against the Separatists, he concluded. That suffering had resulted was a "pity," but the Separatists had greater reason to blame themselves for it than the government.[30]

In his second letter, Johnson took up Dickinson's charge that Anglicans had unchurched Dissenters, including Presbyterians, and thereby precipitated violence. Johnson concluded, first, that it was not episcopacy but opposition to it, or rebellion against it, that had caused such "horrid" incidents. Second, he explained that even if Anglicans were guilty, they had acted in the heat of battle, when the blame for such unfortunate actions could be laid at the feet of both sides. Writing in calmer times, Johnson offered, their differences were not sufficient to warrant their continued separation. After all, he pointed out, Dickinson and other Presbyterians had agreed that Anglican orders were good and its bishops were at least presbyters. If, on the other hand, as Anglicans had insisted, presbyters were not bishops, and they had not been properly ordained, then the entire Presbyterian order was of questionable authority, and its members would do well to return to the Church of England.[31]

The second response to *The Scripture Bishop* appeared under the title *The Scripture Bishop, or the Divine Right of Presbyterian Ordination and Government, Considered in a Dialogue Between Praelaticus and Eleutherius, Examined in Two Letters to a Friend* (1733). It listed no publisher, no place of publication, and no author, but it has been attributed to Arthur Browne. A native of Ireland, Browne was ordained by the Bishop of London and made a missionary of the SPG. In 1729, he was settled at the Anglican church in Newport, Rhode Island. From Newport, one year later, he removed to Providence where he wrote *The Scripture Bishop . . . Considered,* which took the form of two letters "to a friend." Its tone was set at the start, when Browne variously referred to Dickinson and his fellow Presbyterians as "passing for ministers without Christ's approval," as "architects of schism," and as "laying hay and stubble upon the foundation of Christianity, at once mocking God and deceiving the people."

As Wetmore and Johnson had before him, Browne responded to Dickinson's criticism of the Church of England's persecution of Dissenters by referring to the vengeance that had been reaped by them on the Anglicans in England when the Dissenters gained power. To that, however, Browne added the behavior of Dissenters in New England, which he described as being "notorious for her barbarities and cruel persecutions" and as continuing "to persecute honest and well-meaning Christians, members of the true church, by robbing them of their estates towards the support of schismatical teachers" and to "yearly imprison their bodies for refusing to comply with her wicked and unjust demands."[32]

Dickinson's response, *The Scripture Bishop Vindicated,* took aim at Browne's attack on New England. Dickinson agreed that some persecution had taken place in the earliest days of settlement. Laws had been passed "against certain seducers, crowding in among them, who threatened no less than the dissolution of their government," but even in those instances, he explained, the severity of the laws had been exaggerated. Actions toward Quakers, for example, were scarcely justifiable, he allowed, but Quakers were "profane insolent disturbers of solemn public worship," as well as "open deriders and subverters of the Christian faith and . . . of civil government."[33]

Further, Dickinson continued, persecution in New England dissipated in time, as leaders of that church "grew sensible of their error." They became more tolerant of the various sects that entered among them, and after passage of the English Toleration Act no laws were allowed that would "violate liberty of conscience." In reference to Quakers, Baptists, and Anglicans, Dickinson pointed out, several laws were passed creating a relatively nonexclusionary establishment involving merely a common tax for ministerial salaries imposed in each community by majority rule. If Anglicans constituted the majority in any community, their minister would have a legal claim to the salary. It was a system allowed by the laws of the England, he continued, and it was common practice not only in England but in those colonies where the Church of England had been established. Moreover, Dickinson added, the laws of Massachusetts and Connecticut had been further liberalized. Not only were Anglican ministers allowed to raise whatever funds they might among their followers but, where an Anglican minister was settled in a community, he was eligible to receive that part of the tax paid for the support of the ministry by members of his own congregation (28, 30).

Dickinson reminded his readers that New England had been founded by those who sought refuge from the impositions of the Church of England. Nevertheless, all God-fearing men who wished to join in the services of any congregation, even Anglicans, were readily received. Anglicans were treated with "exemplary candor, charity and civility," and if, as was the case, it took many years before the Church of England conducted public services, it was due only to their insufficient numbers or the absence of a ministry by which a congregation might be gathered. Where they wished to establish their own church, they were allowed to do so, and no impediment was offered that was not also applied to their dissenting neighbors (30–31).

In *The Scripture Bishop* Dickinson had noted, largely in passing, that the people had a natural right to commit their most important affairs to those they approve. In that particular case, he argued that the Church of England's imposition of ministers upon congregations was "a lordship" of which Christ and the apostles would not have approved. In referring to Dickinson's comment on natural rights, Browne had suggested that Dickinson would do well to consider that man was no longer in a state of nature but rather in a state of grace. In *The Scripture Bishop Vindicated,* Dickinson asked what difference that would make. Having moved to a state of grace, would man no longer be answerable to the dictates of the laws of nature? Dickinson insisted that as people have the natural right to care for their bodies, they have the natural right to care for their souls, that they be "fed with the food of life, not destroyed or rendered unhealthy by the ignorance, errors, scandals, or other insufficiency" of their ministers: "If I have a natural right to judge for myself, in the affairs of my eternal safety, and must stand or fall at last by my own opinion and conduct, and not by another man's, I have equally a natural right to choose the means that I think most conducive to my eternal well being, and [which] cannot be determined by any other person against my own opinion and conscience" (47–48).

In 1733, Thomas Foxcroft took up his pen once again in response to Wetmore and Johnson, and, though originally published separately, in time Dickinson's *Scripture Bishop Vindicated* and Foxcroft's *Eusebius Inermatus* were combined in a single volume. For the moment, however, both sides in the debate fell silent.

The third phase of Dickinson's pre–Great Awakening clash with colonial Anglicans was initiated by his Elizabeth Town rival, Anglican minister Edward Vaughn. In 1736 Vaughn invited the Reverend John Beach of New Town, Connecticut, to preach in his Elizabeth Town pulpit. Beach, a Yale graduate, had, under the influence of Samuel Johnson, declared his conformity to the Church of England in 1732. Ordained in England in the same year, he became a member of the SPG and was assigned to the Anglican congregation at New Town. At Vaughn's request, Beach preached at Elizabeth Town on two Sundays to a gathering of some three to four hundred people, "no doubt," as Nelson Burr has written, "to the wide-eyed dismay of the Dissenters."[34]

In the same year, an Anglican church was founded in nearby Newark, and many Presbyterians were taken into the Anglican fold not only because of the lure of Anglican theology but also, and possibly primarily because of, anger over an incident involving Colonel Josiah Ogden. Ogden, a wealthy and influential resident, had represented the town in the colonial assembly and been a pillar of the Presbyterian Church. On one occasion, however, he had chosen to rescue his rainsoaked and rotting wheat on the Sabbath, in consequence whereof he was censured by the church for failing to properly observe the Sabbath and placed in the stocks. Joined by a number of those sympathetic to his cause, Ogden protested the church's actions, and a divided congregation resulted, providing fertile ground for the Anglicans. Dickinson, who was one of those sent by the Synod of Philadelphia in a failed effort to mediate the quarrel, was invited by those of the Newark Presbyterian Church that remained to defend Presbyterianism against Anglican criticism. His sermon, which was delivered on June 2, 1736, was entitled *The Vanity of Human Institutions in the Worship of God.*[35]

As in his earlier commentaries, Dickinson represented the Presbyterian-Anglican controversy in broader, philosophically prerevolutionary political terms, presenting a position that he believed was both "agreeable to the Council of God" and founded upon "the unalienable rights of mankind." Implied in his defense of Presbyterianism, or his attack on Anglican prelacy, was the suggestion that Calvinism in general and Presbyterianism in particular were at least loosely consistent with Lockean political theory, wherein human rights are granted by God, not by government. God has "lifted [man] from his self-imposed squalor and sin and given the nobility of a son of God," Dickinson wrote, and, in doing so, he has given man a "notion of independence and responsibility to God alone," whereby he should be "contemptuous of subjugation in any form" and prepared to defend the "natural ability and just claim of all men everywhere to make their own private decisions in matters of conscience and religion."

In *The Vanity of Human Institutions* Dickinson applied this philosophical framework to two specific matters. First, he pointed out, as Presbyterians shared in the liberty wherewith Christ made men free, those who were considering leaving the Newark congregation for the Church of England should realize that in doing so they would part with that liberty and "take upon them a yoke of bondage." Second, he urged those who had chosen to remain within Presbyterian ranks to exercise both "charity and mutual forbearance in the affairs of conscience and salvation." He reminded them that one of their greatest complaints against the Church of England had been the latter's refusing its communion to Presbyterians, excommunicating those who refused to comply with Anglican rites and ceremonies, and declaring incapable of salvation those who rejected prelacy. From such an experience, Dickinson argued, "we have good reason to conclude, that they are safest who are most charitable, and that the error is on the damning side."[36]

Dickinson, of course, went on to recapitulate his previously stated defense of Presbyterianism and criticism of the Church of England. He concluded his sermon, however, with a reminder to the Newark congregation's Reformed heritage, recalling their ancestors' "errand into the wilderness" and their responsibilities, therein:

> Many of my audience are the posterity of those who left their delightful country and pleasant habitations, crossed the Atlantic with their families, came into a howling wilderness among innumerable multitudes of barbarous savages, encountered the most amazing trials, difficulties and discouragements, to fly from the imposition of those things, and to worship God in peace and purity according to their own institutions. And how remarkably were they owned of God! How signal were the appearances of his providence in their favor. Would it not therefore be every way our interest to imitate their purity and piety in worshipping the God of our fathers, that he may be with us as he was with our fathers, that he may remember the kindness of our youth, and the love of our espousals, when we came after him into the wilderness, into a land not sown?[37]

John Beach responded to Dickinson with *A Vindication of the Worship of God According to the Church of England* (1736). He sidestepped the issue of unalienable rights and resistance to government and establishment. He avoided any further substantive discussion of the Anglican Church's doctrine, polity, and history, save to state once again that it did not seek to impose its ordinances and ceremonies on anyone. Instead, he vindicated the people of Newark's right to worship according to the Church of England, if they should so choose.

In particular, Beach took issue with Dickinson's concluding remarks. He argued that although it was true that many Dissenters did flee what they called persecution, that flight did not make them any more blessed than the Catholics of Canada. Once in the colonies, they persecuted, banished, or executed those who did not conform to their way of worship, whether they were Anglicans, Baptists, or Quakers. Moreover, he continued, colonial Dissenters had not crossed the Atlantic for Presbyterianism but for "Brownism or Independency," and if, as Dickinson had suggested, the congregation were to honor the ways of their forefathers, they were free once again to make a break, in this case to the Anglican fold.[38]

Over the course of the next two years, Beach would issue one more response and Dickinson would issue two. Beach took issue with a charge Dickinson had made, almost in passing in his Newark sermon, that some Anglican ministers had become Arminian. Dickinson continued to hammer away at the abuses witnessed under the Anglican establishment, but otherwise there was little left to say until the Great Awakening lent further substance and renewed urgency to their quarrel.[39]

In the previous chapter, Douglas Jacobson was cited as suggesting that Dickinson's essays written during the subscription controversy and Samuel Hemphill affair placed him among the theoretical founders of denominationalism in America. Reflecting on his role in the Presbyterian-Anglican debate, Thomas J. Curry has come to a similar conclusion. Curry has referred to the public debate as suggestive of the growing controversy concerning the relationship between church and state in America, and he has credited Dickinson's tracts with advancing the cause of religious toleration by both criticizing Anglican persecution of dissent in Old England and pointing with approval to liberalization of the Puritan establishment in New England. Dickinson's work, Curry has concluded, reflects a growing disillusionment with, and opposition to, an establishment of church and state, which, in time, led to passage of the First Amendment.[40]

It is fair to suggest that by 1738, though more for scriptural and experiential than theoretically enlightened reasons, Dickinson had come to reject that element of his Separatist heritage which favored establishment.

He denied that which had been taught in the Dissenters' Confession of 1596, for example, namely, that it was the duty of government "to suppress and root out" all false religion and to "establish and maintain by their laws every part of God's word, his pure religion and true ministry . . . protecting and maintaining . . . the good, punishing and restraining the evil."[41]

In his struggle with the Church of England, Dickinson—perhaps because he was living in an area free of establishment and rich in competing churches—extended the position he had taken during the subscription controversy to speak out against any religious establishment that imposed its ordinances in matters of religion on the individual conscience and against the loss of civil, even unalienable, rights for those who dissented. Such an establishment, Dickinson concluded, assumed "the character of that one lawgiver, who only can save or destroy, and take from us the liberty, wherewith Christ has made us free."[42]

5

ARGUING FOR THE REASONABLENESS OF CHRISTIANITY

ONE OF THE GREATEST REVOLUTIONS in religious history, Sydney Ahlstrom has written, occurred in the seventeenth and eighteenth centuries when quietly, even imperceptibly, men confronted the momentous issues of the Enlightenment. That quiet revolution, Ahlstrom has explained, initiated the spiritual transition from a period in which American culture was still recognizably medieval in its outlook to one of distinctly modern religious ideas. Jonathan Dickinson played an important role in that revolution.[1]

Dickinson's response to the Enlightenment has not been as prominent in the histories of the period as that of Jonathan Edwards. After all, he was not as thorough in his consideration of the issues raised by the Enlightenment. But, at least on the specific issue of free will, Dickinson's work both preceded and influenced that of Edwards. Indeed, Jon Pahl has gone so far as to suggest that by the time Edwards entered the fray, due in large part to Dickinson, the question had already been decided or at least a consensus, or "harmony in discord," had been reached.[2]

The Enlightenment significantly influenced Dickinson. That influence has already been seen in our discussion of the subscription controversy, the Samuel Hemphill affair, and the first phase of Dickinson's Anglican debates; other examples will be pointed out when we turn to the Great Awakening. Two other publications, however, are commonly cited as those wherein Dickinson addressed the ideas of the Enlightenment without reference to any other precipitating event: *The Reasonableness of Christianity* (1732) and *Familiar Letters to a Gentleman* (1745). It is to them that we now turn.

Central to the challenge posed by the Enlightenment to Calvinism was the apparently irreconcilable conflict between the former's insistence on man's free will and the latter's doctrine of God's sovereign free grace. That conflict, that paradox or conundrum of free will and divine providence, dominated the intellectual production of colonial America. It provoked a debate which, as Jon Pahl has put it, "defined the boundaries of thought and action in early America as fully as military conflicts defined geographical boundaries." Moreover, by the end of the colonial period, the debate came to transcend the field of religious inquiry to encompass political ideology, or the search for an acceptable line between absolute freedom and tyranny. In short, the rhetoric of the American Revolution and of the ordering of liberty in the new republic had its roots in the debate over free will. The debate peaked during the Great Awakening, but at least for Jonathan Dickinson it began a decade earlier.[3]

As Norman Fiering has written, there were three parts to the problem of reconciling the doctrines of God's sovereign free grace and free will: predestination by free grace and man's inability to effect his own salvation; development of a determinist hypothesis based on the concept of natural law; and the question of whether will and intellect are separate or inseparable. Though present earlier, all three moved to the fore in the British colonies of North America during the Great Awakening. The first arose in response to the growing appeal of Arminianism, the second with the widespread consideration of the controversial writings of such men as Thomas Hobbes and John Locke, and the third as an issue that divided not only New from Old Light/Old Side but also moderate from radical New Light/ New Side.[4]

Pahl has described the response to this problem as a fivefold typology. At the extremes stood the determinists, or those who precluded any human agency, and the indeterminists, who insisted that man was entirely a free agent. Two more commonly held intervening, but opposed, positions resulted from attempts to mediate between the two extremes while retaining substantial portions of one or the other. On the one hand, Calvinists allowed man only a limited degree of liberty within what they called an "inclining necessity." Their opponents, notably those Anglicans with whom Dickinson would be engaged during the Great Awakening, posed the concept of "innate liberty," which shifted the emphasis from determinism to free will while retaining elements of both.

The central position, Pahl argues, resulted in large measure from the Dickinson-Anglican debates of the Great Awakening. The consensus that arose from that debate incorporated elements of both positions. The advocates of this "harmony in discord" allowed, if somewhat paradoxically, for both freedom and fatalism, for both God's order and human spontaneity. As Pahl has put it, they set man free but they limited that freedom to an "aristocracy of grace," those whom God had elected to the covenant of grace. Second, it is important to establish that Dickinson was well along in formulating his position years before the Great Awakening began and likely would have continued to develop it even if the Awakening had not occurred.[5]

Calvinists did not deny man sufficient freedom, or moral autonomy, to be held responsible for his sins. Most believed that man was moved by council rather than coaction. They defined freedom as the absence of constraint or compulsion in behavior. Where the debate raged between Calvinists and exponents of the Enlightenment, however, was over how free will was employed, what choices were possible, and whether freedom was an act of the will or of the intellect and the will inseparably bound. Dickinson and Edwards concluded that the will (or affections) and the intellect (or rational soul) were two powers of the mind but that they were only notionally so and should not be seen as distinct agents with different provinces and authorities capable of performing separate actions.[6]

Given Dickinson's frequent reference to him in both of the works to be considered here, there is little doubt but that John Locke provoked him, as he did Edwards, into making his position known. Norman Fiering is no doubt correct, however, in debunking the myth that reading Locke was "the central and decisive event" in Edwards's intellectual life; neither was it in Dickinson's. Both were far more influenced by an eclectic array of seventeenth-century British moral philosophers widely read in New England. But, at least with Dickinson, Locke's *Essay Concerning Human Understanding* (1690) represented the tendencies toward positivism and skepticism incorporated in the new psychological empiricism, and it is to that work, if only as representative, that Dickinson directed his response. In the specific case of Dickinson's *Reasonableness of Christianity*, much the same can be said of Locke's essay of the same title, published in 1695.[7]

In the eighteenth century, Ahlstrom has written, "there gradually came to prevail among the educated classes a climate of opinion in which moderate common-sense prevailed." Locke's *Reasonableness* was consistent with that climate. To Dickinson, however, Locke's treatise, in its attempt to bring theology into line with the new psychological empiricism, was latitudinarian, if not Deistic. Indeed, Dickinson suggested that it may have contributed to the formulation of rationalistic Christianity and, even later, natural religion. Though he purposefully employed the same title, Dickinson had no such intent. His goal was to defend the essentials of traditional Calvinist Christian doctrine as representing "a simultaneous commitment to faith and reason."[8]

Dickinson sought to describe a simple, intelligible Christianity derived from Scripture. He employed an epistemology and concept of freedom of the will that provided for a "wholeness of mind, spirit, and emotion." More specifically, he attempted to show by scriptural evidence that the single article of faith is that Jesus is the Messiah, the promised Savior, and that to have faith in him, to repent of one's sins, and to endeavor after a sincere obedience to the Savior's commandments are the only conditions required of anyone for salvation.[9]

Dickinson and Edwards stood at the crossroads of Puritanism and the Enlightenment. In appropriating certain ideas of the Enlightenment, they sought the middle ground between the two threats of Arminianism and Antinomianism. Dickinson's *Reasonableness of Christianity* provided not only the author's critique of the Enlightenment but also a moderate Calvinist theologian's attempt to appropriate and temper Enlightenment ideas, thereby signifying his tacit endorsement of Enlightenment rationalism. As such, Dickinson was akin to that group of New England ministers identified by John Corrigan as the "Catholick Congregational Clergy," who drew upon aspects of Reformed doctrine that had developed in seventeenth-century New England as well as ideas from English scientists, latitudinarians, physico-theologians, and Cambridge Platonists to develop a theology that stressed reason, purpose, and unity in nature.[10]

Dickinson's readers, to use his own words, were those "whose favorite topic is the religion of nature." To them, he offered some "rational considerations" of "the being and attributes of God, the apostasy of man, and the credibility of the Christian religion," as well as a vindication through scriptural proof of the divine mission of God "against the most important objections, whether of ancient or modern infidels."[11]

Thomas Foxcroft of Boston, another of Corrigan's "Catholick Congregational Clergy," provided a preface for *The Reasonableness of Christianity.* Quite likely, he also assisted in its Boston publication. Foxcroft hailed Dickinson's book as "seasonable for this skeptical day" in that it "engage[d] the heart, as well as employ[ed] the mind" and demonstrated the reasonableness of Christianity "to the utter confusion of all atheistical pretenses" and "to the manifest confutation and shame of all deistical exceptions." In that it was "calculated [in] every way to the true principles of reason," Foxcroft wrote, *The Reasonableness of Christianity* would point to the "guilt and folly" of unbelievers, as well as to their vanity in pretending to natural religion, while ridiculing divinely supported revelation.[12]

Chastened by Dickinson's sermons, Foxcroft continued, would be those "libertine moralists" and "pharisitical and bigoted papists," who "take the Christian profession upon blind trust, and not out of conviction and rational choice"; those who "adulterate the institutions of Christ" by mixing within it "their own presumptuous devices, or their anomalous and spurious inventions"; those "unevangelical and (pretended) rational Christians . . . [who] teach the principles or practice the duties of natural religion, with little or no explicit reference to a redeemer"; those "heretical and wild opinionists, who professedly receive gospel revelations" but "miserably abuse, torture, and pervert the scripture, to their own and others' destruction"; those "enthusiastical perfectionists (spirited men, falsely so called) who act in religion by no certain stated rule, but by a variable fanatic impulse . . . and vainly boast of those superior lights and refinements, which they think supersede all necessity of ministerial teaching and outward ordinances"; and those "many carnal and inconsistent hypocrites," who "though perhaps orthodox scripturally, punctual devotionists, and precise zealots for some disputed matters of doctrine . . . yet are shameful delinquents in point of morality, and live in open defiance to some essential precepts of the gospel" (i–xii).

Tellingly, Dickinson opened the first sermon, which addressed the being and attributes of God, with the following passage:

> Reason is the dignifying and distinguishing property of human nature, whereby man, above the rest of the lower creation, is qualified to know, obey, and enjoy his creator; by which alone he is capable of that faith, without which it is impossible to please God, and even of believing that first article, that God is, as well as that He is a rewarder of those that diligently seek him. Whence it follows, that He who has made us rational creatures, expects from us a reasonable service, and cannot be pleased with that faith, practice, or hope, that is grounded on education, or common opinion, and not the result of rational reflection, or enquiry.

Given that, Dickinson explained that his plan for *The Reasonableness of Christianity* was to inquire into the grounds of Christianity in order to offer "some rational evidence of the truth of Christianity" and, thereby, the reasonableness of its truths, rather than relying on our receiving them on trust (1–2).

Dickinson cited John Locke as having written that although man can have no innate idea of God, he can create for himself an idea of God through his natural abilities; through those ideas which he does have on existence, duration, and powers; or through ideas gathered from experience, extended to infinity. In response, Dickinson began by offering a similar perspective. He wrote that although God's sublime nature and perfection are invisible to the human eye and beyond even "the most exalted understanding," God has provided man with demonstrative evidence of both, including his holiness, justice, goodness and truth, in the works of his creation (3–4).

In what amounts to a cosmological proof of God's existence, Dickinson explained that in the case of our knowing God, we see the cause by the effect. He assumed that the world around us exists, and that in its "amazing magnificence, luster and harmony," it is neither its own efficient cause or the product of chance. As it had to have proceeded from an author, and not from an author unequal to the work, it must have been the work of an infinitely wise and powerful being (4, 7–8).[13]

Dickinson made essentially the same case for man. He began with some "unquestionably evident" assumptions, namely, that man has a being and that he has not always existed. From those assumptions, he reasoned that, as with the world itself, it is absurd to accept that man created himself or was the product of chance. As with the world, we must have our original from some cause. It is even more the case for "such noble, immaterial, thinking substances, as our souls," Dickinson added, as surely they could not have been the result of natural generation, any more that any material substance can give being to a spiritual one (5–7).

Dickinson rejected the theory that the world has existed eternally and that all beings in the world continue by an infinite and eternal series and succession of necessary causes and effects. If, indeed, the world is eternal, he suggested, it must have a necessary existence, and consequently it would be impossible for either the world, or any part of the world, to be anything else than what it was been, or that it has been anything else than it is now. Nothing can be contingent, and the world in all its glory and perfection must have "forever continued by mere accident without any cause or reason." It must be now, as it has always been, without any addition, diminution, or alteration (8–10).

Such a position, Dickinson argued, is "the height of absurdity." Things exist whose existence is contingent, or for which there is no apparent reason or necessity from their nature for their existence any more than there is for their nonexistence. All the world's constituent parts are not infinite and eternal, as they would be if their creation were necessary, and just as clearly they have not existed for all time without any variation or change or, for that matter, without succession, as would be the case if they were necessarily created. The world has had a beginning, Dickinson insisted, and consequently an author, or efficient cause (9–13).

Dickinson identified those attributes of God which we are able to discern from nature or from God's creations. To begin with, God is eternal, spiritual, and perfect. We know this because, building on what has just been established as to the noneternal nature of things, "what [has] not eternally existed, [has] had a beginning, and what [has] had a beginning must be produced by something else." As there cannot have been a time when there was absolutely nothing, the cause of all things must be an eternal, uncaused, and independent being. We know the cause of all things must be a spiritual being because we are thinking substances, capable of thought, reason, and reflection, and such powers cannot be derived from "dead unactive matter" or matter incapable of thought. And, finally, we know that the cause of all things must be a perfect being, because that being must have "all the perfections of all the innumerable intelligent beings that now are or ever have been in the world" (13–16).

Dickinson suggested that we know from nature that God, the first cause of all things, is infinite and, because God is infinite, that there must be only one God. Although we can have but an imperfect view of the universe, Dickinson reiterated, pointing to our limited knowledge of the planets and stars, we can sense the "prodigious magnitude and amazing extent" of the universe and know that it can only have been created by an infinite creator. This is as it must be, he reasoned, as that creator must be present at all times in every part of that incomprehensible space we call the universe. Given that infinite character, whereby God would also be supreme, there must be only one God; two infinite, or supreme, beings would constitute a contradiction. Dickinson discounted the possibility of a plurality of coordinate gods, as that would suggest either a conjunct creation or separate creations, both of which would belie the idea of one first cause (17, 19, 21–22).

Because the world was created out of nothing, and because of its many perfections, Dickinson wrote, we can conclude that God is omnipotent and infinitely wise. First of all, he explained, creating something from nothing is beyond even the united powers of every finite being. Secondly, whatever perfections exist in creation, either among its various parts or in total, must be first eminently in the creator, "for it is clearly evident that what had its being and beginning from another must have all the properties of its being from the same source." Put another way, Dickinson reasoned that he who has endued man—indeed, heaven and earth—with so much wisdom must have more wisdom himself than all the men in the world (24–25).

Finally, following the same line of reasoning, Dickinson argued that one could reasonably conclude that God is omniscient. The creator and governor of such a "magnificent world with such order and regularity" must have all things of the present and future in his view at once. Being the architect, he must have possessed all of its innumerable parts before he even began. "How else could they all subsist? And what else could keep them from destruction and confusion?" (29).

Dickinson concluded his sermon by noting that he could, if he so wished, continue along the same lines of reasoning to show that we can deduce from the world around us and from all the evidence it provides that God is infinitely good, just, perfect, holy, merciful, and loving. Instead, he chose to offer some "practical inferences" from what he had offered, namely, that, given all such attributes, God should be worshiped in a similarly glorious manner. Joining elements of his Calvinist evangelicalism and enlightened rationalism, Dickinson suggested that such worship should grow out of a "deep impression of our own nothingness," of our "natural unworthiness," of our "moral pollution," and of our being "vile worms and indigent creatures," and be a "rational acknowledgment" of our dependence on God for our very life and breath and for all that we hope and treasure (30–32).

Dickinson's second sermon provided "rational evidence" of our apostasy from God and of our recovery through Christ, the mediator. As the Calvinist interpretation of the Fall and the Redemption will be more fully explained in our discussion of the Great Awakening, we need only consider at this point in what way Dickinson saw his interpretation as based on "rational evidence." In brief, Dickinson insisted that Christ died for the ungodly, those in a state of enmity or opposition to God. As it would be inconsistent with God's merciful nature to have created man in a state of corruption and pollution, such a state must have been the result of the rebellion and apostasy of our first parents, of whom we are the corrupt stock. For similar reasons, namely, God's divine compassion, it also stands to reason that we were rescued from the impotence that accompanied such a state, that our deliverance was purchased by the blood of Christ (ii, 38–39, 56–57).

He that has purchased our deliverance is entitled to our "subjection and obedience," Dickinson insisted, but how can we know God's will in such matters? Has he given us any manifestation of his will? Dickinson insists that he has, and we can find it through Scripture or divine revelation and by "the light of nature." As we know that God is of infinite rectitude and justice, for example, any act of injustice must be contrary to God's nature; as he is of infinite goodness and mercy, any act of "bitterness, wrath, hatred, [or] cruelty" must be contrary to his will, and so on (40–42).

As it is also "agreeable to the very dictates of reason" that there are such things in nature as virtue and vice, right and wrong, Dickinson wrote, and that as our "leading affections and passions . . . are manifestly irregular and vicious," it is our first and chief inclination to accept those things that are most repugnant to the holiness of God and to what He rightfully expects of us and to act in such a way that is opposite to both as well as to our duty and happiness. At our "tender age," without restraint and government over our natural inclinations, without "perpetual instructions and admonitions" planting the seeds of virtue in our minds, we would have been the authors of our own destruction. In our more advanced age, however, we face destruction if we fail in the engagement between reason and passion, in our attempt to regulate our appetites (44–46).

Dickinson suggested that the "greatest part" of this world, "against the light of their own reason," live in sin against, and disobedience to, God. "Custom or education may so darken their understandings, as to satisfy their minds in this stupid idolatry," he wrote, but their reason, if it were to be consulted, would certainly teach them the folly of their ways. Yet, it has not been consulted in most cases, he reasoned, as theirs is "a wicked and depraved nature." When our nature is polluted and our faculties are depraved, our reason is nonplussed, Dickinson wrote, and our best rational inquiries are fruitless and in vain: "Here let the Deist try his skill. Let him without the assistance of revelation, draw up a perfect system of the laws of nature. Let him consult the means of restoring our lost innocency and of keeping our affections and passions under the government of religion and reason. Let him call in the help of the philosophers of Greece and Rome for his assistance in this arduous undertaking. And in the conclusion, he'll have but his labor for his pains and continue in the same inextricable labyrinth" (46, 54).

It is consistent with God's justice that men in such a state are denied God's favor or are the recipients of his displeasure, but as Dickinson had already noted, "it is the height of stupidity to imagine, that Infinite Wisdom should make so noble a being, for no higher purpose than to condemn his attributes, spurn his authority, and maintain a course of opposition to him." That man has been created for some future state seems clear from a contemplation of our natures, namely, the spiritual substances, or souls, within us, Dickinson argued. Our souls being immaterial, they are also incorruptible and "naturally immortal," intended to outlive our bodies: "Now can it be imagined that God has made so superior a creature as man, endowed him with a rational and immortal soul, and with such elevations of mind, only to act a short part in this world, and to just propagate his kind and then return to an eternal state of insensibility and inactivity?" Clearly not! Therefore, while we are in this world, Dickinson concluded, we must be in a state of probation or candidates for another world where we will meet the rewards of our life on earth (49–50, 53).

What reasonable satisfactions, then, can be found in Christianity? What "adequate provisions" can we find in it for the recovery of fallen man? Dickinson offered the following proposition. Christ, the eternal Son of God, "beholding our apostate and perishing state," out of his divine compassion died for us, purchasing with his own blood our deliverance or

providing our ransom so that God might be just in pardoning and justifying us though we be sinners. As both God and man, Christ represented
both the parties at odds and mediated between them. Dickinson insists
that such revelations are entirely worthy of God. As we are unworthy of
any such consideration by God, however, we would do well "to reflect upon
these divine obligations with a rapture of soul" (62–66, 68, 74).

In his third sermon Dickinson considered evidence from Old Testament prophecy of the Messiah in Jesus Christ, of his life, death, and resurrection. In his final sermon, however, he addressed the question of whether
it was reasonable to accept as having actually occurred those miracles attributed to Christ and the apostles in the New Testament. Dickinson defined a miracle as "a work effected in a manner unusual, or different from
the common and regular method of providence, by the interposition either
of God himself, or of some intelligent agent superior to man; for the proof
or evidence of some particular doctrine, or in attestation to the authority of
some particular person." He allowed that by this definition any references
to miracles by Christ, as the second person of the Godhead and when acting in his divine nature, could be readily believed. But, he continued, what
about those said to have been performed by the apostles? (117–18)

Such miracles, Dickinson argued, could only have resulted from
Christ's having extended the power of performing miracles through the
Holy Ghost to the apostles. By those miracles, Christ intended to ensure
the success of the apostles' ministry. Thus, they are distinguished in Scripture from the miracles performed by Christ, but they were, nevertheless,
"in their own nature, miracles of the highest kind, such as could not have
been wrought by the united power and skill of all created spirits." That
they had their intended effect, Dickinson points out, can be gauged by the
multitude of conversions that resulted (122–26, 133–37).

Directly addressing those that might be attracted to the "religion of
nature," Dickinson argued that Christ's and the apostles' miracles, which
were many in number and performed in view of multitudes, were not matters of speculation or of science, wherein the understandings of observers
might be imposed on. They were, instead, "matters of fact, that came under
the immediate cognizance of their senses; such as they could see, hear, and
feel, and be ascertained of, by all possible means of certainty." They would
not, and could not, be deceived, as they had little if anything to gain by
deception, and in the case of the apostles and many of the multitude, they
sealed their testimony on the verity of the miracles they observed with their
blood (141–46).

Further proof of Christ's and the apostles' miracles, Dickinson continued, lies in their having been reported by sacred, and later highly reli-

able, writers. The authors of the New Testament could be trusted, Dickinson assured his readers, because they were sacred penmen. But even those who were not divinely inspired, namely, the earliest historians of the church, could not deceive their contemporaries, those who had been present during the events they sought to describe. The miracles were performed openly before the world, including the enemies of Christ, who would have allowed no deception in their reporting, and as those reports were made public soon after their occurrence, there was every opportunity for those who would quarrel with them to protest any fraudulent comments. Yet, he pointed out, none has been offered (147–49, 154–56, 162–63).

In conclusion, Dickinson offered that all of the foregoing proves to any reasonable person that Christ is our Savior, that he came into the world to save his people from their sins, and that it is madness to reject or neglect him, thereby casting ourselves into hell. That, beyond such basic tenets, the conflicting teachings of so many "sects and parties among professed Christians" have caused much confusion, Dickinson allowed, is unfortunate. All he could recommend to the bewildered were two general rules by which they could act as Christ would have them. First, he suggested, all must labor to ensure "a true and lively faith in Jesus Christ," without which no one will be saved. Second, all must demonstrate the truth and sincerity of their faith "by a holy and heavenly life." Faith without holiness, Dickinson reminded his readers, "is as a carcass without breath" (164–73).

Henry May has written that once American Calvinists sought to fight for the reasonableness of Christianity on terms laid down by the Enlightenment, the trek through Arminianism to Arianism and Socinianism to Deism and, further, to infidelity had begun and could not be turned back. If that is true, *The Reasonableness of Christianity*, being Dickinson's first concerted attempt in that direction, as well as one of the earliest treatises on the subject in colonial America, may be seen as initiating that inexorable trek. At the very least, *The Reasonableness of Christianity*, Dickinson's continued insistence on central Calvinist principles notwithstanding, quite likely played into the hands of Arminians, Deists, and Skeptics.[14] Before drawing any such conclusion, however, we turn to Dickinson's other primary published response to the ideas of the Enlightenment.

Familiar Letters to a Gentleman, upon a Variety of Seasonable and Important Subjects in Religion appeared in 1745, and it was Dickinson's most widely read publication. It has been described as "a powerful and highly popular apologetic and heuristic piece for eighteenth-century Calvinism in America and Scotland," and, indeed, between 1745 and 1842, *Familiar Letters* went through six editions in America and five in Scotland.

Familiar Letters consists of some nineteen letters in which Dickinson improved upon a number of positions he had taken in *The Reasonableness of Christianity*, on the Enlightenment and its relationship to Christianity in general and Presbyterian Calvinism in particular. This time, however, Dickinson wrote from the perspective of the post-Awakening period and from his experiences in that event. As Leigh Eric Schmidt has put it, before the Awakening, in *The Reasonableness of Christianity*, Dickinson felt called upon to defend Christianity against a rationalism that would destroy it; in the wake of the Awakening, he felt compelled to defend Christianity against "a religion which would destroy rationalism."[15]

As a follow-up to *The Reasonableness of Christianity, Familiar Letters* furthered the position of the "Catholick Congregational Clergy" on reason and on freedom of the will. As a follow-up to the Great Awakening, it provided a defense of the Awakening against those whose abuse of the enthusiasms it generated had called into question even its more orderly attainments. As he put it in his opening lines, the extravagances and ecstatic raptures of some "late pretenders to extraordinary attainments in religion" had cast such a blemish upon the Awakening that many were in danger of questioning Christianity itself rather than merely doubting "the manifestly false pretenses and enthusiastic flights" of those who had claimed such attainments. Failure to make such a distinction, Dickinson continued, had given rise to "violent opposition" to the Awakening and to the doctrines of special grace and of experimental piety. It had bred not only rejection and opposition but even contempt for such doctrines "under the opprobrious character of New Light, as if they had never before been heard of, or professed among us." This Dickinson described as "one of the darkest symptoms upon this land," as it led people to question not only the validity of the Awakening but also "the experiences of vital religion, which are necessary to constitute them Christians."[16]

Finally, Dickinson noted his intention of addressing the dangerous tendencies of Antinomianism, which, he suggested, had come to prevail in some parts of the country, "especially under the name of Moravianism." The quarrel between the Moravians and the New Side Presbyterians will be discussed in a later chapter. For now, it need only be noted that although early in the Great Awakening, the more radical New Side Presbyterians and the Moravians had been somewhat in sympathy, in time New and Old Siders alike became increasingly concerned with the activities of the sect and of their recently arrived leader, Count Nikolaus Ludwig von Zinzendorf. To the Presbyterians, Moravianism came to represent little more than Antinomianism and separatism in their worst forms and, though espousing an ecumenical spirit in their evangelizing, many came to fear that the Moravians were preparing for a full-scale assault on the Presbyterians (ii–iii).

The first of Dickinson's "familiar letters" singled out the danger of infidelity or those who, while railing against "priestcraft, cant, and enthusiasm," would ridicule "all pretenses to vital piety" and explode all gospel doctrines respecting future rewards and punishments as "unreasonable or unintelligible dreams and fiction." Dickinson saw this as debasing mankind to the level of the beasts and as denying his hopes for "eternal and inexpressible happiness" (6).

In his second letter, Dickinson turned again to the subject of the evidences—rational, if not Lockean—of the Christian religion. As in *The Reasonableness of Christianity*, he began by agreeing that "faith must be built upon evidences that will reach the understanding, as well as foster passions of the soul." Such evidences, he insisted, could be found in Christianity. They were, for example, in the Mosaic history of the creation of man as the offspring of God; in the revelation of the origins of man's "irregular affections and vitiated appetites and passions"; in the intimations of the means of man's recovery from his state of sin; in the prediction of a savior, by whom man is to obtain redemption; in the record of the miracles which Christ performed, attesting to his divine mission; in Christ's declaration that he is the Son of God and that he rose from the dead and ascended into heaven; in the extraordinary qualifications of the disciples for their work, including their familiarity with many different languages, by which to converse with every nation; in their prophetic spirit, by which they could foretell the future; and in their success in converting the multitudes (11–18).

Such evidences should be sufficient not only for the Deists to allow that Christianity is in every way worthy of God and agreeable to his glorious perfection, Dickinson insisted, but for all men to allow that Christianity is suitable for the perfection of man's nature. The evidence for this can be seen in Christianity's influence upon the hearts and lives of those who sincerely profess it, whereby they are "distinguished from the rest of the world," and in the triumph of Christianity and the doctrines of the cross over their "bitter opposition" (19).

In his third and fourth letters, Dickinson returned to his earlier discussion of prophecies of the birth, life, passion, resurrection, ascension, and future kingdom of Christ the Savior. In his fifth and sixth letters, however, he took up that with which he had not dealt in *The Reasonableness of Christianity*, as it had been made an issue by the Great Awakening, namely, the internal evidences of the "real" Christian or of the marks by which can be distinguished him who has been chosen by God to be lifted out of his carnal state. It is a subject, as we shall see, with which Dickinson and others, such as Jonathan Edwards in his *Distinguishing Marks of a Work of the*

Spirit of God (1741), struggled during the Great Awakening in the face of Old Light/Old Side criticism.

Dickinson's first mark of conversion was the passing away of "old things," as the "spirit of the mind" is renewed and a new man created "in righteousness and true holiness." It is a "distinguishing change of state," Dickinson insists, seen in a person's new "thoughts and dispositions," "desires and affections," "views and apprehensions," "confidence and dependence," and "joys and satisfactions." No person has ever failed to obtain such a blessing, Dickinson added, who has "by faith unfeigned brought his soul to Christ, and depended upon him, for his sanctifying renewing influences" (62–65).

Dickinson's second mark, or evidence, of the true Christian was the spiritual warfare or "intestine war" of the chosen with his remaining corruptions. The true Christian's new affections cry out against the imperfections that remain in his heart and in his outward conduct. Nothing is more grievous to such a person than the continued prevalence of corruption, as well as the "deadness, formality and distractions" that accompany his holy duties. He commits himself to continuous battle, where all others cheerfully and with ease and comfort submit to the injunctions of their conquerors and resign themselves voluntarily to their enemies, "as all careless and secure sinners do into the hands of sin and satan" (65–67).

Dickinson allowed that he who had been chosen by God cannot doubt the change of state he has experienced. At the same time, however, he suggested, such conviction is not complete. As grievous imperfections remain, the true Christian continues to be apprehensive of his spiritual state. As "violent and impetuous temptations" and "horrendous blasphemous thoughts" continue to be injected into the mind of the chosen, his soul continues to be distressed and his heart disquieted. He fights on, however, against his failings, and in the end he is comforted by the thought that he is being continually led on to victory by the "captain" of his salvation (65, 67–68).

This led Dickinson to the third of his distinguishing characteristics, which is the "comfort, peace and joy" of the "true" Christian's religious life. Christ has promised that his "yoke is easy and his burden light," Dickinson explained, and he has offered his disciples peace such as the world cannot afford them. What doubt can remain in the heart of a Christian, Dickinson asked, when he feels such promises fulfilled unto him and when he has been comforted by Christ (69)?

Dickinson responded to those who would argue that such a witnessing of the Holy Spirit is a delusion, or the product of "enthusiasm or heated imagination," by suggesting that, as the blind can have no idea of light or color, they who are in spiritual darkness cannot see or understand "the light of the knowledge of the glory of God." Once again, he allowed that, as even the "true" Christian remains in a militant state, he is not always comforted and confident. But the true Christian can rest assured that he will be strengthened for spiritual encounters and offered sufficient comfort to prove an anchor for his soul and "to keep him sure and steadfast in the most tempestuous seasons" (69–72).

Dickinson's final internal evidence can be found in the manner in which the "great change" is wrought and carried on in the heart of the "true" Christian. Dickinson explained that there is a vast difference in the various methods of divine operation that turn sinners from the power of Satan to God, but that in every case recorded in Scripture the change is verified by the recipient's change of heart and behavior. Where he was once "careless and secure" in "pursuit of his lusts" and "hardened against all [God's] solemn warnings," he is now thoroughly awakened out of his security and "put upon a serious and lasting inquiry" as to how he might be saved. His conscience can no longer be quieted by "imperfect performances," and he is made "deeply sensible" of his defects and impurity and that his own efforts are fruitless and vain. He realizes that he is at Christ's mercy and that he must come to Christ with unqualified faith in, and dependence upon, him (72–73).

Once again, in response to the critics of the Awakening, Dickinson acknowledged that there are some "convinced sinners" whose religious impressions wear off and whose efforts fall short of the effects he has described. But in all those "whose convictions are abiding and effectual" his internal evidences apply. The result is a thorough and lasting change both of heart and life that cannot be imputed to the "irregular sallies of an overheated imagination." As shown in Scripture, it is the means proposed by Christ for our salvation (74–75, 77).

Where the foregoing might cover the likes of the unrepentant, events of the Awakening encouraged Dickinson to qualify or limit any undue confidence or self-righteousness on the part of the repentant. Although Christ has offered to sanctify the hearts of those who sincerely trust in him, he wrote, he has never promised to make them infallible in all their conduct. Therefore, if some such sanctified men, though zealous in their efforts to serve God, through "heated imaginations or erroneous apprehensions of their duty" should err in their ways or act counter to the "true interests of Christ's kingdom," their error is in their opinion, not in their will; they have been misled by their heads, not by their hearts. "They may have had real experiences in true and vital piety . . . [but at a given particular time] their imaginations are imposed on by enthusiasm and delusion" (80–82).

In his seventh letter, Dickinson turned to a vindication of God's sovereign (free) grace, a doctrine he would explore in greater detail in several other pieces during the Great Awakening. Dickinson's purpose here, he suggested, was to answer some of the arguments that had been raised against the doctrine by those under the influence of the Enlightenment—liberal Anglicans, Arminians, Deists, and the like. The specific topic Dickinson singled out to address was that of preparation, which he posed in the following manner: "If we are of ourselves capable of no qualifying conditions of the divine favor, or (to use my own words) if we must feel that we lie at mercy, and that all our own refuges, and all our endeavors in our own strength to relieve our distressed souls, are fruitless and vain, you can't tell to what purpose any of our endeavors are, or what good it will do us to use any means for our salvation" (92).

Dickinson suggested that the "lost, impotent, deplorable state" just described is the case for every unrenewed sinner, every natural man. Natural man is in such a hopeless state that he has no alternative but to lie at the mercy of God. His nature is so corrupt and defiled that he cannot atone for his sins through any performance with his own powers. And, as his sins are repugnant to the perfect, pure, and holy God, they continuously increase the difficulty and danger of his case. This will remain the case, Dickinson continued, as long as he is in an unrenewed state with a corrupt heart and affections and he lives by the natural dispositions of his soul without any true interest in Christ. Given that, we should not despair of the purpose or consequence of our endeavors but rather take heart in Christ's promise, as recorded in Scripture, that he who seeks Christ in faith and sincerity shall be saved (92–95, 97).

Dickinson reminded his readers that although Christ died in order to purchase for man his capacity to make an atonement for himself, he did not sacrifice himself so that God might be pleased with what is contrary to his nature and pacified with such duties as can be no better than "impure streams from a corrupt fountain." Fear necessarily follows such a realization, Dickinson allowed, but though fear may be motivation enough to restrain some of the exercises of a person's sinful appetites or passions, it is not sufficient to totally and permanently change the object of those sensual appetites. Such a change can only result from a thorough renovation of the powers of the soul, and natural man is incapable of effecting any such renovation (95–96).

It does not follow, however, Dickinson continued, that man can lay no claim to the renewing and sanctifying influences of the divine grace necessary to his salvation. Scripture promises that "he who seeks shall find" or, as Dickinson would put it, he who seeks shall find even though he seeks amiss, as long as he does so in faith and sincerity. Dickinson realized that this still begged the question of man's inability to act in faith and sincerity, but it did pose an alternative to doing nothing. Simply put, they who have made no attempt to receive Christ by faith can claim no interest in him or in any of his saving benefits (96–98).

What Dickinson sought to establish here was that God is the "fountain and foundation of all grace and mercy"; that man can offer no inducements for that grace and mercy, to engage God's affections, or to change his purposes; and that the only means by which man can seek his mercy is to lie at God's feet and ascribe to him "the infinite perfections of his excellent nature." In doing this, man may not be able to create any change in his relationship to God, but he will be in the position necessary to judge whether or not God has made any change in him, that he has "a design of special favor" for his soul. Given the hopeless state of man to begin with, Dickinson argued that such a posture is the only means by which he may find comfort, safety, and happiness: It is a "just foundation of comfort and hope, in that it obviates the darkness and discouragements, that would otherwise arise from a sense of your guilt and unworthiness, and from your impotence and unavoidable infirmity and imperfection in the service of God" (103–4).

Finally, if it be objected that if God "in sovereignty designs mercy for us," we shall obtain it whether we seek it or not, or that, if not, it is in vain to strive, Dickinson answered that God "never does in sovereignty appoint salvation for any" who neglect the gospel means. In other words, as God has told us in the gospel, we will not be saved by intentionally ignoring or flouting his word. If we must have faith to be saved, we must have faith. If we do not have the heart to earnestly seek "the gracious influences of the spirit of God, we will never find them" (106–7).

"Familiar letters" 8–11 dealt with the distinguishing characteristics of a "true and saving faith," which have already been alluded to and with which Dickinson would deal in greater detail in separately published tracts yet, and more appropriately, to be discussed in the context of the Great Awakening. Similarly, in letters 12–16, Dickinson elaborated on the doctrine of justification by faith, a subject with which he has already sufficiently dealt for our purposes at this point and to which he, and we, shall return in a subsequent chapter on the Great Awakening.

In letters 17 and 18, Dickinson returned to his earlier criticism of what he believed were Antinomian abuses of the doctrine of the nature and necessity of a believer's "union to Christ." In this instance, however, he explained that a believer's union to God should be considered a mystical union that admits of "no clear and full illustration" in this imperfect world.

Its manner, much like that of God incarnate, to whom we are united, is therefore incomprehensible or "above our search and inquiry." Still, Dickinson continued, the reality and certainty of this union is not beyond our knowledge; both are clearly revealed, as are the blessed effects of the union that are experienced by the children of God. We may therefore believe in it though its nature lies beyond human reason to determine (353–54).

Here and elsewhere, Dickinson insisted, true repentance, as compared with a legal repentance, is "the genuine and necessary fruit of a true faith." Here, he reasoned from that proposition, the true believer finds infallible evidence of his union to Christ in the burden he feels for his sins and in his "groan[ing] after deliverance from them." Here and elsewhere, Dickinson argued, there is greater guilt in the sins of believers than in the sins of others. In brief, a person's union to God leads to a continued repentance for his sins, "a life of continued self-abasement and self-judging, and a life of repeated and renewed mourning after pardon of and victory over our remaining corruptions" (375, 377, 379–80).

In his final letter, Dickinson offered some "directions" with which man, given his reasonable nature as well as his total dependence on God, might nevertheless take "a close and comfortable walk with God." First, he suggested, those who would walk with God should remember that every affair and conduct of human life must be calculated for, and subservient to, that one great end of their being. Second, they should carefully attend, without reserve, to the ordinances of God. Third, they should remember that as they "lie at mercy," so they have a "mercy-seat" to which to repair and at which they may "sow in hope." Men have no claim to the mercy of God, but God has infinite mercy, and if they approach him with an abasing sense of their sinfulness, they may do so as well with a "humble confidence in the riches of his infinite mercy" (403–6).

Fourth, Dickinson offered that those who would come into union with God should review their past and present, confess their sins, and "make up all breaches" with their neighbors. Fifth, they should faithfully discharge the respective duties of the several relations they sustain. For some, this may apply to their ministry, which God has placed in their trust. For others, it may refer to their conjugal relationships. In either case, full compliance with the laws of Christianity is key if all are to be allowed to "live together as fellow heirs of the grace of life and to promote each other's spiritual and eternal welfare" (407–11).

Sixth, Dickinson wrote, those who would walk with God should "walk by rule, in an exact observance of stated devotions" and "befriend a life of religion." They should begin their days with God, carry on with meditation and reflection, and end with thanksgiving. On the Lord's Day, as well as on days of humiliation and thanksgiving, the entire time should be spent in the immediate service of God. Toward this end, Dickinson added, it would be wise to keep a written account of one's daily experience of time: "Before you go to bed, recollect and record (at least in some brief hints) the business you have done, the duties performed, the mercies received, the frame of your soul, the dispensations of providence, with the sins and imperfections of the day past." By such a written accounting, a person may always have before him whatever "special reformations" are necessary and what objections he owes God. Dickinson recommended, however, that although such an account of one's sins and imperfections should be understandable to its author, "there may be some occurrences requiring a veil of obscurity to be thrown over them," so that they cannot be understood by others into whose hands the account may fall (412–13, 417–18).[17]

Finally, Dickinson suggested that he who would walk with God must "walk by faith in the Son of God." Whatever else he might do, it is essential that "faith in Christ be kept in daily exercise" and that faith be present in all his duties. If a person does this, and looks to Christ as "the end finisher" of faith, he will find acceptance in God and obtain "the sealings of the blessed spirit," to which Dickinson appended the following prayer: "Thou hast promised, that if I come unto thee, thou wilt in no wise cast me out. Lord, I would come at thy call. Draw me, and I shall run after thee. . . . As a lost perishing sinner, I would therefore look unto thee for pardon, sanctification, and eternal salvation" (418–20).

As has been suggested, *The Reasonableness of Christianity* and *Familiar Letters to a Gentleman,* though written some thirteen years apart, both shed light on Dickinson's response to those ideas of the Enlightenment which challenged basic Calvinist doctrines. There is no escaping the fact, however, that *Familiar Letters* was written in 1745 after the Great Awakening had swept New England and the Middle Colonies. Indeed, it might as well be seen as Dickinson's final defense of the Great Awakening against its critics from various perspectives, radical New Lights/New Siders and Old Lights/Old Siders, Deists, Antinomians, Arminians, and Anglicans. Viewed in that context, *Familiar Letters* provides an appropriate introduction to Dickinson's role in the Great Awakening, to which we now turn.

6

WELCOMING THE
AWAKENING

A "GREAT AND GENERAL AWAKENING," as it was known to its contemporaries, swept the British colonies of North America during the 1730s and 1740s. Possibly more correctly seen as a series of local, yet at its height interrelated, revivals, the Great Awakening became "the revival by which churchmen and historians measure all others." Some historians have proclaimed the Great Awakening one of the first truly intercolonial movements, forging ties as well between evangelicals of the colonies and of Great Britain. Others have found it much overrated as anything but a series of local events, but nevertheless concur that it brought renewed life to many of the churches of colonial America. It also proved to be divisive within those denominations that participated, however, and that included the Presbyterian Church of the Middle Colonies. Jonathan Dickinson was a major player in the Great Awakening. He was a proponent of the Awakening; he "rejoiced in it" and defended it against its Old Side critics. But he also opposed its divisive tendencies. In sum, he became a leader of the moderate New Side.[1]

Charles H. Maxson and Leonard Trinterud have suggested that Dickinson was second only to Jonathan Edwards in his leadership of the Awakening. Leigh Eric Schmidt has called him a distant second, but even he has recognized Dickinson's importance in the following manner: "By dint of perseverance, consistency, and long preparation, Jonathan Dickinson held firm against foes at the extremes—Old Side and New, infidels and enthusiasts, Arminians and Antinomians—and eventually, within colonial Presbyterianism at least, won out over them."[2]

Similarly, David Harlan has suggested that Dickinson did not see the alternatives of New and Old Side as mutually exclusive abstractions. Rather, he saw them as mutually compelling allegiances, and in the end he responded not by aligning himself with one side or the other but "by trying to reconcile their multiple commitments." This, Harlan has pointed out, stands in contrast to the uncompromising Edwards and to Gilbert Tennent, who argued that there was "no such thing for any present as being of neither party; all must be on one side or the other, either for or against."

Harlan and others have suggested that Dickinson, in his ability to perceive such clearly defined abstractions as represented by the opposing sides of the Awakening, steered a middle course, but in doing so he "lurched from one side to the other, leaving behind . . . a series of zig-zag trails that perfectly recorded [his] erratic ambivalence": "Dickinson's wavering course through the Great Awakening epitomizes the experiences of scores of ministers who tried to steer between the extremes of enthusiasm and formalism, between Calvinism and Arminianism, between New Lights and Old Lights. . . . To most it meant having to change their minds, sometimes more than once."[3]

Dickinson did seize the middle ground. That middle ground, however, represented neither the final step in a retreat from the rampant enthusiasms of the Awakening nor an erratic ambivalence. Rather, as Schmidt has written, it represented the staking-out of a moderate New Side position, consistent with Dickinson's preexisting "vision of a renewed social and religious order." Before 1739, Dickinson did not promote the revival. When he did so, however, he acted from a position consistent with his most deeply rooted convictions. Further, when all was said and done, his vision became that of most New Side Presbyterians. When others of the Awakening sought the middle ground, they found Dickinson was already there, that he had been there from the start, and that he had served to define it.[4]

The course and development of the Great Awakening are sufficiently well known as to require here only an outline wherein one can place Dickinson's actions and writings. To begin with, it is important to note that the fires of the Great Awakening had been lit a decade or more before they reached Elizabeth Town. Some have found the first stirrings of the Awakening in the Middle Colonies occurred in the early to mid-1720s among German radical pietists (e.g., Dunkers). Others have pointed to the work of the German-born Dutch Reformed minister Theodorus Frelinghuysen, who in the mid-1720s created a storm in New Jersey's Raritan Valley by seeking to awaken the spiritually dead and contented. Observing and admiring the work of Frelinghuysen was a newly converted and ordained Presbyterian minister, Gilbert Tennent of nearby New Brunswick.[5]

Tennent was converted en route to the Middle Colonies from Ireland in 1716, trained by his father in a Calvinist experimental form of evangelical Puritanism, licensed by the Synod of Philadelphia in 1725, and ordained in 1726 at New Brunswick, some four miles from Frelinghuysen. He proved particularly susceptible to Frelinghuysen's uniquely pietistic perspective, with emphasis on the necessity of personal conversion and subsequent holiness of life. By 1728, Tennent was conducting services in Frelinghuysen's church, and from Frelinghuysen, it has been argued, Tennent learned his peculiarly stirring "direct and pungent" method of preaching.[6]

The Awakening within the Presbyterian Church of the Middle Colonies, however, may be said to have begun with John Tennent at Freehold, New Jersey, in 1730. By 1735 all the Tennents—William Sr., William Jr., Gilbert, and John (though John would die only two years after initiating the revival at Freehold)—had spread its flames to Presbyterian churches in New Brunswick, Staten Island, and beyond. Most of the group that initially coalesced around the Tennents in their promotion of the Awakening came to be known as the Log College men because they studied under William Tennent Sr. at the school in Neshaminy, Pennsylvania, to which the name was derisively attached. By the height of the Awakening, Tennent graduated at least nineteen men, from whom came the leadership of the radical Awakening among Presbyterians in the Middle Colonies.[7]

To be sure, the Log College men looked to their Scotch-Irish tradition. Marilyn Westerkamp has argued convincingly for causal and correlative factors between the Great Awakening among Presbyterians in the Middle Colonies and seventeenth- and eighteenth-century revivals in Ireland and Scotland. Leigh Eric Schmidt has pointed to precedents in those sacramental occasions in Scotland known as Holy Fairs.[8] As Martin Lodge has pointed out, however, Gilbert Tennent's formative adult years were spent in New York rather than in Ireland or even Pennsylvania. His religious associations were with New Englanders rather than with his fellow Scotch-Irish Presbyterians, who, especially at the outset of the revival, were not only unmoved by but hostile toward the doctrine of new birth or of saving closure with Christ. Not surprisingly, then, Tennent's theology, which would be shared by the other Log College men, was also consistent with that of English Puritan divines. With some important qualifications, it would be welcomed not only by New Light New Englanders but also by those New Side Presbyterians of New England extraction in the Middle Colonies.[9]

At first, the Presbyterian revivals spread rapidly and faced little opposition. It was hoped that they might serve to counter the widely mourned course of declining piety and spiritual concern. In 1733, Gilbert Tennent elicited from the Synod of Philadelphia a show of support for the revivals as a means whereby ministers might reinstall "the declining power of godliness" in their congregations. In 1735, he secured a synod resolution whereby presbyteries were urged to diligently examine all candidates for the ministry and those among the laity seeking admission to the Lord's Supper for "experiences of a work of sanctifying grace in their hearts." The synod instructed ministers "in the most solemn and affecting manner" to convince their charges of "their lost and miserable state" and of the necessity of their diligently employing those means necessary to obtain the sanctifying influences of the spirit of God whereby they would be saved.[10]

The fires of the Awakening were fanned by itinerancy. Although in its first years the Log College men generally did not go uninvited into areas presided over by regular pastors, the large number of vacant congregations provided them with an effective opportunity for spreading the word. When they availed themselves of that opportunity, trouble followed. On May 27, 1737, Gilbert Tennent delivered a terrifying sermon at Maidenhead, New Jersey, where the congregation was experiencing an awakening and the pulpit was vacant. The congregation was within the bounds of the Presbytery of Philadelphia, but, although invited by the congregation, Tennent did not ask permission of the presbytery. One week later, Dickinson and nearly all of the New England group being absent, the Synod of Philadelphia responded by passing a measure by which no minister or probationer could preach in any vacant congregation, nor be invited by the congregation to do so, without the consent of his own presbytery and that of the presbytery within which the congregation was located. On October 23, 1737, however, once again without permission, if in a more temperate manner, Tennent returned to Maidenhead.[11]

In 1738, the New England group having returned, the Log College men were successful in securing from the Synod of Philadelphia an agreement whereby any member of that body could preach in a vacant congregation to which he was invited without permission of the appropriate presbytery, provided no member of that presbytery objected to his presence as likely to promote division. In the bargain, the Log College men (e.g., Gilbert and William Tennent Jr., Samuel Blair, John Cross, and Eleazer Wales) were given their own New Brunswick Presbytery, and the New England–based Presbyteries of Long Island and East Jersey were joined into the Presbytery of New York. Dickinson was the oldest and most distinguished member of the latter body.

The Synod of 1738 also ruled, however, that any ministerial candidate within its bounds without a degree from a New England or European college was to be examined by a committee of the synod. Although he, Dickinson, and other New Siders were appointed by the synod to examine ministerial candidates north of Philadelphia, Gilbert Tennent protested. He claimed, to no avail, that the measure was a thinly veiled attempt to wreck his father's Log College. It also emasculated the just established

Presbytery of New Brunswick, he argued, whose right it was, according to precedent and previously adopted rules governing such procedures, to license and ordain ministerial candidates independent of synod control. At its first meeting of August 8, 1738, the New Brunswick Presbytery declared the act unconstitutional and proceeded to examine and license the Log College graduate John Rowland.[12]

In the meantime, the Awakening continued to spread and to draw closer to Elizabeth Town. In August 1739, fellow New Englander Aaron Burr, who had been converted during the Edwardsean revival in Connecticut, brought the Awakening to Newark, only a few miles from Elizabeth Town, and by the spring of 1740 Dickinson was assisting Burr. In October 1739, however, Dickinson was directly confronted by the forces of censoriousness and separatism, the tendency of the awakened not only to be critical of others not so called but also to denigrate ministers they judged unredeemed. In Woodbridge, New Jersey, John Pierson, a fellow New Englander, came under attack from a group within his congregation. Possibly influenced by the events at Newark or by the Tennents themselves, if indirectly, they charged him with not being sufficiently zealous in the cause of the revival. On October 10, on behalf of the Presbytery of New York to which both Pierson and Dickinson belonged, Dickinson delivered a sermon to Pierson's congregation. In that sermon, he not only came to Pierson's defense but he also warned against the seeds of separatism that such criticism sowed. Without denigrating the accomplishments of the Awakening, he spoke out against its excesses.[13]

In *The Danger of Schisms,* as it subsequently was entitled in print, Dickinson allowed that not all ministers are created alike in their "gifts, graces, or ministerial qualifications." Some are graced "with brighter capacities and more eminent degrees of learning," and we esteem them accordingly. The problem arises, he continued, when those who prefer one despise and deprecate the other, resulting in an injustice, an injury, and an indignity as those of lesser gifts become the object of contempt and abuse.

"Are all [ministers] sons of thunder?" Dickinson asked, employing a phrase used by George Whitefield to describe Gilbert Tennent. Obviously not. It has pleased God to create each minister differently, as he has created hearers with a variety of tastes and sentiments. Accordingly, men are to esteem and value all God's ministers who are discharging the trust he has committed to them, as they are all ministers of Christ and "stewards of the mysteries of the kingdom." Further, men are not to depend on the means of salvation, Dickinson continued, but on "the God of means," for "if ever God [should] bestow saving grace upon us, it will be in his own way." God is the dispenser of the means of life, not man, and if men are unable to find spiritual edification under a faithful minister of Christ, whether or not of the most eminent capacities, it is their fault.

"There is . . . a mutual covenant between a minister and his congregation," Dickinson reminded those present, "whereby they are as well obliged to his support, as he to the discharge of his important trust." If separations in violation of that covenant were to be allowed, he reasoned, the church would be "brought to an utter dissolution." People would abandon their ministers and disperse from parish to parish until there would be no such thing as a united congregation. Those who would create such divisions, he charged, despite their pretense of bringing others to a more gifted minister whereby their eternal interest might be better promoted, break the peace of the churches and cause confusion, discord, and division.[14]

Though allowing that even at this early date Dickinson was a man "of warm personal piety" and that he knew the "ecstasy of spiritual gratification," David Harlan has seen *Danger of Schisms* as revealing the depth of Dickinson's commitment "to the established order and the extent to which he would sacrifice evangelical piety to maintain ecclesiastical order."[15] Closer to the mark, however, are Leonard Trinterud and Leigh Eric Schmidt, who have pointed out that although, in *Danger of Schisms,* Dickinson denounced the excesses of the revival, he did not denigrate its experiential piety. What Dickinson attacked in his sermon was not revivalism but "the inchoate practice of condemning fellow ministers as unconverted." It was fundamentally an enjoinder to respect traditional ministerial authority in order to sustain "the Gospel of Peace" and vital piety and to avoid the chaos and dissolution that would follow any rejection of settled ministers in order to follow roving prophets. Until that was ensured, Schmidt has insisted, the censoriousness of the Awakening would be like "a dead fly in the apothecary's ointment," seriously compromising any contribution it might make to the Presbyterian Church.[16]

On November 2, 1739, George Whitefield arrived in Philadelphia, ostensibly to raise money and supplies for his orphanage in Georgia. It was Whitefield's second of seven visits to the colonies, and his reputation preceded him. Three years after receiving his degree from Oxford, he was already admired in England for his eloquent preaching of the new birth. He was also resented for his abuse of less fervent ministers. Though ordained an Anglican minister, he had become associated with Charles and John Wesley, and as a result many Anglican pulpits had been closed to him. He had then taken to the streets and fields, establishing for himself a practice that became his trademark.[17]

Whitefield preached to "multitudes" in Philadelphia's Anglican church and from the courthouse steps, impressing even the likes of the skeptical

Benjamin Franklin, who would publish Whitefield's sermons and journal and become a lifelong friend. A building was constructed in his honor, open to any of whatever denomination who sought to carry on the spirit of the work Whitefield had begun, and William Tennent Sr. solicited his help in spreading the flames of the Awakening.[18] Whitefield did not initiate the Great Awakening in the colonies, but he became its leading promoter.[19]

Whitefield's tour of the colonies, widely reported in the colonial press, enhanced the Awakening not only in affecting the hearts of those who flocked to see him but also in providing a link that turned isolated instances into a more general phenomenon. But it also aroused further opposition, especially when Whitefield joined in the attack on unconverted ministers. His fellow Anglican ministers began to accuse him of disorderly conduct. In Charleston, South Carolina, an Anglican commissary actually called him before an ecclesiastical court. When Whitefield reached New York in the fall of 1739, the Anglican minister there denied him his pulpit, whereupon Whitefield accepted an invitation from Ebenezer Pemberton to preach in the city's Presbyterian church.[20]

On November 14, accompanied by Gilbert Tennent, George Whitefield passed through Elizabeth Town on his way to New York City. Though not specifically mentioned by either Whitefield or Dickinson, the two no doubt met on that occasion, and Dickinson followed up on that visit with a letter to Whitefield, then in New York, inviting him to address the people of Elizabeth Town upon his return. On November 19, Whitefield returned to Elizabeth Town and met with the town's Anglican minister, Edward Vaughan, who, Whitefield learned later, had preached against him. Vaughan made it clear that he would not allow Whitefield into his pulpit.[21]

Whitefield dined with Dickinson, accepted his offer, and at noon climbed into Dickinson's pulpit to address upwards of seven hundred people. Of his sermon, Whitefield wrote in his journal: "God was pleased to open my mouth against both ministers and people among the dissenters, who hold truth in unrighteousness, contenting themselves with a bare speculative knowledge of the doctrines of grace, but never experiencing the power of them in their hearts."[22]

In a May 24 letter to a close friend, the Reverend Thomas Foxcroft of Boston (Whitefield would not appear in Boston until September 1740), no doubt in response to his friend's request for his impressions of the man, Dickinson wrote that he found Whitefield to be "a young man of ingenuity, of great seriousness and zeal, [and] of indefatigable and even inimitable industry and laboriousness in his endeavors to save poor perishing sinners from eternal destruction." He described Whitefield's Elizabeth Town sermon as "excellent" and concluded that it had "affected multitudes."[23]

Within a few days of Whitefield's visit to Elizabeth Town, although the exact date cannot be established, Dickinson returned to his pulpit and offered to his congregation and some ministers also in attendance his earliest known Awakening sermon. Noting that it would never be published, David Harlan has speculated that Dickinson delivered "Who Is on the Lord's Side?" extemporaneously and that it reflected the excitement of the moment. Whitefield's November 1739 sermon had so moved Dickinson, Harlan has explained, that he abandoned completely the conservative position he had assumed in October. He "collapsed the cautiously drawn out conversion experience into a single ecstatic moment . . . and recklessly mobilized the 'Children of God' in a crusade to root out the corruptions of everyday life."[24]

Two points, however, serve as necessary correctives to Harlan's assessment. First, what Dickinson had to say in praise of the Awakening in "Who Is on the Lord's Side?" was not substantially different from what he had written earlier, though perhaps in less heated terms, most notably in *The Reasonableness of Christianity* (1732). Second, while urging those in his congregation to take the Lord's side, as in *The Danger of Schisms,* Dickinson reminded them that they should nevertheless continue to attend to their religious duties and to avoid schism within their ranks.

Dickinson began his sermon with the observation that all mankind is divided into the children of God and the children of the devil. The latter group, which is larger, he explained, consists of those united in vassalage to the devil, who "extends his government not only over the pagan . . . but also over the greatest part of those that profess subjection to our blessed redeemer . . . [yet] remain destitute of a saving faith in Jesus Christ."[25]

As those listed under the devil's banner were so visibly gaining ground in the world, Dickinson continued, it was high time for "all that wish well to Sion" to be on the Lord's side. He urged the ministers of Christ to zealously inquire of their flock who would espouse God's cause. And he urged the laity to appear on the Lord's side by distinguishing themselves from those "horrid apostates" who, even at the moment of their deliverance from bondage, even at the time of their receiving the Law from his very lips, turned away from God. Toward that end, Dickinson posed the following subjects for their consideration: What's implied in being on the Lord's Side? In what manner one should distinguish oneself by appearing on the Lord's side? For what reasons one should appear on the Lord's side? (2–5)

In taking up the first subject, Dickinson provided the standard Calvinist/Puritan response. He suggested that those who are on the Lord's side have made a profession of faith and given themselves up to God. The Word of the Lord is in their hearts and consciences, and all the faculties of their souls are subjected to him. They have, through the influence of God's spirit, undergone "a great and wonderful change," whereby they have been convinced of their danger, guilt, and misery and of the need to "flee from the Kingdom of Satan into the Kingdom of God's dear Son." They have been brought, "loathing and self-condemning," to lie at God's feet—God, the "fountain of grace and life"—convinced that both their person and services are justly liable to be rejected by God and that they have nothing of their own to recommend them to God or to merit his mercy. And they have cast themselves upon Christ wholly relying on him to justify them by his righteousness and through the power of faith in their souls (6, 8–9, 12).

There is no way to tell whether or not divisions, such as those seen at Woodbridge and elsewhere, occurred at Elizabeth Town during its awakening. There is no evidence that they did, but while on the subject of what is implied by being on the Lord's side Dickinson condemned the "schisms, contentions, parties, and factions" as well as "the judging, censoring and condemning" that had come to prevail among those that professed to have the cause of God in their hearts. Who was responsible for such confusions? Certainly not those who are of "that Kingdom which is righteousness, peace and joy in the Holy Ghost." Such people may differ among themselves on lesser points of religion or on the method of pursuing that end upon which all who are of that kingdom agree, but they agree in all the essentials. They have been sanctified by Christ, and they "keep the unity of the Spirit in the Bond of Peace" (13).

Taking up the question of in what manner and why those in his congregation should distinguish themselves by appearing on the Lord's side, Dickinson suggested that they should do so by carefully and conscientiously discharging their duty in the education and government of their families. It had been the want of family education and government, Dickinson explained, that had opened the "sluices [to] that torrent of sin and guilt that [had] overflow[ed them]." Further, they should be examples of piety and virtue, by which they would promote the cause of God and godliness and commend religion to others by showing its beauty in their own lives. And, as to why they should so distinguish themselves, Dickinson pointed out that they were obligated to appear on the Lord's side because by so distinguishing themselves they would reflect the honor and glory of God. Not to do so—to, instead, "ungratefully value the love of the world and the esteem of wicked men"—would be to bring dishonor to their religion (18–19, 23–24).

Dickinson noted that George Whitefield's November visit to Elizabeth Town was spoken highly of and that some seemed to have been affected by Whitefield's sermon. But, he asked those in his congregation, has it been "effectual for your saving conversion to God"? Or "are you yet [to] come to a resolute conclusion, that whatever course any others take, as for you, and your houses, you will serve the Lord?" If not, he warned, they continued to serve the devil (34–35).

Dickinson exhorted the elderly, "upon the borders of the eternal world," the young, in need of giving up their "youthful lusts and sensual pleasures," and those who had already "taken the vows of the Lord upon them," to "enquire after the way of salvation." He urged them to cast themselves at "the footstool of divine grace" and to do so immediately. He warned them not to grow negligent or careless in their efforts to let their resolutions wear away or to return "like the dog to his vomit and the sow that is washed to her wallowing in the mire" (38–39).

Dickinson concluded his sermon, however, by exhorting those ministers present to appear "with the greatest ardor and diligence . . . in the cause of God":

> The awful bonds of office we lie under oblige us to this and we cannot be faithful to God, to the souls of men, nor to our own souls, if we don't lay out ourselves to the utmost to promote a work of conversion and reformation, to pull down the kingdom of Satan in the hearts of men, to turn them from darkness unto light, and from the kingdom of Satan unto God. To this end, we must add unto our most fervent prayers the most zealous endeavors to pluck poor perishing souls out of the fire. We must, both in public and private, warn sinners of their dreadful danger and endeavor to show them their dreadful perishing necessity of an interest in Christ. We must instruct the ignorant, endeavor to redeem the living, and guide all in the way of life. (40)

On December 23, 1739, one month after he had delivered "Who Is on the Lord's Side?" and two months after he had spoken at Woodbridge on the dangers of schisms that accompanied the awakening, Dickinson was called upon to deliver both messages at Connecticut Farms. Connecticut Farms, which had only recently been separated from Dickinson's charge, was a bit ahead of Elizabeth Town in its experiencing both the first stirrings of a revival and its divisiveness. The sermon was entitled *A Call to the Weary and Heavy Laden to Come unto Christ for Rest.*

"The apostasy of our first parents has plunged all their miserable offspring into a gulf of wo[e], and brought upon them a dreadful weight of distress and misery," Dickinson began, initiating a more detailed assessment of the Awakening's conversion morphology than he had attempted in either of his earlier works. "By this we are [so] universally polluted and defiled, [that] all the members of our bodies, and all the faculties of our souls . . . are loathsome and abominable in the sight . . . of God." It was the classic Calvinist/Puritan position, which leads unalterably to the conclusion that we are "under the power and dominion of our lusts"; that "sin reigns in our mortal bodies"; that we are "under the empire of Satan, and led captive by him at his pleasure"; that we are "enemies to God" and the "children of His wrath"; and that "we have omnipotent vengeance engaged against us."[26]

Where then can man turn for help? Not to our own powers, Dickinson argued, not even if we resolve to seek a new life. "We cannot bring a clean thing out of an unclean," and if we depend on ourselves for salvation, "we shall yet pine away in our iniquities." Even if we turn to God with prayers, tears, reformations, or anything else within our power, we will fail. God is "a consuming fire to all unsanctified sinners," and as long as we are in an unsanctified, natural state we cannot avoid eternal destruction (3–4).

Such a state, Dickinson continued, should fill the soul of every convinced sinner with perplexity and confusion and make him groan under his burden. At the same time, however, it should "fill us with admiring and adoring apprehensions of the unspeakable love of God, in giving his son to save us, of the unspeakable love of our glorious redeemer, who in due time, when we were yet without strength, died for the ungodly; and who is graciously proclaiming of poor distressed sinners the glad tidings. . . . 'Come unto me, all ye that labor and are heavy laden, and I will give you rest'" (4).

Sinners are not qualified to receive that "rest" Christ has promised, Dickinson explained, until they are brought to an awakened sense of their sin, guilt, and perishing condition. They can be brought to such an awakened sense, or conviction, either by the gracious influence of the spirit of God or by a dreadful experience of God's eternal wrath. Accordingly, convictions may begin in the soul "by the means of some awakening providence," by Christian conferences, by public or private ordinances, or even by the immediate influences of the spirit of God, without any known means or outward occasion. Most often, however, Dickinson pointed out, God has chosen to initiate convictions through the ministry of the gospel (6–7).

Dickinson allowed that convictions ordinarily begin in the soul and lead to "terror and amazement." They lead the sinner to see that he is controlled by his iniquities and that he cannot depend upon himself to be saved. All who would be saved, then, must first despair of salvation, but that despair can differ in manner, degree, and duration. Some are more sudden than others; some result in sinners being "more sorely broken with distressing and distracting terrors" of their guilt, the wrath of God, and their prospective damnation; some gain great hope by which they are kept from "sinking under such unalterable anguish"; some agonize for years under "horrors of conscience"; and others are brought more quickly to "the footstool of God's mercy," where they rest with comfort in an absolute dependence upon Christ alone for justification (7–9).

In such an active/passive doctrine, of course, Dickinson conveyed the widely recognized central tension within the Calvinist/Puritan scheme of faith and salvation, preparation or contingency and God's sovereign free grace—the relative roles of human responsibility and God's sovereignty. Due to man's corruption, he is unable to come to Christ by his own power or actions. He must do so through faith. Through faith, which is solely God's gift and not of man's own making, God grants man the assistance of divine grace by which he can endeavor "to lye at his foot stool" or to obtain those gracious influences, whereby he may receive God and have power to become a child of God. In sum, man must endeavor through faith to find God, but he is incapable on his own merits of gaining that faith. This is the means of salvation Christ has provided. It is men's only hope, but for those who might despair of it Dickinson offered: "We cannot, it's true, ever do this [secure faith through our own natural unsanctified will] so as to give us a claim to those divine assistances. . . . [Nevertheless, it] is more than possible for such humbled souls . . . to endeavor to cast themselves at the footstool of the Lord Jesus Christ; to have the work of faith with power wrought in their souls; and in that way they have all possible encouragement, that if they thus seek they shall find" (20–22).

Having addressed the issues of justification and sanctification, Dickinson turned to assurance and told his congregation that the rest which the Lord bestows on the "weary and heavy laden souls" that come to Him is a freedom and deliverance from all the miserable and deadly effects of their fallen apostate state. It is the freedom that Christ purchased and tendered for all such sinners from the guilt and damning power of sin. The "curse of the Law" is taken off such souls, and they are reconciled to God through Christ's death on the cross. Where every unconverted sinner is under a sentence of eternal damnation, the converted have been freed by Christ from that danger and prepared for an eternal triumph over it (22–24).

Corruptions will remain with the converted, Dickinson continued, but "they shall reign no more." The devil will continue to use all his wiles, but they who have come to Christ will be enabled by him to stand against the devil and "to quench all his fiery darts": "The flesh will yet lust against the spirit; and many imperfections accompany their highest attainments; but with the mind they will serve the law of God, though with the flesh the law of sin. Though they must yet keep in their harness, they are sure of a

victory. 'Sin shall no more have dominion over them; for they are not under the law, but under grace'" (23–24).[27]

Often, Dickinson's words are best allowed to speak for him, with
little or no elaboration. What follows are three such instances, wherein
Dickinson's evangelical approach approximates that which we have come
to associate with Jonathan Edwards's *Sinners in the Hands of an Angry God,*
representative or not, preached at Enfield, Connecticut, in 1741. In the
first instance, Dickinson issued a warning to his listeners: "Indeed, my dear
Brethren, this is your case, the dreadful flames of God's burning vengeance
are as it were flashing about your ears; sleep but a little longer, and you are
fixed forever in that fire that shall never be quenched."

In the second, he spoke to those who would not heed his words and
yet hoped to be saved: "What grounds have you for this hope? Can you
hope that God will violate his word for your sake, and sacrifice his truth
and justice to your lusts? Can you hope that God will make new terms of
salvation for you, that were never proposed to any in the world; and that
you shall be saved in a way contrary to his nature, to his law, and to the
whole tenor of the Gospel covenant?"

And, in the third, he responded to those who might complain of his
preaching hell and damnation: "I assure you, that it's not from any delight
in your disquiet or uneasiness, that I set these awful truths before you. I
would leave you in an undisturbed tranquility, if your precious souls were
not in danger. But it is from a sense of duty to God, it's from compassion to
your perishing souls, that I thus warn you of your approaching ruin" (26–
27).[28]

More typically softening his approach, however, Dickinson assured
the unrepentant of the congregation that no matter how long they had
been in a state of sin, it was not too late to be saved. No case is a total loss,
he explained, because it is neither the number nor even the severity of sins
that makes the case for sinners desperate; instead, it is "their impertinent
continuance in them." Dickinson reminded his listeners that God was calling them, and that if they were to accept his invitation and come to Christ,
he would not cast them out. On the one hand Dickinson offered: "You can
make sure to yourselves that your day of grace is not past." On the other
hand, as if to retain that essential tension created by dependence on God's
sovereign free grace, thereby avoiding charges of Arminianism or
preparationism, he added, "for if you have a heart to do this, it's certain you
are not yet given up to a hard heart, and a reprobate mind" (28–30).[29]

Dickinson concluded his sermon at Connecticut Farms with essentially the same message he had conveyed to the people of nearby Woodbridge.
He warned them to avoid divisions, and he charged those who had insti-

gated discord with neither having dedicated themselves to God nor having won the spiritual graces that lead to love of one another. Dickinson suggested that those whom he charged might answer that those they had reproached and vilified were "formal hypocrites"; that it was their duty both to God and to the hypocrites to tell them of it and to awaken them to a sense of their danger; and "that the society in general being such formalists, ought to be broken up, that it may be settled upon a better foundation." Much as he had said two months before, Dickinson responded that whether or not people are "formal hypocrites" is left to God to judge, not man. Their charge was to practice charity toward all and to do nothing that might further divide them, as that, he warned, was clear evidence of their unrepentant state (38–40).

On April 28, George Whitefield returned to Elizabeth Town for his final visit. He was returning from a trip south and with him was Gilbert Tennent, who, on March 8, 1740, had delivered his blistering Nottingham sermon, *The Danger of an Unconverted Ministry*. Dickinson described that visit in a letter to Thomas Foxcroft, dated May 24, 1740. Dickinson's response to Whitefield's first visit, some five months earlier, it will be recalled, had been quite positive. Following Whitefield's second visit, he offered a different opinion.

By Whitefield's estimate there were about two thousand in attendance at his second Elizabeth Town sermon, including some ten Dissenting and two Anglican ministers, who did not "tarry very long." Dickinson wrote that many "stumbled" over Whitefield's comments and that few, if any, were affected. Although, in his letter, Dickinson continued to hope that Whitefield's efforts would "awaken all of the sacred profession to a more active diligence" in God's work, leading to a "glorious success," he also made it clear that he could not "stand surety" for all Whitefield had expressed, "particularly his making assurance to be essentially necessary to a justifying faith; and his openly declaring for a spirit of discovering converts and [those] who are close-hearted hypocrites."[30]

No doubt adding to Dickinson's concern was Whitefield's dealing "very plainly" with the Presbyterian clergy in attendance, many of whom, he was convinced, preached the doctrines of grace to others without being converted themselves. In the midst of their own laity, Whitefield condemned them as "close-hearted hypocrites" and "the bane of the Christian church," and he prayed for their souls. (There is no indication whether or not Dickinson was among those singled out for Whitefield's wrath.) Whitfield concluded his sermon with the following note: "No doubt, some were offended, but I care not for any sect or party of men. As I love all who love the Lord Jesus, of what communion soever; so I reprove all whether Dissenters, or not Dissenters, who take His word into their mouths, but never felt Him dwelling in their hearts."[31]

While the Awakening gained momentum in Elizabeth Town, it continued in full force in Newark, and Dickinson worked with Aaron Burr toward its complete flowering. The Newark revival was largely successful and peaceful, but it had its voices of dissent. In all, Dickinson wrote, there is good reason to conclude that there were many who experienced a saving change at Newark, but there were nonetheless too many who, though at first under convictions, had grown "careless and secure" and failed to find a new life. And there were those who through "false pride and rash zeal" had made "high pretenses to religion" and grown censorious, thereby "opening the mouths of many who opposed the revival."[32] On May 7, nine days after George Whitefield's second visit to Elizabeth Town, Dickinson offered to the Newark congregation his sermon *Witness of the Spirit,* in which he addressed those voices of censoriousness and opposition.

The popularity of *Witness of the Spirit* can be gauged by its having gone through three editions by 1743, all of which, attesting to the readership Dickinson had cultivated in both the Middle Colonies and New England, were published in Boston. Its subtitle would suggest that the sermon might be reminiscent of Jonathan Edwards's observations on the Northampton revival, *Faithful Narrative of Surprising Conversions* (1736), which appeared in an American edition in 1738 and with which Dickinson no doubt was familiar. And, indeed, Dickinson, like Edwards, noted that his sermon was offered "on occasion of a wonderful progress of converting grace in those parts." At the same time, Dickinson wrote that he intended to show "in what way and manner the Spirit himself beareth witness to the adoption of the children of God," and that became the sermon's dominant element.[33]

Alan Heimert and Perry Miller have called *Witness of the Spirit* the "first sustained analysis of the psychology of conversion" of the Awakening, and in that sense it may be seen as an earlier and perhaps more prudent or moderate statement on assurance and religious affections than Edwards's *Distinguishing Marks of a Work of the Spirit of God,* published one year later. Similarly, it might be seen as an earlier and less complex statement on the same subject as Edwards's *Treatise Concerning Religious Affections,* written during the winter of 1742/43, which was arguably the best explanation of religious psychology in early American literature. As Heimert and Miller have concluded, although the younger minister would soon eclipse his efforts, Dickinson anticipated Edwards in his search for a consistent philosophy of the revival. He was also among the first to give the Awakening intellectual credibility.[34]

Without a doubt, *Witness of the Spirit* was a temperate sermon, but its evangelical doctrine had much more in common than in conflict with that espoused by the Log College men. Keith Hardman has suggested that in *Witness of the Spirit* Dickinson was the first to offer a compromise between evangelical demands for sudden conversion and the long-standing Calvinist emphasis on preparation. Having reached a similar conclusion, Leonard Trinterud has argued that with its publication Dickinson not only aligned himself with the revival and against its opponents but also, as he did so from a moderate position, he charted the future character of American Presbyterianism.[35]

In *Witness of the Spirit,* as in his earlier works, Dickinson provided both due recognition of the powerful influence of the "witness of the spirit" and warnings of the abuses to which it had led. On the latter point, in this instance, however, he focused to a much greater extent on the doctrine of assurance, as taught by Whitefield, Tennent, and others of the Log College. Dickinson chastised them for having pretended "to spiritual influences which want a new bible for their justification" and pointed out to them that those tremors of the soul they had often indelibly associated with conversion may not necessarily come from God but rather, and more likely, from "enthusiastic heats, from working up the animal passions, or else from diabolical delusions."[36]

In *Witness,* Dickinson offered seven ways by which we may know, or at least take some comfort in believing, that we are the children of God or that the spirit of God is within us. First, he insisted that, in this as in all other matters, Scripture is man's infallible guide and that it offers all that is necessary on the subject. Consequently, men must not accept anything as the "witness of the spirit" that is not agreeable with Scripture, and they must "try" their state or test their qualifications for salvation by it (3–4).

Second, Dickinson wrote, the spirit bears witness that we are the children of God by its sanctifying and renewing influence on our hearts: "If we are renewed in the spirit of our mind; if old things are passed away, and all things are become new in our souls; if we have put on the new man, which is renewed in knowledge after the image of Him that created us; we have the witness of the spirit himself to our adoption." Such a renewal, Dickinson explained, leads men to a conviction of their sin and misery, as well as a deep impression of their dangerous perishing circumstances as long as they remain an enemy of God. It lifts men out of the "carnal state of security and unconcern" in which dwell the "heirs of eternal perdition" or the "far greatest part of the world of mankind." In the context of his previously detailed conversion morphology, Dickinson pointed out that such conviction is the first operation of the spirit toward a sinner's sanctification (5, 7–9).

Third, Dickinson wrote, the spirit employs in men a "lively faith" in Christ, by which they are brought to look to the "fullness and sufficiency" in Christ and to receive them on Christ's own terms as revealed in the gospel. By such a "lively faith," he explained, men are led away from those futile efforts previously noted, to depend on Christ alone as the author of their salvation (11).

Fourth, Dickinson told the Newark congregation, the spirit reveals itself to men in its bringing about in them a sincere love of God. The carnal minds of men bear enmity toward God until the spirit of God reforms their sinners' nature, sanctifies their affections, and enables their souls to live in the love of God. When that happens, men "love what God loveth, and hate what He hateth." They take to heart "the flourishing and prosperity of his kingdom and interest in the world," and they diligently exert themselves in their respective stations to promote both (12–13).

Dickinson's fifth means of the spirit is found in man's love of the children of God. This is not a natural love based on any relationship or friendship, or on any kindness done one by another, he explained. Nor does it imply that a person must love or approve of the errors and imperfections of others. Rather, it means that he must love the "gracious qualifications" of those whom he has reason to believe are the children of God. In sum, "if we love the image of Christ wherever we see it, or wherever we think we see it . . . if we love the brethren as brethren, love their company, love community and fellowship with them in religious exercise, and love an imitation of them . . . it is a witness for us, that we are born of God" (14–15).

Being chosen of God provides a sixth manner by which the spirit of God reveals itself to men, Dickinson continued, and that is in its giving men, through faith, a victory over the world. They become spiritually minded, and they overcome their natural love of earthly things. Their interest in the world and in temporal things shrinks to nothing when compared with their interest in the eternal, in a future state, and in God's favor (15–16).

Finally, the spirit bears witness to itself in bringing about in men a spirit of supplication. In such men, prayer is their "very breath and vital air." They employ themselves in prayer with a special diligence and delight, not only to quiet their consciences but to have fellowship with God the Father and his Son, Jesus Christ. Provided with the opportunity to approach God and to "complain of the deadness of their hearts," those with the spirit of supplication pray that they may thereby be victorious over their corruptions, gain further evidence of God's favor, and earn more of the gracious influences of God's spirit (17–18).

By all seven means, Dickinson wrote, the spirit of God bears incontestable witness to men of their having been chosen the children of God and of the safety and goodness of their state. But, he continued, men are liable to be deceived, and many, in fact, had been imagining that they were the children of God when they were not. Even some of those who had experienced terrors of the heart and had been awakened from "carnal security," he added, had fallen short of an interest in Christ, had their impressions wear off, and "returned to folly, like a dog to his vomit." Therefore, he argued, men must seriously, impartially, and frequently reexamine themselves to determine whether they possess the characteristics of the children of God, while they depend on the spirit of God (7, 8, 12–14, 19).

In conclusion, Dickinson addressed two key and hotly debated issues that lay at the core of the Awakening: Do all the children of God have clear and satisfying evidence of their sanctified state? And is such evidence absolutely necessary? In answer to the first question, Dickinson pointed out that the influence of the spirit of God on the soul is a sensible, or perceptible, operation, of which it is impossible for anyone who has been convinced of his guilt and danger and brought out of a state of carnal security to be unaware (25–26).

Nevertheless, Dickinson continued, in answer to the second question, there are those who feel such spiritual influences but remain not only uncertain of their conversion to God but also subject to a "dreadful gloom," a "melancholy habit," and "an unhappy course of darkness and fear." By way of example, he pointed to those whose sense of unworthiness makes them afraid to accept any comforts of the soul that belong to them as the result of the presence of grace. They see such "glad tidings" as news too good for them. "They know how hard it is to distinguish between the remains of sin in the children of God and the reign of sin in refined hypocrites." Troubled by the frequent recurrence of "deadness and dulness" in the performance of their duty to God, Dickinson explained, such people are afraid of being deceived as to the true state of their souls. Quite pointedly, in terms of that assurance taught by those of the radical Awakening, Dickinson warned: "Whoever therefore teaches such doctrine, that every converted person must necessarily know that he is converted and will enjoy the light of God's countenance, while walking uprightly, I conceive . . . do offend against the generation of God's children, go contrary to the constant doctrine of the most eminent Protestant divines from the Reformation to this day, and contrary to the blessed oracles of truth" (26–27).

Before turning to the tumultuous year of 1741, it would be useful to further discuss the state of affairs in Elizabeth Town during the "Awakening of 1740." Earlier, reference was made to Dickinson's account of Whitefield's two visits to Elizabeth Town, in a letter to Thomas Foxcroft written only a few weeks after the English divine's second visit. Three years later, in another letter to Foxcroft, Dickinson provided a more detailed and less passionate assessment.

Dickinson opened his letter, dated August 23, 1743, by noting that before the Awakening religion in Elizabeth Town was "in a very low state." The people were generally "careless, carnal and secure," and there was little of the "power of godliness" among them. In the fall of 1739, Dickinson continued, Whitefield moved his congregation toward a "general thoughtfulness about religion" and prompted them "to make the extraordinary zeal and diligence of that gentleman, the common and turning topic of their conversation," but no one was brought "under conviction" or to "any new and special concern about their salvation."

Dickinson reported that he continued to labor unsuccessfully in Elizabeth Town through the winter of 1739/40. In what he admits to Foxcroft was an "afflicting and discouraging" situation, his congregation remained "secure and careless, and could not be awakened out of their sleep." Dickinson assumed that he was laboring in vain and that he had "spent [his] strength for nought."

During the late winter and early spring of 1740, however, an "uncommon concern" among the younger members of his congregation arose. Dickinson tried to provide them with "some affecting sense of their misery, danger, and necessity of a savior." He offered them frequent lectures, but still there was no visible success. Whitefield came and went for the second time, and then, in June 1740, "a remarkable manifestation of the divine presence" appeared among Dickinson's flock. He offered Foxcroft the following description:

> Having at that time invited young people to hear a sermon, there was a numerous congregation convened which consisted chiefly of our youth, though there were many others with them. I preached to them a plain, practical sermon, without any pathos or pungency, or any special liveliness or vigor, for I was then in a remarkably dead and dull frame, till enlivened by a sudden and deep impression which visibly appeared upon the congregation in general. There was no crying out or falling down (as elsewhere has happened) but the inward distress and concern of the audience discovered itself by their tears and by an audible sobbing and sighing in almost all parts of the assembly. There appeared such tokens of a solemn and deep concern as I never saw in any congregation whatsoever.

From that point on, Dickinson wrote, he heard no more of his young people meeting "for frolics and extravagant diversions," as had been common. Instead, they met for religious exercises. Public worship was carefully and constantly attended by people of all ages, and "a serious and solemn attention to the ministry of the word was observable in their very countenances." The number of those seeking spiritual guidance from Dickinson increased until, during the late summer of 1740, more went to Dickinson in one day than had done so over the course of the previous six months.

Dickinson reported that although the degree and duration of distress or terror varied, all were first brought to a deep sense of their sin, guilt, and danger, to despair of their inability to save themselves, and to a realization of their total dependence on God before they obtained any satisfying discovery of safety in Christ. However, in terms of the growing rift between those of the moderate and radical Awakening, and his leadership in the former, Dickinson insisted that at Elizabeth Town there was "very little appearance of those irregular heats . . . which are so loudly complained of in some other parts of the land." Only two or three instances of such outbursts had occurred, and they were "easily and speedily regulated."

Although cautious to assume the conversion of anyone, true to that which he wrote elsewhere on a more theoretical level, Dickinson cited as evidence of the positive effects of the Elizabeth Town revival "the fruits of its trees" produced over time. Writing in 1743 of what had begun three years earlier, Dickinson noted that, although the general concern of his congregation had worn off, and most had returned to "security and insensibility," a "considerable number" were still marked by serious impressions. Approximately sixty of his congregation had actually received a saving change, and to that he added an unspecified number from an adjoining parish, perhaps Connecticut Farms.

Dickinson attached a note to his letter to Thomas Foxcroft reporting that he was gratified by the declaration of the last convention of ministers in Boston, as it suggested to him that there still existed a number among those ministers who were willing to give God "the glory of this special grace so eminently displayed of late."[37] This most likely referred to a meeting and subsequent statement by the New England ministers in Boston on July 7, 1743, something to be considered in the following chapter. For now, suffice to say, the note indicates Dickinson's lasting support for the Awakening and his continued ties with those of similar sentiments in New England.

7

ESTABLISHING THE
MODERATE AWAKENING

As shown in the previous chapter, the year 1740 brought the Great Awakening to its height in the Middle Colonies in general and in the Presbyterian Church in particular. The years 1741 and 1742, however, witnessed the rise of radical forces within the Awakening, the reaction of the Old Side, schism, and Dickinson's emergence as leader of the moderate Awakening. It also was the year in which Dickinson published two of his most important theological treatises on subjects seasonable to the Awakening, *The True Scripture Doctrine* and *A Display of God's Special Grace*.

To begin, however, let us review the events that led to the rupture of 1741. In 1738, the Log College men of the New Brunswick Presbytery protested and then ignored the Synod of Philadelphia's licensing act by examining and licensing the Log College graduate John Rowland. When the synod met in 1739, it found the New Brunswick Presbytery "disorderly," admonished it not to continue such divisive actions, and refused to recognize Rowland as a minister within the bounds of the synod until he submitted to synodical examination.[1] When Rowland refused to submit and the Log College men persisted in their "disorderly" behavior, relations between the two groups quickly deteriorated.

Over the course of the next two years a series of developments served to harden their antagonistic positions. To cite just three, the newly established, largely New Side Hopewell congregation openly defied attempts by the Old Side Presbytery of Philadelphia to settle an Old Side minister among them.[2] Whitefield twice toured the Middle Colonies, lavishing high praise on the Log College men while denouncing their opponents.[3] And in March 1740 Gilbert Tennent delivered his now legendary sermon, *The Danger of an Unconverted Ministry*, in which he labeled unawakened clergy "hypocritical varlets," "lepers," "plague-sores," "dead dogs," and "worms."[4]

Two months later, at the Philadelphia Synod of May 1740, the Old Side gathered for a counterattack and the New Brunswick group mustered for their defense. Joining the New Brunswick ministers were the "awakened" of Philadelphia, who crowded into the gallery of the city's Presbyterian church to observe the synod's deliberations and to make their sentiments known. The city was alive with New Side preaching; Society Hill alone averaged fourteen sermons a week, and no one was allowed to preach unless he was of unquestioned New Side principles. Jonathan Dickinson was not among them. He had become suspect as the result of his sermon at Newark, *Witness of the Spirit.* Still, upon his arrival in Philadelphia, Dickinson wrote glowingly about how the revival had brought about an "amazing transformation in the city." Never to his knowledge, he reported, had the people shown so great a willingness to attend sermons nor had the preachers demonstrated greater zeal and diligence. Religion had become the subject of most conversations, books of devotion were in demand, and the singing of psalms and prayer superseded all other forms of entertainment.[5]

When the Synod of Philadelphia met, neither the Old Side nor the New Brunswick men were disposed to exercise any considerable discretion. Only the New Englanders, with John Pierson chosen moderator, strove for peace and harmony. The issue before the synod remained the examination of candidates for the ministry. Both New and Old Siders agreed that the synod was the proper judge of the qualifications of its own members, but there agreement ended. The synod voted to continue its measure on licensing, and the New Brunswick group continued to protest. The New England group voted with the majority.[6]

Faced with the prospect of a divided body, the synod adopted two compromise positions. First, it repealed as unenforceable the itinerancy law of 1738. Second, it clarified its just confirmed measure on synodical examination, explaining that although it did not intend by its actions to deny presbyteries the right to license ministers, the synod retained its right to examine its own members. In this case, the synod explained, men who were licensed by presbyteries but who failed to take or pass synodical examination, though recognized as gospel ministers, would be denied membership in the synod. In the words of Leonard Trinterud, such preachers would comprise "an extralegal though tolerated group," a lower rank that could serve freelance in restricted areas but that posed no challenge to the synod. Those immediately affected would be the likes of the aforementioned John Rowland.[7]

Peace not yet having been reached, other proposals having been offered but rejected, Samuel Blair took the floor and called for a closed session. In denying his motion, the Old Side majority insisted that whatever he had to offer might just as well be offered in open session. Blair did just that. He openly denounced the Old Side position, and then Gilbert Tennent attacked the "doctrinal and spiritual declension of the church" under Old Side leadership.

In brief, Tennent, much like Blair, charged "a number" of members of the synod with being in a "carnal state"; being "unsound in some principal doctrines of Christianity, that relate to experience and practice," especially as they relate to regeneration, free will, and the covenant of grace; preaching in a "powerless and unsavory" and legalistic and contented manner, as well as being "afraid to use the terrors of the Lord to persuade men"; opposing God's servants and work in a "pharisee and devil-like" manner; insisting that there is no infallible knowledge of one's spiritual state; and allowing men into the ministry without examining them as to their "Christian experience." Tennent brought the charges, though "distressing" to his heart, he explained, for the same reason he had protested "against all restraints in preaching the everlasting gospel in this degenerate state of the church": "Rules which are serviceable in ordinary cases, when the church is stocked with a faithful ministry, are notoriously prejudicial when the church is oppressed with a carnal ministry. Besides the remarkable success that God has given of late to Mr. Whitefield's travelling labors, and several others in this country, makes me abhor the slavish schemes of bigots, as to confinement in preaching the blessed Gospel of Christ."[8]

When the Old Siders asked Tennent and Blair to specify their charges and to identify the people to whom they referred as "unsound in doctrine" or "immoral in practice," Tennent and Blair asked for time and for a regular trial. No agreement being reached on that—prompting Leonard Trinterud to conclude that, at that point, neither side wanted a trial—the Synod of 1740 came to an end. In its concluding moments only a few voices could be heard exhorting the membership to be more faithful and to be at peace. Among those voices was that of Jonathan Dickinson.[9]

Tension between the Old and New Side grew worse. The New Brunswick Presbytery continued to license without regard to the synod, and the Donegal Presbytery brought charges against New Siders Alexander Craighead and David Alexander for "intrusions," unexcused absences from presbytery meetings, and imposing new terms of communion on their congregations. The resulting trial, which took place in December 1740, was at best an embarrassment, at worst a fiasco.

Craighead and Alexander openly defied the presbytery. During Alexander's hearing, while he attacked his judges on the floor of the church to the delight of the lay audience, Craighead harangued a large crowd in a tent adjacent to the church on the Donegal clergy's delinquencies and moral failings. The next day, when Craighead was tried, Alexander returned the favor, this time aided by Samuel Finley, who had been licensed by the

Presbytery of New Brunswick that August. The lay audience forced the presbytery to adjourn before it completed its questioning of Craighead. Nevertheless, both Craig and Alexander were suspended.[10]

Similar difficulties arose at the same time at a meeting of the New Castle Presbytery. First, some of its members challenged Samuel Blair and Gilbert Tennent, then in attendance, to further explain the charges they had brought to the Synod of Philadelphia, at least so far as to state whether or not they had aimed at any of the members of the New Castle Presbytery, in which case a trial could take place. They refused, whereupon members of the presbytery presented to the assembly a list of questions wherein they condemned a number of statements by George Whitefield as being of unsound doctrine. Samuel Blair attempted to defend Whitefield by arguing that Whitefield's remarks only appeared to be in error as they had been taken out of context, but the presbytery rejected his defense and the questions were published in September 1741 under the title *The Querists*.[11]

Defenses of George Whitefield soon appeared, but in late October Whitefield himself responded with *A Letter . . . to Some Church Members of the Presbyterian Persuasion*. Whitefield had just returned from a tour of New England, where he was generally well received by the New Lights but where he also provoked the concerns of some of their leaders. Upon his visit to Northampton, Jonathan Edwards, for example, cautioned Whitefield against rebuking unregenerate ministers and pronouncing persons unconverted, and he warned him against "giving way to every motion of his soul as if of divine origin."

Without abandoning his evangelical position, Whitefield responded to *The Querists* by taking a much more moderate stance on the Awakening than he had at any point thus far. He denied that he, as charged, had espoused the doctrine of universal redemption, but he also thanked the authors of *The Querists* for giving him the opportunity to correct his printed mistakes, especially as to Calvinist doctrine in which, he admitted, he had little training. He even retracted any other "unguarded expressions" he may have made that were subsequently found to be indefensible.[12]

When the authors of *The Querists* replied to Whitefield with further exceptions to his statements, as well as to the revival itself (Gilbert Tennent's Nottingham sermon, *The Danger of an Unconverted Ministry*, was the subject of particular criticism), Whitefield's defenders continued to rally to his and their own support. Particularly enthusiastic defenses of Whitefield and of the Awakening came from the pens of Samuel Blair, in *A Particular Consideration of a Piece Entitled, The Querists* (1741), and of Samuel Finley, in *Christ Triumphing and Satan Raging* (1741).[13]

At Whitefield's urging, Gilbert Tennent had undertaken an evangelistic tour of New England December 13, 1740, to March 2, 1741. It has been said that "an uncommon interest and success" greeted Tennent's labors in New England. Milton Coalter has described Tennent's tour as his finest hour. In Boston, phenomenal crowds greeted him, and in New Haven over half of the Yale College students were awakened by his preaching. A large number of New England clergy, including Dickinson's close friend and ally Thomas Foxcroft, welcomed Tennent. Others, such as Yale rector Thomas Clap and the influential Charles Chauncy, shunned him. In explaining his actions, Clap later asserted that Jonathan Edwards had revealed to him that the Log College men had schemed with Whitefield to bring over from England a group of "godly" young men to be trained at the Log College for service in New England. Although subsequently denied by Edwards, to which Clap admitted that he might have surmised some of the details, Clap nevertheless, coincidentally with Tennent's visit, succeeded in heightening the fears of many of the New England clergy of the Log College men.[14]

In April 1741, at a meeting of the Donegal Presbytery, John Thomson presented an overture in which he lamented the sad state of affairs in the colonial Presbyterian Church and offered some proposals toward restoring order, namely, strengthening the authority of church government. He proposed that the presbytery adopt rules that local churches might employ in disciplining their members; that lay persons be obliged to subscribe to the Westminster Confession of Faith and Catechisms and promise to submit to the government of the Presbyterian Church before being admitted to the sacraments; that all who would be admitted to the sacraments pledge not to attend "disorderly preachers"; and that no clerical member of the presbytery go to hear such preachers or allow any of them into his pulpit. Any violations, the overture continued, would be seen as worthy of the same censures as drunkenness, adultery, or fornication. The overture was carried by "a great majority preparing the way for the Synod of 1741."[15]

At the May 1741 meeting of the Synod of Philadelphia, from which the entire New England delegation was mysteriously absent,[16] Robert Cross, on behalf of nineteen synod Old Siders, initiated the much anticipated fray with his *Protestation*. He declared that the New Brunswick men—with their "unscriptural, antipresbyterial, uncharitable, [and] divisive practices"—were responsible for the "dreadful divisions, distractions, and convulsions" that had seized the "infant church" and that threatened its very existence. He warned that unless the New Brunswick group gave "suitable satisfaction" to the synod, particularly to those signing the *Protestation,* the latter would not consider themselves bound by any future act of the synod made by or with the New Brunswick men. Referring specifically to the Westminster

Confession, Catechisms, and Directory, as adopted by the synod in 1729 and 1736, Cross suggested that members of the New Brunswick Presbytery had no right to be members of the synod, as their principles and practices were opposed to those of the synod in matters of government and order. Continued union with them, Cross insisted, would be "most absurd and inconsistent," and the resulting schism would be of their making.[17]

The specific charges lodged against the New Brunswick men were that the principles of church government elaborated by them in their response to the Synod of Philadelphia the year before, whereby church officers and judicatories were deprived of all authority, were heterodox and anarchical; that their protest against the synod's rule on the examination of ministerial candidates was an act of contempt toward the synod; that their intrusions into other congregations without the concurrence of the ministers of those congregations or of the presbyteries to which the congregations belonged had sown seeds of division; that their sermons, in such cases, had led to alienation and "unjust prejudices" between the laity and their "lawfully called pastors"; that their judgments and condemnations of their brethren in the ministry (to wit Gilbert Tennent's Nottingham sermon was noted by way of example) had been rash and unfair; that their concept of God's call to the ministry as consisting of "some invisible motions and workings of the spirit" rather than being that by which men are "regularly ordained and set apart" was wrong; and that their preaching on the terrors of the law and on the assurance of salvation had led their listeners to unacceptable, "hideous," and "convulsion-like" behavior as well as unsound decisions as to their supposedly gracious state.[18]

No formal vote was taken, or at least recorded, and confusion reigned for years thereafter as to what actually had happened at the Synod of 1741. The protestors would say that they had declared that the New Brunswick men had no right to sit in the synod whether they were in the majority or minority and that the New Brunswick men countered with the argument that those of the majority should constitute the synod, only to find themselves in the minority, at which point they withdrew. The New Brunswick men, on the other hand, would claim that they had not asked the protesters to withdraw but that they had been excluded. They also would explain, however, that after the *Protestation* was entered and subscribed and the moderator had commanded silence, thereby preventing the New Brunswick men from speaking in their defense, they had thought it "expedient" to withdraw. Finally, they would allege that the protesting ministers were in the minority of those present at the synod and that those who did not sign the *Protestation* had no intention of subscribing.[19]

That Gilbert Tennent believed Cross and the other protesters had conspired to expel the New Brunswick group comes as no surprise, but he was not alone, nor was that sentiment limited to the men of that presbytery. George Gillespie, present at the Synod of 1741, a member of the New Castle Presbytery, and a proponent of the revival, in a letter to the absent Jonathan Dickinson and the Presbytery of New York, wrote that he believed the synod had ejected the Log College men illegally and without precedent in order to stop the revival. The roots of the trouble, he asserted, could be found in the synod's act of 1738, wherein the presbyteries were deprived of their essential right to examine candidates for ministerial ordination. Any claim that the act was intended only to ensure the existence of a learned ministry was false, Gillespie argued. He suggested, instead, that it was intended to ensure rule by the synod, and therein lay the problem. If the synod could take away one right, it could take away all on the same grounds. Whereas he once agreed with those who had argued that Gilbert Tennent was intent on dividing the church, having met with Tennent before the opening of the synod, Gillespie had come to believe that Tennent had exonerated himself from any such charge. The Cross *Protestation* had opened Gillespie's eyes "so that now it plainly appeareth who were hottest for a division, to wit, the protesters." Gillespie looked to the Presbytery of New York, as the only New Siders who had not antagonized the Old Side, to reunite the synod.[20]

Similarly, that Tennent's actions and motives would be questioned by Old Siders is not surprising, but the Old Side Scots and Scotch-Irish were not alone in criticizing the New Brunswick men. In a letter of June 25, 1741, to John Pierson of Woodbridge, New Jersey, intended for Dickinson's eyes as well, Jedediah Andrews offered similar sentiments. Andrews noted that he had received letters from Dickinson and Pierson, in which both said that, as so many of their group were to be absent from the Synod of 1741, it would be unreasonable to initiate any further debate on the contested act concerning ministerial examination and licensing. The appeal for repeal of the act was offered. But, Andrews ventured, if it had been carried and the act rescinded, the synod would have been "deluged" by ministers sympathetic to the New Brunswick cause and all others silenced.[21]

Andrews left it to Pierson and Dickinson to decide what influence such a prospect had on those who brought forth the *Protestation*, but he did say that he and those closer to Philadelphia had found the confusions that the New Brunswick men had caused "perfectly astonishing," even making them "weary" of their lives: "They have called themselves members with us, but have been continually acting against us, and endeavoring to make all that don't follow them to be looked on as carnal, graceless, unconverted hypocrites, to destroy our usefulness and bring as many as possible over to them. . . . Both town and country are full of Antinomian notions, which if we say anything against, in pulpit or out, 'tis almost as much as our lives are worth, and we feel ourselves bound in conscience to give people warning and endeavor to preserve them from destruction."

Andrews continued to condemn the New Brunswick men for preaching that "moral law is no rule to believers"; that the unconverted must not be pressed to do their duty to God, as all they do is sin; and that there is no need to urge the converted to do their duty because they will do it, anyway. The New Brunswick group was in an "enthusiastic frenzy," Andrews wrote, as they elevated those they deemed converted and condemned all others. They claimed to be following what they had learned from George Whitefield, and that, Andrews added, he did not dispute: "I feared things would come to this pass from the beginning. . . . Some people blamed me then (thinking people would take the good and leave the bad) that now justify me and say that I saw further than they."

As if from one New Englander to another, anticipating Dickinson's return to the fray, Andrews charged the New Brunswick men with attacking "all solid religion" and tending "to pervert the good principles derived to us from our forefathers." He enclosed a copy of the *Protestation* with his letter, adding that if action had not been taken, the synod would have degenerated into "a babel both as to principles and practices." He called for charity between him and Pierson and Dickinson, even if they did not agree in all things, and confirmed that he remained in accord with the doctrines of their New England predecessors and of the Reformed churches.[22]

The Awakening had driven a wedge into the Presbyterian Church in the Middle Colonies. The day after their ejection, the New Brunswick men and others who left the Philadelphia Synod to join them gathered into the Conjunct Presbyteries of New Brunswick and Londonderry. The Log College men realized what they had to do, and sought to do it, but, as Trinterud put it, they failed in the short run to accomplish it. The "new order" was not to be born until the Dickinson group joined forces with them, and that was four years away.[23]

February 1742 witnessed the turning point in the Great Awakening in the Middle Colonies. In that month, Dickinson received a written retraction from Gilbert Tennent. In a letter dated February 12, Tennent confessed "in the openest manner" that he had mismanaged his affairs thus far in the Awakening and that he could not justify the "excessive heat of temper" he had sometimes shown. Having just returned from another trip to New England, where he had witnessed the abuses of the Awakening, Tennent wrote that it was a time of "great spiritual desertion" for him but that out of it he had been given "a greater discovery" of himself than he had ever had before. He indicated that he was subject to conflicting thoughts concerning the debates before the Synod of Philadelphia and that he "would to God the breach were healed." He particularly blamed, or credited, the Moravians and James Davenport for this realization. The former awakened him to the dangers of anything that tended toward enthusiasm and division in the church; the latter alerted him to the Awakening's excesses.

Tennent wrote that he believed that Davenport's making judgments about an individual's gracious state was unscriptural and of an "awful tendency to rent and tear the church." Echoing Dickinson's already publicly expressed sentiments on the subject, he explained that such judgments were predicated on the false assumption that a certain and infallible knowledge of the estate of a man is attainable. The result had been schismatical, and it had set terms of communion that Christ had not established.

For much the same reason, Tennent went on to denounce, as had Dickinson some three years before, the exposing of unconverted ministers and the setting up of separate meetings "upon the supposed unregeneracy of pastors." Such actions had caused great harm; such meetings were "enthusiastical, proud, and schismatical," and they were based on the assumption that unconverted ministers were of no use as instruments of good in the church. Tennent rejected the sending out of "unlearned men" to teach others upon the supposition of their piety, as tending to bring the ministry into contempt, to breed enthusiasm, and to cause confusion. He also expressed his abhorrence of all pretense to immediate inspiration or following immediate impulses as "an enthusiastical, perilous ignis-futuus" and the practice of "singing in the streets" as "a piece of weakness and enthusiastical ostentation."

Tennent ended his letter to Dickinson with a reference that suggests a realization of the role Dickinson had assumed in the Awakening by that time, as well as knowledge of Dickinson's pending trip to New England: "I wish you success, dear sir, in your journey. . . . May your labors be blessed for that end."[24]

David Harlan has suggested that Tennent's letter to Dickinson was made possible by Dickinson's persistence, as well as by three separate challenges that together had drained Tennent of his confidence and placed him on the defensive. The first challenge arose when John Cross was charged with adultery. As early as 1734–35, Cross had led a revival at Baskingridge, New Jersey, for which he earned praise and support from Gilbert Tennent and George Whitefield. In time, however, as Martin Lodge has written, Cross began sowing more than evangelical seeds. Though so charged by members of his congregation, the New Brunswick Presbytery, to which the congregation belonged and which had licensed Cross in 1739, found Cross not guilty of "the complete act of adultery." It did judge him "very detestable" and guilty of "unclean speech and carriage," however, and on June 24, 1741, the New Brunswick Presbytery suspended Cross from his ministerial office.[25]

In a letter to Foxcroft on April 12, 1742, Dickinson lamented that John Cross had come to be "an unhappy instrument of great prejudice to the interest of religion." In his letter of August 23, 1743, wherein he described the 1739–40 awakening in Newark to Foxcroft, Dickinson added that Cross's "dreadful scandals" had "proved a means to still farther harden many in their declension and apostasy" and to oppose the workings of the spirit among them." He added, "That unhappy gentleman having made so high pretensions to extraordinary piety and zeal, his scandals gave the deeper wound to vital and experimental godliness." As Leigh Eric Schmidt has suggested, the Cross affair added "flesh and blood to the danger of extremes and showed the ease with which one could be sucked into the Charbydis of infidelity or destroyed by the Scylla of Antinomianism." It helped lead Tennent, as he noted in his letter to Dickinson, to repudiate the practice of licensing men solely "upon the supposition of their piety."[26]

The second of the challenges Harlan put forth occurred after the Cross case was resolved, when "the spectre of evangelism-gone-berserk" confronted Tennent again, this time in the person of James Davenport. As minister of a church at Southold, Long Island, in 1741 and 1742, Davenport had become one of the most notorious New Light itinerant ministers. Preaching in fields, pastures, or streets, invited by local ministers or not, Davenport would scream at the top of his lungs and sometimes throw off his clothes in response to which his followers would sing and dance along behind him. As one of Davenport's contemporaries wrote to a fellow minister: "Were you to see him in his most violent agitations, you would be apt to think that he was a madman just broke from his chains."

In fact, in May 1742 Davenport was arrested by the Connecticut General Assembly, declared "disturbed in the rational faculties of his mind," and sent back to Long Island. In June, Davenport went to Boston, where he explained his actions to the associated pastors of Boston and Charlestown. They promptly denounced Davenport's dependence on impulses, his condemning ministers he believed unregenerate, his singing in the streets, and his encouragement of lay exhorters. Davenport thereupon denounced the ministers as unconverted and exhorted the people to separate from them, whereupon he was arrested, declared *non compos mentis,* and deported.[27]

In 1742, Davenport and Timothy Allen founded "an alternative school of the prophets"—an alternative to Yale, that is—to be known as the "Shepherd's Tent" in New London, Connecticut. Although it did not last long, the school did come to represent the views of the most radical of the Awakening, especially on collegiate education, and that earned Davenport, its fund-raiser, and Allen, its teacher, the considerable enmity of both Old and New Siders. Yale rector Thomas Clap took steps to suppress it, persuading the already sympathetic Connecticut General Assembly to pass measures by which such schools were outlawed. Timothy Allen was arrested and jailed for a short time, but the school managed to survive into mid-1743 before Allen and Davenport alienated even their closest allies. One of Tennent's earliest substantive condemnations of Davenport comes in his February 12 letter to Dickinson.[28]

The third challenge to Tennent's commitment to the more radical form of revivalism came from the Moravians and their leader, Count Nikolaus Ludwig von Zinzendorf. Although the Moravians, of German origin, had been in Pennsylvania since the mid-1730s, during the initial years of the Awakening, in large part due to the galvanizing influence of Whitefield's tour of the Middle Colonies, they informally joined forces with the Log College men. They employed the methodology of the New Siders in attacking the unconverted much as Tennent and Davenport had and in urging greater itinerancy on the part of the converted, ministry and laity alike. On the other hand, true to their theology, resisting any change such as Whitefield was willing to undergo, the Moravians rejected Calvinist doctrine.

The arrival in Pennsylvania in November 1741 of Count Zinzendorf exacerbated things. Zinzendorf not only sought to expand the ranks of the awakened and the role of the Moravians among the awakened but he also urged a certain ecumenical, or at least interdenominational, union among the converted, whereby he would be propelled into a position of leadership for the entire movement. During the winter of 1741/42, the New Brunswick men met with Zinzendorf. From that meeting, bewildered by the count's mystical philosophy and bothered by his methods of evangelism, his directions given to religious seekers, and his use of lay preaching, the New Brunswick men concluded that the Moravians were preparing for a full-scale assault on the Presbyterians. Dickinson had long been, and would continue to be, critical of the Moravians.[29]

When he received Gilbert Tennent's letter, Dickinson was about to go to Boston for assistance in ending the divisiveness of the Awakening in the Middle Colonies. Dickinson certainly found divisiveness in New England as rampant and deleterious. On July 27, 1742, he wrote to Thomas Foxcroft that he had found "great confusion" in areas such as New Haven, where Satan had "found the means to turn men's minds from their greatest concern to contrivance to maintain their factions and contentions."[30]

Along the way to Boston, most likely in an attempt to intercede on behalf of the recently expelled New Light David Brainerd, Dickinson met with Yale rector Thomas Clap. We will take up the matter of David Brainerd in a later chapter. For now, it is important to note that the two no doubt discussed the Awakening and its impact on Yale and New Haven, as well as its divisive effects on both the Congregationalists of New England and the Presbyterians of the Middle Colonies. Clap, it will be recalled, was active in suppressing the Awakening in Connecticut, particularly at Yale.[31]

Although there is no direct evidence to prove it, it would seem that upon his visit to New Haven, Dickinson gave Tennent's letter to Clap. Once again, without any real evidence, it would also appear that Clap was responsible for having the letter published in the July 22, 1742, issue of the *Boston Weekly News-Letter*. Whether Tennent's letter was intended for use by Dickinson while on his peace mission or for publication, as it came to pass, remains uncertain. Leonard Trinterud has suggested that it was, on both counts. Tennent, however, later stated that his letter was written without "the least thought" of its publication.[32]

Regardless of their opposing views of the Awakening, Clap and Dickinson continued to correspond. Upon his return to Elizabeth Town, for example, but before his meeting with the Philadelphia Synod in 1742, Dickinson received a letter from Clap dated May 3, 1742, in which he reported that the same problematic state of affairs persisted in New Haven. Some ministers continued to belittle the gracious state of others and to refuse communion with them. About ten or twelve "in the government," Clap wrote, were prepared to "make for an open separation" and were taking steps, through separate meetings, toward that end. They were even encouraging the students at Yale to join them, promising that they would license those students who would leave the college without regard to a degree. Such licensing, he had heard, was to begin at the next convention of the Separatists.

Clap wrote that the First Society of New Haven, which had been badly divided into New and Old Lights, had sought advice from the Reverends William Russell of Middletown, Connecticut, and Jonathan Edwards. Russell and Edwards had advised them to "settle a colleague"—Aaron Burr was recommended—with the Reverend Joseph Noyes. In his opposition to the Awakening, Noyes had incurred the disfavor of a large segment of his congregation, and Burr would undoubtedly appeal to that group. Clap added that the Old Lights of the congregation welcomed the plan, as would most of the Separatists. Four or five of the leading dissenters remained bent on separation, he wrote, but if Burr were to accept their invitation, few in the congregation would leave. Such a solution would "save this town and college from many disorders and confusion," Clap explained to Dickinson, whereupon he asked for Dickinson's help in securing Burr's services. Clap ended with a note to Dickinson no doubt reflecting the optimistic mood of the moment: "I am very glad that there is a prospect of a union in your synod"[33]

From New Haven, Dickinson proceeded to Boston to confer with Thomas Foxcroft, Benjamin Colman, Joseph Sewall, Thomas Prince, John Webb, William Cooper, and Joshua Gee, all New Lights. Then Dickinson traveled to Northampton to see Jonathan Edwards. No records of these meetings have survived, but judging by his letter to Thomas Foxcroft of April 12, 1742, it would appear that he and the New Lights with whom he met resolved, by employing Gilbert Tennent's letter of retraction, to attempt a reconciliation between the two warring factions within the Synod of Philadelphia. For continued good relations between the Synod of Philadelphia and the Presbytery of New York, the presbytery would demand that the synod withdraw its support for Cross's *Protestation.* In return, the New Brunswick men would offer to the synod a recantation of those errors which had precipitated the schism.[34]

On May 27, 1742, at the Synod of Philadelphia Dickinson, who had been chosen moderator, successfully moved that the synod appoint a committee to meet with the New Brunswick brethren "in order to accommodate their differences and heal the breach between them." Dickinson and others from the New and Old Side were duly appointed and directed to "try all methods consistent with gospel truth" toward that end. The meeting between the New Brunswick ministers and the synod committee occurred that afternoon, and the next morning the synod reconvened and resolved to continue negotiations as an "interloquitur of ministers," or a committee of the whole.

It has been suggested that Gilbert Tennent may have been willing to offer a retraction on the most divisive issues, but further attempts at reconciliation promptly floundered over the question of who would judge the matter of the New Brunswick removal from the synod. The New Brunswick men would submit their case only to those in the synod who had not subscribed to the *Protestation,* namely, the New York Presbytery. The protesting brethren responded that they were willing to explain their conduct to those who had been absent, as well as to the public, but that they would be judged only by the synod as it was then constituted, namely, those who had not been excluded. They would not be held accountable only by those absent from the 1741 synod "or by any [other] judicature on earth."[35]

No agreement having been reached after two days, the groups adjourned from the end of the day on Saturday, May 29, until Monday morning, at which time the New York Presbytery entered a formal protest, quite likely authored by Jonathan Dickinson. The protest declared the New England group's sentiments that the synod's excluding of the New Brunswick men without benefit of trial was "illegal and unprecedented," contrary to the rules of the gospel, and "subversive" of the church's constitution. They protested the refusal on the part of those responsible for the expulsion to submit their actions for trial at the Synod of 1742, and asserted that until they were excluded "by a regular and impartial process" the New Brunswick ministers should be considered full members of the synod. Finally, and interestingly, as suggesting what really lay behind all of this and where Dickinson and the New Englanders stood, the protestors of 1742 noted, "We protest against all passages in any of the pamphlets which have been lately published in these parts, which seem to reflect upon the work of divine power and grace, which has been carrying on in so wonderful a manner in many of our congregations, and declare to all the world, that we look upon it to be the indispensable duty of all our ministers to encourage that glorious work with their most faithful and diligent endeavors. And in like manner, we protest and declare against all divisive and irregular methods and practices, by which the peace and good order of our churches have been broken in upon."

From their protest and from what we have seen issuing from Dickinson's pen thus far, it would seem that Dickinson and the New England clergy were in substantial agreement with the charges brought against the New Brunswick men, but they nevertheless condemned their exclusion from the synod—or at least the method by which it was accomplished. Having failed to receive the support of a majority of the synod and finding no satisfaction for the points of which they complained, the New Englanders withdrew. The synod itself concluded with a plea from Francis Alison, one of the protestors of 1741. Alison made it clear that he believed members of the New York Presbytery were infringing on the rights of the synod by calling the other members of the body to account for, and to judge the legality of, actions made in their absence. Still, giving up his rights in the matter, as he put it, Alison urged that the matter be submitted to the next synod so that the merits of the case for which the New Brunswick men had been excluded might be fairly tried and concluded.[36]

On August 3, 1742, in a letter to John Pierson, Jedediah Andrews voiced even stronger sentiments. He continued to condemn the New Brunswick men and to fault the New York Presbytery's protest on their behalf. He argued, however, that the presbytery could not have had a clear picture of the problem before the synod, or it would not have taken such a position. Moreover, he blamed "one man who in an ostentatious, noisy manner" sought not, as he said, to reconcile the two factions but rather to clear his presbytery's name and thereby to escape responsibility for the schism. The person to whom Andrews referred may have been Dickinson, but, if so, he was wrong. Only a week before, Dickinson had written to Thomas Foxcroft that he was still hopeful that a reconciliation could be effected, if only "terms of amicable agreement" could be reached, and that he intended to continue to pursue the matter.[37]

By mid-1742, publication of Gilbert Tennent's letter being the turning point, Jonathan Dickinson assumed the leadership of the Great Awakening among the Presbyterians of the Middle Colonies. Gilbert Tennent continued to defend himself and the Awakening and to denounce those that opposed it, but in more moderate terms. He also praised Dickinson's works and insisted that he had always had a deep sense of his own weakness and a sincere intention of working for God's greater glory.[38]

In 1744 Tennent became pastor of the New Side Congregation that worshiped in George Whitefield's Philadelphia tabernacle. He strove to counteract the "deflated spirit" and backsliding of the new converts, but he increasingly shifted from his earlier polemics to a renewed emphasis on doctrine and Presbyterian order. As a result, in a tabernacle devoted to the followers of Whitefield of all denominations, Tennent soon stood accused of "turning back to Old Presbyterianism" and to "a state of dead forms."[39]

On August 19, 1742, Tennent wrote a letter to Benjamin Franklin for publication in the *Pennsylvania Gazette*. In that letter, which appeared on September 2, he took issue with those who had gloated over or misconstrued the concessions he had made in his letter to Dickinson. Tennent continued to disclaim any belief in the use of "unlearned men" in the ministry "upon the supposition of their piety," of singing in the streets, and of any pretense to immediate inspiration or revelation. But he also explained that by his confession of mismanagement of the affair in the synod, he was referring to his "manner of performing" rather than the "matter or substance" of that for which he was contending. He wrote that he had intended to be critical of Davenport's "method of proceeding," not of his piety and integrity; that although he had admitted that knowledge of the spiritual state of others was at best probable, ministers still "ought to enquire into the state of their flock"; and that although he had agreed that separating from, or "openly exposing ministers, sound in doctrine [and] blameless in life," is unscriptural and likely to cause discord, it remained true that unconverted ministers are not likely to be as "serviceable to the salvation of mankind" as those who are converted. When unregenerate ministers "conspire to blacken and oppose habitually the late memorable revival of God's work in this land," Tennent wrote, those who "fear God" cannot stand by "contentedly."[40]

The defense of the Awakening in the Middle Colonies now fell more fully, however, on the shoulders of Jonathan Dickinson. No doubt buoyed by Tennent's letter, Dickinson sensed the possible return to denominational peace. In a letter to Foxcroft, he expressed his hope that the schism would be healed through the intercession of the New York Presbytery and Tennent's new "cool and catholic spirit." Presumably with the Synod of 1742 in mind, scheduled to begin one month later, Dickinson wrote that he was "ready to submit to proper terms of peace." Even after he failed in that instance, and even though the synod remained disunited and all attempts at union proved fruitless, Dickinson informed Foxcroft that he hoped events would yet "quickly take a more favorable turn." He still believed that the major part of the body favored reunion, if they could but "hit upon terms of an amicable agreement."[41]

David Harlan has written that Tennent's capitulation brought to a close Dickinson's struggle with the radical New Siders and his criticism of their excesses and initiated his efforts to defend the accomplishments of the Awakening. It changed his focus, Harlan has contended, from "subduing the evangelicals to creating a broadly inclusive party of moderation and unity based on acceptance of the revivals as a work of God." In his April 12 letter to Foxcroft, for example, Dickinson wrote of the "astonishing wonders of His grace, that have been lately displayed in this land," which he hoped would not only continue but spread more widely. As we shall see, Dickinson had not yet finished his struggle with the radicals, and he had been defending the accomplishments of the Awakening as well as attempting to subdue the evangelicals in favor of moderation and unity for three years. No doubt adding to his role as defender of the moderate Awakening, however, were his *True Scripture Doctrine,* published in 1741, and *A Display of God's Special Grace,* which appeared in 1742.[42]

The True Scripture Doctrine consisted of five discourses on what Dickinson considered to be important points of Christian faith, including eternal election, original sin, grace in conversion, justification by faith, and perseverance of the elect—upon all of which Dickinson had already written. As they were important elements in the debates surrounding the Great Awakening, however, he found it necessary to comment once again. It was preceded by a rather lengthy preface, wherein Thomas Foxcroft wrote that he knew of no one better qualified than Dickinson for this work in defense of the gospel, "contending earnestly for the faith of God's elect," and that he expected Dickinson's "superior and established character," as well as the importance of the divine subjects with which Dickinson would deal, to "solicit the attention of every serious and impartial inquirer."[43]

Foxcroft reiterated the old jeremiad of a backsliding New Israel and announced that a righteous but loving God had blessed his people with "a very remarkable dispensation of grace," signaling a revival of his work and a "renewing [of] our days as of old." He expressed his sorrow that "the good seed of the word" had brought forth so little fruit elsewhere in the world, but he foresaw those seeds would find good ground in America and bring forth fruit "unto perpetuity." Much as the fall of "old pagan Babylon" had brought about a renewed spirit of God in the world, he wrote, the fall of the "new popish Babylon" would be accompanied by the loss of "her American interest," which, when diverted from her, would "serve the City of God."[44]

As has been noted in our earlier discussion of *The Reasonableness of Christianity,* while never losing his Calvinist moorings, Dickinson did incorporate some of the ideas of the Enlightenment. He did so, especially on free will, in search of the middle ground between the twin threats of Antinomianism and Arminianism.[45] In *The True Scripture Doctrine* Dickinson responded to those who had criticized his doctrine of election, therein, as taking away man's liberty or as being inconsistent with that freedom that must necessarily be supposed of a rational and accountable being. He insisted that his doctrine placed no constraints on a man's affections, appetites, or inclinations, and that man continues to act voluntarily and spontaneously in all his moral conduct. Consistent with God's absolute decree, man is free, Dickinson insisted, but he is also subject to eternal decree. God has decreed that man may "act freely and at full liberty" in choosing his own salvation. But, Dickinson asked, "Is it a contradiction for any event to be infallibly necessary with respect to a rational being, and that being to be notwithstanding in a state of freedom?" Clearly not, Dickinson answered. The elect must will the means of their salvation, God having given them such a will. Others will not, but both are in a state of freedom, as "they cannot will the contrary to what they do."[46]

Dickinson wrote that he disagreed with those who had attributed freedom, or want of freedom, to the will. The will is but a property or faculty of the mind, and it cannot be the subject of other properties or faculties, any more than can our other intellectual powers. Free agency implies personality, he argued, which has nothing to do with the will. Further, there is a difference between an act and an intelligent agent, the latter only being the subject of freedom or the want of it. Therefore, to attribute either of these to the will "is to make that the agent, or person, when it is indeed no more than a personal act, or the person acting in a way of choice."

With this in mind, Dickinson took on those divines who had argued that the will of man has full freedom with respect to things natural, but not in respect to things spiritual, because in the latter case supernatural grace is required. He suggested that such divines had inaccurately attributed freedom to the will. Dickinson agreed with them as far as they insisted that man does not have the power to will the exercise of saving grace until God represents it to him as "most fit to be chosen," conquers his natural aversion to it, and excites him to will it. God does just that, however, when by "the powerful agency of divine grace" he overcomes "our contrary inclinations and represents [to us] such a life most worthy of our approbation and pursuit."[47]

In 1742, Dickinson published the popular *Display of God's Special Grace,* in which, in the form of a dialogue between a minister and a member of his congregation, Dickinson defended as from the Holy Spirit "the work of God, in the conviction and conversion of sinners, so remarkably of late begun and going on in these American parts." A second "conference" was attached, wherein Dickinson considered "sundry Antinomian principles," which had "begun to appear in sundry places." *A Display* appeared anonymously. As Dickinson explained in a letter to Foxcroft on April 12, he intended to make it "more serviceable," as those who would read it not knowing by whom it had been written would consider the subject and not the author. He also thanked Foxcroft for having written the preface to *A Display* and expressed his hope that his words of praise would not expose him to criticism.

David Harlan has discussed both the structure and content of *A Display.* Dialogues, Harlan has explained, which had been popular among the ancients, had fallen from favor among modern philosophers. Quoting David Hume, he pointed out that the form was no longer being used because it tended to convey the image of pedagogue and pupil; to become combative, reducing one of the figures to "impotent silence"; and to become a monologue of limited analytical, systematic, and methodical use. Dickinson's *Display,* Harlan suggested, was an exception.

In *A Display,* Harlan has argued, Dickinson was successful in carrying on a "real dialogue, with real give and take, in which both characters are forced to retreat and modify their arguments several times in the course of the exchange." Theophilus, the moderate revivalist, prevails, but his position changes, as does that of his opponent, Epinetus. Both grow in understanding and—not surprisingly, in view of what he has written elsewhere—Harlan has described that growth as the product of Dickinson's "ambivalence and uncertainty," as he moved between positions that were more mutually compelling than mutually exclusive. Moderates, who were less concerned with consistent theology than with religious peace and unity, and who, along with Dickinson, tried to steer a middle-of-the-road course through the turmoil of the Great Awakening, Harlan has written, were very much attracted to *A Display.*[48]

A *Display* was first published in Boston, prefaced by an "attestation" by the Boston ministers Benjamin Colman, Joseph Sewall, Thomas Prince, John Webb, William Cooper, Thomas Foxcroft, and Joshua Gee, with whom Dickinson had met during his visit to Boston. In that "attestation," the Boston ministers posed the crucial question with which they, Dickinson, and indeed leading ministers of the New and Old Side alike had to deal: Given that "uncommon religious appearances" had occurred in the land, "among people of all ages and characters," was it the work of God?[49]

To answer such a question, the Boston ministers allowed, one must have both knowledge of Scripture and "an experimental acquaintance with the things of the spirit of God." One such person, they wrote, was Jonathan Edwards. (They cited his 1741 *Distinguishing Marks of a Work of the Spirit of God*, which had "met with deserved acceptance and been of great use.")[50] Another, a "dear and reverend brother in a different part of the country," also "exceedingly well adapted to serve the same design," was Jonathan Dickinson. The Boston ministers wrote that if Dickinson had thought it proper to add his name to *A Display*, it would have been sufficient recommendation of the work. As he had not, they offered their recommendation and added that, by it, they wished to be understood as offering a public testimony to the Awakening, as a glorious display of divine power and grace, excluding those disorders, errors, and delusions which were only the "unhappy accidents sometimes accompanying it."[51]

Added to the second printing of *A Display* (1743), this time published in Philadelphia, and to which Dickinson attached his name, was an "attestation" signed by the New Brunswick men: Gilbert and William Tennent, Samuel Blair, Richard Treat, Samuel Finley, and John Blair. As with the Boston ministers, the New Brunswick men offered their public testimony "to the reality and truth" of the Awakening as the work of God. And if anyone should inquire as to what they meant by the "work of God," they added: "We think the judicious author of the following dialogue, has given a plain and pertinent answer to this inquiry, which we declare our high approbation of."

In *A Display*, they attested, Dickinson had "with much judgment and solid reasoning . . . baffled the common cavils of opposers of the work of God, and answered the objections of the scrupulous." They continued, "We cannot but highly approve of his description of the nature and necessity of conviction, establishing it upon the impregnable basis of Scripture and reason. His account of regeneration, faith, and consolation, is likewise exactly agreeable to our sentiment." The ministers wrote that they also concurred with Dickinson's attack on Antinomianism, reasserting their belief that sanctification is evidence of justification and necessary to eternal salvation and that assurance is not essential to faith but only "a separable fruit" of it.

Like their counterparts from Boston, the New Brunswick ministers recommended Edwards's *Distinguishing Marks* as well as *Some Thoughts Concerning the Present Revival of Religion in New England* (1742). They also cited, however, the Scots James Robe, who wrote *A Short Narrative of the Extraordinary Work at Cambuslang in Scotland* (Edinburgh and Philadelphia, 1742), and Alexander Webster, who wrote *Divine Influence the True Spring of the Extraordinary Work at Cambuslang and Other Parts of the West of Scotland* (Edinburgh, 1742; Boston, 1743). In this we have not only another representation of the joined forces of New England and of the Scotch-Irish of the Middle Colonies but also recognition of the disparate sources of their "new light" and of the internationalization of the Awakening.[52]

As it was a much briefer and less detailed treatment of the same subject Dickinson dealt with in his previously published revival pieces, and to which we will return in the next chapter, *A Display* need not detain us here, save to conclude that, as David Harlan has argued, the sum product of all Dickinson's revival pieces up to and including *A Display* was to discredit enthusiastic Calvinists and to unify the disorganized moderates by defining a middle course through the turmoil of the revivals. Dickinson rallied the moderates around the middle course so effectively, Harlan has found, that he "brought the revivalists to submission." Alan Heimert and Perry Miller have offered a similar assessment, suggesting that because of his defense of the Awakening and his criticism of Antinomianism, he brought the Awakening to an end.[53]

The "enthusiastic Calvinists" were not easily quieted, however. Dickinson warned Foxcroft that radical New Lights might be so angered by *A Display* that they would launch a "censorious attack" on him. Two years later, in another letter to Foxcroft, Dickinson acknowledged that attack and the "repeated trials" to which he had been exposed. It is to those attacks and Dickinson's defense that we now turn.[54]

8

DEFENDING THE
MODERATE AWAKENING

JONATHAN DICKINSON SPENT the final years of his life defending the moderate Awakening, both by trying to heal the breach that had occurred within the Synod of Philadelphia and by responding to critics of the moderate Awakening from both the Old Light/Old Side and New Light/New Side ranks. He tried to convince the Synod of Philadelphia that its expulsion of the New Brunswick ministers was irregular and to find grounds upon which compromise could be reached and the excluded brethren readmitted. At the same time, he further staked out his position in the Awakening against detractors from his old nemeses, the Anglicans and Baptists, as well as from evangelical radicals and even a more moderate New Sider.

Dickinson opened the Synod of 1743 with a sermon, the transcript of which has not survived but whose contents can be surmised from the synod records, which note that Dickinson's text was I Corinthians 1:10: "I appeal to you, brethren, by the name of our Lord Jesus Christ, that all of you agree and that there be no dissensions among you, but that you be united in the same mind and the same judgment." On the sixth day of the session, the Presbytery of New York presented an overture lamenting the schism that had occurred within the church as "the scandal of our holy profession" and as encouraging "dangerous errors and delusions." It also put forth proposals for reconciliation.

The New York Presbytery's overture suggested that, as the process by which the New Brunswick men had been excluded was irregular, the protestation should be withdrawn and the excluded allowed to return. It recommended that all future candidates for the ministry not having graduated from a New England college submit to the synod's rules on examination; that, in regard to itinerancy, every pulpit be open to all regular ministers of the church; that it be considered unbrotherly and divisive for one minister to refuse his pulpit to another except for reasons approved by the appropriate presbytery or synod; that any further separations within congregations or attempts to "alienate the hearts of the people from their pastors" be just grounds for censure by the presbytery or synod; and that a minister with a complaint against any of his brethren for any reason should present his complaint to that individual "in a private way" or, failing that, "make regular charges" before the presbytery or synod. Finally, the New York ministers urged their synodical brethren to forgive all past differences and to adopt a plan of union. If reunion could not be achieved, they added, a second synod should be formed and members given a choice as to which synod they would prefer to join.[1]

Although a majority of synod members were willing to accept certain terms of the proposal, they rejected the first and third, thereby voiding the entire package. They justified exclusion of the New Brunswick men both for the reasons of the time and for their conduct since, and they insisted that it was incumbent on the excluded to give satisfaction for their actions and security against further offenses before any reconciliation could be effected. Further, they preferred to retain the synod's earlier ruling whereby no preacher would be allowed into any pulpit not his own without the approval of his own presbytery and of the presbytery within the bounds of which he was to preach. Finally, the synod noted that although they could not sanction the creation of a new or second synod, as it would only perpetuate the schism, if the Presbytery of New York should form such a body, they hoped to "cultivate a truly Christian disposition towards them," as far as any contentious separation would allow. Dickinson's only recorded response was that as long as the New Brunswick men were excluded he could not see his way clear "to sit and act as though . . . [those that remained] were the Synod of Philadelphia."[2]

In the end, the synod voted to send a message to the excluded brethren, expressing its interest in reconciliation "on reasonable terms." The synod demanded, however, that the New Brunswick men submit to its determinations in all matters and, toward that end, that they renounce the contrary principles expounded in their "Apology." The Conjunct Presbyteries, as they then called themselves, rejected the synod's terms for reconciliation and demanded instead that as a prerequisite for any deliberation toward reconciliation the synod withdraw the "illegal protest" they had made against them in 1741, thereby returning all to an equal footing.[3]

The failure of the Synod of 1743 to move toward reconciliation no doubt hastened the rapprochement between Gilbert Tennent and Dickinson begun in 1742. In August 1743 the Presbytery of New York met with the Conjunct Presbyteries and agreed on expansion of the New Side's work into Connecticut and Gilbert Tennent's answering the call of the Presbyterians of Whitefield's tabernacle in Philadelphia. Following the Synod of

1743 Dickinson gave Gilbert Tennent permission to reissue his *Display of God's Special Grace,* this time in Philadelphia, with an additional attestation by the New Brunswick men, thereby tying the pamphlet and its author closer to their cause.[4]

Members of the New York Presbytery being absent from the Synod of 1744, no further steps toward reconciliation were taken. Once again, it is not clear why they were absent. Keith Hardman has ventured that perhaps they felt that their support of Gilbert Tennent's pastorate at Whitefield's tabernacle was too explosive. In letters from Dickinson and Experience Mayhew to Thomas Foxcroft, we learn that Dickinson had been seriously ill in late 1743 and early 1744.[5]

In a letter dated May 6, 1745, Dickinson reported to Thomas Foxcroft that he, Pemberton, and John Pierson had been delegated once again by the Presbytery of New York to seek accommodation between the Synod of Philadelphia and the excluded New Side ministers at the upcoming meeting of the synod but that he despaired of any reconciliation because "jealousy" and "prejudice" were too deeply seated within the synod. Anticipating the failure of his efforts, Dickinson announced that he and others had agreed to erect a new Synod of New York. Correspondence between the two synods would be maintained, however. In this way, Dickinson hoped, divisions within the church would be "quieted and buried."

As planned, then, on the second day of the Synod of 1745, May 23, Dickinson, Pemberton, and Pierson, on behalf of the Presbytery of New York, formally requested that the Synod of Philadelphia appoint a committee to meet with them to prepare an overture "removing any grounds of dissatisfaction or difference between them and the synod." A committee was appointed, consisting of nine Old Siders and the three New Siders, and two days later it presented an overture which the synod voted "a proper plan for accommodation."

In sum, the Synod of Philadelphia continued to hold the New Brunswick ministers guilty of the same transgressions. Moreover, it continued to insist that the synod had done nothing illegal in 1741; that the synod had offered to the New Brunswick men "proposals of peace," which they had rejected; and that the offending brethren had continued to behave in a manner "to the great scandal of religion." The synod voted a set of "fundamental articles and agreements," to which all who would remain part of that body should subscribe, but they were much the same as had been offered as terms of readmission to the New Brunswick ministers by the Synod of 1743.[6]

The ministers of the New York Presbytery refused to subscribe to the "fundamental articles and agreements" and petitioned the Synod of Philadelphia to be allowed to leave and to erect another synod. They sought the synod's consent, the New York ministers explained, so that they would not be seen as setting up the second synod in opposition to the first and in order that there might be "a foundation for the two synods to consult and act in mutual concert with one another hereafter, and maintain love and brotherly kindness with each other." The synod acknowledged that the proposal deeply concerned them, as had their long-standing differences with the New York ministers. The synod asserted that they felt there was "no just ground" for the action, but as that synod which the ministers of the New York Presbytery proposed to erect would be on friendly terms with that of Philadelphia, if it were to be done, they would "endeavor to maintain charitable and Christian affections towards them, and show the same upon all occasions by such correspondence and fellowship as we shall think [our] duty, and consistent with a good conscience."

On September 19, 1745, in Elizabeth Town, New Jersey, Jonathan Dickinson presided as moderator over the first meeting of the Synod of New York. It drew together members of the Presbytery of New York and of the Conjunct Presbyteries of New Brunswick and Londonderry (to be reformulated into the Presbyteries of New Brunswick and New Castle), the latter two groups consisting of those who had been cast out of, or who had withdrawn from, the Synod of Philadelphia in 1741. The forces of the Awakening, led by Dickinson, Gilbert Tennent, Samuel Blair, Samuel Finley, and others, were thereby joined in one ecclesiastical body.[7]

In view of the subscription controversy and other matters of disagreement within the Synod of Philadelphia before 1741, as well as of the stated reasons for the exclusion of the New Brunswick men and for the withdrawal of the ministers of the New York Presbytery, it is worth noting, if only in passing, that the articles of union approved at the first meeting of the Synod of New York adopted the Westminster Confession and Catechisms "in such manner as was agreed unto by the Synod of Philadelphia in the year 1729," or according to Dickinson's Adopting Act. Further, the articles reasserted the authority of presbyteries in matters of ministerial examination and licensure, and they refrained from adopting any educational requirement in such matters that would have militated against graduates of the Log College (which closed its doors that year). Ministers would be admitted to the Synod of New York if they submitted to the synod's discipline, had a "competent degree" of ministerial knowledge, and were "orthodox in their doctrine, regular in their lives, and diligent in their endeavors to promote the important designs of vital godliness."

Dickinson was responsible for establishing the Synod of New York, but he never ceased to work for a reunion of the two ecclesiastical bodies.

In 1745, Dickinson proposed that a committee be appointed to meet with the Synod of Philadelphia to consider terms of agreement and correspondence. At the New York Synod of 1746, Dickinson and Pierson reported that they had failed to attend the meeting of the Synod of Philadelphia in 1746 due to an outbreak of smallpox in that city but that they had written to the synod and received a response.[8]

The minutes of the New York Presbytery do not indicate the nature of the response. Records of the Synod of Philadelphia, however, note that the agreed upon response to Dickinson's letter would include a proclamation of "regard and friendship" for the New Side Synod as well as a pledge of their interest in pursuing those methods by which both might "promote the glory of God, the interest of Christ's kingdom, and welfare of the churches in these parts." But they would not accept Dickinson's offer of any closer relations until they were presented with the New York Synod's plan of union and general agreements by which it had admitted and would admit new members.[9]

Further light is shed on the Philadelphia Synod's response to Dickinson in its letter of May 30, 1746, to Yale's president, Thomas Clap. The synod reported that it had excluded from its ranks the "ringleaders of its divisions" and "the destroyers of good learning and gospel order," and that the expelled had formed a separate body by which they had licensed and ordained men "that were generally ignorant and warm in the divisive schemes." It noted that members of the Presbytery of New York—"whom we esteem and regard, particularly Messrs. Dickinson, Pierson, and Pemberton"—had always blamed the Old Side for the separation and, "through some unhappy bias," become the "warm advocates" of the separated. Having failed to gain readmission for the excluded brethren, the New York ministers had withdrawn from the Synod of Philadelphia and erected the Synod of New York, the letter continued, "declaring that they had no other ground to do so but our excluding those members in a way they disliked."

The Synod of Philadelphia acknowledged receipt of Dickinson's letter, in which he urged correspondence between the two synods, that two or three of the members of each synod attend the annual meetings of the other, and that every third year delegates of both synods meet together "to order public affairs for the glory of God, and good of the church." It also offered the following summary of its response to that letter: "The proposals seem fair, but until these dividers of our churches, who chiefly make up that body [the Synod of New York], declare against the late divisive, uncharitable practices; till they show us in what way they intend to have their youth educated for the ministry, and be as ready to discourage all such methods of bringing good learning into contempt as the shepherd's tent, we shall be shy to comply with their proposals."[10]

Little else is recorded of Jonathan Dickinson's direct involvement in the affairs of the Synod of New York in 1746 or 1747, the final years of his life, save that he attended both and delivered the opening sermon in 1746. The text of Dickinson's sermon has been lost, but according to synod records it was drawn from Psalms 24:4: "Who shall ascend the hill of the Lord? And who shall stand in this holy place? He who has clean hands and a pure heart, who does not lift up his soul to what is false, and does not swear deceitfully."[11]

Before proceeding, it should be noted that in the midst of all this, on April 20, 1745, Jonathan Dickinson suffered the loss of his wife of some thirty-seven years. Joanna, who was sixty-three years old when she died, had borne Jonathan eight children, six of whom survived her. Dickinson, all of whose daughters but Martha, the youngest, had married and moved away, was chastened and "almost left desolate" by the loss, he wrote to Thomas Foxcroft, but, at least for the moment, he was in better physical health than he had been for months. He was active, and although his health would once again grow worse—his periods of ill health becoming more frequent and prolonged—the three concluding years of Dickinson's life were productive and rewarding. He remarried on April 7, 1747, taking as his second bride the widow Mary Crane, age twenty-seven.[12]

At the same time that he was fighting to heal the breach within the Presbyterian ranks to organize the Synod of New York, Dickinson continued to defend the Awakening against what he deemed the errors of Arminianism and Antinomianism. In reference to the first, Dickinson prepared two brief tracts, which did not appear in print before 1823. (They were published by the American Tract Society, which did not come into existence until that year.) Clearly intended for a popular audience, both *Marks of Saving Faith* and *Marks of True Repentance* restated points he had made earlier on the difference between a saving and a dead faith or between an evangelical and a legal repentance.[13]

Dickinson's more substantial defense of the Awakening against its Arminian detractors, however, appeared in his response to Anglican critics, thus renewing that public discourse which had begun decades earlier. Anglicans, for the most part, were opposed to the Great Awakening. As we have seen, by way of example, when the Reverend George Whitefield joined forces with the New Light/New Side, he was denounced and turned away from Anglican pulpits.[14]

The main event of Dickinson's reengagement with the Anglicans over matters related to the Great Awakening began in 1746. A prelude to that event, however, occurred in 1743, at once recalling Dickinson's earlier defense of infant baptism against proponents of adult baptism and challenging him to publicly reconcile his paedobaptist position with his insistence on the necessity of a second regenerative experience. In that year, Anglican divine Daniel Waterland published a pamphlet entitled *Regeneration Stated and Explained According to Scripture and Antiquity in a Discourse* (1740) in London. Dickinson responded with *The Nature and Necessity of Regeneration.*

Waterland was reacting to evangelicals on both sides of the Atlantic who were preaching that God's method for saving those under Christian dispensation is by free grace, whereby we are not saved by any righteousness on our part in our unassisted state but rather by the freely given cleansing, regenerating, and renewing of the Holy Ghost. Waterland insisted, however, that the regeneration to which Scripture referred was baptism. Christian baptism, he explained, is wrought by the Holy Spirit, and it signifies "death unto sin, and a new birth unto righteousness." It constitutes a new birth, whereby man is "translated from his natural state in Adam, to a spiritual estate in Christ." As there can be only one baptism per person, Waterland reasoned, it is the first and the only entrance to the spiritual estate allowed any man.

Waterland admitted that not all who are baptized are ultimately saved. Some fall after being baptized or regenerated, either by desertion or disobedience. Such individuals may later be improved, but he insisted it would be improper to refer to those who have such an experience as having been regenerated, as that would imply that they had been baptized again. Further, to call it a second regeneration is "mischievous," as it tells people that they ought to be regenerated a second time, rather than to repent or amend their ways. The likely result, he offered, supporting the commonly held criticism of New Light/New Side pride and censoriousness, would be "self-flattery indulged too far" or people who wrongly believe they are "divinely inspired, divinely illuminated, [and] divinely conducted."[15]

The first part of Dickinson's response to Daniel Waterland consisted of a sermon on regeneration preached at a meeting of the New York Presbytery in Newark on January 15, 1743. In that sermon, Dickinson charged Waterland with certain Arminian errors (errors he found common among many Anglican divines of the day), especially in his comparison of baptism and the adult conversion experience. Dickinson denied Waterland's assertion that through baptism a person has all the properties and character of a new birth and is therefore regenerate. He pointed out that Scripture speaks of two kinds of regeneration: baptism, which may be without holiness, and a change of heart, which is productive of a holy life and which is the "necessary fruit of regeneration." While recognizing the importance of the first, Dickinson emphasized the necessity of the second for eternal life.

Dickinson took issue with Waterland for suggesting that the second form of regeneration can come about through moral suasion or through outward means that lead to the improved exercise of man's natural abilities, moral virtues, and religious duties. By nature, unregenerate man is spiritually dead, he insisted, and therefore he cannot find the new principle without God's help. What God offers through the new principle is illumination. He gives light of the knowledge of the glory of God, whereby the darkness of the mind is dissipated, and we are given "a lively realizing and sensible view of divine things," which, in turn, actuates the powers and faculties of the soul toward conformity to God.

The new principle, Dickinson continued, brings a man, in all spiritual respects, into a new state of existence. It creates in him a new spiritual capacity in that it renews his understanding, whereby he is able to spiritually discern that which before he could never see. His will is renewed, because he becomes aware of Christ's excellencies and of his own necessities. His will bows in obedience to Christ and comes unto Christ for life and into compliance with the gospel offer. His affections, appetites, and passions are renewed, and new desires and new delights replace those of the flesh and of "lusts and pleasures."[16]

In 1744, James Wetmore, the Anglican divine of Rye, New York, who earlier engaged Dickinson in defense of his church, responded to *Nature and Necessity* with *A Letter Occasioned by Mr. Dickinson's Remarks upon Dr. Waterland's Discourse on Regeneration*. Wetmore accused Dickinson of not only sowing confusion among the people concerning baptism but also trying to persuade his "credulous readers" that the Anglican doctrine of baptism was both inconsistent with Scripture and an effective bar to salvation. In brief, as he added little to Waterland's treatment of the subject, Wetmore argued that sincere believers in Christ, those who have faith, or (as Waterland had put it) those who have "a good conscience and a good life" may "hope to enter into a state of favor with God" when they are baptized. The faith to which he referred, that which is required of those who would be baptized, Wetmore explained, consists of belief in that which is reported about Christ in the gospel and a sincere desire to practice the duties of a Christian life. Such a doctrine of baptismal regeneration was not only consistent with Scripture and with the teachings of the ancient church fathers, Wetmore pointed out, but, contrary to what Dickinson had implied, it could be found in the Church of England's Article 27 and in the practices of the Church of England since the Reformation.[17]

Dickinson responded to Wetmore with *Reflections upon Mr. Wetmore's Letter in Defense of Dr. Waterland's Discourse on Regeneration* (1744), but the debate was not further advanced until he published *A Vindication of God's*

Sovereign Free Grace. This appeared in 1746 in response to three treatises that had been published the previous year by John Beach, Henry Caner, and Samuel Johnson. We are already acquainted with John Beach and Samuel Johnson. Beach's and Johnson's efforts to expand Anglican membership in New England and New Jersey, as well as to establish an American episcopacy, it will be recalled, had attracted Dickinson's attention a decade earlier. Henry Caner, classified by Sydney Ahlstrom as among "the flower of Massachusetts Anglicanism," was a Yale graduate who had studied theology with Samuel Johnson and in 1727 been ordained in England by the Church of England. Upon his ordination, Caner was appointed by the Society for the Propagation of the Gospel in Foreign Parts as its missionary to Fairfield, Connecticut. He also served the Anglicans of nearby Norwalk, the home of Jonathan's brother Moses Dickinson.[18]

The purpose of Beach's and Johnson's sermons, *A Sermon Showing that Eternal Life Is God's Free Gift* and *A Letter from Aristocles to Authades, Concerning the Sovereignty and Promise of God,* was to show that "eternal life is God's free gift, bestowed upon men according to their moral behavior" and that "free grace and free will concur in the affair of man's salvation" in that God has chosen to give his Holy Spirit to anyone who seriously seeks it. Beach, in particular, condemned those who had "magnif[ied] the free sovereign and rich grace of God" to the point where those who believed in man's moral agency were seen as enemies to the grace of God. Johnson took issue with those who had argued that God, by an "eternal, arbitrary and absolute determination," without any consideration of their good or ill behavior, has determined the eternal fate of men. Such a position, Johnson insisted, implied a design by which the majority of men are "under a necessity of being eternally miserable, antecedent to any consideration of their demerit," and even of necessarily being sinful that they might be miserable, as "he that wills the end, must will the means."[19]

Henry Caner, in his *True Nature and Method of Christian Preaching,* added a new dimension to the debate by considering the most effective and scriptural means of preaching. He described the method by which Anglican ministers preached, like that of Christ and his apostles, as including reasoning, "persuasives to duty," "dissuasives from vice," and rules for the conduct of one's life. He referred to it as a method that informed the mind or understanding of the "great truths of and duties of the gospel." In contrast, Caner continued, New Light/New Side ministers insisted that preaching the "terrors of the law" was necessary for the awakening and conviction of sinners. Though deserved by some, to employ such methods, Caner wrote, was "highly wicked." It tended only "to amuse people with a set of obscure and difficult terms and phrases, without meaning." The attention of some may have been awakened by such a method, he pointed out, but they had not been brought any closer to salvation.[20]

In his 1746 response to Beach and Johnson, *A Vindication of God's Sovereign Free Grace,* Dickinson reiterated his explanation of the Fall and of original sin. He continued to insist that Adam's sins had been imputed to man and that mankind therefore is in a degenerate state in which he cannot effect his own salvation. Dickinson argued that in their suggesting that grace is so free that it is not confined or restrained to an elect number, and that if a man wishes to be saved he must merely "walk worthy of God's electing love," implies that there is in every man the power of self-determination, or of choosing or refusing to comply with the suggestions of the Holy Spirit whereby he might live forever. As he had all along, Dickinson denied man that ability and insisted that God's will, or saving grace, is absolute and irresistible.[21]

Did Christ, then, really die only for those that came to be called the elect? Did his death not only purchase for the elect the privilege of being saved if they believe but also the faith whereby they will believe and be saved? Yes, Dickinson continued to insist. Moreover, such an offer on Christ's part, wherein Christ had done more for some than for others and had purchased for some, but not for others, special grace whereby they alone would be made willing to comply with the gospel offer, was not unfair. The wicked were still at fault for their own destruction. For such people, Dickinson explained, "Christ wrought out a sufficient redemption . . . , exhibited himself, and freely offered his saving benefits in the gospel . . . , but they willfully rejected both him and them. . . . They rejected, abused, and sinned away all these advantages from no other necessity but the indulgence of their lusts and the perverseness of their wills, and finally perished."[22]

Beach and Johnson had denied the irresistible nature of converting grace. Man must choose to be saved, they reasoned, and if converting grace is irresistible, those who receive it have no choice as to whether they will comply with the Holy Spirit or resist it. Dickinson argued that conversion is brought about by "the special illumination and influence of the spirit of God," whereby the converted have an effectual discovery not only of their own sin and misery but of the glorious nature of God, the author of salvation. A decision therefore may be involved on the part of those who receive converting grace, but it is an irresistible decision—those who are made aware of their condemned estate cannot but be willing to accept a pardon when they realize that there is one freely offered.

Put in Enlightened terms, Dickinson suggested that it is a process whereby the understanding is enlightened, the mind is renewed, and the sinner is brought into a willing compliance with the gospel offer. He acts from "the clearest light and purest reason, from the most rational convictions, and the noblest motives impressed by the spirit of God." There is no force involved. He complies willingly with the spirit of God and the way of salvation, as it satisfies all his wants and desires. To suggest that this is not irresistible, Dickinson added, is to achieve exactly what Beach and Johnson had argued against, namely, to rob man of his freedom, to make man "a mere engine," rather than to make of him an intelligent being.[23]

Dickinson was briefer in his comments on the work of Henry Caner. He accepted the first of Caner's two major points—that when a minister preaches to the unconverted heathen, repentance of their former wicked lives and faith in Christ are the proper doctrines to be inculcated—but he rejected the second—that when preaching to those who are already Christian and who have professed their faith in Christ, one should no longer insist on faith but on practice. Dickinson responded that it cannot automatically be assumed that a person who professes Christianity is a true believer in Christ, any more than it follows that such professors are in a justified or sanctified state. It may be, as Caner had written, that good works and a holy life naturally accompany or flow from faith. It may not be the case, however, Dickinson argued, that the former necessarily indicates the presence of the latter or that grace signifies both.[24]

Beach and Johnson responded to Dickinson with *God's Sovereignty and His Universal Love* and *A Letter to Jonathan Dickinson,* both of which appeared in 1747, the year Dickinson died. Beach charged Dickinson with espousing Antinomian principles. Johnson accused him of implying that, first, because God knew Adam would disobey, he must necessarily have willed his disobedience, and for the same reason that he must necessarily have willed all the sins of those who ever were or ever will be in the world; second, that God approves of, and takes pleasure in, the sins and death of every sinner; and, third, that there is no such thing as liberty or free agency for God or man.[25]

Dickinson's response, *A Second Vindication of God's Sovereign Free Grace,* appeared posthumously in the form of letters to Beach and Johnson. Dickinson completed the first on August 28, 1747, less than six weeks before his death; the second was finished by his brother Moses. In both instances, Jonathan and Moses Dickinson merely denied the "consequences," or doctrines, that Beach and Johnson had inferred from Jonathan's previously stated points and reiterated what he had written earlier.[26]

Moses Dickinson, by the way, was pastor of the Congregational church at Norwalk, Connecticut. Jonathan's younger brother by some seven years, he had graduated from Yale in 1717. Following in his brother's footsteps, he was ordained in 1717 by the churches of Hopewell and Maidenhead,

New Jersey. Unlike his brother, however, Moses left New Jersey after only eight years to serve the congregation at Norwalk. Although not as active in its defense, Moses, like his brother, was a moderate New Light in a congregation that was favorably disposed to the Awakening.[27]

As the quarrel between colonial Anglicans and Presbyterians, especially over the relationship between free will and God's sovereign free grace, did not begin with Jonathan Dickinson, it did not end with his death. Though the continuing story lies beyond the scope of this study, it is worth noting, first of all, that Dickinson's *Second Vindication* elicited at least one more round of responses by Beach and Moses Dickinson.[28] Second, Dickinson's *Vindication* influenced what was perhaps the most highly regarded of all Calvinist tracts on God's sovereign free grace and free will: Jonathan Edwards's *Freedom of the Will* (1754). Edwards first considered writing *Freedom of the Will* in 1746, in the midst of what he called "the Arminian controversy." For the Arminian perspective, Edwards turned to Samuel Johnson and John Beach. Among his primary Calvinist sources was Jonathan Dickinson.[29]

Dickinson's defense of the New Light/New Side was not limited to his continued public discourse with the Anglicans. The Awakening also revived, if in a far less substantive manner, his earlier encounter with the Baptists. Among colonial Baptists as a whole, as among Anglicans, supporters of the Great Awakening were few and its critics many, the latter seeing the Awakening as "the fruit of fanaticism and the devil." Nevertheless, the revival gave those Baptists who supported it such power that the denomination fairly leaped into a position of influence. It has been suggested that the Great Awakening "released the initial impulse for itinerant evangelism among the Baptists." In New England in the years following the revival, it also swelled their ranks with disaffected New Lights called Separatists.[30]

In the Middle Colonies few New Side Presbyterians became Baptists. The most common explanation for that is the formation of the more flexible and liberal New York Synod, which provided an alternative within the church absent in New England. It is also the case, however, that many Baptist churches closed their communion to anyone not of their own fellowship, something the more tolerant New Side Presbyterians resented, and that there was no civil pressure on potential schismatics to join another denomination, as was the case in New England. Thus, once the first flush of evangelical unity passed, interdenominational rivalries recurred and New as well as Old Siders stepped to the fore in defense of their churches.[31]

One of the most notable examples of Presbyterian-Baptist rivalry during the Great Awakening occurred in New Jersey in 1743. It took the form of debates between New Side Presbyterian minister Samuel Finley and Baptist minister Abel Morgan at Cape May, where since 1742 a revival had brought about "a remarkable stir of the religious kind" and gathered together both Presbyterian and Baptist evangelicals. What was said during the Cape May debates found its way into print through a series of publications by the disputants. The two issues upon which they had focused, but which had also divided Dickinson and John Gale twenty years earlier, were, as Finley put it, "Whether the infants of such as are members of the visible church have a right to the ordinance of baptism?" and "Whether baptism be rightly administered by pouring water on the person baptized?" As had Dickinson and his Puritan predecessors, Finley responded affirmatively to both, in much the same terms.[32]

Jonathan Dickinson's *Brief Illustration and Confirmation of the Divine Right of Infant Baptism* appeared at approximately the same time as Samuel Finley's *Charitable Plea for the Speechless* (1746). Dickinson would have been aware of the Cape May debates, and he may have been influenced by that course of events to enter the fray. Due to the timing, however, it is unlikely that either Finley or Dickinson read one another's work before composing their own essays. By the time Abel Morgan made his written reply to Finley in 1747, he had read both, and he responded to both. Attached to Morgan's *Anti-Paedo Rantism* was an appendix devoted entirely to Dickinson's pamphlet, written by Morgan's stepbrother, the Baptist minister Benjamin Griffith of Montgomery, Pennsylvania.[33]

In brief, in addition to continuing to defend the two above noted propositions, Dickinson warned anyone who might be tempted by the Baptists to deny his baptism that to do so would be to vacate the covenant and to assume the condition of being unbaptized. It would imply that those ministers who had baptized him as an infant, and who continued in that office, were neither in covenant with God nor ministers and therefore were unable to administer baptism or any other sacred ordinance. And, finally, it would offend "all of the generations of God's children," in that by casting doubt on those entrusted by Christ to carry out God's ordinances, the church would be left without the instituted means of life and salvation, while the "greatest part" of Christianity would be relegated to "a state of heathenism, without any hope of salvation but from the uncovenanted mercies of God."[34]

In his *Anti-Paedo Rantism* Morgan quoted Dickinson, especially where Dickinson's comments supported Samuel Finley's, which was always the case. Otherwise, Morgan relegated criticism of Dickinson to Benjamin Griffith.

In his brief appendix, Griffith wrote that enough had already been offered on the mode and subject of baptism and that he would prefer to challenge Dickinson on the question of at what time infant baptism was first universally practiced in the church. Consistent with earlier Baptist statements on the subject, with much the same evidence, Griffith asserted that it had occurred sometime between three and four hundred years after the birth of Christ. Dickinson, it may be recalled, had insisted that it had begun earlier, perhaps even during apostolic times.

Dickinson had questioned what had become of Christ's promise "to be with his ministers always, in the administration of this ordinance," if, as the Baptists had allowed, infant baptism, which had been practiced exclusively by the Christian Church for over one thousand years, was contrary to the Word of God and therefore ineffectual. Griffith responded by allowing that during that time "the true church and spouse of Jesus Christ" had been in the wilderness and that there were few "faithful ministers" within its ranks. Both had reappeared during the Reformation, however, and thereafter the Baptists stood on as good ground as other Protestants in promoting the glory of God.[35]

Dickinson died in the same year that Morgan's and Griffith's critiques appeared, but the debate between the Baptists and Presbyterians continued. Finley's answer to Morgan and Griffith, *A Vindication of the Charitable Plea for the Speechless,* was published in 1748, but it did not include any defense of Dickinson's pamphlet. Morgan's final volley came in 1750, under the title *Anti-Paedo Rantism Defended.* Morgan continued to do battle with Samuel Finley, but Dickinson was the most liberally cited of all others, making it clear that the importance of Dickinson's involvement in the Baptist-Presbyterian debate of the 1740s, in contrast to that of the 1720s, lay not in what he had to say but in the leadership position he had assumed among colonial Presbyterians and even among colonial Calvinists.[36]

An equally serious challenge to the moderate Awakening came from within New Light/New Side ranks, posed by those who, rather than charging Dickinson with Antinomianism, criticized him for professing Arminian principles. Dickinson clarified his position relative to those critics in a letter of November 28, 1743, to Thomas Foxcroft. Dickinson's comments were prodded by his reading of *Enthusiasm Described and Cautioned Against* (Boston, 1742), by the Old Light penman Charles Chauncy.

As the title suggests, Chauncy had been critical of the enthusiastic excesses of the Awakening, and in his letter to Foxworth Dickinson agreed: "I must first inform you . . . I heartily concur in the doctor's testimony against those enthusiastic heats, divisive practices, and other irregularities and extravagances which he complains of; and have from the beginning borne my part, according to my capacity and opportunity, both publicly and privately, in testifying against them. And I pray to God [Chauncy's] book may be blessed as a means of suppressing these things."

He ascribed such sinful excesses to the devil, having transformed himself into "an angel of light," or to "enthusiastic guides" playing upon the weaknesses of human nature in its zeal for God. But if there had been those who, in "pretence to an extraordinary change" or having misapplied the principle of love to God, were guilty of extravagance, Dickinson continued, there were also those who had avoided such "irregular heats" and exhibited "good evidences of a real change." He had seen such cases "in this place" (presumably Elizabeth Town) and its environs and heard of them elsewhere, and based on such evidence he continued to believe that the Awakening was "a glorious work of divine grace."

It was the excesses of Antinomianism, then, that Dickinson addressed in his unpublished manuscript "The Danger of the Enthusiasm of the Present Times," written before July 1746, the date upon which Thomas Foxcroft received it. And it was Dickinson's criticism of those excesses there and elsewhere that precipitated one of the most heated debates among New Lights or New Siders of the Great Awakening, that between Dickinson and Andrew Croswell.

Andrew Croswell, Massachusetts born and Harvard educated, was minister of the Congregational church at Groton, Connecticut. By 1742, he was well known not only for his support of the radical tenets of the Awakening but also for his assertion that most of his contemporary Congregational ministers had abandoned the doctrines of the Reformation and become "less Orthodox than Arminius." To a large extent, Croswell is best known as a supporter of James Davenport, but he deserves greater recognition than that. As Leigh Eric Schmidt has written, Croswell "was more persistent and visible, provoked more controversies, itinerated longer, and published more tracts than any other incendiary New Light, including James Davenport. In his writings one finds the fullest articulation of the theology and spirituality of the radical Awakening."[37]

In October 1742, in response to Dickinson's *Display of God's Special Grace,* Croswell took on Dickinson in what Leigh Eric Schmidt has called the climax of Croswell's "rhetorical campaign for the radical Awakening." Much as ministers of New England and the Middle Colonies had attested to Dickinson's work, the Reverends Timothy Allen, Timothy Symmes, and John Curtis attested to Croswell's work. An additional note revealed that Eleazar Wheelock and Benjamin Pomeroy had "in conversation" condemned *A Display* as well. In a preface to *Mr. Croswell's Reply,* the subscribers declared that Dickinson's teachings would have a direct tendency to make "thousands of Pharisees . . . easy and quiet in their minds, and so speak peace to themselves while God hath no peace for them."

Croswell called Dickinson's *Display* "the worst Arminian performance

that ever was written"! He attacked Dickinson's qualified acceptance of assurance and his insistence upon preparation in the conversion experience
and upon justification by sanctification as Arminianism and legalism. Further, in his criticism of radical New Lights and New Siders, Croswell accused Dickinson of creating an Antinomian extreme that either did not
exist or that at least was inappropriate to that for which Croswell and his
cohorts stood. No one, for example, who was "zealous for the work of God,"
Croswell argued, could be charged with not caring how wickedly they might
act because they had been justified from eternity.[38]

Croswell argued that to provide sinners with directions by which to
prepare for coming to Christ, as Dickinson had, naturally leads one to
imagine that if they follow those directions God will be inclined to save
them. Not only is this "legal way" misleading, Croswell insisted, but it also
lessens their conviction. He made it clear that he was not opposed to all
directions. Ministers may teach sinners to pray or even to "cry to God night
and day for a new heart and an interest in Christ." But as sinners have a
propensity to take comfort from such duties, a minister's pleading for the
performance of any other duties, even when he makes it clear that they
must not rest upon such duties, as Dickinson had, is likely only to keep
them from Christ, "to marry them to the law and their natural spouse."

Contrary to that with which Dickinson had charged radicals in general, Croswell insisted that he did not believe that assurance is necessary to
being in a justified state. People may have the "habit of faith," he explained,
yet "for a time walk in total darkness." When men exercise true faith, however, they are always sensible of it. To argue to the contrary, as he suggested
Dickinson had, Croswell wrote, namely, that men may be good Christians
even though they have never had any clear manifestations of the love of
God, and that persons must find out their justification by their sanctification, constituted the "most horrible pages in the whole book": "Nay there
is not one disciple of [Jacobus] Arminius, but will subscribe [that] doctrine
with heart and hand." Croswell did not deny that holiness is the mark of a
justified state, but he insisted that it is only so when joined with the "witness of the spirit and the divine sealing which the scriptures make the common privilege of all believers."

Finally, Croswell argued that acts of duty toward God without "witness of the spirit" can be readily identified as they are marked by a selfish-
ness and lack of gratitude consistent with someone who has not yet realized
that God has freely given his Son to man. He remains full of spiritual pride,
as he has never been sufficiently humbled and disabused of all self-suffi-
ciency and brought to true repentance. He who has the "witness of the
spirit," however, Croswell added, realizes that God loves him for Christ's

sake through all his vileness. He is moved to loathe himself and to be filled with self-revenge for his ingratitude. And, though God has forgiven him— indeed, because God has forgiven him—he cannot forgive himself, any more than he can stop fearing his continued abuses of God's will.[39]

Dickinson responded to Croswell with *A Defense of . . . A Display of God's Special Grace* (1743), a defense no doubt made more urgent in Dickinson's mind by the increasingly wild antics of the radical revivalists. In the fall of 1742, the Synod of Philadelphia appointed Dickinson to a commission that was to investigate charges brought against James Davenport by his congregation in Southold (Long Island), New York. Upon his arrival in Southold in February 1743, Dickinson wrote, in a letter to Thomas Foxcroft, he had found Davenport's congregation "in utmost confusion, [and] Antinomianism in its worst form making a horrible progress among the people." Davenport, Dickinson wrote, had acknowledged and attempted to justify charges made against him by the congregation. The commission found Davenport's justification unacceptable, however, and concluded that it could find no reason to require the congregation to continue under Davenport's ministry "without any reformation of those irregularities." Consistent with Dickinson's proclivity for avoiding separation wherever possible, the commission advised the congregation to be patient in the coming winter months, in hope that their pastor would recognize his mistakes and mend his ways. But, failing any change by spring, the commission authorized the congregation to seek another minister "in the most peaceable manner" possible.[40]

Further, on March 14, 1743, Yale rector Thomas Clap wrote to Dickinson informing him of another "pretty remarkable piece of news." The Separatists and Antinomians of New London, under the leadership of Andrew Croswell and Timothy Allen, had called James Davenport to preach to them. On the Sabbath after Davenport's arrival, Clap reported, they built a bonfire before the town's church, then consisting of Nonseparatists, in which, as the worshipers were leaving, they burned an unspecified number of Dickinson's books, most likely including *A Display of God's Special Grace.* One of the ministers prayed over the bonfire and told everyone that it was God's mercy that they had avoided the errors contained in such books, and that if they had not, they would have been in similar flames. According to Clap, the gathering concluded with Davenport commanding the ministers to pull off their gowns, and others their short cloaks and wigs, and to pile them up for burning.[41]

Dickinson began *A Defense* by insisting that, Croswell's protestations notwithstanding, those whom he had labeled Antinomians did exist in Massachusetts and Connecticut. He wrote that it grieved him, however, that his criticism of those individuals had led to their public dispute, as he believed that Croswell had "the character of a zealous friend to vital piety," and that he would have preferred to work with him rather than against him, whereby the opposition was being fed in the process. More specifically, Dickinson explained that he and Croswell seemed to agree that people should be sensible of their sin and misery, that they should have the prospect of God's vengeance made clear to them so that they might fly to Christ for refuge, and that sinners must have convictions if they are to come to Christ. Further, he could not quarrel with Croswell's assertion that, before they are able to take such saving steps, sinners must be convinced that they are absolutely unable to come to Christ or that they are absolutely "lost in the wilderness."[42]

Dickinson asserted, however, that he had not contradicted himself on the point by insisting that, though men must come to Christ immediately, they must first be convinced of their own impotency. While men remain in a natural state, insensible of their danger and need of a savior, he explained, they are nevertheless duty bound to do all that is necessary to awaken themselves out of their security. Where Croswell had argued that such a doctrine tended to persuade sinners that if they behaved in a certain manner, God would be inclined to save them, thereby providing them with a false sense of security, Dickinson answered: "Sinners must [first] be directed to get a knowledge of the gospel, and an acquaintance with the way and terms of salvation therein proposed, lest they hope for salvation, they know not how or why. For, how can they believe in him, of whom they have not heard?" (9–13).

Dickinson felt most compelled to defend his doctrine of assurance. Croswell had been critical of his assertion that a holy life is good evidence of a person's justification. Dickinson allowed that the justified continue to be tempted by Satan and that, quite commonly, they still sin and fall into a state of melancholy and despair. But, he insisted, they are not abandoned. Dickinson agreed that men cannot accept uncertainty as to their spiritual estate, that they need assurance, and that assurance among the elect is a relatively common occurrence. Still, he insisted, if men look to such evidence absolutely and without doubt or questioning, without further effort and self-examination, they may be greatly deceived. The true joy of assurance can only arise from, and rises only in proportion to, the evidence we have of our justified state in sanctification (14–20, 22, 39–40).

Croswell had written that assurance, or "a persuasion of our justified state," is essential to the exercise of saving faith but not necessarily to the "being" of it. Dickinson found such logic problematic. If assurance is essential to the first exercise of saving faith, he reasoned, it must precede justification. If it precedes justification, we are receiving assurance of our justified state before we are actually justified. Dickinson preferred to believe that at the same instant that we receive Christ, we have a "special saving interest in him," and we receive assurance, but not before (22–23).

Dickinson argued that Croswell's position on assurance was not only illogical but could also lead to Antinomianism, licentiousness, or at least a false sense of security. If it were true that persuasion of one's justified state is linked only to the exercise of saving faith, he wrote, then those who are so persuaded could conclude that they are justified regardless of whatever other manifestations may be wanting. They could be led to "a false hope and peace," though they continue in sin and imperfection. They could even be transported with joy in expectation of eternal happiness, when in reality they remain destined for "eternal perdition" (23, 31–32).

It may be recalled that Croswell accused Dickinson and the Boston ministers of opposing God's work in the Awakening. Dickinson denied the charge and instead indicted those "unhumbled hearts" that could not bear to stoop to the sovereignty of God, those whose self-esteem and self-flattery would not allow them to accept their dangerous and miserable state. Moreover, Dickinson continued, God's work in the Awakening had been weakened by those who, in their zealous support of the cause, had pretended to extraordinary inspirations and special impulses and engaged in "censorious invectives" against ministers and others of sound piety and doctrine. They had done more, Dickinson insisted, than all the united efforts of their enemies to bring down upon themselves and the Awakening "obloquy and reproach" (35–36).

Dickinson had published *A Display* anonymously, and in concluding his *Reply,* Croswell noted that he would take no notice of anyone who responded to him without listing his name. Dickinson, indeed, added his name to the second edition of *A Display,* but, almost as if to further irritate Croswell, he published *A Defense* under the name Theophilus, the protagonist of *A Display.* And, sticking to his word, Croswell did not respond.[43]

Several months after his public parry with Andrew Croswell, Jonathan Dickinson exchanged letters privately with Experience Mayhew. Mayhew, of the five "missionary Mayhews," spent his entire life on Martha's Vineyard in Massachusetts. In 1694, after being licensed to preach, he was employed by the Society for the Propagation of the Gospel to serve the Indians of that island, at which he was quite successful.

Mayhew was a moderate in the Awakening who had taken issue with radical New Lights and New Siders on much the same grounds as Dickinson. He was also a moderate Calvinist who deviated from strict orthodoxy in speaking for a measure of free will against the doctrine of total depravity and God's sovereign free grace. It was this which led Mayhew in August 1743 to write to Thomas Foxcroft, expressing his exceptions to some passages in Dickinson's *True Scripture Doctrine*. It seems from his letter that in a conversation between the two in Boston Foxcroft had invited Mayhew to comment on those passages with which he disagreed. Further, it would appear that Foxcroft had mentioned showing Mayhew's comments to Dickinson. Mayhew wrote that he did not want to offend so "worthy" and "learned" a person as Dickinson, whom he held in "very high esteem," but that he would be pleased to consider anything Dickinson might offer in response.

Mayhew's questions dealt with Dickinson's treatment of the will. He was unsatisfied with Dickinson's limited use of Locke's treatment of human understanding in his Calvinistic scheme on the will. He saw Dickinson as more directly reflecting the ideas of Thomas Hobbes. Specifically, Mayhew questioned Dickinson's statements that the power to will, or to choose, that which appears to us "unfit to be chosen" is inconsistent with our being free agents, and that the power to will or choose "that which is indifferently either the one or the other of . . . two contrary objects" is so far from freedom that it is entirely inconsistent with it or with any being that is perfectly free. Dickinson had argued, it may be recalled, that a free agent must necessarily choose what his understanding, appetites, and affections represent to him as the fittest object of his choice and that to do otherwise would be to suppose that a power extrinsic to him must move him "as a clock or watch is moved." Mayhew responded that by such a definition, human freedom was imperfect. He saw no reason why a man must be like a clock or watch simply because he has the power to will that which he does not will or not to will that which he does. Further, he continued, if a man's judgments, appetites, or affections in a particular situation are not already unalterably fixed, he would have the power to choose either object.

Mayhew, like Dickinson, spoke of the faculties of the human mind separately, but in matters of faith he had difficulty maintaining a distinction between them. He insisted that the soul, or the "seat of liberty," is but one single substance or essence and that whatever act it performs it performs as the entire soul. The soul, according to Mayhew, includes all of those elements Dickinson had noted (but not seen as necessarily or clearly joined into one faculty): the will, understanding, and affections. "The soul understands, wills, chooses, loves, desires, etc.," Mayhew wrote, and at the same time that it knows whether something is true (or not), it wills it or consents to it (or not).[44]

Dickinson responded to Experience Mayhew in a letter to Thomas Foxcroft in December 1743. He recalled that the central point with which

Mayhew had found fault was Dickinson's observations on the power to will, but he was particularly concerned with Mayhew's having suggested that he had taken a position consistent with that of Thomas Hobbes. In that Dickinson, like Edwards, subscribed to a Hobbesian doctrine of the will as a single-staged notion of agency, Mayhew was largely correct. Dickinson, however, responded that the opposite was true. He agreed with Mayhew that the soul is but one single individual substance and that whatever act it performs is performed by the entire soul, but he disagreed with Mayhew's approach to the soul as consisting of separate faculties that ought to be considered as acting jointly and with one consent. Moreover, he pointed out that what Hobbes had written had led him to "wild notions of fatality and irresistible destiny," something Dickinson had clearly avoided.[45]

Dickinson and Mayhew continued their correspondence, but no accord was reached on their differing views concerning free will, a disagreement which divided other moderate Calvinists as well. Mayhew's second letter, also to Thomas Foxcroft, was written in August 1744, and in the same year Mayhew put his ideas into print with *Grace Defended*.[46] Dickinson wrote "some brief remarks" on Mayhew's treatise, but they were never published. They have survived in manuscript form, bearing no date, but written sometime between April 9, 1746, the date upon which Dickinson indicated in a letter to Foxcroft that he felt bound to reply to Mayhew, and September 26, 1746, when Foxcroft received the manuscript.[47] On September 5, Dickinson wrote to Foxcroft that he was working on the response to Mayhew and that he was sending Foxcroft a "rough draft" for his opinion as to its appropriateness for publication. Perhaps Foxcroft found its publication inappropriate.

In its initial stages, as David Harlan has pointed out, most ministers aligned themselves with neither the Old nor the New Lights and New Siders. "Regular Lights," as Samuel Mather labeled them, saw both the limitations of the first and the dangers of the second. Dickinson provided the middle ground to which, by the mid-1740s, they and those disillusioned with both the radical New and the Old Side were attracted. As Leigh Eric Schmidt has suggested, Dickinson's model served as the centripetal force that pulled the radical New Siders back to a more centrist position, from the countervailing centrifugal forces of Antinomianism and enthusiasm.[48]

By 1746, however, the moderate Awakening in the Middle Colonies was being played out in the field of education, and once again Dickinson was in the forefront of that endeavor. It is to that subject that we turn next for our concluding chapter.

9

FOUNDING THE
COLLEGE OF NEW JERSEY

Calls for the founding of a college to train ministers for the Presbyterian Church in the Middle Colonies could be heard during the 1730s, but the primary impetus came during the Great Awakening. If the first calls were made by those in the Synod of Philadelphia who sought unity and uniformity through the establishment of a local institution from which they might gather orthodox men of faith for an increasing number of vacant pulpits, the final call was sounded by those New Siders who separated from that body over what that orthodoxy should be and how it should be ensured. Jonathan Dickinson was the acknowledged leader of that group. He and others of the Presbytery of New York founded the College of New Jersey, later to be known as Princeton, and Dickinson briefly served as the college's first president.

Thomas Pears has determined that before 1735 approximately 63 percent of the Presbyterian ministers who entered the Synod of Philadelphia had been educated abroad; another 28 percent had graduated from New England colleges. To be more specific, of the 78 ministers who joined the synod by 1735, 23 had graduated from the University of Glasgow, 9 from Edinburgh, 17 from other colleges abroad which Pears could not identify, 17 from Yale, and 5 from Harvard. Of the remaining 7 ministers, 4 were products of the Log College and 3 were unaccounted for.[1]

Beginning in 1735 the process by which ministers were supplied to the Middle Colonies began to change. Fewer candidates presented themselves from Scotland, and the possibility of sending native sons abroad, or even to New England, for collegiate education remained remote because of distance and cost. At the same time, the need grew in the Middle Colonies for trained, orthodox Presbyterian ministers. Simply put, the growth in population exceeded the available clerical supply, and many of those who did present themselves from abroad were instigating what appeared to be more frequent incidents of inappropriate behavior or unorthodox teaching. Thus, a sense of urgency developed for the creation of an institution for ministerial education closer to home.[2]

At first, ministerial education in the Middle Colonies was provided by individual ministers who held degrees from colleges abroad or in New England. In addition to their ministerial duties, they would privately tutor young men in the classics and in divinity. Jonathan Dickinson did so in Elizabeth Town, Aaron Burr in nearby Newark, Samuel Blair at Faggs Manor, Pennsylvania, and Samuel Finley in Nottingham, Maryland. And of course there was the controversial Log College operated by William Tennent. None of these colonial ministerial schools had a charter, academic standing, or authority to confer degrees. The Log College did supply at least sixteen candidates for the ministry, but it soon became inextricably linked to the radical wing of the Great Awakening.[3]

The need for an educational institution of some kind was undoubtedly the source of some conversation among Presbyterians in the Middle Colonies for years before the Great Awakening. The lack of such an institution, as we have seen, lurked in the background during synodical debates over the Adopting Act of 1729. The immediate path toward establishment of a college, however, began in earnest in 1738, and it was precipitated by concern over the Log College. In that year, as a preface to its overture on the examination of ministerial candidates, the Synod of Philadelphia acknowledged that it had been laboring "under a grievous disadvantage for want of the opportunities of universities and professors skilled in the several branches of useful learning." Most prospective students, the synod explained, lacked the circumstances that would enable them to attend colleges in Europe or New England, and that was proving to be detrimental to church and society.

The Synod of Philadelphia proposed that before anyone who had not earned a degree from a European or New England college was encouraged by a presbytery to prepare for the ministry, he should be examined by a committee of the synod on his knowledge of the several branches of philosophy, divinity, and languages. The synod explained that by this measure it hoped to "banish ignorance" and to fill the infant church with "men eminent for parts and learning." The New Brunswick men, however, protested the action as a blatant attempt to suppress the Log College.[4]

By 1739, both the New Side and the Old Side had come to realize that the future would be with the side that could control education. That year, the Synod of Philadelphia adopted an overture for the erection of a school or seminary. The Tennents and their supporters having made their earlier protest and absented themselves, the measure was carried unanimously and a committee was appointed to implement it, consisting of Jonathan Dickinson and Ebenezer Pemberton, of New England and the Presbytery of New York; Robert Cross, from Ireland and the Presbytery of Philadelphia; and James Anderson of Scotland and the Presbytery of Donegal. Two of the four were to go to Europe, and Pemberton was to travel to Boston "to prosecute this affair with proper directions." Those directions would be formulated by a commission of the synod with correspondents from every presbytery.[5]

This commission met in Philadelphia on August 15, 1739. Ten members of the synod were present, but among the six commission members listed as missing were those of the Presbyteries of New York and New Brunswick, including Dickinson, Pemberton, and Gilbert Tennent. Pemberton sent a letter to the commission explaining his absence, which was sustained, but the others did not. On August 16 the commission voted not to take any action. It explained that too many preparatory letters and instructions remained to be written, especially if some were to be sent to Europe seeking assistance, and that the matter was too important to be decided in the absence of so many commission members. The commission voted to send a letter to Benjamin Colman in Boston, seeking the support of the Boston brethren in their endeavor, but otherwise it decided to leave final disposition of the matter to the entire synod, which was scheduled to convene in Philadelphia in September. In the meantime, letters were to be sent to the Presbyteries of New York and New Brunswick "ordering their attendance" at the appointed time.[6]

The outbreak of hostilities between England and Spain (King George's War, as the American phase of the War of the Austrian Succession was called) forced cancellation of the synod's September meeting. According to the minutes of a meeting of the synod commission held on June 2, 1740, however, Benjamin Colman had responded to the commission with a letter in which he assured the synod of the associated brethren of Boston's readiness to "concur" in its "laudable proposal." The commission ordered Jedediah Andrews to continue to correspond with the Boston brethren, but there is no record of any further action being taken before the schism of 1741, which made it impossible to pursue the matter any longer as a united body.[7]

It was not until 1743 that the Synod of Philadelphia returned to the issue of erecting a seminary within its bounds. On May 31, the synod voted to write once again to the General Assembly of the Church of Scotland and to "lay before them the low and melancholy condition" of the church in the Middle Colonies. They informed the General Assembly of their need for probationers to fill their numerous vacancies and urged the Assembly to send ministers and probationers with enough money to tide them over for a few years. Finally, the synod requested support for erecting in the Middle Colonies a seminary or "school for educating young men" for the ministry.

Although it was not proposed by the Synod of Philadelphia, the Presbyteries of Philadelphia, New Castle, and Donegal met on November 16, 1743, to consider means by which men might be educated for the ministry within the confines of the Middle Colonies. On May 25, 1744, they made their recommendation to the synod. They proposed that a school be opened to which anyone might send their children to have them instructed, gratis, in languages, philosophy, and divinity. Toward that end, they asked that every congregation within the bounds of the Synod of Philadelphia be asked for contributions to pay for a master teacher and tutor and to defray the cost of books and other necessary supplies. Finally, they recommended that Francis Alison be appointed master of the school. Alison was one of the finest classical scholars in British North America.

The synod agreed with the proposal and appointed a board of trustees to manage the affair for the first year. Although provision was made for later additions to the board, possibly due to their absence, no one was appointed from the Presbytery of New York. Within the year, a school was established at New London, Pennsylvania, and on November 24, 1743, a note appeared in the *Pennsylvania Gazette,* which announced that the school had been created for "the promotion of learning, where all persons may be instructed in the languages and some other parts of polite literature without any expenses for their education."

On August 20, 1745, after the Presbytery of New York had withdrawn, a commission of the Synod of Philadelphia asked Jedediah Andrews and Robert Cross to write to Rector Thomas Clap and the trustees of Yale College providing them with information on the synod school. The synod had recommended a closer working relationship between the schools, whereby its graduates would be sent to Yale for college degrees. Clap, in response, while voicing his readiness to help promote the cause of religion and learning among the Presbyterians of the Middle Colonies, requested further information on the synod school's "plan and constitution."[8]

The letter, adopted by the Synod of Philadelphia on May 9, 1746, presented a summary of developments concerning its newly erected school. It reported that thus far the school's accomplishments had exceeded its expectations and that it hoped to obtain assistance from England, Ireland, and elsewhere, with which it would be able to found a college, but that "the troubles of the times" hindered any such application. The synod acknowledged that it had not yet obtained a charter for the school but that it had reason to hope that it might, "if there be occasion."

The synod assured Clap that the school was being regulated in as similar a manner to Yale as circumstances would allow, but that it was willing to make any changes the Yale president or trustees might require in order to secure the college's cooperation. On a related matter, however, the synod offered Clap its assurance that it found just as offensive as he the actions of certain students the college had recently expelled. This would be a reference to students disciplined for their New Light activities, in general, and quite likely to include David Brainerd. The synod reminded Clap that the "Tennent party," which had been involved in the Brainerd affair, had left the Synod of Philadelphia to join others also involved in the fray in the Synod of New York.[9]

Correspondence between the Synod of Philadelphia and Clap continued for a time, but nothing came of the proposed cooperative effort between the synod school and Yale. Shortly after the May 30 letter, Francis Alison, in a similar letter, sought help from Francis Hutcheson of Glasgow University, but once again there is little evidence of any significant results. The school never overcame its severe financial needs, and after nine years, in 1752, Alison left to accept a position at the newly organized College of Philadelphia. The synod school was moved to Newark, Delaware, and placed under the care of one of Alison's former students, Alexander McDowell, but it never became a college.[10]

Before turning to the Synod of New York's efforts to establish a college, it is necessary to provide further information on the David Brainerd affair, to which we have previously referred only in passing. Thomas Clap became rector of Yale College in 1740, in the midst of the Great Awakening. At first, he welcomed the revival. He made college facilities available to various New Light/New Side ministers, but soon after Gilbert Tennent's tumultuous visit in the spring of 1741 he began to withdraw his support and to clamp down on New Light activity in the college. In the spring of 1742, when such activity continued, Clap suspended classes and ordered the students home. Thus began a tenure of office which, as Norman Pettit has described it, was one of the most "decisively constructive" and troubled in Yale's history.[11]

As we have seen, in his letter to Jonathan Dickinson dated May 3, 1742, Clap accused those who, he believed, were aggravating the separation between New and Old Lights in Connecticut of seeking a similar separation at Yale. In the same month, he informed the Connecticut General Assembly, which had been asked by the governor to inquire into events on the Yale campus, that "sundry students" under the "instigation, persuasion, and example of others" had "fallen into several errors in principle and disorder in practice," which could prove "hurtful to religion" and "inconsistent with the good order and government of that society." Some students, he explained, had fallen into the practice of rashly judging and censuring others, including the trustees, rector, and tutors of the college. They had refused to attend classes and religious exercises and, instead, turned to those to whom such instruction had not been committed. Some students, Clap continued, had been going into New Haven and nearby towns, sometimes for several days and "before great numbers of people" to teach and exhort much as ministers of the gospel.

In response, the Connecticut General Assembly recommended that the rector and tutors continue to instruct the students "in the true principals of religion," to keep them from "all such errors as they may be in danger of imbibing from strangers and foreigners," and to do everything in their power to prevent students from coming under the influence of those who would "prejudice their minds against the way of worship and ministry established by the laws" of the colony. Finally, in order to maintain "order and authority," the Assembly instructed the rector to dismiss any student who refused to submit to the laws, orders, and rules of the college.[12]

Clap pushed through regulations whereby, among other things, students were forbidden to attend the off-campus sermons of certain New Light evangelicals or to question the spiritual state of the college's rector, trustees, or tutors. David Brainerd was among the first to violate those regulations. Brainerd, one of Yale's awakened students, in the controversial spirit that followed the tumultuous winter of 1741/42, made some impolitic comments concerning the spiritual state of certain faculty. To be more specific, he was alleged to have said that tutor Chauncey Whittelsy had "no more grace than a chair" and to have wondered aloud why Clap "did not drop down dead" for forbidding students to follow Gilbert Tennent to Milford, Connecticut, upon one of his visits and then for fining those who did. Brainerd admitted having made the comment about Whittelsy, but when he refused to make a public confession (the penalty for a first offense in such a matter), he was expelled only a few months before he was to have graduated.[13]

Dickinson, Aaron Burr, and Jonathan Edwards interceded on Brainerd's behalf to no avail. Brainerd became a cause célèbre for the New Lights and New Siders, as well as a symbol of both the piety and the victimization of the awakened. Jonathan Edwards edited and published Brainerd's diary as a model of the conversion experience, and Brainerd's expulsion from Yale added resolve to the New York New Siders' quest for a college more sympathetic to their needs.[14]

In the meantime, however, Brainerd went to study for the ministry with the Reverend Samuel Mills of Ripton, Connecticut, and in July 1742 he was licensed as a probationer by the New Light Ministerial Association of the Eastern District of Fairfield County. In April 1743, Dickinson, Burr, and Pemberton hired him as an Indian missionary, and finally in June 1744, although he had not completed his degree, the Presbytery of New York ordained Brainerd at Newark, New Jersey.[15]

By the middle of the eighteenth century, Congregationalists and Presbyterians were already working as Indian missionaries, as were Anglicans, Quakers, Moravians, and Baptists. The Great Awakening stimulated New Light/New Side interest in such missionary efforts, however, especially as those missionaries might employ experimental religion in the conversion process. Cooperative efforts were arranged between Scotland's Society for Propagating Christian Knowledge (SPCK), chartered in 1709, and ministers in New England and the Middle Colonies.[16]

Jonathan Dickinson, Aaron Burr, and Ebenezer Pemberton were the first Middle Colony New Side Presbyterians to become correspondents of the SPCK. Related communication between Dickinson and Pemberton dates to 1729, but in 1740 all three wrote to the society of the "deplorable and perishing condition" of the Indians of Long Island, New York, and Pennsylvania. In 1741 the SPCK authorized them to organize a Board of Correspondents, which would be committed to the establishment of missions in all three places. Joining them on the board would be laymen from the Presbytery of New York and ministers of the Presbytery of New Brunswick. Among the first missionaries commissioned by the board were John Sergent in 1741, Asariah Horton in 1742, and David Brainerd in 1743.[17]

For the years he served the Indians of western Massachusetts/eastern New York, in the area known as the Forks of the Delaware, and of central New Jersey, Brainerd and Dickinson remained close friends. He visited Dickinson several times before the latter's death, some suggesting that he sought Dickinson's counsel both on the state of his soul and on his mission to the Indians. He preached from Dickinson's pulpit, took up collections for his mission, and officiated at Dickinson's marriage to his second wife, Mary Crane, in Newark. Brainerd died two days after Dickinson at the home of Jonathan Edwards in Northampton, Massachusetts, where he had gone to seek the hand of Edwards's daughter, Jerusha.[18]

Dickinson was pleased with David Brainerd's efforts among the Indians. On April 9, 1746, for example, Dickinson told Thomas Foxcroft of the "most wonderful work of grace making a triumphant progress" among the Indians under Brainerd's ministry. But, as with Edwards, Brainerd may have meant even more to Dickinson. Norman Pettit, who has also suggested that the role Dickinson played in Brainerd's life was equal to, if not greater than, that of Edwards, has written: "No other man, apart from Edwards, took such an interest in Brainerd's plight," and "none was so vividly aware of how perfectly he served the Side Presbyterian cause": "He [Brainerd] personified, on the one hand, what Tennent's Log College (which Dickinson now disliked) had failed to produce, and, on the other hand, what Dickinson's own college, Yale, had refused to tolerate. In short he stood for what a new college in the Middle Colonies might strive to produce, a sound reason for founding the College of New Jersey."[19]

To return to our discussion of the founding of the College of New Jersey, it should come as no surprise to the reader that establishment of a school for ministerial education was a high priority for members of the Synod of New York. What is surprising is that the actions they took toward that end were, at least officially, nonsynodical. In fact, there is no record of any discussion of the college by the Synod of New York until 1751, and then the reference is only to a request from the college's trustees for the synod's help in persuading Ebenezer Pemberton's congregation to allow him to go to Europe seeking financial support.[20]

As previously noted, the Synod of New York's articles of union provided that all who had achieved "a competent degree of ministerial knowledge, were orthodox in doctrine, regular in life, diligent to promote vital godliness, and willing to submit to the discipline" could become members. Moreover, several ministers who had been trained at the Log College and either had been, or likely would have been, barred from membership in the Synod of Philadelphia had joined the New York Synod's ranks.[21]

Two problems remained, however. First, the rapid growth of the Synod of New York created a demand for ministerial candidates that was impossible to satisfy as it was dependent on Harvard, Yale, and colleges in Great Britain. Second, fears lingered on the part of those from the New York Presbytery as to perceptions of the Synod of New York as anti-intellectual. Attacks on "Pharisee-Teachers" and empty "head knowledge" by the New Brunswick group were seen by many as a rejection of a learned ministry.[22]

New York Presbytery members of the Synod of New York thus took on the task of establishing a college, and the leadership in that endeavor was provided by those who had been selected for the task by the Synod of Philadelphia in 1739—Jonathan Dickinson and Ebenezer Pemberton. Dickinson, at that point in his life, has been described as "in all respects the best adapted to superintend and conduct the education of youth," "better qualified than most of his brethren," and "the best scholar, the most effective writer, and of the soundest judgment in the church." Charles Augustus Briggs put it this way: "No better man could have been found to lay the foundation of Presbyterian higher education in America. He was head and shoulders above his brethren in the ministry in intellectual and moral endowment."[23]

As early as March 1745, Dickinson and a group of ministers and laymen of the New York Presbytery, acting independently, drew up plans for a college. On November 20, Jonathan Edwards wrote from Northampton to an unnamed correspondent in Scotland (likely John McLaurin of Glasgow) that a plan for educating young men for the ministry was afoot involving the Reverends Dickinson, Burr, Blair, and Finley and that the group planned to seek a charter for the college from the king. In fact, sometime in late 1745 or early 1746, they applied to New Jersey royal governor Lewis Morris for the charter. Morris, aptly described by one early historian of Princeton as "a zealous Anglican and a strict observer of the precedents and commissions of his office," denied the request. Among the explanations offered were that he doubted that he had the right to grant such a charter without permission from London, and that even if he had such authority it would be impolitic to grant an act of incorporation for an educational institution to ministers and laymen not of the Church of England.

Support for Morris's rejection of the petition was unequivocal among New Jersey Anglicans who opposed the chartering of any Dissenter institutions, whether they be colleges or even local churches. The long-standing animosity between Anglicans and Dissenters, and Dickinson's prominent role in that quarrel, have already been discussed, but in Morris's case, his action was personally consistent as well. Earlier, as chief council of New York, he had been a member of the Provincial Council when it twice refused a charter to the First Presbyterian Church of New York for the same reason—that there was no precedent for conferring that privilege on a company of Dissenters.[24]

Only a few months prior to receipt of the Dissenters' application, Anglicans were not united in their opposition to the College of New Jersey. On March 25, 1745, for example, the college recorded subscriptions totaling 185 pounds from some ten prominent New Yorkers and New Jerseyites, seven of whom were Anglicans. It would seem that they did not fear New Light Presbyterian exclusivity. Why then the split between Anglicans and Presbyterians over the college later that year?

One possibility is that Presbyterians and Anglicans came to disagree over the governing of the college. A letter from William Livingston of New Jersey, dated December 9, 1745, described the collapse of what might have been an Anglican-Presbyterian alliance: "A project of erecting an academy [the college] . . . was last year set on foot and seemed to devour all before it, so that the projectors had a prospect of collecting sufficient funds by subscription, but when all came to all they quarreled about the government of it. The Presbyterians not being able to brook that it should be managed by the long-gowns, and the churchmen opposing its being governed by the Dissenters."[25]

A second possible explanation involves the renewal of the Anglican-Presbyterian quarrel over Anglican establishment. At about the same time that Dickinson, Burr, and others petitioned Governor Morris for a charter for the College of New Jersey, Anglicans of New Jersey and of other colonies once again launched a drive to secure an American bishop. The volatility of that issue, and Dickinson's response to it, have already been discussed. Its impact on the chartering of the College of New Jersey should not be underestimated. As Alison Olson has discovered, the "Presbyterian interest" in establishing the College of New Jersey was the same political faction dominated by the Newark and Elizabeth Town "liberals," and the champions of the Anglican church in East Jersey were the East Jersey proprietors themselves.[26]

A third possible cause of Anglican opposition to the chartering of the College of New Jersey may have been the New Jersey antiproprietary land riots of 1745 and 1746. Three of the college subscribers of 1745—Robert Hunter Morris, Joseph Murray, and Andrew Johnston—were East Jersey proprietors. Robert Morris, New Jersey's chief justice and son of Lewis Morris, became one of the college's most outspoken opponents. Most of the rioters were from the Newark and Elizabeth Town congregations of Aaron Burr and Jonathan Dickinson, two leaders of the college movement.[27]

The quit rent controversy dates to the "Concessions and Agreement of the Lord Proprietors" of 1665, under which the settlers of East Jersey were legally entitled to their land and which required that beginning in 1670 landowners were to pay one half-penny per acre yearly for their land. The settlers, called the associates (e.g., the Elizabeth Town associates), and their descendants argued that they had received permission to settle in New Jersey and patents for their land from New York governor Richard Nicolls in 1664 and that this agreement included no provision for quit rents. The East Jersey proprietors, beginning with Lord John Berkeley and Sir George Carteret, however, pointed out that the duke of York had granted them the land in question some five months before the Nicolls patent was issued, thereby nullifying that patent. The associates insisted that they had entered into their purchase agreement in good faith and that the Nicolls grant was binding on both parties. They even argued that King Charles had no right to pass on to the duke of York the land in question, because he had neither conquered nor bought out the Indians who remained in possession of the land. In brief, they never paid the quit rent.[28]

New Jersey became a royal colony in 1702, but the proprietors retained all rights and privileges due them relative to the land they continued to own and to that which they had patented and sold, including their claim to quit rents. The new royal government supported them in those rights, but to no avail. By the 1730s, attempts at reconciliation having failed, the number of related lawsuits grew to the point where the proprietors opted to settle the entire affair through England's Court of Chancery. In 1736, however, Lewis Morris became governor of New Jersey. He was a leading proprietor in both the East and West Divisions. He appointed his son chief justice and his daughter's father-in-law receiver general of quit rents. Under Morris's governorship, matters grew worse.[29]

Beginning in 1741 actual ejection cases were brought against Elizabeth Town landowners who insisted on rights to their land based on the Nicolls grant, and in 1742, in what was known as the Clinker Lot Case, the jury ruled in the proprietors' favor. In 1743, fearing other such decisions, as well as the unbearable cost of several pending court cases and the prospect of having the soon-to-be submitted proprietors' bill in Chancery decided against them, the Elizabeth Town freeholders decided to appeal the entire matter to the king. In September 1745, however, five months after the proprietors' bill was actually filed, but before the matter was resolved, riots broke out. Violence erupted in Newark, the home of the Provincial Court, when protesters broke into the town jail to free a prisoner who had been incarcerated in a related matter. Indictments were brought against many of the rebels, and some were jailed. In January 1746, mobs broke into the same jail and released its prisoners, only to have further indictments follow. Violence continued for another six years before calm was restored.[30]

Although there is little direct evidence linking Dickinson to the quit rent controversy, he was almost certainly involved. Moreover, it is likely that he was actively involved at about the same time that he and other prominent Presbyterian ministers and laymen from northern New Jersey and New York City were petitioning the governor of New Jersey for a college charter. In reference to the quit rent controversy, one source has offered that Dickinson was "more than an average lawyer." Another has referred to him as an adviser in legal difficulties and explained that "he greatly aided his parishioners in their strife before the courts for their homes, when their titles were attacked by the East Jersey proprietors."[31]

Edwin Hatfield, historian of Elizabeth, New Jersey, has been the most specific. He has written that as early as 1729 Dickinson subscribed to "a paper designed to unite more closely and effectively his townsmen in their opposition to the pretensions of the East Jersey Proprietors." From that point on, Hatfield continued, Dickinson proved himself "an invaluable counselor and organizer in defense of popular rights. In all the straits and trials, growing out of the litigations with which they were disturbed, he ever stood with them, and never shrank from any responsibilities thus devolved upon him."[32]

No document directly related to the quit rent controversy has been found bearing Dickinson's name. His name does not appear, for example, on any of the lists of special committees formed to defend the rights of those with claims under the Nicolls grant. But, then, as a minister, that would not have been unusual. In 1743, when 309 freeholders of Elizabeth Town and the surrounding area petitioned the king to intervene in the quit rent controversy, not one of the ministers of the seven congregations involved signed their names.[33]

The ministers of Newark and Elizabeth Town, the best educated residents of those communities, probably did assist their flocks, however, by advising them and writing their pamphlets and letters of defense. Various letters that appeared in the newspapers of the day charged that some of the pamphlets published during the riots of 1745 and 1746 to vindicate the rioters were written by the ministers of Elizabeth Town and Newark, which would include Dickinson and Burr. Those same letters argued that, as the authors had not heard any of the ministers in those communities condemn the actions of the rioters in their congregations, they thereby approved and encouraged their lawless behavior. Other letters, however, written in response, called such accusations false and insidious. They insisted that the ministers were opposed to the riots, that they had admonished the rioters from their pulpits and told them "that heaven looked with disfavor on their acts," and that one minister had gone so far as to ride a considerable distance in order to confront some rioters and to "convince them that they should confess their guilt and plead for a pardon."[34]

Given the preponderance of circumstantial evidence for Presbyterian ministerial involvement in the quit rent controversy, then, there is little reason to be surprised at Governor Morris's rejection of their college petition of 1745 or 1746. On May 21, 1746, however, Morris died and was succeeded on an interim basis by Provincial Council president John Hamilton. On September 5, 1746, Jonathan Dickinson wrote to Thomas Foxcroft noting that some unnamed events seemed auspicious, and it would seem that at least one of those auspicious events was tied to the interim governor. Not quite three months later, on November 24, he wrote to Foxcroft once again and reported that he and his fellow trustees had obtained a charter "with full and ample privileges for a college in the province" and that he expected the trustees to meet in Elizabeth Town that week "in order to promote the settlement of the college."

John Hamilton, like Morris, was an Anglican, an East Jersey proprietor, and a loyal servant of the crown. Moreover, he was deeply troubled by the quit rent difficulties. Upon assuming office, he urged the Assembly to stop the riots, proposed that a committee be established to resolve the matter, and warned that if peace were not restored, the resentment of the king and Parliament might be "too heavy for us to bear." The riots continued into 1747. But, whether because of his greater tolerance for Dissenters than Morris had shown or because of his support for educational causes, he granted a charter for the College of New Jersey on October 22, 1746. Having no precedent to guide him, Hamilton sought neither legislative nor crown approval, thereby providing the College of New Jersey with the first college charter to be so enacted in the British colonies of North America.[35]

The granting of the college charter was noted in Book C of the New Jersey Commissions and Charters, but an official copy of the charter was never filed. There is no explanation for this oversight, but a commonly accepted theory is that the charter was so controversial and so quickly objected to by prominent and influential Anglicans that neither the governor nor the college trustees were anxious to publish it in its entirety. Any plan to publish the charter was further delayed by Hamilton's death in June 1747.[36]

Although the actual text of the charter of 1746 has been lost, surviving transcriptions, excerpts, and summaries suggest that it provided for a self-perpetuating board of trustees with authority to receive bequests and other gifts; to erect buildings; to appoint faculty and other officers, as were "usual in any of the universities or colleges in the realm of great Britain"; to make such laws and ordinances for the governing of the college as were necessary, provided those laws were not repugnant to the laws of the realm and of the province; and to award any degree conferred by British universities. There was no provision requiring governmental involvement in the administration of the college, nor was it required that all trustees live within the Province of New Jersey. The charter further stipulated that prospective students were not to be barred from the college on account of their "speculative principles of religion"; put another way, "those of every religious profession [were to] have equal privilege and advantage of education."[37]

Establishment of the College of New Jersey was not delayed by the controversy that surrounded the granting of the first charter. Solicitation of funding began almost immediately. Representative was a letter written on January 30, 1747, by Jonathan Dickinson to Captain Theophilus Howell of Bridgehampton, Long Island. In that letter, Dickinson acknowledged that he had not yet met Howell but that from what he had heard of him he was encouraged to write for his subscription and that of his friends for "such a pious design" as the College of New Jersey. Dickinson explained to Howell that he hoped the college would "prove as well a seminary of vital piety as of good literature" and that it would serve to "promote the interests of the Redeemer's Kingdom" and to provide qualified people to fill the numerous vacancies in all provinces, even as far away as Virginia. Dickinson reported that the college was dependent on contributions, from "charitable well disposed persons," and that people had subscribed so liberally that the college was to open in the spring.[38]

On February 2, 1747, an announcement was placed in the *New York Gazette* and the *New York Weekly Post Boy,* which read that a charter for founding the college had been granted on October 22, 1746, to Jonathan Dickinson of Elizabeth Town, John Pierson of Woodbridge, Ebenezer Pemberton of New York City, and Aaron Burr of Newark, all ministers of the Presbytery and Synod of New York, as well as to "some other gentlemen" who were to join them as college trustees. Notice was given that the charter secured "equal liberties and privileges . . . to every denomination of Christians, any different religious sentiments notwithstanding," and that those who sought admission and were "qualified by preparatory learning" were to apply by the end of May 1747.[39]

On April 20, 1747, an article in the *Weekly Post Boy* announced that the trustees of the College of New Jersey had appointed Jonathan Dickinson president of the college, which would open during the fourth week in May at Elizabeth Town. On August 13, 1747, in both the *Pennsylvania Gazette* and the *Pennsylvania Journal,* notice appeared that the college had opened. The notice read that Caleb Smith, a Yale graduate (class of 1743) who had been studying divinity with Dickinson in preparation for the ministry, had been appointed tutor and that the college had been located in Elizabeth Town until a building could be erected in a more central place in the province.[40]

The August 13 article identified those "other gentlemen" who had been named by the charter of 1746. They were laymen William Smith, a prominent New York lawyer; William Peartree Smith, then of New York but later of Elizabeth Town, referred to by one historian as "a man of leisure and wealth and given to good works"; and Peter Van Brugh Livingston, a wealthy and influential New York merchant and Council member. All, save the Harvard-trained Pemberton, were Yale graduates, and all were Presbyterians living within the bounds of the Presbytery of New York.

Finally, the article of August 13 reported that the charter had allowed for the appointment of five additional trustees, and that (presumably, sometime between the February and April *New York Gazette* articles) those men had been chosen as well. They were the Reverends Gilbert Tennent, William Tennent Jr., Samuel Blair, and Samuel Finley, who were all Log College graduates, and the Reverend Richard Treat, who had earned his degree at Yale but later rallied in defense of the Log College.[41]

It has been suggested that the original seven trustees, those who were most visibly active in pursuing the charter, sought to organize the college on a plan far larger than that of the Log College, and that they were committed to the idea that supervision of the college should lie beyond the confines of any single church judicatory, or synod, even their own. Not only had that been the case with both Harvard and Yale but, some would argue, it stood to reason that if that were done and if the Synod of Philadelphia could be persuaded to send its prospective ministers to the college, they might also be convinced not to pursue their own plan of converting their New London school into a college. Some of those who have subscribed to this interpretation further suggest that the Log College men were not likely to agree on either of those points, and therefore they were not included among the petitioners.[42]

On the other hand, it has been persuasively argued that although there were good reasons for not including the names of the Log College men on the original petitions and charter, the college charter of 1746 was designed to allow for their participation on the board of trustees at a later date. Those who support this position argue that the time had come for the Log College men to support a new college, especially if it were to be under the influence of those they trusted. Samuel Blair's and Samuel Finley's academies could not fill the needs of the Synod of New York, and although the exact date is not known, the Log College was closed by the time the New York men petitioned for their college.[43]

That the Log College men were not listed among the original petitioners for the College of New Jersey, or appointed to the first board of trustees, can be seen as the result of the antagonism against them that still existed among a considerable number of Presbyterians and Anglicans. Neither the original petitioners for the college nor the Log College men wished to add any other source of difficulty to what was already a problematic request of the governor of New Jersey. Dickinson's letter of March 3, 1747, noted above, lends some credence to that position. Upon election to the board of trustees of the College of New Jersey, however, the Log College men acted on its behalf as avidly as they had for their alma mater. They actively solicited funds both at home and abroad. Davies and Tennent even visited England for that purpose.[44]

Succeeding Acting Governor John Hamilton was Jonathan Belcher, a man in whom New Jersey Dissenters and Jonathan Dickinson rejoiced, as he was one of them. Stephen Crane and Matthias Hetfield, both prominent in the Elizabeth Town Presbyterian Church, for example, were in London at the time and made a personal appeal to Benjamin Avery for Belcher's appointment. Avery, a leader of the Protestant Dissenting Deputies, organized in 1732 to lobby Parliament in matters of interest to Protestant Dissenters from the Church of England, was largely responsible for Belcher's appointment. He also supported establishment of the college in New Jersey. On April 25, 1747, Avery wrote to Jonathan Dickinson offering his congratulations on the appointment of Belcher as governor, to which he added: "He cannot be altogether a stranger to you; and from his known zeal for the rights and liberties of mankind, both civil and religious, you and your friends may reasonably hope to enjoy your several privileges and immunities unmolested under his administration."[45]

In a letter to Thomas Foxcroft, dated November 24, 1746, Dickinson wrote: "There is for ought I can hear a universal satisfaction and rejoicing in this province upon the agreeable news of Mr. Belcher's being appointed our governor. . . . As to the ministers of our profession, I'm confident there is not one in the province but what rejoices at the agreeable tidings. There is nowhere to be found a ministry more united in sentiment than those of this province." Foxcroft must have voiced some concern over the reception certain Presbyterian Old Lights might offer Belcher upon his arrival, as Dickinson added: "The ministers you seem afraid of belong to Pennsylvania." Dickinson concluded this letter by noting that he intended to write Belcher a letter of congratulations. In August 1747, he would entertain the newly arrived governor in his home.

Jonathan Belcher, born in 1682, was a wealthy native son of Cambridge, Massachusetts, whose father, Andrew Belcher, had been a member of the Massachusetts Provincial Council. He graduated from Harvard in 1699, whereupon he took up the mercantile trade and served in the Massachusetts Council. In 1722 Belcher was appointed his state's colonial agent in England, but he returned to Boston in 1730 as governor, a post he held until 1741.

During his term as Massachusetts governor, Jonathan Belcher showed considerable interest in higher education and religion. He served on Harvard's board of overseers and was openly warmed by the evangelical fires of the First Great Awakening. In the former capacity he worked toward reconciliation of the college's contending and divisive liberal and conservative factions, but he was also known for his attacks on what he saw as the "poisonous notions" of Arminianism, Arianism, and Socinianism, which threatened to destroy the "noble pious principles" on which the college had been founded. In the latter, having himself undergone a heartfelt conversion experience with which any evangelical would have been pleased, he openly welcomed George Whitefield's visits to Massachusetts.[46]

King George II appointed Belcher governor of New Jersey in July 1746, but he did not assume office until August 8, 1747. He took up residence in Burlington, New Jersey, where, on August 20, he met for the first time with his legislature. Like his successors, Belcher had to face the continued quit rent disorders. He immediately let it be known that he was prepared to do whatever was necessary to suppress the rioters. He demanded action from the New Jersey Assembly, which had been reluctant to respond to the pleadings of either the proprietors or associates, and he wrote to London of the need for action against the rioters. Alison Olson has argued, however, that privately Belcher began working with the Elizabeth Town associates to finance the sending of a special agent to London to plead their case. Further, she has found that he arranged with his friend and fellow merchant, Jeremiah Allen, to be their agent and that he had secured a loan from Allen's brother to pay for Allen's services.[47]

On August 25, the New Jersey Assembly responded that it would appoint a committee to meet with Council representatives to consider the matter. Within six months it adopted a resolution castigating the rioters for their contempt of the law and passed three bills designed to stop the disturbances, which Belcher signed into law. Those laws prescribed a fine and prison sentence for jail breaking, releasing prisoners, or dispossessing anyone of their property. Rather than declare a state of rebellion and implement the death penalty, as the proprietors and Council had proposed, however, the Assembly delayed all proceedings of trials resulting from the first law, if the person charged gave bond of good behavior and sought to amicably settle affairs with his accuser. Finally, the Assembly provided amnesty for all who had participated in the public disturbances during the previous two years and against whom charges had not yet been brought.[48]

The matter was not resolved, but for the moment the riots stopped, and Belcher was able to turn his attention to the College of New Jersey. On September 16, 1747, he wrote to the Reverend Thomas Bradbury of London that the people of New Jersey were "in a poor situation for educating their children," that he was "putting forward the building of a college" in New Jersey "for the instruction of youth in the principles of true religion and good literature," and that he had "a good prospect of bringing it to pass." On September 18, he wrote a similar letter to the Committee of the West Jersey Society, but added a reference to a quarrel his plan had generated "between the gentlemen of the Eastern and those of the Western Division" as to where the college should be placed. He had managed to bring both sides into agreement, he concluded, to have it built at Princeton.[49]

Although there was some consideration of appealing the issuance of the college charter of 1746 to a court of chancery, opponents of the College of New Jersey, mostly adherents to the Church of England, took their complaints, instead, to the bishop of London under whose jurisdiction lay the province of New Jersey. They told the bishop that they had had no opportunity to respond to petitions for the college, and they asked him to quash the charter granted by Acting Governor Hamilton because it violated English law governing the religious practices of Dissenters.[50]

Typical was the letter of March 26, 1747, to the bishop of London written by Dickinson's old nemesis, James Wetmore of Rye, New York. In that letter Wetmore referred to the Presbyterians as "the most bitter enemies of the church" and insisted that the college they had founded would negatively affect the state of religion in New York and New Jersey. He argued that as the charter was "inconsistent with our constitution," the bishop should suppress it or at least instruct the governor of New Jersey to have the president and tutors licensed by the bishop. He explained that he did not believe that any governor commissioned by the king would have granted such a patent, but that it had been done upon the death of Governor Morris by the president of the Council, to whom application was made "so privately that our clergy had no opportunity to enter a caveat against it." The incorporators were all followers of "Mr. Whitefield's doctrines and methods," Wetmore reported, and "Mr. Dickinson, the leader of them, who is said to be president of the college, has distinguished himself by his virulent writings against the Church of England, beyond all the Dissenters in America." Hamilton's action, Wetmore concluded, would only lead to the propagation of those doctrines under a royal charter.[51]

Although the bishop of London did not act in response to the New Jersey Anglicans, their opposition continued. Governor Belcher, in the meantime, decided to intervene. According to one possibly apocryphal story, when a group of Anglicans met with him to protest the charter, Belcher responded: "Pray gentlemen, make yourselves easy, if their charter is not good, I'll get them a better!"[52] Apocryphal or not, Belcher accepted the legality of Hamilton's charter, and he let it be known that if the trustees wished to continue to operate on the basis of the charter of 1746, he would support them. Belcher's political experience persuaded him, however, that the charter of 1746 should be enhanced if it were to withstand continued criticism. He therefore acted on three fronts: to provide the college with a better charter, to secure a more visible and permanent home, and to attract much needed financial assistance.

Even before the College of New Jersey opened at Elizabeth Town, its trustees stated their intention of constructing new buildings as quickly as possible. "It will not in common reputation be esteemed a college," they wrote, "till some public buildings are built for the use of such college." They stipulated that those buildings should be erected in and, thereby the college relocated to, Princeton, which was halfway along the main road between New York and Philadelphia.[53]

Belcher readily agreed with the trustees. On September 18, 1747, he wrote to the Committee of the West Jersey Society expressing his preference for the move and suggesting that the relocation would add to land values and promote the interest of the West Jersey proprietors. On October 2, Belcher wrote to a friend in Boston that he believed Princeton to be the best location for the college, but he added that a new charter was needed as well. On October 8, he wrote nearly identical letters to Jonathan Dickinson, Ebenezer Pemberton, and William Peartree Smith acknowledging receipt from Dickinson of a college catalog (long since lost) and suggesting that the three meet with him in Burlington for the purpose of devising "a lottery or anything else" to present to the Provincial Assembly "for the service of our infant college." "I say our infant college," Belcher explained, "because I am determined to adopt it for a child and to do everything in my power to promote and establish so noble an undertaking." Belcher could not know, of course, that on the day before he penned his letter to Dickinson, Dickinson had died. When he was so informed, he wrote the following note to Pemberton: "The death of that eminent servant of God, the learned and pious Dickinson, is a considerable rebuke of Providence, and is to remind us that we have such precious treasure in earthen vessels, and that our eyes and hearts must be lifted to the great head of the church, who holds the stars in his right hand. Then let us not despond or murmur."[54]

The presidency of the college and the college itself would be transferred to the Reverend Aaron Burr and to Newark. As our concern is with Dickinson, the history of the college need not detain us further except to mention that Dickinson's death did not alter Belcher's plans for the college. Belcher pushed forward, but not without resistance. He postponed his immediate plan for placing his lottery proposal before the New Jersey Assembly, due to the accumulation of other business before that body, and when he finally brought it to the Assembly, it was rejected. He pushed forward on the new charter as well. In this he was more successful, having it approved by the Provincial Council on September 14, 1748.[55]

Historian William A. Dod has written that the roots of the College of New Jersey can be traced to the influence of religion—an influence "so vital and so urgent" that no other influence could have brought about the same result. Ashbel Green has suggested, however, that the curriculum of the college was calculated to establish a solid basis for all the liberal professions and that it was accompanied by such religious and moral teaching and discipline "as were equally proper for all youth, whatever might be their prospects or character in future life." The two, of course, are not mutually exclusive positions, but surviving records suggest that even though Dickinson agreed with both, he was especially concerned with ministerial education.[56]

In a letter to Capt. Theophilus Howell dated January 30, 1747, Dickinson wrote, upon receipt of the charter but before the doors of the college actually opened that day, that he hoped the college would "prove as well a seminary of vital piety as of good literature" and that he especially sought to provide qualified ministerial candidates for the church's many vacancies. In a letter dated March 3, 1747, he wrote that the "great and chief design" of the college was the education of "pious and well qualified" ministerial candidates and "that vital piety may by that means be promoted in our churches." It may be that Dickinson, in his search for funding, was offering prospective donors what they wanted to hear and what they would be willing to support, but there can be little doubt that he meant what he said. Of the six students who graduated in the College of New Jersey's first class, that of 1748, five became Presbyterian ministers. Of the second class of seven, five became ministers.

Much like Harvard and Yale, however, the College of New Jersey was to be more than a seminary. The charters of Harvard and Yale clearly noted that they were to train men both for the ministry and for the state. The College of New Jersey's charter made no mention of training men for the ministry, and entrance to the college was to be without reference to any particular religious profession. That the trustees not only accepted but were committed to this liberal admission policy can be seen in a letter from Jonathan Dickinson to an unidentified person dated March 3, 1747, wherein he wrote: "This is a natural right that cannot be justly denied to any." As Aaron Burr wrote in a letter to Philip Doddridge in London, dated October 8, 1749, his first priority was religion. But, he added, this was due to the "importance of having men of real religion" not just in the pulpit but in the "public stations in life" other than the ministry. By the time eight classes had graduated, only 52 percent of the graduates became ministers, and the number was declining rapidly.[57]

The "General Account" of the College of New Jersey, prepared in 1752 for Tennent and Davies to take with them to Great Britain for their fund-raising campaign, put it this way: "It will suffice to say that the two principal objects the trustees had in view were science and religion. Their first concern was to cultivate the minds of the pupils in all those branches of erudition, which are generally taught in the universities abroad; and to perfect their design, their next care was to rectify the heart, by inculcating the great precepts of Christianity, in order to make them good."[58]

As the minutes of the trustees for the period from May to October

1747 have not survived, little is known of the college during the months of Jonathan Dickinson's presidency. Thomas Jefferson Wertenbaker has described it in its simplest terms: the president was Jonathan Dickinson, the tutor was Caleb Smith, the dorms were Dickinson's house and those of his neighbors, the library consisted of Dickinson's books, the lecture hall was Dickinson's parlor, and the refectory was his dining room.[59]

There is no record of admission requirements, of curriculum, or even of the number of students he and Smith taught. The public notice of May 1747 simply stated that admission would be offered to "all persons suitably qualified." Upon the occasion of the November 9, 1748, commencement, formal standards of admission to the College of New Jersey were adopted, and there is no reason to believe that they varied a great deal from those used by Dickinson only one year before. Aaron Burr stated, "None may expect to be admitted into the College but such as being examined by the President and Tutors shall be found able to render Virgil and Tully's Orations into English, and to turn English into true grammatical Latin, and so well acquainted with Greek as to render any part of the four Evangelists in that language into Latin or English, and to give the grammatical construction of the words."[60]

Most likely what was offered to the students of the College of New Jersey in 1747 in the way of a curriculum was what Dickinson had been offering the pupils of his classical school, which was drawn from what he had learned at Yale and from what was taught at Harvard. That, in turn, was patterned after what was being taught at universities in Great Britain such as at Cambridge's Emmanuel College, founded in 1584 to educate ministers in the Puritan tradition, or even at England's "dissenting academies," which had been established in the homes of Dissenting divines after the Restoration, when Dissenters were ousted from Oxford and Cambridge.[61]

The earliest references to the curriculum of the College of New Jersey by Dickinson's successor, Aaron Burr, refer to languages, the liberal arts and sciences, and theology. Assuming the school followed the pattern of other colleges of the time, that would include Latin, Greek, mathematics, astronomy, logic, rhetoric, and what were then known as natural philosophy and mental and moral philosophy. More specifically, Burr referred to recitations of Xenophon, Watts, and Cicero; the study of Horace and Virgil; work on Hebrew grammar, which he felt was being neglected at Yale, and on the Greek Testament; mastery of the syllogistic method; and courses in geography, rhetoric, ontology, and elementary mathematics.[62]

Neither is there any record of the exact number of students who entered the College of New Jersey in May 1747. Aaron Burr later wrote that at its inception the school included "some students" formerly in private schools, no doubt training for the ministry. Some, if not most of them, were already studying with Dickinson, but, as indicated in a letter written by Dickinson upon receipt of the college charter, he was expecting more students to be attracted to the college.[63]

Most estimates suggest that Dickinson and Smith taught between eight and ten students. The greatest number attributed to them is twenty. It is a matter of record that some twenty students enrolled in the college when it moved to Newark following Dickinson's death in October 1747 and that the first class to be prepared for graduation in May 1748 consisted of six students. No doubt most of those who graduated in October and quite likely others who were enrolled when the college moved to Newark had been Jonathan Dickinson's students.[64]

EPILOGUE

JONATHAN DICKINSON DIED on Wednesday, October 7, 1747, at 4 A.M., leaving his second wife, five daughters, and his son, Jonathan Jr. He was approaching his sixtieth year. Ebenezer Pemberton, his ministerial colleague and friend, wrote his death notice, which appeared on October 12, 1747, in both the *New York Weekly Post Boy* and the *New York Gazette*. He announced that Dickinson—"the eminently learned, faithful, and pious minister of the gospel, and President of the College of New Jersey"—had died of "a pleuritic illness."[1]

Dickinson's contemporaries remembered him as a scholar and a man of God or as a man who served both the mind and the soul. They described him as "a most solemn, weighty and moving preacher"; "industrious, indefatigable, and successful in his ministerial labors"; "serious but affable in his intercourse"; "courteous in his manners, and . . . sufficiently easy of access . . . [but] never tolerant towards undue liberties." They recognized him as a man "controlled by principle and impelled to action by high purposes"; a man "eminent for the warmth and strength of his devotional feelings," as well as for his "uniform consistency"; and a man of "calm temperament" whose "faculties and attainments were made to yield the very best results to a resolute will."[2] As Pemberton put it, "In [Dickinson] conspicuously appeared those natural and acquired moral and spiritual endowments which constitute a truly excellent and valuable man, a good scholar, an eminent divine, and a serious devout Christian. . . . He boldly appeared in the defense of the great and important truths of our most holy religion and the gospel doctrines of the free and sovereign grace of God. He was a zealous promoter of godly practice and godly living."[3]

In his eulogy, the Reverend John Pierson of Woodbridge, whom Dickinson had once publicly defended against the disaffected New Siders of his congregation, offered similar praise. As a gospel minister, Pierson explained, Dickinson was a man of "true and vital piety"; a man who made "the glory of God, the honor and interest of Christ, the spiritual good and eternal happiness of immortal souls, the great and governing design of his ministry"; and a man who persevered in his "unshaken resolution and unfainting constancy" in the face of whatever hardships and reproaches confronted him.

As a scholar in service to the church, Pierson described Dickinson as a man of "superior and elevated genius," who possessed intellectual powers "far above the common level." He hailed Dickinson as "no ordinary figure in the learned world" and "no stranger to the most celebrated authors therein," as well as a person who exercised "a due sagacious judgment of things," showed "a warm zeal in the cause of the truth," and was "very careful to hold fast" the truth when "many corrupt opinions and soul destroying errors" threatened to prevail.

Finally, Pierson recalled Dickinson's strength and courage as being second to none. For his efforts, Pierson explained, Dickinson bore the unreasonable reproaches, censures, and injurious treatment of others with "Christian meekness." Dickinson was "slow to anger," "knew how to rule his spirit," and was not of a "litigious disposition." He could sacrifice anything for peace except "truth and duty." Once truth and duty were challenged, Pierson continued, Dickinson insisted on "refuting pernicious errors" and on "defending and establishing important laboring truths of the gospel." In doing so, he employed "a clear cool thought and unwavering principle." He penetrated deeply into difficult and perplexing cases, and resolved them judiciously by confirming "truths by irrefragable arguments" in so "clear and advantageous light" that he "put gainsayers to confusion and silence."[4]

Not surprisingly, as they knew him best, Pemberton and Pierson well summarized, for their generation, Jonathan Dickinson's life, labors, and accomplishments. Some two and a half centuries later, I have sought to do the same for my generation. As noted at the start, my primary goal has been to provide the first intellectual biography of the man Alan Heimert and Perry Miller have called the "most powerful mind of his generation of American divines."[5] In doing so, however, I have emphasized Dickinson's role in early American Presbyterian history. Three points should be made on my taking this approach.

First, by emphasizing Dickinson's place in Presbyterian history, I did not intend to suggest that Dickinson's was a parochial point of view. I simply meant to underscore the important—if often neglected—point that, as with nearly every other leading divine of the time, Dickinson operated from a denominational base that gave rise to, and helped define his response to, those issues with which he would deal. His story, in other words, is unintelligible without reference to the history of that institution that nurtured and in turn was nurtured by him.

Second, it should be recalled that to be a Presbyterian leader was not to be relegated to the margins of colonial American society. Rather, it was to assume a position of considerable importance. Presbyterians constituted the second largest religious group in the British colonies. They were second only to New England Congregationalists, to whom, as we have seen, Dickinson was inextricably linked by both early training and later contacts. They were the largest group in the Middle Colonies, and both were part of the Reformed tradition to which most colonial Americans belonged.

And, third, although alluded to earlier, it should be underscored that the experience described herein was not unique to Presbyterians. Indeed, it was merely one of many groups that would eventually undergo such an ordeal, thereby providing what might be seen as a case study of the early American religious experience—a case study in which Dickinson played a key role.

As noted in the introduction to this study, Leonard Trinterud has shown that, in the first half of the eighteenth century, Presbyterians endured a "fiery ordeal of ecclesiastical controversy" out of which was born a new order, an American tradition. "The entire history of the [American Presbyterian] Church," Trinterud has written, "has been shaped by that which its founding fathers thought and did during its first half-century." It began with the transplanting to America of two religious groups similar in theology and polity but different in tradition and divergent in their allegiances. They sought to replicate in the wilderness their native churches, but in time they found common ground upon which to build an American understanding of Presbyterianism.[6]

What exactly constitutes the American religious understanding, of course, has been the subject of considerable debate. Common to most proposals, however, is the resolution of what has come to be seen as the classical dilemma not only of American religious history but of the American experience as a whole. How, the founding fathers of church and state must have asked, were they to create institutions that would satisfy America's simultaneous longing for freedom and need for order or, as it is currently phrased, America's seemingly irreconcilable obsession with individualism and need for commitment?[7]

It is the search for a resolution to that dilemma that underscores and ties together Dickinson's responses to the major ecclesiastical issues of the formative years of American Presbyterianism, each of which has been addressed in this book. In his first public debates with the Baptists, he defended infant baptism, not only because he believed it was scriptural and consistent with the teachings of the early church but because he was convinced it served as a cohesive force within the religious community. Two decades later, he defended the need for a more personal adult conversion experience, making it clear that membership in "God's visible household" was not enough to guarantee personal salvation.

In the subscription controversy, Dickinson fought to accommodate individual conscience in the matter of ministerial subscription to the Westminster Confession, only shortly thereafter to clearly establish the limits of that freedom within those boundaries needed to protect the religious community he had helped build. In his Anglican debates, Dickinson asserted Presbyterian legitimacy, at the same time that he defended its right to dissent from the established Church of England. In doing so, he called into question the very idea of union of church and state, and he advanced that line of reasoning that culminated in the creation of American denominationalism.

In his consideration of the issues raised by the Enlightenment, he argued that free will was not inconsistent with the Calvinist doctrine of God's sovereign free grace, that which bound together those of the Reformed tradition. At the same time he insisted that, properly understood, freedom as defined in the Reformed tradition provided the appropriate balance between the extremes of determinism and human agency, tyranny and absolute freedom. And, in his response to the Great Awakening, he became a proponent of the revival's potential to effect in the hearts of men the sanctifying influence of the spirit of God, necessarily an intensely personal experience, while he steadfastly opposed the individualistic antinomian extremes to which it tended. In sum, Dickinson sought, found, and institutionalized—in the genius of the New Side New York Synod he established—a renewed religious order encompassing both spiritual gratification and ecclesiastical order.[8]

Finally, the point should be made once again that Dickinson's ultimate success was achieved from a moderate position. Avoiding the extremes of those around him, thereby perhaps relegating himself to a less prominent place in history, Dickinson paved the way for the future of American Presbyterianism by moving forward in a progressive but cautious, evolving but consistent, and creative but institutionally responsible manner. Though hardly the "stuff" of legend, it may well be the substance of history—that which provided for the creation, out of diversity and adversity, of a new order.

NOTES

INTRODUCTION

1. Leonard J. Trinterud, *The Forming of an American Tradition: A Re-examination of Colonial Presbyterianism* (Freeport, N.Y.: Books for Libraries Press, 1949), 7. One of the earliest to offer a thesis similar to Trinterud's was Charles Augustus Briggs, in *American Presbyterianism: Its Origins and Early History* (New York: Scribner, 1885), 216. Among the most recent is Leigh Eric Schmidt, "Jonathan Dickinson and the Making of the Moderate Awakening," *American Presbyterians* 63 (winter 1985): 344.

2. Edwards and Erskine are quoted in several places, but both are in Edwin F. Hatfield, *History of Elizabeth, New Jersey* (New York: Carlton and Lanahan, 1868), 352. A topic that merits further research is Dickinson's reception, or the extent to which he was read and was influential, abroad. Given his prominence in the colonies and the surprisingly effective transatlantic ministerial/church network of the time, there can be little doubt that he was known. The extent to which he was read and the degree of his influence, however, are more difficult to assess. At least two of Dickinson's major works were published in Scotland. *Sermons and Tracts,* a collection of six pieces previously issued separately in the colonies, was published in Edinburgh in 1793. *Familiar Letters to a Gentleman upon a Variety of Seasonable and Important Subjects in Religion,* published in the colonies in 1745, appeared in Edinburgh in 1757 and was republished in Glasgow as late as 1829. On the transatlantic network of communication, see Susan O'Brien, "A Transatlantic Community of Saints: The Great Awakening and the First Evangelical Network, 1735-1755," *American Historical Review* 91 (Oct. 1986): 811-32.

3. Ashbel Green, *Discourses Delivered in the College of New Jersey* (Philadelphia: E. Littell, 1822), 13; Trinterud is quoted in Schmidt, "Jonathan Dickinson," 342; Alan Heimert and Perry Miller, eds., *The Great Awakening: Documents Illustrating the Crisis and Its Consequences* (Indianapolis: Bobbs-Merrill, 1967), xxxi.

4. Published works on Dickinson by Bryan F. Le Beau include "'The Acrimonious Spirit' among Baptists and Presbyterians in the Middle Colonies during the Great Awakening," *American Baptist Quarterly* 9 (Sept. 1990): 167-83; "Joseph Morgan's Sermon at the Ordination of Jonathan Dickinson and the Clerical Literature of Colonial New England and New Jersey," *New Jersey History* 109 (spring/summer 1991): 55-81; "The Subscription Controversy and Jonathan Dickinson," *Journal of Presbyterian History* 54 (fall 1976): 317-35

Other published studies include David C. Harlan, "The Travail of Religious Moderation: Jonathan Dickinson and the Great Awakening," *Journal of Presbyterian History* 61 (winter 1983): 411-26; Harlan, "A World of Double Visions and Second Thoughts: Jonathan Dickinson's *Display of God's Special Grace," Early American Litera-*

ture 21 (fall 1986): 118-30; Schmidt, "Jonathan Dickinson," 341-53; and Leslie W. Sloat, "Jonathan Dickinson and the Problem of Synodical Authority," *Westminster Theological Journal* 8 (June 1946): 149-65.

To these published works, should be added Keith Jordan Hardman, "Jonathan Dickinson and the Course of American Presbyterianism, 1717-1747" (Ph.D. diss., University of Pennsylvania, 1971); Herbert L. Samworth, "Those Astonishing Wonders of His Grace: Jonathan Dickinson and the Great Awakening" (Th.D. diss., Westminster Theological Seminary, 1988); and Philip W. Ott, "Christian Experience as Seen in the Writings of Jonathan Dickinson" (M.A. thesis, Princeton Theological Seminary, 1963).

5. See, for example, the necessary corrective for such studies offered by Harry S. Stout in *The New England Soul: Preaching and Religious Culture in Colonial New England* (New York: Oxford University Press, 1986), 4.

6. See Le Beau, "Subscription Controversy."

I. BECOMING ESTABLISHED

1. Edwin F. Hatfield, *History of Elizabeth, New Jersey* (New York: Carlton and Lanahan, 1868), 294-96; Nicholas Murray, *Notes, Historical and Biographical, Concerning Elizabeth Town, Its Eminent Men, Churches, and Ministers* (Elizabeth Town, N.J.: E. Sanderson, 1844), 53. As there is no record of his predecessor having resigned in 1704, Melyen probably shared the Elizabeth Town pulpit with John Harriman until Harriman died in 1705. Henry C. Ellison, *Church of the Founding Fathers of New Jersey: A History* (Cornish, Maine: Carbrook Press, 1964), 34-35. See also Mary E. Alward, "Early History of the First Presbyterian Church of Elizabeth, New Jersey," in *Proceedings of the Union County Historical Society* (Elizabeth, N.J.: Union County Historical Society, 1924), 155.

2. Richard Webster, *A History of the Presbyterian Church in America, from Its Origin until the Year 1760* (Philadelphia: Joseph M. Wilson, 1857), 358; Sylvester Judd, *History of Hadley: Including the Early History of Hatfield, South Hadley, Amherst, and Granby, Massachusetts* (Springfield, Mass.: H. R. Huntington, 1905), 34; Richard B. Sewall, *The Life of Emily Dickinson* (New York: Farrar, Straus and Giroux, 1987), 17; George Frisbie Whicher, *This Was a Poet: A Critical Biography of Emily Dickinson* (Amherst: Amherst College Press, 1992), 22-23. The lineage of poet Emily Dickinson has been traced to Nathaniel's second son (of nine), Samuel Dickinson.

3. For discussions of the Wethersfield strict Congregationalists and the Hartford controversy, see John Putnam Demos, *Entertaining Satan: Witchcraft and the Culture of Early New England* (New York: Oxford University Press, 1986), 349-51; Sewall, *Emily Dickinson,* 17.

Hatfield, *History of Elizabeth,* 326; William B. Sprague, "Jonathan Dickinson," in *Annals of the American Pulpit,* ed. William B. Sprague (New York: Robert Carter, 1868), 3:14; Franklin B. Dexter, "Jonathan Dickinson," in his *Biographical Sketches of the Graduates of Yale College* (New York: Henry Holt, 1885-1912), 1:45; John E. Pomfret, "Jonathan Dickinson," in *Dictionary of American Biography,* 5:301.

4. Jonathan Dickinson's grandfather, Nathaniel, served in 1667 on a committee to establish a grammar school in Hadley. Judd, *History of Hadley,* 55; Sewall, *Emily Dickinson,* 17.

5. Moses King, *King's Handbook of Springfield, Massachusetts* (Springfield: James D. Gill, 1884), 126-28.

6. Hatfield, *History of Elizabeth,* 326-27; Dexter, "Jonathan Dickinson," 1:45; William L. Kingsley, *Yale College: A Sketch of Its History* (New York: Henry Holt, 1879), 1:26.

7. Richard Warch, *School of the Prophets: Yale College, 1701-1740* (New Haven: Yale University Press, 1973), 48; Kingsley, *Yale College,* 1:26.

8. Warch, *School of the Prophets,* 48; Hatfield, *History of Elizabeth,* 326-27; Dexter, "Jonathan Dickinson," 1:45; Roland H. Bainton, *Yale and the Ministry: A History of Education for the Christian Ministry at Yale from the Founding in 1701* (New York: Harper, 1957), x; Ebenezer Baldwin, *Annals of Yale College* (New Haven: Hezekiah Howe, 1831), 10, 12, 19-20.

9. Bainton, *Yale and the Ministry,* 1; Warch, *School of the Prophets,* 12-14, 34.

10. Baldwin, *Annals of Yale College,* 25; Warch, *School of the Prophets,* 39-40, 192-93, 198-237, 244; Bainton, *Yale and the Ministry,* 7-8, 39-41; Kingsley, *Yale College,* 1:17, 25-26.

11. Kingsley, *Yale College,* 1:392-93; Dexter, "Jonathan Dickinson," 1:48. See Jonathan Dickinson, *Observations on that Terrible Disease Vulgarly Called the Throat Distemper with Advice as to the Method of Cure: In a Letter to a Friend* (Boston: S. Kneeland and T. Green, 1740); and Stephen Wickes, *History of Medicine in New Jersey and of Its Medical Men, from the Settlement of the Province to A.D. 1800* (Newark: Martin R. Dennis, 1879). On Dickinson's role as physician see Bryan F. Le Beau, "The 'Angelical Conjunction' Revisited: Another Look at the Preacher-Physician in Colonial America and the Throat Distemper Epidemic of 1735-1740," *Journal of American Culture* 18 (fall 1995): 1-12. Also see Patricia A. Watson, *The Angelical Conjunction: The Preacher-Physician of Colonial New England* (Knoxville: University of Tennessee Press, 1991).

12. Warch, *School of the Prophets,* 226-27, 192, 234-37.

13. Kingsley, *Yale College,* 2:15; For a standard source on the Puritan concept of covenant, see Perry Miller, *Errand into the Wilderness* (New York: Harper and Row, 1956), 48-98. See also George M. Marsden, *Religion and American Culture* (New York: Harcourt Brace Jovanovich, 1990), 49.

14. Warch, *School of the Prophets,* 195, 270; Baldwin, *Annals of Yale College,* 27.

15. Dexter, "Jonathan Dickinson," 1:45; Hatfield, *History of Elizabeth,* 327; Pomfret, "Jonathan Dickinson," 5:301.

16. Sprague, "Jonathan Dickinson," 3:14; David C. Harlan, "The Travail of Religious Moderation: Jonathan Dickinson and the Great Awakening," *Journal of Presbyterian History* 61 (winter 1983): 412; Judd, *History of Hadley,* 34. Abigail Dickinson married Thomas Ingersoll of nearby Westfield, Massachusetts. They had no children, By 1711 the couple had moved to Springfield where Abigail died in 1717. Dexter, "Jonathan Dickinson," 1:45; Henry M. Burt, *The First Century of the History of Springfield* (Springfield, Mass.: privately printed, 1899), 316-17.

17. Warch, *School of the Prophets,* 195-96.

18. Hatfield, *History of Elizabeth,* 327-28; Ellison, *Church of the Founding Fathers,* 36.

19. Hatfield, *History of Elizabeth,* 327-28; Sprague "Jonathan Dickinson," 3:14; Dexter, "Jonathan Dickinson," 1:45-46; Pomfret, "Jonathan Dickinson," 5:301; Everard Kempshall, *The Centennial of the Anniversary of the Burning of the Church Edifice of the First Church of Elizabeth, New Jersey: Caldwell and the Revolution: A Historical Sketch of the First Presbyterian Church of Elizabeth, Prior to and During the War of the Revolution* (Elizabeth: Elizabeth Daily Journal, 1881), 19-20; Ellison, *Church of the Founding Fathers,* 36.

20. For a comparison of Morgan's ordination sermon with others of the time see Bryan F. Le Beau, "Joseph Morgan's Sermon at the Ordination of Jonathan Dickinson and the Clerical Literature of Colonial New England and New Jersey," *New Jersey History* 109 (spring/summer 1991): 55-81. See also J. William T. Youngs Jr., "Congregational Clericalism: New England Ordination before the Great Awakening," *William and Mary Quarterly,* 3d ser., 31 (July 1974); 487-89; and James W. Schmotter, "The Irony of Clerical Professionalism: New England's Congregational Ministers and the Great Awakening," *American Quarterly* 31 (summer 1979): 151, 153.

21. Joseph Morgan, *The Great Concernment of Gospel Ordinances, Manifested from the Great Effect of the Well Improving or Neglect of Them* (New York: William and Andrew Bradford, 1712).

22. Murray, *Notes Concerning Elizabeth Town,* 53, 56; Webster, *Presbyterian Church in America,* 359; Ezra Hall Gillett, *History of the Presbyterian Church in the United States of America* (Philadelphia: Presbyterian Publishing Committee, 1864), 1:39, 46; Sprague, "Jonathan Dickinson," 3:14; Frederick Lewis Weis, "The Colonial Clergy of the Middle Colonies: New York, New Jersey, and Pennsylvania," in *Proceedings of the American Antiquarian Society* (Worcester, Mass.: American Antiquarian Society, 1957), 208; Alward, "First Presbyterian Church," 147, 158; Hatfield, *History of Elizabeth,* 329.

23. Abigail was born 16 June 1711; Jonathan Jr. 19 September 1713; Temperance on 11 May 1715; Joanna on 27 February 1717; Elizabeth on 3 March 1721; Mary on 15 October 1722; and Martha on 18 May 1725.

24. Murray, *Notes Concerning Elizabeth Town,* 45; Kempshall, *Burning of the Church Edifice,* 13-14; William T. Hanzsche, "New Jersey Molders of the American Presbyterian Church," *Journal of the Presbyterian Historical Society* 24 (June 1946): 71; Douglas Jacobsen, *An Unprov'd Experiment: Religious Pluralism in Colonial New Jersey* (Brooklyn: Carlson, 1991), 25-26; Theodore Thayer, *As We Were: The Story of Old Elizabethtown* (Elizabeth: Grassmann, 1964). In the final chapter it will be necessary to present a more detailed account of the controversy surrounding the purchase of lands in New Jersey by New Englanders.

25. Edwin Scott Gaustad, *Historical Atlas of Religion in America,* rev. ed. (New York: Harper and Row, 1976), 2; Hanzsche, "New Jersey Molders," 72-73; Thayer, *As We Were,* v, 6; Murray, *Notes Concerning Elizabeth Town,* 45-47; Kempshall, *Burning of the Church Edifice,* 3; Ellison, *Church of the Founding Fathers,* 38; Alward, "First Presbyterian Church," 147, 150, 153.

26. Hatfield, *History of Elizabeth,* 204; Keith Jordan Hardman, "Jonathan Dickinson and the Course of American Presbyterianism, 1717-1747" (Ph.D. diss., University of Pennsylvania, 1971), 5; Thayer, *As We Were,* 28.

27. Murray, *Notes Concerning Elizabeth Town,* 47-48; Alward, "First Presbyterian Church," 153; Hanzsche, "New Jersey Molders," 72; Alan Heimert and Andrew Delbanco, eds., *The Puritans in America: A Narrative Anthology* (Cambridge: Harvard University Press, 1985), 218; Hatfield, *History of Elizabeth,* 204-5, 280-81.

28. Leonard J. Trinterud, *Forming of an American Tradition: A Re-examination of Colonial Presbyterianism* (Freeport, N.Y.: Books for Libraries Press, 1949), 7, 15-16; Warch, *School of the Prophets,* 57.

29. Trinterud, *American Tradition,* 16, 19. On the Half-way Covenant, see Robert G. Pope, *The Half-way Covenant: Church Membership in Puritan New England* (Princeton: Princeton University Press, 1969).

30. Trinterud, *American Tradition,* 16, 18, 29.

31. Warch, *School of the Prophets,* 55-57; Williston Walker, *The Creeds and Platforms of Congregationalism* (Boston: Pilgrim Press, 1969), 495-504.

32. *Records of the Presbyterian Church in the United States of America,* ed. William H. Roberts (Philadelphia: Presbyterian Board of Publication and Sabbath School Work, 1904), vi; Trinterud, *American Tradition,* 31.

33. Trinterud, *American Tradition,* 33. By 1750, two Congregational churches remained in New Jersey; fifty-one churches were Presbyterian. Gaustad, *Historical Atlas of Religion,* app. B.

34. Trinterud, *American Tradition,* 34.

35. *Records,* 39, 43; Sprague, "Jonathan Dickinson," 3:14.

36. *Records,* 45, 48, 49, 53; Kempshall, *Burning of the Church Edifice,* 20; Ellison, *Church of the Founding Fathers,* 36; Pomfret, "Jonathan Dickinson," 5:301.

37. Trinterud, *American Tradition,* 330-31; Pomfret, "Jonathan Dickinson," 5:301; *Records,* 56, 59, 64; Hatfield, *History of Elizabeth,* 331.

38. Jonathan Dickinson, *Remarks upon Mr. Gale's Reflections on Mr. Wall's History of Infant Baptism: In a Letter to a Friend* (New York: T. Wood, 1721), 3-4.

39. Peter O. Wacker, *Land and People: A Cultural Geography of Preindustrial New Jersey: Origins and Settlement Patterns* (New Brunswick, N.J.: Rutgers University Press, 1975), 186; Gaustad, *Historical Atlas of Religion,* 10; Robert G. Torbet, *A History of the Baptists* (Philadelphia: Judson Press, 1950), 221; William H. Brackney, ed., *Baptist Life and Thought, 1600-1980: A Source Book* (Valley Forge, Penn.: Judson Press, 1983), 109.

40. Walter B. Shurden, "The Baptist Association in Colonial America, 1707-1814," in *Perspectives in Churchmanship: Essays in Honor of Robert G. Torbet,* ed. David M. Scholer (Macon, Ga.: Mercer University Press, 1986), 106; John T. Christian, *A History of the Baptists of the United States: From the First Settlement of the Country to the Year 1845* (Nashville: Sunday School Board of the Southern Baptist Convention, 1926), 24-25; Brackney, *Baptist Life and Thought,* 15, 23, 119.

41. William G. McLoughlin, *New England Dissent, 1630-1833: The Baptists and the Separation of Church and State* (Cambridge: Harvard University Press, 1971), 1:6, 28; Christian, *Baptists of the United States,* 25, 44; Albert H. Newman, *A History of the Baptist Churches in the United States* (New York: Scribner, 1915), 79-88; Jesse L. Boyd, *A History of Baptists in America prior to 1845* (New York: American Press, 1957), 22, 31; Robert C. Newman, *Baptists and the American Tradition* (Des Plaines, Ill.: Regular Baptist Press, 1976), 9; Gaustad, *Historical Atlas of Religion,* 3, 10; Torbet, *A History of the Baptists,* 221.

42. Christian, *Baptists of the United States,* 79, 126-27; Kenneth Silverman, *The Life and Times of Cotton Mather* (New York: Harper and Row, 1984), 299-306.

43. Norman H. Maring, *Baptists in New Jersey: A Study in Transition* (Valley Forge, Penn.: Judson Press, 1964), 13-17; John E. Pomfret, *Colonial New Jersey: A History* (New York: Scribner, 1973), 115-16; Henry C. Vedder, *A History of the Baptists in the Middle States* (Philadelphia: American Baptist Publication Society, 1898), 41-42, 44-45, 70-71; Torbet, *A History of the Baptists,* 219, 226, 230; Christian, *Baptists of the United States,* 89, 94, 149; H. K. Neely, "Baptist Beginnings in the Middle Colonies, 1684-1776," in *The Lord's Free People in a Free Land,* ed. William R. Estep (Fort Worth, Tex.: Southwestern Baptist Theological Seminary, 1976), 27-29, 31, 35-36; Morgan Edwards, ed., *Materials Towards a History of the Baptists* (1770, 1792; rpt. Danielsville, Ga.: Heritage Papers, 1984), 1:79, 80-98; Hardman, "Dickinson and American Presbyterianism," 66; Brackney, *Baptist Life and Thought,* 117; John B. Frantz, "Religion

in the Middle Colonies: A Model for the Nation," *Journal of Regional Cultures* 2 (fall/winter 1982): 14.

44. Brackney, *Baptist Life and Thought,* 25, 97-98; Torbet, *A History of the Baptists,* 219, 232; William H. Brackney, *The Baptists* (Westport, Conn.: Greenwood Press, 1988), 67; Maring, *Baptists in New Jersey,* 37; R. Newman, *Baptists and the American Tradition,* 10. See also A. Newman, *Baptist Churches,* 38-47, 48-56.

45. Thomas Cooper, "William Wall," in *The Dictionary of National Biography,* 20:554; William Wall, *The History of Infant Baptism,* vols. 1 and 2 in *The History of Infant Baptism, Together with Mr. Gale's Reflections and Dr. Wall's Defense,* ed. Henry Cotton (Oxford: Oxford University Press, 1836), 1:vi, viii-ix (hereafter pages will be cited in the text); William Wall, *A Conference between two Men that had Doubts about Infant Baptism* (London: Joseph Downing, 1706).

46. Cooper, "William Wall," 554; James McMullen Rigg, "John Gale," in *Dictionary of National Biography,* 7:814.

47. John Gale, *Reflections on Mr. Wall's History of Infant Baptism,* vol. 3 in *The History of Infant Baptism, Together with Mr. Gale's Reflections and Dr. Wall's Defense,* 14, 15, 22.

48. Ibid., 3:95, 147, 190, 210, 216, 242-43, 264, 405, 419.

49. Ibid., 3:425-26.

50. Ibid., 3:60-61, 569-70.

51. See McLoughlin, *New England Dissent,* 1:29; Christian, *Baptists of the United States,* 167-68.

52. Dickinson cited Galatians 3:14 and 29 and Romans 4:11-13 and 11:17-20. Dickinson, *Remarks upon Mr. Gale's Reflections,* 49-50, 52-53.

2. ACCOMMODATING FREEDOM OF CONSCIENCE

1. *Records of the Presbyterian Church in the United States of America,* ed. William H. Roberts (Philadelphia: Presbyterian Board of Publication and Sabbath School Work, 1904), 68.

2. Edward A. Dowey, *A Commentary on the Confession of 1967 and An Introduction to the "Book of Confessions"* (Philadelphia: Westminster Press, 1968), 216.

3. The Westminster Standards are reprinted in vol. 3 of Philip Schaff's *Creeds of Christendom* (New York: Harper, 1919).

4. Robert Ellis Thompson, *A History of the Presbyterian Churches in the United States* (New York: Christian Literature, 1895), 26; Marilyn J. Westerkamp, *Triumph of the Laity: Scots-Irish Piety and the Great Awakening, 1625-1760* (New York: Oxford University Press, 1988), 13, 78, 80, 87; Richard Webster, *A History of the Presbyterian Church in America, from Its Origin until the Year 1760* (Philadelphia: Joseph M. Wilson, 1857), 97; Leonard J. Trinterud, *The Forming of an American Tradition: A Re-examination of Colonial Presbyterianism* (Freeport, N.Y.: Books for Libraries Press, 1949), 41-42; Alexander Blaikie, *A History of Presbyterianism in New England* (Boston: Alexander Moore, 1881), 58.

5. Webster, *Presbyterian Church in America,* 99, 103; Trinterud, *American Tradition,* 42; Elizabeth I. Nybakken, "New Light on the Old Side: Irish Influences on Colonial Presbyterianism," *Journal of American History* 68 (March 1982): 819; Westerkamp, *Triumph of the Laity,* 89, 98.

6. This movement of Scot and Ulster Scot Presbyterianism is explained in

Trinterud, *American Tradition,* 15-37. See also Henry H. Ford, *The Scotch-Irish in America* (New York: Peter Smith, 1944); and Wayland Dunaway, *The Scotch-Irish of Colonial Pennsylvania* (Chapel Hill: University of North Carolina Press, 1944).

7. The Cambridge and Savoy Platforms are explained in Williston Walker, *The Creeds and Platforms of Congregationalism* (Boston: Pilgrim Press, 1969). For a discussion of platforms and subscription in England and New England, see C. Gordon Bolan, *The English Presbyterians in New England* (Boston: Alexander Moore, 1882); and Blaikie, *A History of Presbyterianism in New England.* Alan Heimert and Perry Miller, eds., *The Great Awakening: Documents Illustrating the Crisis and Its Consequences* (Indianapolis: Bobbs-Merrill, 1967), xxxii.

8. Charles Hodge, *The Constitutional History of the Presbyterian Church in the United States of America* (Philadelphia: William S. Martien, 1839), 1:98-100, 130; Trinterud, *American Tradition,* 30.

9. See, for example, *Records,* 63, 65-67; Trinterud, *American Tradition,* 38.

10. Lawrence E. Brynestad, "The Great Awakening in the New England and Middle Colonies," pt. 1, *Journal of the Presbyterian Historical Society* 14 (June 1930): 85; James Hastings Nichols, "Colonial Presbyterianism Adopts Its Standards," *Journal of the Presbyterian Historical Society* 34 (March 1956): 56.

11. Included in Webster, *Presbyterian Church in America,* 99-100.

12. Ibid., 320, 326, 328-30; Ezra Hall Gillett, *History of the Presbyterian Church in the United States of America* (Philadelphia: Presbyterian Publishing Committee, 1864), 1:38-39, 44-45; *Records,* 67, 73; Alan Heimert and Andrew Delbanco, eds., *The Puritans in America: A Narrative Anthology* (Cambridge: Harvard University Press, 1985), 383-84; Trinterud, *American Tradition,* 23.

13. Nichols, "Colonial Presbyterianism," 56; Nybakken, "New Light on the Old Side," 815; David C. Harlan, "The Travail of Religious Moderation: Jonathan Dickinson and the Great Awakening," *Journal of Presbyterian History* 61 (winter 1983): 412; Keith Jordan Hardman, "Jonathan Dickinson and the Course of American Presbyterianism, 1717-1747" (Ph.D. diss., University of Pennsylvania, 1971; Westerkamp, *Triumph of the Laity,* 150.

14. Jonathan Dickinson, *A Sermon Preached at the Opening of the Synod at Philadelphia, September 19, 1722* (Boston: T. Fleet, for S. Gerish, 1723).

15. *Records,* 73-74.

16. Hodge, *Constitutional History,* 1:114, 144; Nichols, "Colonial Presbyterianism," 56.

17. *Records,* 76, 78-79; Maurice W. Armstrong et al., eds., *The Presbyterian Enterprise: Sources of American Presbyterian History* (Philadelphia: Westminster Press, 1956), 21-22.

18. Nichols, "Colonial Presbyterianism," 57; Webster, *Presbyterian Church in America,* 102.

19. The text of Thomson's proposal is not in the synod records. It is included in John Thomson, *An Overture Presented to the Synod* (Philadelphia: Franklin and Meredith, 1729), 31-32. See also Charles Augustus Briggs, *American Presbyterianism: Its Origins and Early History* (New York: Scribner, 1885), 211; Webster, *Presbyterian Church in America,* 103.

20. "Records of the Presbytery of New Castle upon Delaware," pt. 5, *Journal of the Presbyterian Historical Society* 15 (Dec. 1932): 178.

21. Heimert and Miller, *Great Awakening,* 110-11; *Records,* 91.

22. Jonathan Dickinson, *Remarks upon a Discourse Intitled An Overture Presented to the Reverend Synod of Dissenting Ministers Sitting in Philadelphia, in the Month of September, 1728* (New York: J. Peter Zenger, 1729).

23. Andrews's letter is included in Webster, *Presbyterian Church in America,* 105-6.

24. Ibid., 108; Hardman, "Dickinson and American Presbyterianism," 62. Craighead's brother, Robert, had been moderator of the Irish synod that adopted the Pacific Acts in 1720. Nichols, "Colonial Presbyterianism," 55.

25. Hardman, "Dickinson and American Presbyterianism," 67; *Records,* 94-95. By way of example, one of the excluded sections of chapter 23 authorized civil magistrates, indeed made it their duty, to suppress "all blasphemies and heresies, all corruptions and abuses in worship and discipline." Nicols, "Colonial Presbyterianism," 64. The Reverend Daniel Elmer, recently arrived from New England, was not prepared to subscribe, but he did so in 1730.

26. Webster, *Presbyterian Church in America,* 107; *Records,* 94-95; Trinterud, *American Tradition,* 48-52.

With the exception of E. H. Gillett and Leslie Sloat, who have proclaimed John Thomson the victor, most historians agree with the preceding analysis, which suggests that the Adopting Act of 1729 was a compromise attributable, in large part, to Jonathan Dickinson. See, for example, Gillett, "Adoption of the Confession of Faith," *Biblical Repertory and Princeton Review* 30 (Oct. 1858): 682-84; Leslie W. Sloat, "Jonathan Dickinson and the Problem of Synodical Authority," *Westminster Theological Journal* 8 (June 1946): 162-65; Hodge, *Constitutional History,* 1:105, 180; Frederick W. Loetscher, "The Adopting Act," *Journal of the Presbyterian Historical Society* 13 (Dec. 1929): 342; and Trinterud, *American Tradition,* 48. While agreeing that the Adopting Act resulted from Dickinson's efforts, Elizabeth Nybakken has concluded that the compromise was more readily accepted by the Scots and Ulster Scots because it so closely followed the Irish Pacific Articles. Nybakken, "New Light on the Old Side," 816, 820-21.

27. Martin E. Lodge, "The Crisis of the Churches in the Middle Colonies, 1720-1750," *Pennsylvania Magazine of History and Biography* 95 (Apr. 1971): 210-11, 213-16. More recently, Patricia Bonomi has made much the same point in *Under the Cope of Heaven: Religion, Society, and Politics in Colonial America* (New York: Oxford University Press, 1986), 132, 134.

28. Hodge, *Constitutional History,* 1:189; Trinterud, *American Tradition,* 50.

29. *Records,* 98, 105-7. See also Hodge, *Constitutional History,* 1:173-75.

30. *Records,* 109-11.

31. Ibid., 115.

32. Ibid., 118-19.

33. Ibid., 126-27; Hodge, *Constitutional History,* 1:185; Webster, *Presbyterian Church in America,* 113.

34. Gillett, "Confession of Faith," 683-85; Ashbel Green, "Letter to Presbyterians," *Christian Advocate* 11 (Aug. 1833): 364, 366; Nichols, "Colonial Presbyterianism," 60; Sloat, "Synodical Authority," 162-65; Trinterud, *American Tradition,* 4, 49.

35. See, for example, Trinterud, *American Tradition,* 66-67.

36. *Records,* 100, 106-7, 136, 138-39.

37. Ibid., 97, 100, 102, 107, 113, 123, 131, 136, 144, 150, 160, 163, 166, 172, 178.

38. Ibid., 104-5, 108-9; Hodge, *Constitutional History,* 1:230-31; Melvin H.

Buxbaum, *Benjamin Franklin and the Zealous Presbyterians* (University Park: Pennsylvania State University Press, 1975), 93.

39. Hodge, *Constitutional History,* 1:231-32; *Records,* 121-22, 129-30, 132-33; Trinterud, *American Tradition,* 67.

40. George M. Marsden, *Fundamentalism and American Culture: The Shaping of Twentieth-Century Evangelicalism, 1870-1925* (New York: Oxford University Press, 1980), 110. See also Cedric B. Cowing, *The Great Awakening and the American Revolution: Colonial Thought in the Eighteenth Century* (Chicago: Rand McNally, 1971), 56; and Bonomi, *Under the Cope of Heaven,* 157-60.

3. DEFENDING THE NEED FOR LIMITS

1. Melvin H. Buxbaum, *Benjamin Franklin and the Zealous Presbyterians* (University Park: Pennsylvania State University Press, 1975), 93; Charles Hodge, *The Constitutional History of the Presbyterian Church in the United States of America* (Philadelphia: William S. Martien, 1839), 1:230; *Records of the Presbyterian Church in the United States of America,* ed. William H. Roberts (Philadelphia: Presbyterian Board of Publication and Sabbath School Work, 1904), 104-5; Merton A. Christensen, "Franklin on the Hemphill Trial: Deism versus Presbyterian Orthodoxy," *William and Mary Quarterly,* 3d ser., 10 (July 1953): 425.

2. *Records,* 109; Buxbaum, *Benjamin Franklin,* 81; Robert Ellis Thompson, *A History of the Presbyterian Churches in the United States* (New York: Christian Literature, 1895), 27-28; William S. Barker, "The Hemphill Case, Benjamin Franklin, and Subscription to the Westminster Confession," *American Presbyterians* 69 (winter 1991): 245; James Hastings Nichols, "Colonial Presbyterianism Adopts Its Standards," *Journal of the Presbyterian Historical Society* 34 (March 1956): 60.

3. Benjamin Franklin, *Some Observations on the Proceedings against the Reverend Mr. Hemphill; with a Vindication of His Sermons,* in vol. 2 of *The Papers of Benjamin Franklin,* ed. Leonard W. Labaree (New Haven: Yale University Press, 1960), 38-39; Franklin, "Dialogue between Two of the Presbyterians Meeting in This City," ibid., 27, editor's note; Christensen, "Franklin on the Hemphill Trial," 427n 13; Buxbaum, *Benjamin Franklin,* 94; Richard Webster, *A History of the Presbyterian Church in America, from Its Origin until the Year 1760* (Philadelphia: Joseph M. Wilson, 1857), 111; Barker, "Hemphill Case," 246.

4. Carl Van Doren, *Benjamin Franklin* (Westport, Conn.: Greenwood Press, 1973), 131-32; Nichols, "Colonial Presbyterianism," 61; Franklin, "Dialogue between Two Presbyterians," 27; Christensen, "Franklin on the Hemphill Trial," 424; Buxbaum, *Benjamin Franklin,* 82.

5. Franklin, *Observations,* 40; Webster, *Presbyterian Church in America,* 111; Andrews's letter is included in Christensen, "Franklin on the Hemphill Trial," 426; *Records,* 104-5.

6. Van Doren, *Benjamin Franklin,* 131-32; Esmond Wright, *Franklin of Philadelphia* (Cambridge, Mass.: Belknap Press, 1986).

7. Benjamin Franklin, *Autobiography,* ed. John Bigelow (1868; rpt. Garden City, N.Y.: Dolphin Books, n.d.), 169-70.

8. Buxbaum, *Benjamin Franklin,* 1; Alfred Owen Aldridge, *Benjamin Franklin and Nature's God* (Durham, N.C.: Duke University Press, 1947), 101.

9. Christensen, "Franklin on the Hemphill Trial," 424, 440; Buxbaum, *Benjamin Franklin*, 1-2, 29; See also Wright, *Franklin of Philadelphia*, 6; Ormond Seavey, *Becoming Benjamin Franklin: The Autobiography and the Life* (University Park: Pennsylvania State University Press, 1988), 156-57.

10. Franklin, "Dialogue between Two Presbyterians," 28-33; Buxbaum, *Benjamin Franklin*, 95-96.

11. Jedediah Andrews having disqualified himself, and Dickinson not being present, the remaining members of the originally appointed synod commission were James Anderson, John Thomson, George Gillespie, Robert Cross, John Pierson, Thomas Creaghead, and Ebenezer Pemberton. Joining them, as "correspondents," were David Evans, Richard Treat, Adam Boyd, Joseph Houston, Andrew Archbold, Robert Jamison, Thomas Evans, Alexander Hutchison, Robert Cathcart, Nathaniel Hubbel, Gilbert Tennent, William Tennent Sr., and William Tennent Jr. Barker, "Hemphill Case," 246-47; *Records*, 107; Franklin, *Observations*, 41-43.

12. Franklin, *Observations*, 37, 41-43; Christensen, "Franklin on the Hemphill Trial," 428-30.

13. Leonard J. Trinterud, *The Forming of an American Tradition: A Re-examination of Colonial Presbyterianism* (Freeport, N.Y.: Books for Libraries Press, 1949), 63; Nichols, "Colonial Presbyterianism," 61.

14. Ebenezer Pemberton, *A Sermon Preached before the Commission of the Synod at Philadelphia, April 20th, 1735* (New York: John Peter Zenger, 1735), 3.

15. In May 1735, the commission printed an extract of its minutes, consisting almost exclusively of samples from Hemphill's sermons and its notes on how they were evidence of the charges brought against him. Testimony by Hemphill, or on his behalf, was not included. Franklin, *Observations*, 46; Christensen, "Franklin on the Hemphill Trial," 430; Barker, "Hemphill Case," 247, Buxbaum, *Benjamin Franklin*, 97.

16. Christensen, "Franklin on the Hemphill Trial," 432; Franklin, *Observations*, 50-52.

17. Franklin, *Observations*, 52-57, 64.

18. Buxbaum, *Benjamin Franklin*, 101; Jonathan Dickinson, *A Vindication of the Reverend Commission of the Synod in Answer to Some Observations on Their Proceedings against the Reverend Mr. Hemphill* (Philadelphia: Andrew Bradford, 1735), 3 (hereafter pages will be cited in the text).

19. Dickinson included with each article those passages from Hemphill's sermons upon which he was condemned.

20. Ibid., 6; Christensen, "Franklin on the Hemphill Trial," 324, 433.

21. Dickinson, *A Vindication*, 47-48. Attached to *A Vindication* is the complete text of those extracts taken from Hemphill's sermons by the commission, as well as what Hemphill had asked to be added "for the better explication of his meaning." Dickinson wrote that the commission had not believed it was necessary to include the entire text when it first published its minutes, as they assumed the extracts were sufficient to show cause for the commission's findings.

22. *Records*, 116-17. Despite the commission's having suspended him from the pulpit, Hemphill preached at least two sermons in Philadelphia on 25 July 1735. Christensen, "Franklin on the Hemphill Trial," 432.

23. *Records*, 117. Richard Webster has written that George Gillespie, a member of the commission, published an attack on Hemphill entitled *A Treatise Against the Deists or Freethinkers: Proving the Necessity of a Revealed Religion*. This pamphlet, which Webster says cannot be located, was published in direct opposition to the wishes of the

synod, as it also included Gillespie's criticism of the commission's "leniency" in its conduct of the hearing. Buxbaum suggests that it was the text of a sermon preached sometime during the commission hearing, therefore grouping it with Pemberton's and Cross's as to its intent and effect. Webster, *Presbyterian Church in America,* 340; Buxbaum, *Benjamin Franklin,* 97; Christensen, "Franklin on the Hemphill Trial," 436.

24. *Records,* 117-19.

25. This author has concluded that Hemphill was responsible for the substance of *A Letter* and that Franklin wrote the preface. However, as the pamphlet is included among the published papers of Benjamin Franklin, in order to avoid confusion, in this and following references, Franklin will be noted as the author of the entire pamphlet. Benjamin Franklin, *A Letter to a Friend in the Country, Containing the Substance of a Sermon Preached at Philadelphia, in the Congregation of the Reverend Mr. Hemphill, Concerning Terms of Christian and Ministerial Communion,* in vol. 2 of *The Papers of Benjamin Franklin,* 65, editor's note.

26. Christensen, "Franklin on the Hemphill Trial," 433, 439. See also Buxbaum, *Benjamin Franklin,* 106.

27. Franklin, *A Letter to a Friend in the Country,* 66-67; Buxbaum, *Benjamin Franklin,* 106.

28. Franklin, *A Defense of Mr. Hemphill's Observations, or An Answer to the Vindication of the Reverend Commission,* in vol. 2 of *The Papers of Benjamin Franklin,* 90, editor's note, 94-95, 96-97, 113; Aldridge, *Benjamin Franklin,* 94; Christensen, "Franklin on the Hemphill Trial," 432; Buxbaum, *Benjamin Franklin,* 94, 107, 109.

29. Dickinson, *Remarks upon a Pamphlet, Intitled, A Letter to a Friend in the Country* (Philadelphia: Andrew Bradford, 1735), 2, 6, 14-15.

30. Obadiah Jenkins, *Remarks upon the Defense of the Reverend Mr. Hemphill's Observations: In a Letter to a Friend. Wherein the Orthodoxy of His Principles, the Excellency and Meekness of his Temper, and the Justice of His Complaints, against the Rev. Commission, Are Briefly Considered; and Humbly Proposed to the View of His Admirers* (Philadelphia: Andrew Bradford, 1735), 16, 19-21.

31. Franklin, *Autobiography,* 170; Franklin, *A Defense of Mr. Hemphill's Observations,* 91, editor's note; Aldridge, *Benjamin Franklin,* 99; Buxbaum, *Benjamin Franklin,* 105.

32. Franklin, *Autobiography,* 170; Wright, *Franklin of Philadelphia,* 49; Van Doren, *Benjamin Franklin,* 132.

33. Buxbaum, *Benjamin Franklin,* 113; Christensen, "Franklin on the Hemphill Trial," 433-34.

34. Martin Marty has suggested that this was Franklin's contribution to a "new American religion, or to what has become the nation's public religion." Martin E. Marty, *Pilgrims in Their Own Land: 500 Years of Religion in America* (New York: Penguin Books, 1986), 156-57.

35. Buxbaum, *Benjamin Franklin,* 98, 102, 113.

36. Nichols, "Colonial Presbyterianism," 61. Leonard Trinterud has argued that pro-subscriptionists may have used the Hemphill affair to advance their call for ironclad subscription, but that "in those presbyteries where the subscriptionist party was the strongest, ministerial discipline was the most lax and conditions generally the worst." Trinterud, *American Tradition,* 63.

37. William S. Barker has called Dickinson's *Vindication* "the most important document for our understanding of confessional subscription." Barker, "Hemphill Case," 248.

38. Douglas Jacobsen, *An Unprov'd Experiment: Religious Pluralism in Colonial New Jersey* (Brooklyn: Carlson, 1991), xvii-xviii, 117-18, 137-38.

4. DISSENTING ON MATTERS OF CHURCH AND STATE

1. Leonard J. Trinterud, *The Forming of an American Tradition: A Re-examination of Colonial Presbyterianism* (Freeport, N.Y.: Books for Libraries Press, 1949), 228; Arthur Lyon Cross, *The Anglican Episcopate and the American Colonies* (Hamden, Conn.: Archon Books, 1964), 1-2, 36-53, 88-113; Sydney E. Ahlstrom, *A Religious History of the American People* (New Haven: Yale University Press, 1972), 134.

2. Cross, *Anglican Episcopate,* 270-71; Nelson R. Burr, *The Anglican Church in New Jersey* (Philadelphia: Church Historical Society, 1954), 12; Ruth H. Bloch, "Religion and Ideological Change in the American Revolution," in *Religion and American Politics: From the Colonial Period to the 1980s,* ed. Mark A. Noll (New York: Oxford University Press, 1990), 44-61. See also Alan Heimert, *Religion and the American Mind: From the Great Awakening to the Revolution* (Cambridge: Harvard University Press, 1966) and Cedric B. Cowing, *The Great Awakening and the American Revolution: Colonial Thought in the Eighteenth Century* (Chicago: Rand McNally, 1971).

3. Rhys Isaac, *The Transformation of Virginia, 1740-1790* (Chapel Hill: University of North Carolina Press, 1982), 197; Jack P. Greene, *Pursuit of Happiness: The Social Development of Early Modern British Colonies and the Formation of American Culture* (Chapel Hill: University of North Carolina Press, 1988), 124, 139.

4. Trinterud, *American Tradition,* 231-32; Isaac, *Transformation of Virginia,* 148, 151. It is interesting to note, in terms of the possible connection to Dickinson's anti-Anglican activity, that on 20 September 1723, the Synod of Philadelphia asked Dickinson to visit Presbyterians in Virginia and to preach to them on as many Sabbaths as possible during the following year. There is no further reference to the trip, but because there is nothing in the synod records to indicate that he did not go, it is reasonable to assume that he did. The synod also appointed Dickinson and Robert Cross to write to the governor of Virginia on the matter of supplying those same people with ministers, but the contents of the letter were never recorded. *Records of the Presbyterian Church in the United States of America,* ed. William H. Roberts (Philadelphia: Presbyterian Board of Publication and Sabbath School Work, 1904), 76; Edwin F. Hatfield, *History of Elizabeth, New Jersey* (New York: Carleton and Lanahan, 1868), 333.

5. John Frederick Woolverton, *Colonial Anglicanism in North America* (Detroit: Wayne State University Press, 1984), 30-31; Cross, *Anglican Episcopate,* 36; Trinterud, *American Tradition,* 229.

6. Woolverton, *Colonial Anglicanism,* 19, 82, 84, 106, 125-26; Cross, *Anglican Episcopate,* 3-4, 12-23, 43, 58; Burr, *Anglican Church,* 154-56; Trinterud, *American Tradition,* 229.

7. Cross, *Anglican Episcopate,* 89-90, 98, 102; Burr, *Anglican Church,* 12; Edwin P. Tanner, "The Province of New Jersey, 1664-1778" (Ph.D. diss., Columbia University, 1908), 597.

8. In 1750 the numbers of Presbyterian churches reached thirty-five in New York, fifty-six in Pennsylvania, and fifty-one in New Jersey. Woolverton, *Colonial Anglicanism,* 28-29; Edwin Scott Gaustad, *Historical Atlas of Religion in America,* rev. ed. (New York: Harper and Row, 1976), 8, app. B.

9. Gaustad, *Historical Atlas of Religion,* 8; Peter O. Wacker, *Land and People: A Cultural Geography of Preindustrial New Jersey: Origins and Settlement Patterns* (New Brunswick, N.J.: Rutgers University Press, 1975), 186; Keith Jordan Hardman, "Jonathan Dickinson and the Course of American Presbyterianism, 1717-1747" (Ph.D. diss., University of Pennsylvania, 1971), 73; John E. Pomfret, *Colonial New Jersey: A History* (New York: Scribner, 1973), 113-14; Tanner, "Province of New Jersey," 582.

10. Woolverton, *Colonial Anglicanism* 16, 123; Joyce D. Goodfriend, "A New Look at Presbyterian Origins in New York City," *American Presbyterians* 67 (fall 1989): 199; Cross, *Anglican Episcopate,* 34.

11. Wacker, *Land and People,* 186; Hatfield, *History of Elizabeth,* 289; Tanner, "Province of New Jersey," 583; Burr, *Anglican Church,* 630; Trinterud, *American Tradition,* 28; Cross, *Anglican Episcopate,* 95; Woolverton, *Colonial Anglicanism,* 21.

12. Henry C. Ellison, *Church of the Founding Fathers of New Jersey: A History* (Cornish, Maine: Carbrook Press, 1964), 34; Hatfield, *History of Elizabeth,* 297-98; Thomas J. Wertenbaker, *The Founding of American Civilization: The Middle Colonies* (New York: Scribner, 1938), 133; Woolverton, *Colonial Anglicanism,* 17; Burr, *Anglican Church,* 4, 12, 54, 101, 152, 156, 522; Tanner, "Province of New Jersey," 584; Cross, *Anglican Episcopate,* 2, 93.

13. Ellison, *Church of the Founding Fathers,* 46c; *Records,* 356.

14. Ellison, *Church of the Founding Fathers,* 522; Hatfield, *History of Elizabeth,* 356-57, 360; Burr, *Anglican Church,* 522; Jonathan Dickinson, *A Brief Discourse upon the Divine Appointment of the Gospel Ministry, and the Methods of Its Conveyance, Thro' the Successive Ages of the Church* (Boston: J. Draper, for D. Henchman, 1738), 48; Samuel A. Clark, *The History of St. John's Church, Elizabeth Town, New Jersey: From the Year 1703 to the Present Time* (Philadelphia: J. B. Lippincott, 1857), 49.

15. Ellison, *Church of the Founding Fathers,* 46c, 46e.

16. Hatfield, *History of Elizabeth,* 332; Perry Miller, *The New England Mind: From Colony to Province* (Cambridge: Harvard University Press, 1953), 471; G. B. Rapelye, "William Vesey," in *Annals of the American Pulpit,* ed. William B. Sprague (New York: Robert Carter, 1869), 5:16; Woolverton, *Colonial Anglicanism,* 128-29.

17. In 1738 Checkley succeeded in being ordained, named a missionary of the Society for the Propagation of the Gospel, and assigned to St. John's Church in Providence, Rhode Island. James McMullen Rigg, "Charles Leslie," in *The Dictionary of National Biography,* 2:958-59; Jon Pahl, *Paradox Lost: Free Will and Political Liberty in American Culture, 1630-1760* (Baltimore: Johns Hopkins University Press, 1992), 63-64; John Checkley, *Choice Dialogues between a Godly Minister and an Honest Country-Man Concerning Election and Predestination. Detecting the False Principles of a Certain Man, Who Calls Himself a Presbyter of the Church of England* (Boston: n.p., 1720), 1-2; Woolverton, *Colonial Anglicanism,* 120; James Truslow Adams, "John Checkley," in *The Dictionary of American Biography,* 4:46.

18. John Checkley, *A Modest Proof of the Order and Government Settled by Christ and His Apostles in the Church* (Boston: Thomas Fleet, 1723), ii-iii (hereafter pages will be cited in the text).

19. Hardman, "Dickinson and American Presbyterianism," 90.

20. Jonathan Dickinson, *A Defense of Presbyterian Ordination, In Answer to a Pamphlet, Entitled, A Modest Proof of the Order and Government Settled by Christ in the Church* (Boston: Daniel Henchman, 1724), i-ii (hereafter pages will be cited in the text).

21. John Checkley, *A Defense of a Book Lately Re-Printed at Boston, Entitled, A Modest Proof of the Order and Government, Etc.* (Boston: T. Fleet, 1724), 53 (hereafter pages will be cited in the text).

22. Jonathan Dickinson, *Remarks upon the Postscript to the Defense of a Book Lately Re-printed at Boston, Entitled, A Modest Proof of the Order* (Boston: D. Henchman, 1724), 2-3.

23. Ibid., 17-18, 27.

24. John Checkley, *A Letter to Jonathan Dickinson* (Boston: n.p., 1725), 1-3 (hereafter pages will be cited in the text).

25. James Truslow Adams, "Samuel Johnson," in *The Dictionary of American Biography,* 118-19; Cross, *Anglican Episcopate,* 106-7.

26. Jonathan Dickinson, *The Scripture Bishop, or the Divine Right of Presbyterian Ordination and Government Considered in a Dialogue between Praelaticus and Eleutherius* (Boston: D. Henchman, 1732), i-ii, 1-4, 6-7.

27. Rapelye, "William Vesey," 16.

28. In his first letter, Johnson indicated that prior to his writing some conversation had taken place on the subject between him and Dickinson. In the second letter, he wrote that Dickinson had responded to his first letter on May 4—1725 presumably—but that Dickinson had indicated that he would take no further notice of what Johnson had to say on the subject. There is no record of any such meeting or correspondence between Johnson and Dickinson. They may have occurred, but the fabrication of such scenarios being quite common, chances are they did not. More likely, it was Johnson's response to Dickinson's comment that the Anglicans had failed to respond to his earlier defense of Presbyterian ordination. James Wetmore, *Eleutherius Enervatus; or, An Answer to a Pamphlet, Entitled, the Divine Right of Presbyterian Ordination. Done by Way of a Dialogue between Eusebius and Eleutherius* (New York: John Peter Zenger, 1733), 4; Timothy Cutler to the Reverend Dr. Gray, 8 November 1734, photostat collection, box 14, Massachusetts Historical Society, Boston. Samuel Johnson, "Letters upon This Subject, Some Time Ago Sent to the Supposed Author of the Pamphlet," in Wetmore, *Eleutherius Enervatus,* 56, 78.

29. Wetmore, *Eleutherius Enervatus,* 8-9, 11.

30. Ibid., 12-14.

31. Johnson, "Letters upon This Subject," 112, 114-15.

32. Charles Burroughs, "Arthur Browne," in *Annals of the American Pulpit,* 5:76-85. Cutler identified Arthur Browne as the author of *The Scripture Bishop.* See Timothy Cutler to the Reverend Dr. Gray, 8 November 1734. Arthur Browne, *The Scripture Bishop, or the Divine Right of Presbyterian Ordination and Government, Considered in a Dialogue between Praelaticus and Eleutherius, Examined in Two Letters to a Friend* (n.p.: n.p., 1733), 3-4.

33. Jonathan Dickinson, *The Scripture Bishop Vindicated. A Defense of the Dialogue between Prelaticus and Eleutherius, upon the Scripture Bishop, or the Divine Right of Presbyterian Ordination and Government* (Boston: S. Kneeland and T. Green for D. Henchman, 1733), 1-2, 14-16, 28, 33, 35, 39 (hereafter pages will be cited in the text).

34. "John Beach," in *Annals of the American Pulpit,* 5:82-83; Burr, *Anglican Church,* 56.

35. Tanner, "Province of New Jersey," 601; *Records,* 110, 115, 121; Wertenbaker, *Founding of American Civilization,* 130-31.

36. Jonathan Dickinson, *The Vanity of Human Institutions in the Worship of God* (New York: John Peter Zenger, 1736), i-iv; Hardman, "Dickinson and American Presbyterianism," 119.

37. Dickinson, *Vanity*, 30.

38. John Beach, *A Vindication of the Worship of God According to the Church of England, from the Aspersions Cast upon It by Mr. Jonathan Dickinson* (New York: William Bradford, 1736), 3-4, 7, 9, 11, 45, 49-53. The term *Brownism* refers to the English divine Robert Browne, whose works [e.g., *Reformation without Tarrying for Any* (1582)] encouraged the establishment of a congregational polity with its communion of the faithful, nonconformity, and, to many, separatism.

39. John Beach, *An Appeal to the Unprejudiced in a Supplement to The Vindication of the Worship of God According to the Church of England, from the Injurious and Uncharitable Reflections of Mr. Jonathan Dickinson* (Boston: n.p., 1737), 2, 5-9, 105-6; Jonathan Dickinson, *A Defense of a Sermon Preached at Newark, June 2, 1736, Entitled, The Vanity of Human Institutions in the Worship of God* (New York: John Peter Zenger, 1737), 3, 9-14; Jonathan Dickinson, *The Reasonableness of Nonconformity to the Church of England, in Point of Worship. A Second Defense of a Sermon, Preached at Newark, June 2, 1736, Entitled "The Vanity of Human Institutions in the Worship of God." Against the Exceptions of Mr. John Beach, in His Appeal to the Unprejudiced* (Boston: S. Kneeland and T. Green, 1738), i, 13-16, 38, 41, 121-22. In 1738 Dickinson wrote *A Brief Discourse upon the Divine Appointment of the Gospel Ministry, and the Methods of Its Conveyance, Thro' the Successive Ages of the Church.* As the title suggests, it encompassed many of the same theological issues, but it was not intended to be part of the public debate.

40. Trinterud, *American Tradition*, 230; Thomas J. Curry, *The First Freedoms: Church and State in America to the Passage of the First Amendment* (New York: Oxford University Press, 1986), 113-14.

41. Excerpts from the Dissenters' Confession of 1596 were taken from Barrie White, "Early Baptist Arguments for Religious Freedom: Their Overlooked Agenda," *Baptist History and Heritage* 24 (Oct. 1989): 3.

42. Curry, *First Freedoms*, 113-14.

5. ARGUING FOR THE REASONABLENESS OF CHRISTIANITY

1. Sydney E. Ahlstrom, *A Religious History of the American People* (New Haven: Yale University Press, 1972), 350-51.

2. Jon Pahl, *Paradox Lost: Free Will and Political Liberty in American Culture, 1630-1760* (Baltimore: Johns Hopkins University Press, 1992), 119. Dickinson's influence on Edwards's *Freedom of the Will* has been noted in the preceding chapter.

3. Ibid., xi-xii, 6, 12-13.

4. Norman S. Fiering, "Will and Intellect in the New England Mind," *William and Mary Quarterly*, 3d ser., 29 (Oct. 1972): 516-17.

5. Pahl, *Paradox Lost*, 6-8.

6. Fiering, "Will and Intellect," 516-17, 553. See also Jonathan Edwards, *A Strict Inquiry into the Freedom of the Will*, ed. Paul Van Buren (New Haven: Yale University Press, 1957), 147.

7. Norman S. Fiering, *Jonathan Edwards's Moral Thought and Its British Context* (Chapel Hill: University of North Carolina Press, 1981), 14, 35-36; James Hoopes, "Jonathan Edwards's Religious Psychology," *Journal of American History* 69 (March 1983): 850.

8. Ahlstrom, *A Religious History*, 353; Charles Gray Shaw, "The Enlightenment," in *Encyclopedia of Religion and Ethics*, 5:313-14; David C. Harlan, "The Travail

of Religious Moderation: Jonathan Dickinson and the Great Awakening," *Journal of Presbyterian History* 61 (winter 1983): 412; Hoopes, "Jonathan Edwards," 850.

9. John Frederick Woolverton, *Colonial Anglicanism in North America* (Detroit: Wayne State University Press, 1984), 103; Keith Jordan Hardman, "Jonathan Dickinson and the Course of American Presbyterianism, 1717-1747" (Ph.D. diss., University of Pennsylvania, 1971), 280.

10. Leigh Eric Schmidt, "Jonathan Dickinson and the Making of the Moderate Awakening," *American Presbyterians* 63 (winter 1985): 347, 353n 34; Henry F. May, *The Enlightenment in America* (New York: Oxford University Press, 1976), 26; John Corrigan, "Catholick Congregational Clergy and Public Piety," *Church History* 60 (June 1991): 210-22.

11. Jonathan Dickinson, *The Reasonableness of Christianity, in Four Sermons, Wherein the Being and Attributes of God, the Apostasy of Man, and the Credibility of the Christian Religion Are Demonstrated by Rational Considerations. And the Divine Mission of Our Blessed Savior Proved by Scripture Arguments, Both from the Old Testament and the New; and Vindicated Against the Most Important Objections, Whether of Ancient or Modern Infidels* (Boston: S. Kneeland and T. Green, 1732), title page.

12. Corrigan, "Catholick Congregational Clergy," 210; Dickinson, *Reasonableness of Christianity,* i, iii, v-vi. Page numbers for *Reasonableness* will be cited hereafter in the text.

13. In *Reasonableness,* Dickinson employed almost exclusively the first-person plural and its possessive form when referring to man. That usage will be retained hereafter to a greater extent than it has thus far.

14. May, *Enlightenment in America,* 13. Schmidt, "Jonathan Dickinson," 347.

15. Schmidt, "Jonathan Dickinson," 353n 39. 248.

16. Woolverton, *Colonial Anglicanism,* 103; Jonathan Dickinson, *Familiar Letters to a Gentleman, upon a Variety of Seasonable and Important Subjects in Religion* (Boston: Rogers and Fowle, 1745), i-iii. Page numbers for *Familiar Letters* will be cited hereafter in the text.

17. The reader will recall our earlier discussion of the likelihood that Dickinson kept a journal, but that if he did, it has been lost.

6. WELCOMING THE AWAKENING

1. Alan Heimert and Perry Miller, eds., *The Great Awakening: Documents Illustrating the Crisis and Its Consequences* (Indianapolis: Bobbs-Merrill, 1967), xiii, xxxiv; Charles Hartshorn Maxson, *The Great Awakening in the Middle Colonies* (Gloucester, Mass.: Peter Smith, 1958), 2; Leigh Eric Schmidt, "Jonathan Dickinson and the Making of the Moderate Awakening," *American Presbyterians* 63 (winter 1985): 341; J. M. Bumsted and John E. Van de Wetering, *What Must I Do to Be Saved? The Great Awakening in Colonial America* (Hinsdale, Ill.: Dryden Press, 1976), 102; Martin E. Lodge, "The Great Awakening in the Middle Colonies" (Ph.D. diss., University of California at Berkeley, 1964), 158, 187, 201, 271. The most persuasive voice in opposition to those who would label the First Great Awakening an intercolonial movement has been Jon Butler. See, for example, his "Enthusiasm Described and Decried: The Great Awakening as Interpretive Fiction," *Journal of American History* 69 (Sept. 1982): 306-8. On the transatlantic evangelical network, see Susan O'Brien, "A Transatlantic Community of Saints: The Great Awakening and the First Evangelical Network, 1735-1755," *American Historical Review* 91 (Oct. 1986): 811-32.

2. Maxson, *Great Awakening*, 24; Leonard J. Trinterud, *The Forming of an American Tradition: A Re-examination of Colonial Presbyterianism* (Freeport, N.Y.: Books for Libraries Press, 1949), 42; Schmidt, "Jonathan Dickinson," 351.

3. David C. Harlan, "The Travail of Religious Moderation: Jonathan Dickinson and the Great Awakening," *Journal of Presbyterian History* 61 (winter 1983): 411-12, 416. See also Bumsted and Van de Wetering, *What Must I Do to Be Saved?* 115; and Lodge, "Great Awakening," 275.

4. Schmidt, "Jonathan Dickinson," 341-42. See also Maxson, *Great Awakening*, 25; and Herbert L. Samworth, "Those Astonishing Wonders of His Grace: Jonathan Dickinson and the Great Awakening" (Th.D. diss., Westminster Theological Seminary, 1988), 114.

5. Lawrence E. Brynestad, "The Great Awakening in the New England and Middle Colonies," pt. 1, *Journal of the Presbyterian Historical Society* 14 (June 1930): 87-88; Bumsted and Van de Wetering, *What Must I Do to Be Saved?* 55; Lodge, "Great Awakening," 91; Maxson, *Great Awakening*, 3-4; John B. Frantz, "The Awakening of Religion among the German Settlers in the Middle Colonies," *William and Mary Quarterly*, 3d ser., 33 (Apr. 1976): 266; Trinterud, *American Tradition*, 54.

6. Lodge, "Great Awakening," 134; Maxson, *Great Awakening*, 14, 17, 28; Milton J. Coalter Jr., *Gilbert Tennent, Son of Thunder: A Case Study of Continental Pietism's Impact on the First Great Awakening in the Middle Colonies* (Westport, Conn.: Greenwood Press, 1986), 1.

7. Jonathan Dickinson participated in the ordination of John Tennent at Freehold in 1730 and composed an elegy in his memory, which later was inscribed on his tombstone. Trinterud, *American Tradition*, 58-64; Bumsted and Van de Wetering, *What Must I Do to Be Saved?* 66.

8. Marilyn J. Westerkamp, *Triumph of the Laity: Scots-Irish Piety and the Great Awakening, 1625-1760* (New York: Oxford University Press, 1988), 14; Leigh Eric Schmidt, *Holy Fairs: Scottish Communions and American Revivals in the Early Modern Period* (Princeton: Princeton University Press, 1989), 3. For another perspective on the Scottish connection, see Michael J. Crawford, "New England and the Scottish Religious Revivals of 1742," *American Presbyterians* 69 (spring 1991): 23-32.

9. Lodge, "Great Awakening," 130-31; Maxson, *Great Awakening*, 22; Trinterud, *American Tradition*, 60.

10. *Records of the Presbyterian Church in the United States of America*, ed. William H. Roberts (Philadelphia: Presbyterian Board of Publication and Sabbath School Work, 1904), 105, 111.

11. Ibid., 134-35. See also Trinterud, *American Tradition*, 69, 73; Charles Hodge, *The Constitutional History of the Presbyterian Church in the United States of America* (Philadelphia: William S. Martien, 1839), 1:247; Lodge, "Great Awakening," 156.

12. Lodge, "Great Awakening," 158-59; Hodge, *Constitutional History*, 1:240, 250; S. D. Alexander, *The Presbytery of New York, 1738 to 1888* (New York: Anson D. F. Randolph, 1887), 3-4; *Records*, 138, 141-42; Trinterud, *American Tradition*, 74. See also Keith Jordan Hardman, "Jonathan Dickinson and the Course of American Presbyterianism, 1717-1747" (Ph.D. diss., University of Pennsylvania, 1971), 175.

13. Trinterud, *American Tradition*, 84, 87, 98; Coalter, *Gilbert Tennent*, 59.

14. Jonathan Dickinson, *The Danger of Schisms and Contentions with Respect to the Ministry and Ordinances of the Gospel* (New York: John Peter Zenger, 1739).

15. Harlan, "Travail of Religious Moderation," 413.

16. Trinterud, *American Tradition*, 87; Schmidt, "Jonathan Dickinson," 353n 50.

17. Richard L. Bushman, ed., *The Great Awakening: Documents on the Revival of Religion, 1740-1745* (New York: Atheneum, 1970), 19.

18. David T. Morgan, "A Most Unlikely Friendship: Benjamin Franklin and George Whitefield," *Historian* 47 (Feb. 1985): 208-18; Trinterud, *American Tradition*, 86; Lodge, "Great Awakening," 170.

19. Heimert and Miller, *Great Awakening*, xxiv; Bumsted and Van de Wetering, *What Must I Do to Be Saved?* 70; Frank Lambert, "The Great Awakening as Artifact: George Whitefield and the Construction of Intercolonial Revival, 1739-1745," *Church History* 60 (June 1991): 233. See also Frank Lambert, "'Pedlar in Divinity': George Whitefield and the Great Awakening, 1737-1745," *Journal of American History* 77 (Dec. 1990): 812-37.

20. On Whitefield's opposition, see the *Pennsylvania Gazette,* 13 December 1739; the *Boston Weekly News-Letter,* 22 November 1739, 30 November 1739, and 6 December 1739; and Trinterud, *American Tradition,* 87-88. Bushman, *Great Awakening,* 20.

21. George Whitefield, *George Whitefield's Journals, 1737-1741,* ed. William V. Davis (Gainesville, Fla.: Scholars Facsimiles and Reprints, 1969), 334, 347. Nicholas Murray has written that Gilbert Tennent preached from Jonathan Dickinson's pulpit. It may have been during this visit, but he offers no date, and no record has survived of the event. Murray, *Notes, Historical and Biographical, Concerning Elizabeth Town, Its Eminent Men, Churches, and Ministers* (Elizabeth Town, N.J.: E. Sanderson, 1844), 43.

22. Whitefield, *Journals,* 347-48.

23. Jonathan Dickinson to Thomas Foxcroft, 24 May 1740, Foxcroft Collection, Firestone Library, Princeton University.

24. Jonathan Dickinson, "Who Is on the Lord's Side?" manuscript, 1739(?), Foxcroft Collection; Harlan, "Travail of Religious Moderation," 414. For a brief review of the pattern, or morphology, of the Puritan conversion experience, see Murray G. Murphey, "The Psychodynamics of Puritan Conversion," *American Quarterly* 31 (summer 1979): 135-47.

25. Dickinson, "Who Is on the Lord's Side?" 1-2 (page numbers hereafter noted in text).

26. Jonathan Dickinson, *A Call to the Weary and Heavy Laden to Come unto Christ for Rest* (New York: William Bradford, 1740), 3 (page numbers hereafter noted in text).

27. The direct quote is from Romans 6:14.

28. This author is aware, and does not wish to challenge those who would argue, that *Sinners in the Hands of an Angry God* may not be representative of Edwards's evangelical approach. The comparison offered here is to that sermon alone.

29. Dickinson, as many other evangelicals, was concerned with, and often addressed directly, the youth of his congregation. Of the young, he noted in *A Call to the Weary,* he had more hope than of the others, as "it has been a constant observation" that most of those brought to a saving interest in Christ are converted in their youth. Leigh Eric Schmidt, however, has suggested that there may have been a more personal motive for Dickinson's message, namely, Dickinson's relationship with his son.

Jonathan Jr. was a member of the Yale Class of 1730. He got himself into enough unspecified difficulty to be demoted to the bottom of his class, but it was not sufficiently severe to prevent him from taking his bachelor's degree on time, and, soon after, his master's. It would seem that upon his return to Elizabeth Town in the mid-1730s, however, the relationship with his father soured. It is reported that his father "prayed daily at the family devotions" for his errant son, who had "deserted his father's house and led a wandering vicious life." In his will, Dickinson passed over his son as executor in favor of his sons-in-law, Jonathan Sergeant and John Odell, and there is no evidence that the son ever collected the portion of his father's estate allotted to him—an equal portion of Dickinson's estate, as divided among the son and his five sisters.

The only surviving reference by Dickinson to his son's absence can be found in a letter dated 24 May 1740 to Thomas Foxcroft, who apparently had inquired into the matter. In that letter, Dickinson offered the following statement: "I heartily thank you for your sympathy for me on account of my son's absence. I have endeavored to resign him as well as others [of] my concerns to the sovereign disposal of a holy providence; and I hope I shall be satisfied with His will, who has the right to deal with me and mine as he pleases." In any event, Dickinson suggested, he was prepared to endure "the bitterest cup my heavenly Father will mix me to drink."

As Schmidt has suggested, Dickinson's efforts at mending his son's ways may very well have failed, and he may have expelled his son, rather than the son having deserted his father, thus leading Dickinson to write, in "Who Is on the Lord's Side?": "If persuasions won't avail we should try severer methods and let none dwell under our roofs, that won't submit to our government lest they bring a curse upon our houses and God be provoked to determine concerning us as of Ely in 1 Samuel 3:13: 'For I have told him that I will judge his house forever for the iniquity which he knoweth because his sons made themselves vile and he restrained them not.'"

Schmidt has reasoned not only that the matter of his errant son must have weighed heavily on Dickinson's mind, as he sought a revival of vital religion through youth and families, but also that the family problem may have given Dickinson a keener sense of the need for moderation. Schmidt has suggested that it reenforced Dickinson's fear of extremes, whether of infidelity or enthusiasm, both of which, it was clear, ended in the same place—in religious or social disorder or in libertinism. Unfortunately, we know too little of Dickinson and his son to be certain.

On the above see Dickinson, *A Call to the Weary*, 42; Schmidt, "Jonathan Dickinson," 344; Hardman, "Dickinson and American Presbyterianism," 6; Richard Webster, *A History of the Presbyterian Church in America, from Its Origin until the Year 1760* (Philadelphia: Joseph M. Wilson, 1857), 360; Franklin B. Dexter, *Biographical Sketches of the Graduates of Yale College* (New York: Henry Holt, 1885-1912), 1:438, 426; Jonathan Dickinson, Last Will and Testament, 16 September 1747, and Mary Dickinson, Papers on the Discharge of Jonathan Dickinson's Will, 31 December 1747 and 13 January 1748, General Manuscripts, Firestone Library, Princeton University; Jonathan Dickinson to Thomas Foxcroft, 24 May 1740, Foxcroft Collection; Dickinson, "Who Is on the Lord's Side?" 19.

30. David Harlan has suggested that Dickinson packed the Elizabeth Town meeting with Whitefield's critics. Harlan, "Travail of Religious Moderation," 414. See also Hardman, "Dickinson and American Presbyterianism," 204.

31. Whitefield, *Journals*, 412.

32. Dickinson to Foxcroft, 24 May 1740, reprinted in Thomas Prince, ed., *The Christian History, Containing Accounts of the Revival and Propagation of Religion in Great Britain and America* (Boston: S. Kneeland and T. Green, 1744), 1:252-54.

33. Jonathan Dickinson, *The Witness of the Spirit . . . Wherein Is Distinctly Shown, in What Way and Manner the Spirit Himself Beareth Witness to the Adoption of the Children of God. On Occasion of a Wonderful Progress of Converting Grace in Those Parts*, 2d ed. (Boston: S. Kneeland and T. Green, 1740).

34. Heimert and Miller, *Great Awakening*, x, 101; Hardman, "Dickinson and American Presbyterianism," 12, 213; Bumsted and Van de Wetering, *What Must I Do to*

Be Saved? 38, 104; Edwards's *Treatise Concerning Religious Affections* was not published until 1746.

35. Trinterud, *American Tradition,* 93; Hardman, "Dickinson and American Presbyterianism," 339.

36. Harlan, "Travail of Religious Moderation," 418; Dickinson, *Witness of the Spirit,* 4, 20, 23 (page numbers hereafter noted in text).

37. Dickinson to Foxcroft, 23 August 1743, reprinted in Prince, *Christian History,* 1:254-58.

7. ESTABLISHING THE MODERATE AWAKENING

1. *Records of the Presbyterian Church in the United States of America,* ed. William H. Roberts (Philadelphia: Presbyterian Board of Publication and Sabbath School Work, 1904), 148; Richard Webster, *A History of the Presbyterian Church in America, from Its Origin until the Year 1760* (Philadelphia: Joseph M. Wilson, 1857), 139, 183-84; Charles Hodge, *The Constitutional History of the Presbyterian Church in the United States of America* (Philadelphia: William S. Martien, 1839), 1:230; (1840), 2:126-28.

2. Leonard J. Trinterud, *The Forming of an American Tradition: A Re-examination of Colonial Presbyterianism* (Freeport, N.Y.: Books for Libraries Press, 1949), 148.

3. George Whitefield, *George Whitefield's Journals, 1737-1741,* ed. William V. Davis (Gainesville, Fla.: Scholars Facsimiles and Reprints, 1969), 144, 350-51.

4. Trinterud, *American Tradition,* 89; Alan Heimert and Perry Miller, eds., *The Great Awakening: Documents Illustrating the Crisis and Its Consequences* (Indianapolis: Bobbs-Merrill, 1967), 72; Martin E. Lodge, "The Great Awakening in the Middle Colonies" (Ph.D. diss., University of California at Berkeley, 1964), 132.

5. Trinterud, *American Tradition,* 96; Webster, *Presbyterian Church in America,* 148, 152. It has been suggested that someone may have made a request on Jonathan Dickinson's behalf that he be permitted to use the Society Hill pulpit but that Gilbert Tennent had refused the request. Although not an unreasonable conjecture, the evidence for it is inconclusive. See, for example, Herbert L. Samworth, "Those Astonishing Wonders of His Grace: Jonathan Dickinson and the Great Awakening" (Th.D. diss., Westminster Theological Seminary, 1988), 148.

6. Trinterud, *American Tradition,* 96; Lodge, "Great Awakening," 201; *Records,* 153.

7. Trinterud, *American Tradition,* 97.

8. Ibid., 98; Webster, *Presbyterian Church in America,* 151; Lodge, "Great Awakening," 201-2; Samuel Blair, *A Vindication of the Brethren Who Were Unjustly and Illegally Cast Out of the Synod of Philadelphia by a Number of the Members* (Philadelphia: Benjamin Franklin, 1744); *Apology of the Presbytery of New Brunswick* (Philadelphia: Benjamin Franklin, 1742). Tennent is quoted in Hodge, *Constitutional History,* 2:145-49.

9. Trinterud, *American Tradition,* 98; *Records,* 154; Webster, *Presbyterian Church in America,* 152. See also George Gillespie, *A Letter to the Reverend Brethren of the Presbytery of New York, or of Elizabeth Town. In Which Is Shown the Unjustness of the Synod's Protest, Entered Last May at Philadelphia, Against Some of the Reverend Brethren* (Philadelphia: Benjamin Franklin, 1742).

10. Trinterud, *American Tradition,* 99-100, 103; Lodge, "Great Awakening," 212-13; Webster, *Presbyterian Church in America,* 162; Hodge, *Constitutional History,* 2:171-72.

11. Trinterud, *American Tradition,* 100; Webster, *Presbyterian Church in America,* 156; *The Querists: Part I* (Philadelphia: Benjamin Franklin, 1741).

12. George Whitefield, *A Letter from Mr. Whitefield to Some Church Members of the Presbyterian Persuasion in Answer to Certain Scruples and Queries Relating to Some Passages in His Printed Sermons and Other Writings* (Boston: S. Kneeland and T. Green, 1740); Trinterud, *American Tradition,* 101; Webster, *Presbyterian Church in America,* 156-57; Lodge, "Great Awakening," 211; Milton J. Coalter Jr., *Gilbert Tennent, Son of Thunder: A Case Study of Continental Pietism's Impact on the First Great Awakening in the Middle Colonies* (Westport, Conn.: Greenwood Press, 1986), 66, 77.

13. *The Querists: Part II* (Philadelphia: Benjamin Franklin, 1741); *The Querists: Part III* (Philadelphia: Benjamin Franklin, 1741). Samuel Blair, *A Particular Consideration of a Piece Entitled, The Querists* (Philadelphia: Benjamin Franklin, 1741); discussed in Trinterud, *American Tradition,* 101. Samuel Finley, *Christ Triumphing and Satan Raging* (Philadelphia: Benjamin Franklin, 1741); discussed in Trinterud, *American Tradition,* 102; Webster, *Presbyterian Church in America,* 161; Coalter, *Gilbert Tennent,* 78-80.

14. Trinterud, *American Tradition,* 101-2; Coalter, *Gilbert Tennent,* 76; Webster, *Presbyterian Church in America,* 157.

15. Trinterud, *American Tradition,* 103.

16. There is no way to explain the absence of the entire New York Presbytery from the Synod of 1741. Milton Coalter has suggested that the New Englanders, caught in the middle of the dispute between the New Brunswick men and the Old Siders, chose to absent themselves in order to discourage any further acrimonious debate. There is little evidence to support such a conclusion, however, and it must be remembered that absence from the synod was not uncommon. There were absences from all the presbyteries except Donegal at the Synod of 1741.

The reader may recall Dickinson's letter to Foxcroft of 23 August 1743, wherein he referred to "one of the greatest mortalities" that had ever been known in that town. The letter suggests that the "throat distemper" (diphtheria) struck Elizabeth Town in 1741 and 1742. As Dickinson was committed to the physical, as well as the spiritual, care of his flock, such a contagion would certainly explain his absence.

Finally, the records of the Synod of 1742 read that the body had considered the absences of the New York Presbytery from the Synod of 1741 and sustained some of the members' excuses. Although no further comment is offered, it would appear that the presbytery was not acting en masse.

Coalter, *Gilbert Tennent,* 82; Charles Hartshorn Maxson, *The Great Awakening in the Middle Colonies* (Gloucester, Mass.: Peter Smith, 1958), 75; Thomas Prince, ed., *The Christian History, Containing Accounts of the Revival and Propagation of Religion in Great Britain and America* (Boston: S. Kneeland and T. Green, 1744), 1:257; *Records,* 162.

17. *Records,* 157; discussed in Trinterud, *American Tradition,* 103.

18. *Records,* 158-59; see also Trinterud, *American Tradition,* 105; Hodge, *Constitutional History,* 2:179-87; Robert Ellis Thompson, *A History of the Presbyterian Churches in the United States* (New York: Christian Literature, 1895), 334-41.

19. *Records,* 158-59; Trinterud, *American Tradition,* 105-6; Coalter, *Gilbert Tennent,* 83; Webster, *Presbyterian Church in America,* 183. See Gilbert Tennent, *Remarks upon a Protestation Presented to the Synod of Philadelphia* (Philadelphia: Benjamin Franklin, 1741).

Most historians have argued that the protestors and those who supported them constituted a majority of the Synod of 1741. See, for example, Trinterud, *American Tradition,* 105; Maxson, *Great Awakening,* 75; Thompson, *Presbyterian Churches,* 32; and Lodge, "Great Awakening," 214.

20. Gillespie, *A Letter to the Reverend Brethren.* See Coalter, *Gilbert Tennent,* 83; Keith Jordan Hardman, "Jonathan Dickinson and the Course of American

Presbyterianism, 1717-1747" (Ph.D. diss., University of Pennsylvania, 1971), 235-36; Trinterud, *American Tradition,* 114; Lodge, "Great Awakening," 216. Gillespie's account of the Synod of 1741 was the first to appear in the newspapers, namely, the *Pennsylvania Gazette* on 11 June 1741.

21. Webster, *Presbyterian Church in America,* 177, 181. See John Thomson, *The Government of the Church of Christ* (Philadelphia: Andrew Bradford, 1741). Milton Coalter has offered this as evidence of the strategically planned absence of the New York Presbytery from the Synod of 1741. Coalter, *Gilbert Tennent,* 82.

22. Webster, *Presbyterian Church in America,* 178-81.

23. Trinterud, *American Tradition,* 110.

24. Webster, *Presbyterian Church in America,* 189-91. Webster includes the complete text of the letter.

Over the course of the previous few months, Tennent had written similar letters to several New England ministers disassociating himself from some specific activities of the radical New Light/New Side, such as lay preaching. None, however, was as general a retraction and, therefore, of as much import as that of February 1742 to Jonathan Dickinson. For an example of the earlier letters, see Tennent's letter to Jonathan Edwards in Sereno E. Dwight, ed., *Memoirs of Jonathan Edwards* in *Works of Jonathan Edwards* (1815, reprint. Edinburgh: Banner of Truth Trust, 1974), 1:liv-lv.

Gilbert Tennent elaborated on most of the same points in *Irencium Ecclesiasticum, or a Humble Impartial Essay upon the Peace of Jerusalem* (Philadelphia: William Bradford, 1749).

25. David C. Harlan suggests that Cross was the father of an illegitimate child: "The Travail of Religious Moderation: Jonathan Dickinson and the Great Awakening," *Journal of Presbyterian History* 61 (winter 1983): 420. See "History of the Presbytery of New Brunswick, Minutes, 1740-1741," *Journal of Presbyterian History* 7 (1913-14): 152; and Webster, *Presbyterian Church in America,* 162.

26. Webster, *Presbyterian Church in America,* 413; Prince, *Christian History,* 1:254; Leigh Eric Schmidt, "Jonathan Dickinson and the Making of the Moderate Awakening," *American Presbyterians* 63 (winter 1985): 349; Harlan, "Travail of Religious Moderation," 420.

27. Harlan, "Travail of Religious Moderation," 420-21; Harlan quotes from the letter as it was published on 5 July 1742, in the *Boston Evening Post.* Hodge, *Constitutional History,* 2:105-6; Coalter, *Gilbert Tennent,* 107; Harry S. Stout and Peter Onuf, "James Davenport and the Great Awakening in New London," *Journal of American History* 71 (Dec. 1983): 556. For the text of the ministerial association's ruling see Richard L. Bushman, ed., *The Great Awakening: Documents on the Revival of Religion, 1740-1745* (New York: Atheneum, 1970), 50-51. Dickinson voiced his approval of the ruling in a letter to Thomas Foxcroft, a member of the ministerial association. See Dickinson to Foxcroft, 27 July 1742, Foxcroft Collection, Firestone Library, Princeton University.

28. Richard Warch, "The Shepherd's Tent: Education and Enthusiasm in the Great Awakening," *American Quarterly* 30 (summer 1978): 177-98.

29. Harlan, "Travail of Religious Moderation," 421; Webster, *Presbyterian Church in America,* 189; Trinterud, *American Tradition,* 114-15; Maxson, *Great Awakening,* 80-84; Coalter, *Gilbert Tennent,* 96-105; Jonathan Dickinson, *Familiar Letters to a Gentleman, upon a Variety of Seasonable and Important Subjects in Religion* (Boston: Rogers and Fowle, 1745), iii.

30. Trinterud, *American Tradition,* 116. Elsewhere in New England, Dickinson found "strange appearances" and "falling into strange fits." In the latter instance he marveled at women who, having fallen into a trance, were able to accurately tell of "sundry

distant events" and, without assistance, to identify those in their neighborhood who had fallen into similar trances, even as to the exact time and circumstance of each occurrence.

31. Norman Pettit, "Prelude to Mission: Brainerd's Expulsion from Yale," *New England Quarterly* 59 (March 1986): 34-35; see also Ross W. Beales Jr., "Harvard and Yale in the Great Awakening," *Historical Journal of Massachusetts* 14 (Jan. 1986): 1-10; Jonathan Edwards, *The Life of David Brainerd,* ed. Norman Pettit (New Haven: Yale University Press, 1985), 38, 41-42.

32. Tennent's letter was reprinted in the *Pennsylvania Gazette* on 12 August 1742, and in the 5-12 August 1742, issue of the Philadelphia *American Weekly Mercury.* Trinterud, *American Tradition,* 116; Gilbert Tennent, *The Examiner, Examined, or Gilbert Tennent, Harmonious* (Philadelphia: William Bradford, 1743), 64.

33. Stephen Nissenbaum, ed., *The Great Awakening at Yale College* (Belmont, Calif.: Wadsworth, 1972), 109-11, 116-17. Aaron Burr did not accept the position in New Haven, and the First Society remained permanently divided. The Separatists eventually secured their own regular minister.

34. Jonathan Dickinson to Thomas Foxcroft, 12 April 1742, Foxcroft Collection. Coincidentally, Edwards was in the process of publishing *Some Thoughts Concerning the Present Revival of Religion in New England,* which was intended to present his views on the proper conduct of the revival. As J. M. Bumsted and John E. Van de Wetering have written, Edwards, in *Some Thoughts Concerning the Revival,* while defending the Awakening, also granted the importance of reason and understanding, something, he hinted, that had been neglected by its more radical proponents. Much as Dickinson had written, and would continue to write, Edwards warned against accepting false evidence of religious experiences and insisted that the revival conform to the model provided for it in Scripture. See Bumsted and Van de Wetering, *What Must I Do to Be Saved? The Great Awakening in Colonial America* (Hinsdale, Ill.: Dryden Press, 1976), 100-101.

One historian of Elizabeth Town has suggested that at some point Edwards preached from Dickinson's Elizabeth Town pulpit. No evidence has been found, however, either to confirm or to date such an event. Nicholas Murray, *Notes, Historical and Biographical, Concerning Elizabeth Town, Its Eminent Men, Churches, and Ministers* (Elizabeth Town, N.J.: E. Sanderson, 1844), 43.

35. *Records,* 162; Webster, *Presbyterian Church in America,* 193; Hodge, *Constitutional History,* 2:198-99.

36. *Records,* 160, 164; Webster, *Presbyterian Church in America,* 177.

37. Jedediah's letter to John Pierson is included in Webster, *Presbyterian Church in America,* 200-201; Dickinson to Foxcroft, 27 July 1742.

38. Webster, *Presbyterian Church in America,* 195-97; Tennent, *Examiner,* 3-5.

39. Trinterud, *American Tradition,* 119-20; Coalter, *Gilbert Tennent,* 165-68.

40. Passages quoted are from Tennent's letter as reprinted in its entirety in Tennent, *Examiner,* 64-66. See also Webster, *Presbyterian Church in America,* 195-97.

41. Webster, *Presbyterian Church in America,* 196-97; Maxson, *Great Awakening,* 84; Dickinson to Foxcroft, 12 April 1742, 27 July 1742, Foxcroft Collection; Coalter, *Gilbert Tennent,* 106.

42. Harlan, "Travail of Religious Moderation," 422.

43. Jonathan Dickinson, *The True Scripture Doctrine, Concerning Some Important Points of Christian Faith, Particularly Eternal Election, Original Sin, Grace in Conversion, Justification by Faith, and the Saints' Perseverance* (Boston: G. Rogers for S. Eliot, 1741), xii-xiii.

44. In this context, Foxcroft called for God's intercession on behalf of the British against the Spanish in the War of Jenkins' Ear. Also, interestingly, in view of what would happen in 1742 among the New Lights and New Siders, James Davenport, referred to as "one of the most celebrated lights of the Reformation," is cited as an exponent of the same "true scripture doctrine" Dickinson had explicated. Dickinson, *True Scripture Doctrine*, i-iv, vii. See also Gerald R. McDermott, "Jonathan Edwards, the City on a Hill, and the Redeemer Nation: A Reappraisal," *American Presbyterians* 69 (spring 1991): 33-47.

45. Schmidt, "Jonathan Dickinson," 347; Harlan, "Travail of Religious Moderation," 412; Bumsted and Van de Wetering, *What Must I Do to Be Saved?* 103-4; Henry F. May, *The Enlightenment in America* (New York: Oxford University Press, 1976), 26.

46. Dickinson, *True Scripture Doctrine*, 31-35.

47. Ibid., 37-38.

48. David C. Harlan, "A World of Double Visions and Second Thoughts: Jonathan Dickinson's *Display of God's Special Grace*," *Early American Literature* 21 (fall 1986): 118-19, 121, 123.

49. Jonathan Dickinson, *A Display of God's Special Grace in a Familiar Dialogue between a Minister and a Gentleman of His Congregation, About the Work of God in the Conviction and Conversion of Sinners, So Remarkably of Late Begun and Going on in These American Parts* (Philadelphia: William Bradford, 1743), i.

50. Ava Chamberlain has pointed to *Distinguishing Marks* as providing the first inklings that Edwards considered radical New Lights a problem for the Great Awakening. Chamberlain, "Self-Deception as a Theological Problem in Jonathan Edwards's 'Treatise Concerning Religious Affections,'" *Church History* 63 (Dec. 1994): 542.

51. Dickinson, *A Display of God's Special Grace*, ii-iii.

52. Ibid., v, viii, and x.

53. Harlan, "Travail of Religious Moderation," 414-16; Heimert and Miller, *Great Awakening*, 177.

54. Harlan, "Travail of Religious Moderation," 415; Dickinson to Foxcroft, 29 August 1744, Foxcroft Collection.

8. DEFENDING THE MODERATE AWAKENING

1. *Records of the Presbyterian Church in the United States of America*, ed. William H. Roberts (Philadelphia: Presbyterian Board of Publication and Sabbath School Work, 1904), 165-68. Discussed in Charles Hodge, *The Constitutional History of the Presbyterian Church in the United States of America* (Philadelphia: William S. Martien, 1840), 2:204-5.

2. *Records*, 168, 172-74; discussed in Hodge, *Constitutional History*, 2:207-8.

3. *Records*, 168-70; discussed in Hodge, *Constitutional History*, 2:209-12.

4. Keith Jordan Hardman, "Jonathan Dickinson and the Course of American Presbyterianism, 1717-1747" (Ph.D. diss., University of Pennsylvania, 1971), 298.

Whitefield's tabernacle had been constructed for the use of all who responded to the New Light without regard to their denominational affiliation. In 1745, a group of trustees led by Moravians, but with Whitefield's support, protested what they saw as Tennent's conversion of the tabernacle into Philadelphia's second Presbyterian church. In response, Tennent and his Presbyterian congregation sought to leave it and build a new house of worship. Tennent asked Dickinson to represent his need for funds to their

New England brethren, which he did in a letter to Thomas Foxcroft. See Dickinson to Foxcroft, 21 January 1746, Foxcroft Collection, Firestone Library, Princeton University. See also Leonard J. Trinterud, *The Forming of an American Tradition: A Re-examination of Colonial Presbyterianism* (Freeport, N.Y.: Books for Libraries Press, 1949), 119.

5. *Records,* 171; Hardman, "Dickinson and American Presbyterianism," 306; Dickinson to Foxcroft, 28 November 1743 and 29 August 1744; Experience Mayhew to Foxcroft, 24 August 1744, Foxcroft Collection.

6. *Records,* 178-80; Hardman, "Dickinson and American Presbyterianism," 307; Hodge, *Constitutional History,* 2:212; Richard Webster, *A History of the Presbyterian Church in America, from Its Origin until the Year 1760* (Philadelphia: Joseph M. Wilson, 1857), 211; S. D. Alexander, *The Presbytery of New York, 1738 to 1888* (New York: Anson D. F. Randolph, 1887), 12.

7. *Records,* 181; Hodge, *Constitutional History,* 2:218-19; Webster, *Presbyterian Church in America,* 213, 215; Robert Hastings Nichols, "The First Synod of New York, 1745-1758, and Its Permanent Effects," *Church History* 14 (Dec. 1945): 247.

8. *Records,* 233-35; Trinterud, *American Tradition,* 144; Webster, *Presbyterian Church in America,* 218.

9. *Records,* 186.

10. Ibid., 188-89; Trinterud, *American Tradition,* 144.

11. *Records,* 235.

12. Jonathan Dickinson to Thomas Foxcroft, 6 May 1745, Foxcroft Collection; Jonathan Edwards, *The Life of David Brainerd,* ed. Norman Pettit (New Haven: Yale University Press, 1985), 441.

13. References in the following letters may be to either tract: Dickinson to Foxcroft, 21 January 1746 and 5 September 1746; Dickinson, *Marks of Saving Faith: The Plain Distinction between a Saving and a Dead Faith* (New York: American Tract Society, n.d.); Dickinson, *Marks of True Repentance, Distinguishing between a Legal and an Evangelical Repentance* (New York: American Tract Society, n.d.).

14. Alan Heimert and Perry Miller, eds., *The Great Awakening: Documents Illustrating the Crisis and Its Consequences* (Indianapolis: Bobbs-Merrill, 1967), xxiv-xxvi; J. M. Bumsted and John E. Van de Wetering, *What Must I Do to Be Saved? The Great Awakening in Colonial America* (Hinsdale, Ill.: Dryden Press, 1976), 116.

15. Daniel Waterland, *Regeneration Stated and Explained According to Scripture and Antiquity in a Discourse* (London, 1740; New York: Hugh Gaine, 1793), 3-6, 8, 11, 20-21, 26-27, 30-31.

16. Jonathan Dickinson, *The Nature and Necessity of Regeneration* (New York: James Parker, 1743), iii-v, 1, 8-9, 12, 14-17, 22-23.

17. James Wetmore, *A Letter Occasioned by Mr. Dickinson's Remarks upon Dr. Waterland's Discourse on Regeneration* (New York: J. Parker, 1744), 3-4, 7, 12, 17-18, 28, 32-33.

18. Jonathan Dickinson, *Reflections upon Mr. Wetmore's Letter in Defense of Dr. Waterland's Discourse on Regeneration* (Boston: J. Draper for S. Eliot, 1744), 6-8, 10-11, 15. Sydney E. Ahlstrom, *A Religious History of the American People* (New Haven: Yale University Press, 1972), 388; William B. Sprague, "Henry Caner," in *Annals of the American Pulpit,* ed. William B. Sprague (New York: Robert Carter, 1869), 5:61-63; Franklin B. Dexter, *Biographical Sketches of the Graduates of Yale College* (New York: Henry Holt, 1885-1912), 165-68.

19. John Beach, *A Sermon Showing that Eternal Life Is God's Free Gift, Bestowed upon Men According to their Moral Behavior, and that Free Grace and Free Will Concur in*

the Affair of Man's Salvation (Newport, R.I.: Widow Franklin, 1745), 3; Samuel Johnson, *A Letter from Aristocles to Authades, Concerning the Sovereignty and the Promise of God* (Boston: Thomas Fleet, 1745), ii, 1-2.

20. Henry Caner, *The True Nature and Method of Christian Preaching, Examined and Stated* (Newport, R.I.: Widow Franklin, 1745), 4-5, 5-7, 34-35.

21. Jonathan Dickinson, *A Vindication of God's Sovereign Free Grace* (Boston: Rogers and Fowle, 1746), 5-6, 8-11, 18-21, 34-35; Jon Pahl, *Paradox Lost: Free Will and Political Liberty in American Culture, 1630-1760* (Baltimore: Johns Hopkins University Press, 1992), 135-36.

22. Dickinson, *A Vindication of God's Sovereign Free Grace,* 22-23, 25-28, 38-39.

23. Ibid., 42-44.

24. Ibid., 50-51, 61-63.

25. John Beach, *God's Sovereignty and His Universal Love to the Souls of Men Reconciled, in a Reply to Mr. Jonathan Dickinson's Remarks upon a Sermon Entitled, Eternal Life God's Free Gift* (Boston: Rogers and Fowle, 1747), 16-17, 31; Samuel Johnson, *A Letter to Mr. Jonathan Dickinson, in Defense of Aristocles to Authades, Concerning the Sovereignty and Promises of God* (Boston: Rogers and Fowle, 1747), 12.

26. Jonathan Dickinson, *A Second Vindication of God's Sovereign Free Grace Against the Exceptions Made to a Former Vindication by Mr. John Beach* (Boston: Rogers and Fowle, 1748), 7-8, 14-21, 28-29.

27. The Norwalk congregation had been disposed to offer the pulpit to Gilbert Tennent, but, having been advised by the Fairfield Ministerial Association that Tennent's services were needed more in New Jersey, they offered it to Moses Dickinson. From 1764 to 1772, Dickinson shared his pulpit with Gilbert Tennent's younger brother, William Jr. See Dexter, "Moses Dickinson," 165; William B. Sprague, "Moses Dickinson," in *Annals of the American Pulpit,* ed. William B. Sprague (New York: Robert Carter, 1857), 1:310-12.

28. John Beach, *A Second Vindication of God's Sovereign Free Grace Indeed. In a Fair and Candid Examination of the Last Discourse of the Late Mr. Dickinson, Entitled a Second Vindication of God's Sovereign Free Grace* (Boston: Rogers and Fowle, 1748), and Moses Dickinson, *An Inquiry into the Consequences Both of Calvinist and Arminian Principles Compared Together. In Which the Principal Things in Mr. Beach's Second Reply to the late Mr. Jonathan Dickinson's Second Vindication of God's Sovereign Free Grace Are Particularly Considered.* (Boston: Fowle, 1750).

Jon Pahl has identified at least a dozen authors, other than those noted in this chapter, who contributed to the public discourse on free will and God's sovereign free grace between 1745 and 1754. Ten of them, however, published their work after Dickinson's death. Pahl, *Paradox Lost,* 134.

29. Jonathan Edwards to Joseph Bellamy, 15 January 1747, in "Six Letters of Jonathan Edwards to Joseph Bellamy," *New England Quarterly* 1 (Apr. 1928): 230-31; Edwards to Bellamy, 11 June 1749, ibid., 234; Edwards to John Erskine, summer 1747, quoted in Pahl, *Paradox Lost,* 149.

30. John T. Christian, *A History of the Baptists of the United States: From the First Settlement of the Country to the Year 1845* (Nashville: Sunday School Board of the Southern Baptist Convention, 1926), 127, 179-80; William G. McLoughlin, *Isaac Backus and the American Pietistic Tradition* (Boston: Little, Brown, 1967), 89-91; C. C. Goen, *Revivalism and Separatism in New England, 1740-1800: Strict Congregationalists and Separate Baptists in the Great Awakening* (New Haven: Yale University Press, 1962), vii, 148, 193, 200-201; William G. McLoughlin, *New England Dissent, 1630-1833: The*

Baptists and the Separation of Church and State (Cambridge: Harvard University Press, 1971), 279, 319, 324-25, 345-46, 349, 422, 436; Edwin Scott Gaustad, *The Great Awakening in New England* (Gloucester, Mass.: Peter Smith, 1965), 120; Albert H. Newman, *A History of the Baptist Churches in the United States* (New York: Scribner, 1915), 243; Charles Hartshorn Maxson, *The Great Awakening in the Middle Colonies* (Gloucester, Mass.: Peter Smith, 1958), 138; Robert C. Newman, *Baptists and the American Tradition* (Des Plaines, Ill.: Regular Baptist Press, 1976), 149; William H. Brackney, *The Baptists* (Westport, Conn.: Greenwood Press, 1988), 13; Heimert and Miller, *Great Awakening,* xlviii.

31. Gaustad, *Great Awakening in New England,* 157-58n 88; Norman H. Maring, *Baptists in New Jersey: A Study in Transition* (Valley Forge, Penn.: Judson Press, 1964), 48; William H. Brackney, ed., *Baptist Life and Thought, 1600-1980: A Source Book* (Valley Forge, Penn.: Judson Press, 1983), 117; Heimert and Miller, *Great Awakening,* l-li.

32. Morgan Edwards, ed., *Materials Towards a History of the Baptists* (1770, 1792; rpt. Danielsville, Ga.: Heritage Press, 1984), 1:83. Samuel Finley had migrated from Ireland in 1734, graduated from the Log College, and became an ardent supporter of the Awakening. Harris Elwood Starr, "Samuel Finley," in *The Dictionary of American Biography,* 6:391; Maring, *Baptists in New Jersey,* 60. Abel Morgan, Baptist minister at Middletown, New Jersey, in the wake of George Whitefield's visit to New Jersey in 1739, had undergone a conversion experience and also become well known for fanning the flames of evangelical religion. A. Newman, *Baptist Churches,* 279; Jesse L. Boyd, *A History of Baptists in America prior to 1845* (New York: American Press, 1957), 46; Edwards, *Materials,* 1:82-83; Maring, *Baptists in New Jersey,* 51-52; Samuel Finley, *A Charitable Plea for the Speechless; or, The Right of Believers' Infants to Baptism Vindicated: And the Mode of It by Pouring or Sprinkling, Justified* (Philadelphia: William Bradford, 1746), 1.

33. Abel Morgan, *Anti-Paedo Rantism; or, Mr. Samuel Finley's Charitable Plea for the Speechless Examined and Refuted: The Baptism of Believers Maintained; and the Mode of it by Immersion Vindicated* (Philadelphia: B. Franklin, 1747), vii. See William H. Allison, "Benjamin Griffith," in *The Dictionary of American Biography,* 7:624. On Griffith's authorship, see Charles Evans, *American Bibliography, 1639-1820* (New York: Peter Smith, 1941), 2:340.

34. Jonathan Dickinson, *A Brief Illustration and Confirmation of the Divine Right of Infant Baptism; In a Plain and Familiar Dialogue between a Minister and One of His Parishioners* (Boston: S. Kneeland and T. Green, 1746), 4-6.

35. Benjamin Griffith, "An Appendix to the Foregoing Work; Being Remarks on Some Particulars in a Late Pamphlet, Entitled, Divine Right of Infant Baptism," in Morgan, *Anti-Paedo Rantism,* 164, 168, 173-74, 265.

36. Samuel Finley, *A Vindication of the Charitable Plea for the Speechless: In Answer to Mr. Abel Morgan's Anti-Paedo Rantism* (Philadelphia: William Bradford, 1748), 113; See Morgan, *Anti-Paedo Rantism Defended* (Philadelphia: Benjamin Franklin, 1750). Maxson, *Great Awakening,* 133; Trinterud, *American Tradition,* 130, 133, 135; Boyd, *A History of Baptists in America,* lv; Hardman, "Dickinson and American Presbyterianism," 69.

37. Leigh Eric Schmidt, "A Second and Glorious Reformation: The New Light Extremism of Andrew Croswell," *William and Mary Quarterly,* 3d ser., 43 (Apr. 1986): 214, 217; Andrew Croswell, *A Reply to a Declaration of the Associated Ministers in Boston and Charlestown with Regard to the Reverend James Davenport and His Conduct* (Boston: Rogers and Fowle, 1742); Bumsted and Van de Wetering, *What Must I Do to Be Saved?* 109; Leigh Eric Schmidt, "Jonathan Dickinson and the Making of the Moderate Awakening," *American Presbyterians* 63 (winter 1985): 350.

38. Andrew Croswell, *Mr. Croswell's Reply to a Book Lately Published, Entitled a Display of God's Special Grace* (Boston: Rogers and Fowle, 1742), 2-5, 7, 9-10, 23; Schmidt, "A Second and Glorious Reformation," 222-23; Bumsted and Van de Wetering, *What Must I Do to Be Saved?* 102.

39. Croswell, *Mr. Croswell's Reply,* 7-12, 18, 20-22.

40. Dickinson's February 1743 letter to Thomas Foxcroft is included in Hardman, "Dickinson and American Presbyterianism," 287-88.

41. Webster, *Presbyterian Church in America,* 204.

42. Jonathan Dickinson, *A Defense of the Dialogue Intitled, A Display of God's Special Grace, Against the Exceptions Made to It by the Reverend Mr. A. Croswell* (Boston: J. Draper, 1743), 1-2, 6-7, 46 (hereafter pages will be cited in the text).

43. Croswell, *Mr. Croswell's Reply,* 23.

44. Cotton Mather and Charles Chauncy, "The Missionary Mayhews," in *Annals of the American Pulpit,* 1:131-33; Richard F. F. Tyner, "Experience Mayhew," in *The Dictionary of American Biography,* 12:453-54; Experience Mayhew, "Reverend Mr. Experience Mayhew's Letter Containing Exceptions Against Some Passages in Mr. Dickinson's Scripture Doctrine," 24 August 1743, Foxcroft Collection. Mayhew cited Hobbes's *The Necessity of All Things* but likely meant *Of Liberty and Necessity* (1654). Conrad Cherry, *The Theology of Jonathan Edwards* (Garden City, N.Y.: Anchor Books, 1966), 14.

45. Dickinson to Foxcroft, 18 December 1743, Special Collections, Mugar Memorial Library, Boston University, 1, 17-18, 20, 23.

46. Mayhew to Foxcroft, 24 August 1744, 1; Experience Mayhew, *Grace Defended, in a Modest Plea for an Important Truth; Namely That the Offer of Salvation Made to Sinners in the Gospel, Comprises in It an Offer of the Grace Given in Regeneration* (Boston: B. Green for D. Henchman, 1744), iii-v.

47. Jonathan Dickinson, "Free Grace Vindicated, in Some Brief Remarks upon a Book Entitled Grace Defended by Experience Mayhew," title page, Foxcroft Collection.

In the year Dickinson died, Mayhew published, on the same subject, *A Letter to a Gentleman on that Question. Whether Saving Grace be Different in Species from Common Grace, or in Degree Only* (Boston: S. Kneeland and T. Green, 1747).

48. David C. Harlan, "The Travail of Religious Moderation: Jonathan Dickinson and the Great Awakening," *Journal of Presbyterian History* 61 (winter 1983): 423; Schmidt, "Jonathan Dickinson," 353n 61.

9. Founding the College of New Jersey

1. Thomas Clinton Pears Jr., "Colonial Education among Presbyterians," pt. 1, *Journal of the Presbyterian Historical Society* 30 (June 1952): 117.

2. Varnum Lansing Collins, *Princeton* (New York: Oxford University Press, 1914), 3-4.

3. Ibid., 5-6; John DeWitt, "Historical Sketch of Princeton University," in *Memorial Book of the Sesquicentennial Celebration of the Founding of the College of New Jersey and of the Ceremonies Inaugurating Princeton University* (New York: Scribner, 1898), 324-25; Pears, "Colonial Education," 117, 122-23.

4. *Records of the Presbyterian Church in the United States of America,* ed. William H. Roberts (Philadelphia: Presbyterian Board of Publication and Sabbath School Work, 1904), 141; Collins, *Princeton,* 7; Pears, "Colonial Education," 124; Thomas Clinton

Pears Jr., "Colonial Education among Presbyterians," pt. 2, *Journal of the Presbyterian Historical Society* 30 (Sept. 1952): 165-66; "An Examination and Refutation of William G. Tennent's Remarks, etc." in Thomas Clinton Pears Jr., ed., *Documentary History of William Tennent and the Log College* (Philadelphia: Presbyterian Historical Society, 1940), 156, 160-61. See also Leonard J. Trinterud, *The Forming of an American Tradition: A Re-examination of Colonial Presbyterianism* (Freeport, N.Y.: Books for Libraries Press, 1949), 327.

5. Thomas J. Wertenbaker, "The College of New Jersey and the Presbyterians," *Journal of the Presbyterian Historical Society* 36 (Dec. 1958): 210; *Records*, 148; Trinterud, *American Tradition*, 84; Charles Hodge, *The Constitutional History of the Presbyterian Church in the United States of America* (Philadelphia: William S. Martien, 1840), 2:261; Richard Webster, *A History of the Presbyterian Church in America, from Its Origin until the Year 1760* (Philadelphia: Joseph M. Wilson, 1857), 255; George H. Ryden, "The Relation of the Newark Academy of Delaware to the Presbyterian Church and to Higher Education in the American Colonies," in *Delaware Notes*, 9th ser. (Newark: University of Delaware Press, 1935), 11.

6. *Records*, 151-52; Trinterud, *American Tradition*, 84; Hodge, *Constitutional History*, 2:261-62; Webster, *Presbyterian Church in America*, 256.

7. *Records*, 151, 154; Collins, *Princeton*, 7-8; DeWitt, "Historical Sketch," 330.

8. *Records*, 170-71, 175-76, 186-87; Hodge, *Constitutional History*, 2:262-63; Webster, *Presbyterian Church in America*, 256; Pears, "Colonial Education," 116, 167-68; Trinterud, *American Tradition*, 137-38.

9. Records, 186-88.

10. Trinterud, American Tradition, 138-39; Hodge, Constitutional History, 2:265; Webster, *Presbyterian Church in America*, 256-57.

11. Jonathan Edwards, *The Life of David Brainerd*, ed. Norman Pettit (New Haven: Yale University Press, 1985), 48, 54; Ross W. Beales Jr., "Harvard and Yale in the Great Awakening," *Historical Journal of Massachusetts* 14 (Jan. 1986): 3; Ralph Henry Gabriel, *Religion and Learning at Yale: The Church of Christ in the College and University, 1757-1957* (New Haven: Yale University Press, 1958), 15-16; Douglas Sloan, ed., *The Great Awakening and American Education: A Documentary History* (New York: Teachers College Press, 1973), 134.

12. Stephen Nissenbaum, ed. *The Great Awakening at Yale College* (Belmont, Calif.: Wadsworth, 1972), 116, 164-66; Sloan, *Great Awakening*, 134-37.

13. Nissenbaum, *Great Awakening*, 4-5, 58-60, 124; Trinterud, *American Tradition*, 123-24; Norman Pettit, "Prelude to Mission: Brainerd's Expulsion from Yale," *New England Quarterly* 59 (March 1986): 34-35; Beales, "Harvard and Yale," 1-10; Edwards, *David Brainerd*, 41-42, 52, 155; Gabriel, *Religion and Learning at Yale*, 16.

14. Trinterud, American Tradition, 123; Edwards, *David Brainerd*, 1, 38, 42, 154-55, 217-20; Charles Hartshorn Maxson, *The Great Awakening in the Middle Colonies* (Gloucester, Mass.: Peter Smith, 1958), 94; Pettit, "Prelude to Mission," 29, 31, 43.

15. Edwards, *David Brainerd*, 40, 52, 56, 157, 174, 251; Maxson, *Great Awakening*, 94-95; Pettit, "Prelude to Mission," 41.

16. Leigh Eric Schmidt, "Jonathan Dickinson and the Making of the Moderate Awakening," *American Presbyterians* 63 (winter 1985): 351; Martin E. Lodge, "The Great Awakening in the Middle Colonies" (Ph.D. diss., University of California at Berkeley, 1964), 281; Edwards, *David Brainerd*, 25, 28-30; Maxson, *Great Awakening*, 92-93; Trinterud, *American Tradition*, 130-31.

17. Maxson, *Great Awakening*, 93; Trinterud, *American Tradition*, 130-31; Webster,

Presbyterian Church in America, 359; John MacLean, *History of the College of New Jersey, 1746-1854* (Philadelphia: J. B. Lippincott, 1887; rpt. New York: Arno Press, 1969), 121; Frederick V. Mills, "The Society in Scotland for Propagating Christian Knowledge in British North America, 1730-1775," *Church History* 63 (March 1994): 20.

18. Edwards, *David Brainerd,* 2, 412, 417, 441; Edwin F. Hatfield, *History of Elizabeth, New Jersey* (New York: Carlton and Lanahan, 1868), 347-48.

19. Jonathan Dickinson to Thomas Foxcroft, 9 April 1746, Foxcroft Collection, Firestone Library, Princeton University; Edwards, *David Brainerd,* 54.

20. *Records,* 244; Collins, *Princeton,* 10; S. D. Alexander, *The Presbytery of New York, 1738 to 1888* (New York: Anson D. F. Randolph, 1887), 14.

21. Maxson, *Great Awakening,* 91.

22. Coalter, *Gilbert Tennent,* 142-43; Sloan, *Great Awakening,* 13, 26, 46; Lawrence A. Cremin, *American Education: The Colonial Experience, 1607-1783* (New York: Harper and Row, 1970), 318. The New Light need to charter colleges in order to counter accusations of their being enemies to learning led to the establishment of other colleges, such as Dartmouth, the College of Rhode Island (Brown), and Queens College (Rutgers).

23. William Armstrong Dod, *History of the College of New Jersey from Its Commencement, A.D. 1746, to the Present Time* (Princeton: J. T. Robinson, 1844), 3; Robert Ellis Thompson, *A History of the Presbyterian Churches in the United States* (New York: Christian Literature, 1895), 36. Briggs is quoted in Keith Jordan Hardman, "Jonathan Dickinson and the Course of American Presbyterianism, 1717-1747" (Ph.D. diss., University of Pennsylvania, 1971), 332.

24. "Jonathan Edwards to an Unnamed Correspondent in Scotland, Northampton, November 20, 1745," in *Jonathan Edwards, Apocalyptic Writings,* ed. Stephen J. Stein (New Haven: Yale University Press, 1977), 448; Collins, *Princeton,* 10-12; DeWitt, "Historical Sketch," 334-35; Alexander, *Presbytery of New York,* 14; MacLean, *College of New Jersey,* 31, 34, 36; Thomas J. Wertenbaker, *Princeton, 1746-1896* (Princeton: Princeton University Press, 1946), 21; Trinterud, *American Tradition,* 124; Hardman, "Dickinson and American Presbyterianism," 326.

25. David C. Humphrey, "The Struggle for Sectarian Control of Princeton, 1745-1760," *New Jersey History* 91 (summer 1973): 79-82.

26. Gary S. Horowitz, "New Jersey Land Riots, 1745-1755" (Ph.D. diss., Ohio State University, 1966), 48; *Minutes of the Board of Proprietors of the Eastern Division of New Jersey,* vol. 2, *1725 to 1744* (Perth Amboy: General Board of Proprietors of the Eastern Division of New Jersey, 1960 reprint), xx-xxi; Peter O. Wacker, *Land and People: A Cultural Geography of Preindustrial New Jersey: Origins and Settlement Patterns* (New Brunswick, N.J.: Rutgers University Press, 1975), 348-49; David S. Lovejoy, *Religious Enthusiasm and the Great Awakening* (Englewood Cliffs, N.J.: Prentice-Hall, 1969), 133, 144; John E. Pomfret, *Colonial New Jersey: A History* (New York: Scribner, 1973), 87-88, 123-45; Alison B. Olson, "The Founding of Princeton University: Religion and Politics in Eighteenth-Century New Jersey," *New Jersey History* 87 (autumn 1969): 150.

27. Humphrey, "Struggle for Sectarian Control," 80, 82; Olson, "Founding of Princeton," 137.

28. Horowitz, "New Jersey Land Riots," 15, 17-18; Donald L. Kemmerer, *Path to Freedom: The Struggle for Self-Government in Colonial New Jersey, 1703-1776* (Cos Cob, Conn.: John E. Edwards, 1968), 190; *Minutes of the Board of Proprietors of the Eastern Division of New Jersey,* vol. 1, *1685-1724* (Perth Amboy: General Board of Proprietors of the Eastern Division of New Jersey, 1949 reprint), 16-28; Pomfret, *Colonial New Jersey,* 7-8; Thomas L. Purvis, *Proprietors, Patronage, and Paper Money: Legislative*

Politics in New Jersey, 1703-1776 (New Brunswick: Rutgers University Press, 1986), 4-8; Theodore Thayer, *As We Were: The Story of Old Elizabethtown* (Elizabeth: Grassmann, 1964), 33.

29. One quit rent case involved Edward Vaughan, Anglican minister of Elizabeth Town. His contested claim to town land, based on a proprietary grant, was heard by the New Jersey Supreme Court and appealed to the governor and council, but no final verdict was ever rendered and the case was dropped. This and other important cases are noted in Thayer, *As We Were,* 58; Pomfret, *Colonial New Jersey,* 154; Hatfield, *History of Elizabeth,* 308; Horowitz, "New Jersey Land Riots, 50-51; Kemmerer, *Path to Freedom,* 191.

It was about this time that the Elizabeth Town records of the proceedings and related land surveys dating to settlement mysteriously disappeared. Each side blamed the other for the loss, according to Hatfield, *History of Elizabeth,* 308-9.

30. The Elizabeth Town associates did not formally respond to the proprietors' Chancery Bill, with *An Answer to a Bill in the Chancery of New Jersey,* until 1752. Hatfield, *History of Elizabeth,* 364-67; *Documents Relating to the Colonial History of the State of New Jersey,* vol. 6, *1738 to 1747,* ed. William A. Whitehead (Newark, N.J.: Daily Journal Establishment, 1882), 297; Ashbel Green, *Discourses Delivered in the College of New Jersey* (Philadelphia: E. Littell, 1822), 281; Horowitz, "New Jersey Land Riots," 62-63, 67-94; Kemmerer, *Path to Freedom,* 196-97, 199; *Minutes of the Board of Proprietors,* 2:xlvi, 90; Purvis, *Proprietors,* 209-12; Pomfret, *Colonial New Jersey,* 154-55, 158-59; Wacker, *Land and People,* 350-52.

As one might expect, at least one historian has suggested that the quit rent controversy generated among the residents of Elizabeth Town a united defense of what they saw as their rights and privileges as freeborn Englishmen and that it made them "bold in upholding the principles of liberty" during the American Revolution. Thayer, *As We Were,* v, 63. For a discussion of the New Jersey land riots as evidence of a strong commitment to the tenets of possessive individualism, rather than as a "levelers" movement against an unjust system of social and economic exploitation, see Jack P. Greene, *Pursuit of Happiness: The Social Development of Early Modern British Colonies and the Formation of American Culture* (Chapel Hill: University of North Carolina Press, 1988), 140.

31. Collins, *Princeton,* 18; DeWitt, "Historical Sketch," 351.

32. Hatfield, *History of Elizabeth,* 334.

33. Hatfield, *History of Elizabeth,* 313, 366-67; Horowitz, "New Jersey Land Riots," 61; Olson, "Founding of Princeton," 136.

34. Horowitz, "New Jersey Land Riots," 71-72. It might be noted that the previously mentioned David Brainerd became embroiled in the New Jersey land riots. At the time that riots erupted in Newark, Brainerd was preparing to settle some of his converts near Cranbury, New Jersey. Given Brainerd's ties to Dickinson and Burr, rumors spread that the Indians were gathering to intervene on the inhabitants' behalf against the proprietors. Paul Harris, "David Brainerd and the Indians: Cultural Interaction and Protestant Missionary Ideology," *American Presbyterians* 72 (spring 1994): 7.

35. Horowitz, "New Jersey Land Riots," 79-80, 91; Kemmerer, *Path to Freedom,* 202; Purvis, *Proprietors,* 212

Harvard and Yale were chartered with the approval of their respective colonial legislatures; the charter for the College of William and Mary was granted by the sovereigns of the same name. Wertenbaker, *Princeton,* 21; Hatfield, *History of Elizabeth,* 369; Hardman, "Dickinson and American Presbyterianism," 327; Collins, *Princeton,* 10-12; DeWitt, "Historical Sketch," 334-35.

36. Henry Clay Cameron, *Jonathan Dickinson and the College of New Jersey* (Princeton: C.S. Robinson, 1880), 24; Collins, *Princeton,* 12.

37. Thomas J. Wertenbaker has found a copy of the original charter of 1746 among the colonial papers of the Society for the Propagation of the Gospel. Wertenbaker, "College of New Jersey," 212. An account of the charter of 1746 can be found in "A Letter to be Made Patent" (with the provincial seal, witnessed by Governor John Hamilton, and dated 22 October 1746) in "Society for the Propagation of the Gospel in Foreign Parts, London: Letter Series B, 1701-1786," General Manuscripts, Firestone Library, Princeton University. See also Collins, *Princeton,* 17; DeWitt, "Historical Sketch," 336.

Provisions of the charter of 1746 are consistent with the general pattern of church-state relations in the area of higher education during the colonial period. As Donald G. Tewksbury has found, colonial government did not assume primary responsibility for the control and support of educational institutions. Control was given to self-perpetuating boards of trustees, without government representation, and support was left to private philanthropy. Where an established church existed, of course, the state was more closely associated with church-related schools on all counts (e.g., Harvard and Yale). Tewksbury, *The Founding of American Colleges and Universities before the Civil War: With Particular Reference to the Religious Influences Bearing upon the College Movement* (New York: Archon Books, 1965), 137-41. Douglas Sloan has found much the same pattern in his study of New Light colleges. Sloan, *Great Awakening,* 26-27.

38. Jonathan Dickinson to Captain Theophilus Howell, 30 January 1747, General Manuscripts, Firestone Library, Princeton University.

39. Cameron, *Jonathan Dickinson,* 25; Collins, *Princeton,* 21; MacLean, *College of New Jersey,* 86.

40. Cameron, *Jonathan Dickinson,* 26. The August 13 article was repeated in the *Pennsylvania Gazette* and *Pennsylvania Journal* on August 17 and September 10, and on August 27, 1747, respectively. Collins, *Princeton,* 13-14; DeWitt, "Historical Sketch," 349. Caleb Smith, a native of Brookhaven, Long Island, later became pastor of the Presbyterians of Newark Mountains. He married Martha, Dickinson's youngest child, who was born to his first wife, Joanna. DeWitt, "Historical Sketch," 349; Cameron, *Jonathan Dickinson,* 37; Hatfield, History of Elizabeth, 349; MacLean, *College of New Jersey,* 116-17.

41. Collins, *Princeton,* 14-15; Wertenbaker, *Princeton,* 16-17. On 3 March 1747, Dickinson wrote to an unidentified correspondent that the seven men "who first concocted the plan and foundation for the college" and who had been named trustees by the charter had been authorized to choose five more to join them in that capacity, and that they were considering the Tennents, Blair, Finley, and Treat. Dickinson explained that he and Pemberton were planning in two weeks to journey to Philadelphia to meet with those gentlemen and to prevail upon them to accept the five. Jonathan Dickinson to [unknown], 3 March 1747, General Manuscripts, Firestone Library, Princeton University.

42. DeWitt, "Historical Sketch," 332-33; Sloan, *Great Awakening,* 25.

43. William Tennent resigned his pastorate in 1742 and offered his property for sale. He died 6 May 1746.

44. Gilbert Tennent, *The Examiner, Examined, or Gilbert Tennent, Harmonious* (Philadelphia: William Bradford, 1743), 16; Jonathan Belcher to [Unknown], 14 November 1748, General Manuscripts, Firestone Library, Princeton University; Trinterud, *American Tradition,* 123; Milton J. Coalter Jr., *Gilbert Tennent, Son of Thunder: A Case Study of Continental Pietism's Impact on the First Great Awakening in the Middle Colonies* (Westport, Conn.: Greenwood Press, 1986), 144; "William Tennent, Sr.; Advertise-

ment for Sale of Plantation (1742)," in Pears, *Documentary History of William Tennent,* 134; Collins, *Princeton,* 16.

45. Wertenbaker, *Princeton,* 25; Maurice W. Armstrong, "The English Dissenting Deputies and the American Colonists, Part 1," *Journal of Presbyterian History* 40 (spring 1962): 24. See also Alison G. Olson, "The Eighteenth-Century Empire: The London Dissenters' Lobbies and the American Colonies," *Journal of American Studies* 26 (Apr. 1992): 41-58; Benjamin Avery to Jonathan Dickinson, 25 April 1747, General Manuscripts, Firestone Library, Princeton University. See also Olson, "Founding of Princeton," 138, 146.

46. Collins, *Princeton,* 21; DeWitt, "Historical Sketch," 341, 345; Dod, *College of New Jersey,* 5; Green, *Discourses,* 262; Hardman, "Dickinson and American Presbyterianism," 329; Kenneth P. Minkema, "The Great Awakening Conversion: The Relation of Jonathan Belcher," *William and Mary Quarterly,* 3d ser., 44 (Jan. 1987): 123; Wertenbaker, *Princeton,* 26.

47. Hatfield, *History of Elizabeth,* 377; Olson, "Founding of Princeton," 143. Although while in Massachusetts Belcher was a Congregationalist, when he moved to New Jersey, he worshiped with the Presbyterians. In 1751, he moved from Burlington to Elizabeth Town where he attended the town's (and Dickinson's) Presbyterian church. In 1753, he gave the church its charter of incorporation, a form of legal recognition not possible before Belcher's governorship. Mary E. Alward, "Early History of the First Presbyterian Church of Elizabeth, New Jersey," in *Proceedings of the Union County Historical Society* (Elizabeth, N.J.: Union County Historical Society, 1924), 159; Thayer, *As We Were,* 79, 88.

48. Purvis, *Proprietors,* 214-18.

49. Belcher to Bradbury, 16 September 1747, and Belcher to the Committee of the West Jersey Society, 18 September 1747, General Manuscripts, Firestone Library, Princeton University; MacLean, *College of New Jersey,* 102; Collins, *Princeton,* 12-13, 21; DeWitt, "Historical Sketch," 338, 341.

50. Collins, *Princeton,* 18-19, 21; Dewitt, "Historical Sketch," 341; "The First History of Princeton," *Princeton Alumni Weekly,* 11 March 1905, 369-71.

51. For the full text of the letter, see "Society for the Propagation of the Gospel," 78. See also *Glimpses of the Presbyterian Church in Colonial Days from Documents of the Society for the Propagation of the Gospel in Foreign Parts,* comp. John T. Faris (Philadelphia: Presbyterian Historical Society, 1943-44), 111.

52. Collins, *Princeton,* 18-19. The issue of Hamilton's age concerned the college's Presbyterian founders as well. In a letter written in April 1748 to Philip Doddridge, Aaron Burr noted that Hamilton's being "superannuated" at the time he granted the Presbyterians their charter, might make the Anglicans' protest more credible. Burr to Doddridge, April 1748.

53. Collins, *Princeton,* 19, 22. Princeton may also have been chosen, one source reports, because the town made the best offer, including free land and a subscription for the erection of a building. DeWitt, "Historical Sketch," 359.

54. Humphrey, "Struggle for Sectarian Control," 85; Collins, *Princeton,* 22-23; DeWitt, "Historical Sketch," 342; MacLean, *College of New Jersey,* 81-83.

55. Collins, *Princeton,* 23; *Glimpses of the Presbyterian Church,* 111-12; Humphrey, "Struggle for Sectarian Control," 86-86; Coalter, *Gilbert Tennent,* 145-46; "Society for the Propagation of the Gospel," 91-93.

In a letter dated April 1748, Aaron Burr told Philip Doddridge that Belcher had already given the college a new charter but that a few matters remained unresolved. In a letter to James Logan of Philadelphia, Belcher reported that he "had been applied to" for a new charter, but he did not indicate that it had been prepared: Belcher to Logan, 12 May 1748, General Manuscripts, Firestone Library, Princeton University.

On the charter of 1748, see MacLean, *College of New Jersey*, 84; Collins, *Princeton*, 24-27, 31, 38; DeWitt, "Historical Sketch," 339, 343-46; Olson, "Founding of Princeton," 140; and Humphrey, "Struggle for Sectarian Control," 84, 86.

56. Dod, *College of New Jersey*, 2; Green, *Discourses*, 293; Wertenbaker, *Princeton*, 87.

57. Hatfield, *History of Elizabeth*, 350; Humphrey, "Struggle for Sectarian Control," 88; MacLean, *College of New Jersey*, 116. Both objectives—to prepare clergy and to train men in "other learned professions" as "ornaments of the state as well as well as the church"—are cited in "The First History of Princeton," 369-71.

58. From "A General Account of the Rise and State of the College Lately Established in the Province of New Jersey in America," the text of which is in Sloan, *Great Awakening*, 177-86.

In the second special petition prepared by Tennent and Davies while they were in England in 1754, the two objectives were reversed, but, then, the second petition was specially designed for distribution in Scotland to clergy and other leaders of the Presbyterian Church just before the annual meeting of the General Assembly of the Church of Scotland. Gilbert Tennent and Samuel Davies, "An Account of the College of New Jersey in 1754" (London, 1754), General Manuscripts, Firestone Library, Princeton University. See also Collins, *Princeton*, 19-20; DeWitt, "Historical Sketch," 319.

59. Wertenbaker, *Princeton*, 25.

60. Collins, *Princeton*, 293-94. See also DeWitt, "Historic Sketch," 355; Francis L. Broderick, "Pulpit, Physics, and Politics: The Curriculum of the College of New Jersey, 1746-1794," *William and Mary Quarterly*, 3d ser., 6 (Jan. 1949): 49.

61. DeWitt, "Historical Sketch," 317-18, 320. Both Dickinson and Burr corresponded with Philip Doddridge, who ran a Dissenting academy at Northampton. Charles Osgood has suggested that England's dissenting academies tended to be in the forefront in breaking from the traditional course of study at English universities to include mathematics, physical sciences, and English rhetoric and literature and that this might account for the comparatively liberal curriculum that developed at Princeton. Charles G. Osgood, *Lights in Nassau Hall: A Book of the Bicentennial, Princeton 1746-1946* (Princeton: Princeton University Press, 1951), 11. See also Wertenbaker, *Princeton*, 80-87; Douglas Sloan, *The Scottish Enlightenment and the American College Ideal* (New York: Teachers College Press, 1971), 67; Broderick, "Pulpit, Physics, and Politics," 44; Wertenbaker, "College of New Jersey," 210.

62. Collins, *Princeton*, 296-97; DeWitt, "Historical Sketch," 355-58; Burr to Doddridge, 8 October 1749. For the curriculum as of 1750, see Sloan, *Scottish Enlightenment*, 63; Broderick, "Pulpit, Physics, and Politics," 45-46, 50-51.

63. Burr to Doddridge, April 1748. Hardman, "Dickinson and American Presbyterianism," 329.

64. Commencement was originally set for the third Wednesday in May, but it was postponed until November, pending final approval of the charter of 1748. Green, *Discourses*, 296; Collins, *Princeton*, 20-21; Cameron, *Jonathan Dickinson*, 35; DeWitt, "Historical Sketch," 348; Dod, *College of New Jersey*, 3, 6; Trinterud, *American Tradition*, 125; MacLean, *College of New Jersey*, 115; Wertenbaker, *Princeton*, 24.

Epilogue

1. Moses Dickinson to Thomas Foxcroft, 13 October 1747, Foxcroft Collection, Firestone Library, Princeton University; John DeWitt, "Historical Sketch of Princeton University," in *Memorial Book of the Sesquicentennial Celebration of the Founding of the College of New Jersey and of the Ceremonies Inaugurating Princeton University* (New York: Scribner, 1898), 349; Edwin F. Hatfield, *History of Elizabeth, New Jersey* (New York: Carlton and Lanahan, 1868), 350; Franklin B. Dexter, "Jonathan Dickinson," in *Biographical Sketches of the Graduates of Yale College* (New York: Henry Holt, 1885-1912), 1:47.

2. Hatfield, *History of Elizabeth,* 352; DeWitt, "Historical Sketch," 349, 351; William B. Sprague, "Jonathan Dickinson," in *Annals of the American Pulpit,* ed. William B. Sprague (New York: Robert Carter, 1868), 3:17.

3. Jonathan Dickinson's "Notice of Death and Burial," written by Ebenezer Pemberton, from the New York *Weekly Post Boy,* 12 October 1747, as quoted in Hatfield, *History of Elizabeth,* 351.

4. John Pierson, *The Faithful Minister: A Funeral Sermon Preached at Elizabeth Town, October 9, 1747. Occasioned by the Death of the Reverend Jonathan Dickinson, Late Pastor of the First Presbyterian Church in Elizabeth Town* (New York: James Parker, 1748), 1-13, 20-21.

5. Alan Heimert and Perry Miller, eds., *The Great Awakening: Documents Illustrating the Crisis and Its Consequences* (Indianapolis: Bobbs-Merrill, 1967), xxxi.

6. Leonard J. Trinterud, *The Forming of an American Tradition: A Re-examination of Colonial Presbyterianism* (Freeport, N.Y.: Books for Libraries Press, 1949), 7.

7. From among the many books on the American religious experience, see, e.g., George M. Marsden, *Religion and American Culture* (New York: Harcourt Brace Jovanovich, 1990), and Martin E. Marty, *Religion and the Republic: The American Circumstance* (Boston: Beacon Press, 1987). Among the more popular recent books on the subject in secular American life is Robert N. Bellah, *The Broken Covenant: American Civil Religion in the Time of Trial,* 2d ed. (Chicago: University of Chicago Press, 1992).

8. In addition to arguing for the genius of the New York Synod, Trinterud attributes the inspiration for that genius to Jonathan Dickinson and William Tennent Sr. See Trinterud, *American Tradition,* 308.

BIBLIOGRAPHY

DICKINSON'S PUBLISHED WORKS

A Brief Discourse upon the Divine Appointment of the Gospel Ministry, and the Methods of Its Conveyance, Thro' the Successive Ages of the Church. Boston: J. Draper for Daniel Henchman, 1738.

A Brief Illustration and Confirmation of the Divine Right of Infant Baptism; In a Plain and Familiar Dialogue between a Minister and One of His Parishioners. Boston: S. Kneeland and T. Green, 1746.

A Call to the Weary and Heavy Laden to Come unto Christ for Rest. New York: William Bradford, 1740.

The Danger of Schisms and Contentions with Respect to the Ministry and Ordinances of the Gospel. New York: John Peter Zenger, 1739.

A Defense of the Dialogue Intitled, A Display of God's Special Grace, Against the Exceptions Made to It by the Reverend Mr. A. Croswell. Boston: J. Draper, 1743.

A Defense of Presbyterian Ordination, In Answer to a Pamphlet, Entitled, A Modest Proof of the Order and Government Settled by Christ in the Church. Boston: Daniel Henchman, 1724.

A Defense of a Sermon Preached at Newark, June 2, 1736, Entitled, The Vanity of Human Institutions in the Worship of God. New York: John Peter Zenger, 1737.

A Display of God's Special Grace in a Familiar Dialogue between a Minister and a Gentleman of His Congregation, About the Work of God in the Conviction and Conversion of Sinners, So Remarkably of Late Begun and Going on in These American Parts. Boston: Rogers and Fowle, 1742.

Familiar Letters to a Gentleman, upon a Variety of Seasonable and Important Subjects in Religion. Boston: Rogers and Fowle, 1745.

Marks of Saving Faith: The Plain Distinction between a Saving and a Dead Faith. New York: American Tract Society, n.d.

Marks of True Repentence, Distinguishing between a Legal and an Evangelical Repentance. New York: American Tract Society, n.d.

The Nature and Necessity of Regeneration. New York: James Parker, 1743.

Observations of That Terrible Disease Vulgarly Called the Throat Distemper with Advice as to the Method of Cure: In a Letter to a Friend. Boston: S. Kneeland and T. Green, 1740.

A Protestation Presented to the Synod of Philadelphia, 29 May 1742. Philadelphia: B. Franklin, 1742.

The Reasonableness of Christianity, in Four Sermons, Wherein the Being and Attributes of God, the Apostasy of Man, and the Credibility of the Christian Religion Are Demonstrated by Rational Considerations. And the Divine Mission of Our Blessed Savior Proved by Scripture Arguments, Both from the Old Testament and the New; and Vindicated Against the Most Important Objections, Whether of Ancient or Modern Infidels. Boston: S. Kneeland and T. Green, 1732.

The Reasonableness of Nonconformity to the Church of England, in Point of Worship. A Second Defense of a Sermon, Preached at Newark, June 2, 1736, Entitled "The Vanity of Human Institutions in the Worship of God." Against the Exceptions of Mr. John Beach, in His Appeal to the Unprejudiced. Boston: S. Kneeland and T. Green, 1738.

Reflections upon Mr. Wetmore's Letter in Defense of Dr. Waterland's Discourse on Regeneration. Boston: J. Draper for S. Eliot, 1744.

Remarks upon a Pamphlet, Intitled, A Letter to a Friend in the Country. Philadelphia: Andrew Bradford, 1735.

Remarks upon the Postscript to the Defense of a Book Lately Reprinted at Boston, Entitled, A Modest Proof of the Order. Boston: D. Henchman, 1724.

Remarks upon Mr. Gale's Reflections on Mr. Wall's History of Infant Baptism: In a Letter to a Friend. New York: Thomas Wood, 1721.

Remarks upon a Discourse Intitled An Overture Presented to the Reverend Synod of Dissenting Ministers Sitting in Philadelphia, in the Month of September, 1728. New York: John Peter Zenger, 1729.

The Scripture Bishop, or the Divine Right of Presbyterian Ordination and Government Considered in a Dialogue between Praelaticus and Eleutherius. Boston: Daniel Henchman, 1732.

The Scripture Bishop Vindicated. A Defense of the Dialogue between Prelaticus and Eleutherius, upon the Scripture Bishop, or the Divine Right of Presbyterian Ordination and Government. Boston: S. Kneeland and T. Green for Daniel Henchman, 1733.

The Second Vindication of God's Sovereign Free Grace Against the Exceptions Made to a Former Vindication by Mr. John Beach. Boston: Rogers and Fowle, 1748.

A Sermon Preached at the Opening of the Synod at Philadelphia, September 19, 1722. Wherein Is Considered the Character of the Man of God, and his Furniture for the Exercise both of Doctrine and Discipline, With the True Boundaries of the Church's Power. Boston: Thomas Fleet for S. Gerish, 1723.

Sermons and Tracts. Edinburgh: M. Gray, 1793.

The True Scripture Doctrine, Concerning Some Important Points of Christian Faith, Particularly Eternal Election, Original Sin, Grace in Conversion, Justification by Faith, and the Saints Perseverance. Boston: G. Rogers for S. Eliot, 1741.

The Vanity of Human Institutions in the Worship of God. New York: John Peter
    Zenger, 1736.
The Vindication of God's Sovereign Free Grace. Boston: Rogers and Fowle, 1746.
*The Witness of the Spirit . . . Wherein is Distinctly Shown, in What Way and
    Manner the Spirit Himself Beareth Witness to the Adoption of the Children
    of God. On Occasion of a Wonderful Progress of Converting Grace in Those
    Parts.* 2d ed. Boston: S. Kneeland and T. Green, 1740.

PUBLISHED WORKS ATTRIBUTED TO DICKINSON

Jenkins, Obadiah. *Remarks upon the Defense of the Reverend Mr. Hemphill's Ob-
    servations: In a letter to a Friend. Wherein the Orthodoxy of His Principles,
    the Excellency and Meekness of his Temper, and the Justice of His Complaints,
    against the Rev. Commission, are briefly Considered; and Humbly Proposed
    to the View of His Admirers.* Philadelphia: Andrew Bradford, 1735.
*A Vindication of the Reverend Commission of the Synod in Answer to Some Obser-
    vations on Their Proceedings against the Reverend Mr. Hemphill.* Philadel-
    phia: Andrew Bradford, 1735.

DICKINSON'S UNPUBLISHED MANUSCRIPTS

"The Danger of the Enthusiasm of the Times." Manuscript, 1746, Foxcroft
    Collection, Firestone Library, Princeton University.
"Free Grace Vindicated, in Some Brief Remarks upon a Book Entitled Grace
    Defended by Experience Mayhew." Manuscript, undated, Foxcroft Col-
    lection, Firestone Library, Princeton University.
"Who Is on the Lord's Side?" Manuscript, 1739(?), Foxcroft Collection, Firestone
    Library, Princeton University.

DICKINSON'S UNPUBLISHED PERSONAL LETTERS AND PAPERS

Avery, Benjamin. Letter to Jonathan Dickinson. 25 April 1747. General Manu-
    scripts, Firestone Library, Princeton University.
Dickinson, Hezekiah. Letter to Jonathan Dickinson. July 1704. General Manu-
    scripts, Firestone Library, Princeton University.
Dickinson, Jonathan. Last Will and Testament. 16 September 1747. General
    Manuscripts, Firestone Library, Princeton University.
———. Fifteen Letters to Thomas Foxcroft. 24 May 1740; 12 April 1742; 27 July
    1742; 27 November 1742; 18 December 1742; 7 February 1743; 28
    November 1743; 29 August 1744; 6 May 1745; 21 January 1746; 9
    April 1746; 25 August 1746; 5 September 1746; 24 November 1746;
    two undated. Foxcroft Collection, Firestone Library, Princeton Univer-
    sity.

____. Letter to Thomas Foxcroft. 18 December 1743. Special Collections, Mugar Memorial Library, Boston University.

____. Letter to Colonel Alford. 28 November 1743. Foxcroft Collection, Firestone Library, Princeton University.

____. Letter to Captain Theophilus Howell. 30 January 1747. General Manuscripts, Firestone Library, Princeton University.

____. Letter to [unknown]. 3 March 1747. General Manuscripts, Firestone Library, Princeton University.

PUBLISHED AND UNPUBLISHED CONTEMPORARY WORKS, PAPERS, LETTERS, AND RECORDS

Alison, Francis. *An Examination and Refutation of Mr. Gilbert Tennent's Remarks.* Philadelphia: Benjamin Franklin, 1742.

Apology of the Presbytery of New Brunswick. Philadelphia: Benjamin Franklin, 1742.

Beach, John. *An Appeal to the Unprejudiced in a Supplement to The Vindication of the Worship of God According to the Church of England, from the Injurious and Uncharitable Reflections of Mr. Jonathan Dickinson.* Boston: n.p., 1737.

____. *God's Sovereignty and His Universal Love to the Souls of Men Reconciled, in a Reply to Mr. Jonathan Dickinson's Remarks upon a Sermon Entitled, Eternal Life God's Free Gift.* Boston: Rogers and Fowle, 1747.

____. *A Second Vindication of God's Sovereign Free Grace Indeed. In a Fair and Candid Examination of the Last Discourse of the Late Mr. Dickinson, Entitled a Second Vindication of God's Sovereign Free Grace.* Boston: Rogers and Fowle, 1748.

____. *A Sermon Showing that Eternal Life Is God's Free Gift, Bestowed upon Men According to Their Moral Behavior, and that Free Grace and Free Will Concur in the Affair of Man's Salvation.* Newport, R.I.: Widow Franklin, 1745.

____. *A Vindication of the Worship of God According to the Church of England, from the Aspersions Cast upon It by Mr. Jonathan Dickinson.* New York: William Bradford, 1736.

Belcher, Jonathan. Letter to Mr. Bradbury. 16 September 1747. General Manuscripts, Firestone Library, Princeton University.

____. Letter to the Committee of the West Jersey Society. 18 September 1747. General Manuscripts, Firestone Library, Princeton University.

____. Letter to Mr. Logan. 12 May 1748. General Manuscripts, Firestone Library, Princeton University.

Blair, Samuel. *A Particular Consideration of a Piece Entitled, the Querists.* Philadelphia: Benjamin Franklin, 1741.

____. *A Vindication of the Brethren Who Were Unjustly and Illegally Cast Out of the Synod of Philadelphia by a Number of the Members.* Philadelphia: Benjamin Franklin, 1744.

Browne, Arthur. *The Scripture Bishop, or the Divine Right of Presbyterian Ordination and Government, Considered in a Dialogue between Praelaticus and Eleutherius, Examined in Two Letters to a Friend* p.: n.p., 1733.

Burr, Aaron. Letter to Thomas Foxcroft. 16 September 1742. Foxcroft Collection, Firestone Library, Princeton University.

———. Three Letters to Philip Doddridge. April 1748; 8 October 1749; 31 May 1750. General Manuscripts, Firestone Library, Princeton University.

Caldwell, John. *An Impartial Trial of the Spirit.* Boston: Thomas Fleet, 1742.

Caner, Henry. *The True Nature and Method of Christian Preaching, Examined and Stated.* Newport, R.I.: Widow Franklin, 1745.

Chauncy, Charles. *Enthusiasm Described and Cautioned Against.* Boston: T. Eliot, 1742.

———. *Letter to Mr. George Wishart.* Boston: Thomas Fleet, 1743.

———. *Seasonable Thoughts on the State of Religion in New England.* Boston: Rogers and Fowle, 1743.

Checkley, John. *Choice Dialogues between a Godly Minister and an Honest Country-Man Concerning Election and Predestination. Detecting the False Principles of a Certain Man, Who Calls Himself a Presbyter of the Church of England.* Boston: n.p., 1720.

———. *A Defense of a Book Lately Re-Printed at Boston, Entitled, A Modest Proof of the Order and Government, Etc.* Boston: Thomas Fleet, 1724.

———. *A Discourse Showing Who is a True Pastor.* Boston: n.p., 1724.

———. *A Letter to Jonathan Dickinson.* Boston: n.p., 1725.

———. *A Modest Proof of the Order and Government Settled by Christ and His Apostles in the Church.* Boston: Thomas Fleet, 1723.

Clap, Thomas. *The Annals or History of Yale College.* New Haven: J. Hotchkiss and B. Mecom, 1766.

Craighead, Thomas. "Craighead Against Confessional Revision." *Journal of Presbyterian History* 45 (June 1967): 125-42.

Croswell, Andrew. *Letter from Rev. Mr. Croswell.* Boston: Rogers and Fowle, 1742.

———. *Answer to Rev. Mr. Garden's First Three Letters.* Boston: S. Kneeland and T. Green, 1741.

———. *Mr. Croswell's Reply to a Book Lately Published, Entitled a Display of God's Special Grace.* Boston: Rogers and Fowle, 1742.

———. *A Reply to a Declaration of the Associated Ministers in Boston and Charlestown with Regard to the Reverend James Davenport and His Conduct.* Boston: Rogers and Fowle, 1742.

———. *What Is Christ to Me, If He Is Not Mine?* Boston: Rogers and Fowle, 1745.

———. *Heaven Shut Against Armimians and Antinomians.* Boston: Rogers and Fowle, 1747.

———. *Second Defense of the Doctrine of Justification.* Boston: Rogers and Fowle, 1747.

Cutler, Timothy. Letter to the Reverend Dr. Gray. 8 November 1734. Photostat Collection, Box 14, Massachusetts Historical Society, Boston.

Davenport, James. *Confessions and Retractions.* Boston: S. Kneeland and T. Green, 1744.

Davies, Samuel. *The Impartial Spirit, Tried Impartially, and Convicted of Partiality.* Williamsburg: W. Parks, 1748.

Dickinson, Mary. Two Letters to John Odell. 31 December 1747; 15 January 1748. General Manuscripts, Firestone Library, Princeton University.

Dickinson, Moses. *An Inquiry into the Consequence Both of Calvinistic and Arminian Principles Compared Together. In Which the Principal Things in Mr. Beach's Second Reply to the Late Mr. Jonathan Dickinson's Second Vindication of God's Sovereign Free Grace Are Particularly Considered.* Boston: Fowle, 1750.

_____. Letter to Thomas Foxcroft. 13 October 1747. Foxcroft Collection, Firestone Library, Princeton University.

_____. Letter to Thomas Foxcroft. 25 April 1749. Foxcroft Collection, Firestone Library, Princeton University.

Documents Relating to the Colonial History of the State of New Jersey, vol. 6, *1738 to 1747.* Edited by William A. Whitehead. Newark: Daily Journal Establishment, 1882.

Edwards, Jonathan. *The Distinguishing Marks of a Work of the Spirit of God.* Edited by C. C. Goen. 1741. Reprint, New Haven: Yale University Press, 1972.

_____. *The Great Awakening.* New Haven: Yale University Press, 1972.

_____. *The Life of David Brainerd.* Edited by Norman Pettit. New Haven: Yale University Press, 1985.

_____. *Memoirs of Jonathan Edwards* in *Works of Jonathan Edwards.* Edited by Sereno E. Dwight. 1815. Reprint, Edinburgh: Banner of Truth Trust, 1974.

_____. *The Religious Affections.* New Haven: Yale University Press, 1969.

_____. *Some Thoughts Concerning the Present Revival of Religion in New England,* in Jonathan Edwards, *The Great Awakening.* Edited by C.C. Goen. 1742. Reprint, New Haven: Yale University Press, 1972.

_____. *A Strict Inquiry into the Freedom of the Will.* Edited by Paul Van Buren. New Haven: Yale University Press, 1957.

_____. *A Treatise Concerning Religious Affections.* Edited by John E. Smith. 1746. Reprint, New Haven: Yale University Press, 1972.

Edwards, Morgan, ed. *Materials Towards a History of the Baptists.* 1770, 1792. Reprint, Danielsville, Ga.: Heritage Papers, 1984.

An Examination and Refutation of Mr. Gilbert Tennent's Remarks on the Protestation Presented to the Synod of Philadelphia, June 1, 1741. Philadelphia: Benjamin Franklin, 1742.

Finley, Samuel. *An Account of the College of New Jersey.* Woodbridge, N.J.: James Parker, 1764.

_____. *A Charitable Plea for the Speechless; or, The Right of Believers' Infants to Baptism Vindicated: And the Mode of It by Pouring or Sprinkling, Justified.* Philadelphia: William Bradford, 1746.

_____. *Christ Triumphing and Satan Raging.* Philadelphia: Benjamin Franklin, 1741.

_____. *Clear Light Put Out in Darkness.* Philadelphia: Benjamin Franklin, 1743.

_____. *A Letter to a Friend.* Philadelphia: Benjamin Franklin, 1740.

_____. *The Successful Minister of Christ Distinguished in Glory: A Sermon Occasioned by the Death of Mr. Gilbert Tennent, Pastor of the 2nd Presbyterian Congregation in Philadelphia.* Philadelphia: William Bradford, 1764.

_____. *A Vindication of the Charitable Plea for the Speechless: In Answer to Mr. Abel Morgan's Anti-Paedo Rantism.* Philadelphia: William Bradford, 1748.

Fisher, Hugh. *A Preservative from Damnable Errors in the Unction of the Holy One.* Boston: n.p., 1730.

Foxcroft, Thomas. *Eusebius Inermatus.* Boston: Daniel Henchman, 1733.

_____. *The Ruling and Ordaining Power of Congregational Bishops or Presbyters, Defended.* Boston: Samuel Gerrish, 1724.

Franklin, Benjamin. *Autobiography.* Edited by John Bigelow. 1868. Reprint, Garden City, N.Y.: Dolphin Books, n.d.

_____. *The Papers of Benjamin Franklin,* vol. 2. Edited by Leonard W. Labaree. New Haven: Yale University Press, 1960.

Gillespie, George. *An Examination and Refutation of Mr. Gilbert Tennent's Remarks.* Philadelphia: Benjamin Franklin, 1741.

_____. *A Letter to the Reverend Brethren of the Presbytery of New York, or of Elizabeth Town. In Which Is Shown the Unjustness of the Synod's Protest, Entered Last May at Philadelphia, Against Some of the Reverend Brethren.* Philadelphia: Benjamin Franklin, 1742.

_____. *Remarks on Mr. George Whitefield Proving Him to Be a Man Under Delusion.* Philadelphia: Benjamin Franklin, 1744.

_____. *A Sermon Against Divisions in Christ's Church.* Philadelphia: William Bradford, 1740.

Gillies, John, ed. *Historical Collections Related to Remarkable Periods of the Success of the Gospel.* 1754. Reprint, Kelso: John Rutherford, 1845.

_____. *Historical Collections Relating to the Revival.* Edinburgh: Banner of Truth Trust, 1981.

Glimpses of the Presbyterian Church in Colonial Days from Documents of the Society for the Propagation of the Gospel in Foreign Parts. Compiled by John T. Faris. Philadelphia: Presbyterian Historical Society, 1943-44.

Hancock, John. *The Examiner, or Gilbert Versus Tennent.* Boston: S. Eliot, 1742.

Harvard College Faculty. *A Letter on Mr. George Whitefield.* Boston: Thomas Fleet, 1744.

Hetfield, Mathias. Letter to Benjamin Avery. 20 March 1748. General Manuscripts, Firestone Library, Princeton University.

_____. Letter to Philip Doddridge. 12 October 1749. General Manuscripts, Firestone Library, Princeton University.

Hetfield, Mathias, and Stephen Crane. Letter to Benjamin Avery. 20 December 1749. General Manuscripts, Firestone Library, Princeton University.

"History of the Presbytery of New Brunswick, Minutes, 1740-1741." *Journal of Presbyterian History* 7 (1913-14): 142-54.

Johnson, Samuel. *A Letter from Aristocles to Authades, Concerning the Sovereignty and Promise of God.* Boston: Thomas Fleet, 1745.

_____. *A Letter to Mr. Jonathan Dickinson, in Defense of Aristocles to Authades, Concerning the Sovereignty and Promises of God.* Boston: Rogers and Fowle, 1747.

Klett, Guy S., ed. *Records of the Presbyterian Church in America, 1706-1789.* Philadelphia: Presbyterian Historical Society, 1976.

McGregore, David. *The Spirits of the Present Day Tried.* Boston: Daniel Henchman, 1742.

Mayhew, Experience. Letter to Thomas Foxcroft. 24 August 1743. Foxcroft Collection, Firestone Library, Princeton University.

_____. Letter to Thomas Foxcroft. 24 August 1744. Foxcroft Collection, Firestone Library, Princeton University.

_____. *Grace Defended, in a Modest Plea for an Important Truth; Namely That the Offer of Salvation Made to Sinners in the Gospel, Comprises in It an Offer of the Grace Given in Regeneration.* Boston: B. Green for Daniel Henchman, 1744.

_____. *A Letter to a Gentleman on that Question. Whether Saving Grace be Different in Species from Common Grace, or in Degree Only.* Boston: S. Kneeland and T. Green, 1747.

Minutes of the Board of Proprietors of the Eastern Division of New Jersey, vol. 1, *1685-1724.* Perth Amboy: General Board of Proprietors of the Eastern Division of New Jersey, 1949.

Minutes of the Board of Proprietors of the Eastern Division of New Jersey, vol. 2, *1725 to 1744.* Perth Amboy: General Board of Proprietors of the Eastern Division of New Jersey, 1960.

Minutes of the Philadelphia Baptist Association from A.D. *1707 to* A.D. *1807.* Edited by A. D. Gillette. Philadelphia: American Baptist Publication Society, 1851.

Morgan, Abel. *Anti-Paedo Rantism Defended.* Philadelphia: Benjamin Franklin, 1750.

_____. *Anti-Paedo Rantism; or, Mr. Samuel Finley's Charitable Plea for the Speechless Examined and Refuted: The Baptism of Believers Maintained; and the Mode of it by Immersion Vindicated.* Philadelphia: Benjamin Franklin, 1747.

Morgan, Joseph. *The Great Concernment of Gospel Ordinances, Manifested from the Great Effect of the Well Improving or Neglect of Them.* New York: William and Andrew Bradford, 1712.

Pears, Thomas Clinton, Jr. *Documentary History of William Tennent and the Log College.* Philadelphia: Presbyterian Historical Society, 1940.

Pemberton, Ebenezer. *A Sermon Preached before the Commission of the Synod at Philadelphia, April 20th, 1735.* New York: John Peter Zenger, 1735.

_____. *Sermon Preached at the Ordination of David Brainerd to the Gospel Ministry.* New Haven: S. Converse, 1822.

Pierson, John. *The Faithful Minister: A Funeral Sermon Preached at Elizabeth Town, October 9, 1747. Occasioned by the Death of the Reverend Jonathan Dickinson, Late Pastor of the First Presbyterian Church in Elizabeth Town.* New York: James Parker, 1748.

Prince, Thomas. *The Christian History, Containing Accounts of the Revival and Propagation of Religion in Great Britain and America.* Vol. 1. Boston: S. Kneeland and T. Green, 1744.

Querists. *Reply to Mr. George Whitefield's Letter.* Philadelphia: Benjamin Franklin, 1740.

Records of the Presbyterian Church in the United States of America. Edited by William H. Roberts. Philadelphia: Presbyterian Board of Publication and Sabbath School Work, 1904.

"Records of the Presbytery of New Castle upon Delaware," *Journal of the Presbyterian Historical Society* 14 (September 1931): 289-308; 14 (December 1931): 377-84; 15 (June 1932): 73-120; 15 (September 1932): 159-68; 15 (December 1932): 174-207.

Robe, James. *The Christian Monthly History.* Edinburgh: R. Fleming and Alison, 1744.

Rowland, John. *An Account of the Revival at Freehold, New Jersey.* Philadelphia: William Bradford, 1742.

"A Short Account of the Rise and State of the College in the Province of New Jersey in America." *New American Magazine.* March 1760, 103-5.

Smith, Josiah. *Humane Imposition Proved Unscriptural, or the Divine Right of Private Judgement.* Boston: Daniel Henchman, 1729.

_____. *No New Thing to be Slandered.* Boston: n.p., 1730.

Society for the Propagation of the Gospel in Foreign Parts, London: Letter Series B, 1701-1786. General Manuscripts, Firestone Library, Princeton University.

Tennent, Gilbert, and Samuel Davies. "An Account of the College of New Jersey in 1754" (London, 1754). General Manuscripts, Firestone Library, Princeton University.

Tennent, Gilbert. *The Danger of an Unconverted Ministry.* Philadelphia: B. Franklin, 1740.

_____. *Declaration of the Presbyteries of New Brunswick and New Castle.* Philadelphia: William Bradford, 1743.

_____. *The Examiner, Examined, or Gilbert Tennent, Harmonious.* Philadelphia: William Bradford, 1743.

_____. *Necessity of Holding Fast the Truth.* Boston: S. Kneeland and T. Green, 1743.

_____. *Irencium Ecclesiasticum, or a Humble Impartial Essay upon the Peace of Jerusalem.* Philadelphia: William Bradford, 1749.

_____. *Remarks upon a Protestation Presented to the Synod of Philadelphia.* Philadelphia: B. Franklin, 1741.

Tennent, John. *The Nature of Regeneration Opened, and Its Absolute Necessity in or to Salvation, Demonstrated in Three Sermons.* Boston: S. Kneeland and T. Green, 1735.

Thomson, John. *The Doctrine of Convictions.* Philadelphia: Andrew Bradford, 1741.

_____. *The Government of the Church of Christ.* Philadelphia: Andrew Bradford, 1741.

_____. *An Overture Presented to the Synod*. Philadelphia: Franklin and Meredith, 1729.

Wall, William. *A Conference between Two Men That had Doubts about Infant Baptism*. London: Joseph Downing, 1706.

Wall, William and John Gale. *The History of Infant Baptism, Together with Mr. Gale's Reflections and Dr. Wall's Defense*. 3 vols. Edited by Henry Cotton. Oxford: Oxford University Press, 1836.

Walter, Thomas. *An Essay upon That Paradox, Infallibility May Mistake*. Boston: Daniel Henchman, 1724.

Waterland, Daniel. *Regeneration Stated and Explained According to Scripture and Antiquity in a Discourse*. New York: Hugh Gaine, 1793.

Wetmore, James and Samuel Johnson. *Eleutherius Enervatus; or, An Answer to a Pamphlet, Entitled, the Divine Right of Presbyterian Ordination. Done by Way of a Dialogue between Eusebius and Eleutherius*. New York: John Peter Zenger, 1733.

_____. *A Letter Occasioned by Mr. Dickinson's Remarks upon Mr. Waterland's Discourse on Regeneration*. New York: J. Parker, 1744.

Whitefield, George. *George Whitefield's Journals, 1737-1741*. Edited by William V. Davis. Gainesville, Fla.: Scholars Facsimiles and Reprints, 1969.

_____. *A Letter from Mr. Whitefield to Some Church Members of the Presbyterian Persuasion in Answer to Certain Scruples and Queries Relating to Some Passages in His Printed Sermons and Other Writings*. Boston: S. Kneeland and T. Green, 1740.

_____. *Works*. Volume I. Edinburgh: Banner of Truth Trust, 1976.

Wigglesworth, Edward. *Sober Remarks on a Modest Proof of the Order and Government Settled by Christ and His Apostles in the Church*. Boston: Samuel Gerrish, 1724.

SECONDARY SOURCES ON DICKINSON

Cameron, Henry Clay. *Jonathan Dickinson and the College of New Jersey*. Princeton: C.S. Robinson, 1880.

Hardman, Keith Jordan. "Jonathan Dickinson and the Course of American Presbyterianism, 1717-1747." Ph.D. diss., University of Pennsylvania, 1971.

Harlan, David C. "The Travail of Religious Moderation: Jonathan Dickinson and the Great Awakening." *Journal of Presbyterian History* 61 (winter 1983): 411-26.

_____. "A World of Double Visions and Second Thoughts: Jonathan Dickinson's *Display of God's Special Grace*." *Early American Literature* 21 (fall 1986): 118-30.

Le Beau, Bryan. "'The Acrimonious Spirit' among Baptists and Presbyterians in the Middle Colonies during the Great Awakening," *American Baptist Quarterly* 9 (September 1990): 167-83.

_____. "'The Angelical Conjunction' Revisited: Another Look at the Preacher-Physician in Colonial America and the Throat Distemper Epidemic of 1735-1740." *Journal of American Culture* 18 (fall 1995): 1-12.

_____. " Joseph Morgan's Sermon at the Ordination of Jonathan Dickinson and the Clerical Literature of Colonial New England and New Jersey." *New Jersey History* 109 (spring/summer 1991): 55-81.

_____. "The Subscription Controversy and Jonathan Dickinson." *Journal of Presbyterian History* 54 (fall 1976): 317-35.

Ott, Philip W. "Christian Experience as Seen in the Writings of Jonathan Dickinson." M.A. thesis, Princeton Theological Seminary, 1963.

Samworth, Herbert L. "Those Astonishing Wonders of His Grace: Jonathan Dickinson and the Great Awakening." Th.D. diss., Westminster Theological Seminary, 1988.

Schmidt, Leigh Eric. "Jonathan Dickinson and the Making of the Moderate Awakening." *American Presbyterians* 63 (winter 1985): 341-53.

Sloat, Leslie W. "Jonathan Dickinson and the Problem of Synodical Authority." *Westminster Theological Journal* 8 (June 1946): 149-65.

SELECTED SECONDARY WORKS

Ahlstrom, Sydney E. *A Religious History of the American People.* New Haven: Yale University Press, 1972.

Aldridge, Alfred Owen. *Benjamin Franklin and Nature's God.* Durham, N.C.: Duke University Press, 1947.

Alexander, Archibald. *Biographical Sketches of the Founder and Principal Alumni of the Log College.* Philadelphia: Presbyterian Board of Publication, 1851.

Alexander, S. D. *The Presbytery of New York, 1738 to 1888.* New York: Anson D. F. Randolph, 1887.

Alward, Mary E. "Early History of the First Presbyterian Church of Elizabeth, New Jersey." In *Proceedings of the Union County Historical Society.* Elizabeth, N.J.: Union County Historical Society, 1924.

Armstrong, Maurice W. "The English Dissenting Deputies and the American Colonists, Part 1." *Journal of Presbyterian History* 40 (spring 1962): 24-37.

_____. "English, Scottish, and Irish Backgrounds of American Presbyterianism, 1689-1729." *Journal of the Presbyterian Historical Society* 34 (March 1954): 3-18.

Armstrong, Maurice W., Lefferts A. Loetscher, and Charles A. Anderson, eds. *The Presbyterian Enterprise: Sources of American Presbyterian History.* Philadelphia: Westminster Press, 1956.

Atwater, Lyman. "The Great Awakening of 1740." *Presbyterian Quarterly and Princeton Review* 5 (October 1876): 678-81.

Bainton, Roland H. *Yale and the Ministry: A History of Education for the Christian Ministry at Yale from the Founding in 1701.* New York: Harper, 1957.

Baldwin, Ebenezer. *Annals of Yale College.* New Haven: Hezekiah Howe, 1831.

Barker, William S. "The Hemphill Case, Benjamin Franklin, and Subscription to the Westminster Confession." *American Presbyterians* 69 (winter 1991): 243-56.

_____. "Subscription to the Westminster Confession of Faith and Catechisms." *Presbyterion: The Covenant Seminary Review* 10 (1984): 1-19.

Barkley, John M. "The Presbyterian Church in Ireland (Part 1)." *Journal of Presbyterian History* 44 (December 1966): 244-65.

Batinski, Michael C. *Jonathan Belcher, Colonial Governor.* Lexington: University Press of Kentucky, 1996.

Beales, Ross W. Jr. "Harvard and Yale in the Great Awakening." *Historical Journal of Massachusetts* 14 (January 1986): 1-10.

Beaver, Robert Pierce. "Methods in American Missions to the Indians in the 17th and 18th Centuries: Calvinist Models for Protestant Foreign Missions." *Journal of the Presbyterian Historical Society* 47 (July 1969): 124-48.

Bellah, Robert N. *The Broken Covenant: American Civil Religion in the Time of Trial.* 2d ed. Chicago: University of Chicago Press, 1992.

Blaikie, Alexander. *A History of Presbyterianism in New England.* Boston: Alexander Moore, 1881.

Bloch, Ruth H. "Religion and Ideological Change in the American Revolution." In *Religion and American Politics: From the Colonial Period to the 1980's,* edited by Mark A. Noll. New York: Oxford University Press, 1990.

Bolan, C. Gordon. *The English Presbyterians in New England.* Boston: Alexander Moore, 1882.

Bonomi, Patricia U. *Under the Cope of Heaven: Religion, Society, and Politics in Colonial America.* New York: Oxford University Press, 1986.

Boudinot, Elias. "An Account of a Remarkable Revival of Religion in Freehold, New Jersey." *Christian Advocate* 2 (September; October 1824): 400-404; 453-55.

Boyd, Jesse L. *A History of Baptists in America prior to 1845.* New York: American Press, 1957.

Brackney, William H. *The Baptists.* Westport, Conn.: Greenwood Press, 1988.

_____, ed. *Baptist Life and Thought, 1600-1980: A Source Book.* Valley Forge, Penn.: Judson Press, 1983.

Brauer, Jerald. "Conversion: From Puritanism to Revivalism." *Journal of Religion* 58 (July 1978): 227-43.

Briggs, Charles Augustus. *American Presbyterianism: Its Origins and Early History.* New York: Scribner, 1885.

Brockway, Robert W. "The Significance of James Davenport in the Great Awakening." *Journal of Religious Thought* 24 (June 1968): 86-94.

Broderick, Francis L. "Pulpit, Physics, and Politics: The Curriculum of the College of New Jersey, 1746-1794." *William and Mary Quarterly,* 3d ser., 6 (January 1949): 42-60.

Brynestad, Lawrence E.. "The Great Awakening in the New England and Middle Colonies." *Journal of the Presbyterian Historical Society* 14 (June; September 1930): 80-91, 104-41.

Bumsted, J. M., and John E. Van de Wetering. *What Must I Do to Be Saved? The Great Awakening in Colonial America.* Hinsdale, Ill.: Dryden Press, 1976.

Burr, Nelson R. *The Anglican Church in New Jersey.* Philadelphia: Church Historical Society, 1954.

———. *Education in New Jersey: 1630-1871.* Princeton: Princeton University Press, 1942.

Burt, Henry M. *The First Century of the History of Springfield.* Springfield, Mass.: privately printed, 1899.

Bushman, Richard L., ed. *The Great Awakening: Documents on the Revival of Religion, 1740-1745.* New York: Atheneum, 1970.

Butler, Jon. "Enthusiasm Described and Decried: The Great Awakening as Interpretive Fiction." *Journal of American History* 69 (September 1982): 305-25.

Buxbaum, Melvin H. *Benjamin Franklin and the Zealous Presbyterians.* University Park: Pennsylvania State University Press, 1975.

Capers, Thomas Stacy. "The Great Awakening in the Middle Colonies." *Journal of the Presbyterian Historical Society* 8 (September 1916): 296-315.

Chamberlain, Ava. "Self-Deception as a Theological Problem in Jonathan Edwards's 'Treatise Concerning Religious Affections.'" *Church History* 63 (December 1994): 541-56.

Cherry, Conrad. *The Theology of Jonathan Edwards.* Garden City, N.Y.: Anchor Books, 1966.

Cheyney, Edward Potts. *History of the University of Pennsylvania, 1740-1940.* Philadelphia: University of Pennsylvania Press, 1940.

Christensen, Merton A. "Franklin on the Hemphill Trial: Deism versus Presbyterian Orthodoxy." *William and Mary Quarterly,* 3d ser., 10 (July 1953): 422-40.

Christian, John T. *A History of the Baptists of the United States: From the First Settlement of the Country to the Year 1845.* Nashville: Sunday School Board of the Southern Baptist Convention, 1926.

Clark, Samuel A. *The History of St. John's Church, Elizabeth Town, New Jersey: From the Year 1703 to the Present Time.* Philadelphia: J. B. Lippincott, 1857.

Coalter, Milton J. Jr. *Gilbert Tennent, Son of Thunder: A Case Study of Continental Pietism's Impact on the First Great Awakening in the Middle Colonies.* Westport, Conn.: Greenwood Press, 1986.

———. "The Radical Pietism of Count Nicholas Zinzendorf as a Conservative Influence on the Awakener, Gilbert Tennent." *Church History* 49 (March 1980): 35-46.

Collins, Varnum Lansing. "George Whitefield and the College of New Jersey." *Princeton University Bulletin* 9 (June 1897): 23-33.

———. *Princeton.* New York: Oxford University Press, 1914.

Cornwall, Robert D. "The Search for the Primitive Church: The Use of Early Church Fathers in the High Church Anglican Tradition, 1680-1745." *Anglican and Episcopal History* 59 (September 1990): 303-29.

Corrigan, John. "Catholick Congregational Clergy and Public Piety." *Church History* 60 (June 1991): 210-22.

_____. *The Prism of Piety: Catholick Congregational Clergy at the Beginning of the Enlightenment.* New York: Oxford University Press, 1991.

Cowing, Cedric B. *The Great Awakening and the American Revolution: Colonial Thought in the Eighteenth Century.* Chicago: Rand McNally, 1971.

Craven, Elijah R. "The Log College of Neshaminy and Princeton University." *Journal of the Presbyterian Historical Society* 1 (June 1902): 308-14.

Crawford, Michael J. "New England and the Scottish Religious Revivals of 1742." *American Presbyterians* 69 (spring 1991): 23-32.

Cremin, Lawrence A. *American Education: The Colonial Experience, 1607-1783.* New York: Harper and Row, 1970.

Cross, Arthur Lyon. *The Anglican Episcopate and the American Colonies.* Hamden, Conn.: Archon Books, 1964.

Curry, Thomas J. *The First Freedoms: Church and State in America to the Passage of the First Amendment.* New York: Oxford University Press, 1986.

Dallimore, Arnold. *George Whitefield.* London: Banner of Truth Trust, 1970.

Demos, John Putnam. *Entertaining Satan: Witchcraft and the Culture of Early New England.* New York: Oxford University Press, 1986.

DeWitt, John. "Historical Sketch of Princeton University," in *Memorial Book of the Sesquicentennial Celebration of the Founding of the College of New Jersey and of the Ceremonies Inaugurating Princeton University.* New York: Scribner, 1898.

Dexter, Franklin B. *Biographical Sketches of the Graduates of Yale College.* 6 vols. New York: Henry Holt, 1885-1912.

_____, ed. *Documentary History of Yale University.* New Haven: Yale University Press, 1916.

Dod, William Armstrong. *History of the College of New Jersey from Its Commencement, A.D. 1746, to the Present Time.* Princeton: J. T. Robinson, 1844.

Drury, Clifford M. "Presbyterian Beginnings in New England and the Middle Colonies." *Journal of the Presbyterian Historical Society* 34 (March 1956): 19-35.

Dunaway, Wayland. *The Scotch-Irish of Colonial Pennsylvania.* Chapel Hill: University of North Carolina Press, 1944.

Dunn, Elizabeth E. "From a Bold Youth to a Reflective Sage: A Reevaluation of Benjamin Franklin's Religion." *Pennsylvania Magazine of History and Biography* 111 (October 1987): 501-24.

Eells, Earnest Edward. "Indian Missions on Long Island, Part IV." *Journal of the Presbyterian Historical Society* 19 (June 1940): 47-64.

Ellison, Henry C. *Church of the Founding Fathers of New Jersey: A History.* Cornish, Maine: Carbrook Press, 1964.

Encyclopedia of Religion. Edited by Mircea Eliade. New York: Macmillan, 1987.

Encyclopedia of Religion and Ethics. Edited by James Hastings. New York: Scribner, 1937.

Fawcett, Arthur. *The Cambuslang Revival: The Scottish Evangelical Revival of the Eighteenth Century.* London: Banner of Truth Trust, 1971.

Fiering, Norman S. *Jonathan Edwards's Moral Thought and Its British Context.* Chapel Hill: University of North Carolina Press, 1981.

_____. "Will and Intellect in the New England Mind." *William and Mary Quarterly,* 3d ser., 29 (October 1972): 515-58.

Finney, William P. "The Period of the Isolated Congregations and the General Presbytery." *Journal of the Presbyterian Historical Society* 15 (March 1932): 8-17.

"The first History of Princeton," *Princeton Alumni Weekly,* 11 March 1905, 369-71.

Ford, Henry H. *The Scotch-Irish in America.* New York: Peter Smith, 1944.

Frantz, John B. "The Awakening of Religion among the German Settlers in the Middle Colonies." *William and Mary Quarterly,* 3d ser., 33 (April 1976): 266-88.

_____. "Religion in the Middle Colonies: A Model for the Nation," *Journal of Regional Cultures* 2 (fall/winter 1982): 9-22.

Fraser, James W. "The Great Awakening and the Patterns of Presbyterian Theological Education." *Journal of Presbyterian History* 60 (fall 1982): 189-208.

Gabriel, Ralph Henry. *Religion and Learning at Yale: The Church of Christ in the College and University, 1757-1957.* New Haven: Yale University Press, 1958.

Gaustad, Edwin Scott. *The Great Awakening in New England.* Gloucester, Mass.: Peter Smith, 1965.

_____. *Historical Atlas of Religion in America.* Rev. ed. New York: Harper and Row, 1976.

Gillett, Ezra Hall. "Adoption of the Confession of Faith." *Biblical Repertory and Princeton Review* 30 (October 1858): 669-92.

_____. *History of the Presbyterian Church in the United States of America.* 2 vols. Philadelphia: Presbyterian Publishing Committee, 1864.

Goen, C. C. *Revivalism and Separatism in New England, 1740-1800: Strict Congregationalists and Separate Baptists in the Great Awakening.* New Haven: Yale University Press, 1962.

Goodfriend, Joyce D. "A New Look at Presbyterian Origins in New York City." *American Presbyterians* 62 (fall 1989): 199-207.

_____. *Before the Melting Pot: Society and Culture in Colonial New York City, 1664-1730.* Princeton: Princeton University Press, 1992.

Green, Ashbel. *Discourses Delivered in the College of New Jersey.* Philadelphia: E. Littell, 1822.

_____. "Letters to Presbyterians." *Christian Advocate* 11 (July, August, September, October, November, December 1833): 318-25, 358-66, 411-22, 458-65, 493-95, 547-53; 12 (January, February, March, April 1834): 27-35, 78-86, 128-33, 181-84.

Greene, Jack P. *Pursuit of Happiness: The Social Development of the Early Modern British Colonies and the Transformation of American Culture.* Chapel Hill: University of North Carolina Press, 1988.

Griffiths, Thomas S. *A History of Baptists in New Jersey.* Hightstown, N.J.: Barr Press, 1964.

Hageman, J. F. *History of Princeton.* Philadelphia: J. B. Lippincott, 1879.

Hall, Timothy D. *Contested Boundaries: Itinerancy and the Reshaping of the Colonial American Religious World.* Durham, N.C.: Duke University Press, 1994.

Hanzsche, William T. "New Jersey Molders of the American Presbyterian Church." *Journal of the Presbyterian Historical Society* 24 (June 1946): 71-82.

Harlan, David C. *Clergy and the Great Awakening in New England.* Ann Arbor, MI: UMI Research Press, 1980.

Harmelink, Herman. "Another Look at Frelinghuysen and His Awakening." *Church History* 37 (December 1968): 423-38.

Harris, Paul. "David Brainerd and the Indians: Cultural Interaction and Protestant Missionary Ideology." *American Presbyterians* 72 (spring 1994): 1-9.

Hatfield, Edwin F. *History of Elizabeth, New Jersey.* New York: Carlton and Lanahan, 1868.

Heimert, Alan. *Religion and the American Mind: From the Great Awakening to the Revolution.* Cambridge: Harvard University Press, 1966.

Heimert, Alan and Andrew Delbanco, eds., *The Puritans in America: A Narrative Anthology.* Cambridge: Harvard University Press, 1985.

Heimert, Alan, and Perry Miller, eds. *The Great Awakening: Documents Illustrating the Crisis and Its Consequences.* Indianapolis: Bobbs-Merrill, 1967.

Henry, Stuart C. *George Whitefield: Wayfaring Witness.* New York: Abingdon Press, 1957.

Hill, Edward Yates. "Some Leaders of the General Synod." *Journal of the Presbyterian Historical Society* 9 (September 1918): 295-307.

Hodge, Charles. *The Constitutional History of the Presbyterian Church in the United States of America.* 2 vols. Philadelphia: William S. Martien, 1839-40.

Hoopes, James. "Jonathan Edwards's Religious Psychology." *Journal of American History* 69 (March 1983): 849-65.

Horowitz, Gary S. "New Jersey Land Riots, 1745-1755." Ph.D. diss., Ohio State University, 1966.

Humphrey, David C. "The Struggle for Sectarian Control of Princeton, 1745-1760." *New Jersey History* 91 (summer 1973): 77-90.

Ingram, George. "The Story of the Log College." *Journal of the Presbyterian Historical Society* 13 (August 1929): 487-511.

Isaac, Rhys. *The Transformation of Virginia, 1740-1790.* Chapel Hill: University of North Carolina Press, 1982.

Jacobsen, Douglas. *An Unprov'd Experiment: Religious Pluralism in Colonial New Jersey.* Brooklyn: Carlson, 1991.

Judd, Sylvester. *History of Hadley: Including the Early History of Hatfield, South Hadley, Amherst, and Granby, Massachusetts.* Springfield, Mass.: H. R. Huntington, 1905.

Kemmerer, Donald L. *Path to Freedom: The Struggle for Self-Government in Colonial New Jersey, 1703-1776.* Cos Cob, Conn.: John E. Edwards, 1968.

Kempshall, Everard. *The Centennial of the Anniversary of the Burning of the Church Edifice of the First Church of Elizabeth, New Jersey: Caldwell and the Revolution: A Historical Sketch of the First Presbyterian Church of Elizabeth, Prior to and During the War of the Revolution* (Elizabeth: Elizabeth Daily Journal, 1881).

King, Moses. *King's Handbook of Springfield, Massachusetts.* Springfield: James D. Gill, 1884.

Kingsley, William L. *Yale College: A Sketch of Its History.* 2 vols. New York: Henry Holt, 1879.

Labaree, Leonard. "Conservative Attitudes Toward the Great Awakening." *William and Mary Quarterly,* 3d ser., 1 (October 1944): 331-52.

Lambert, Frank. "The Great Awakening as Artifact: George Whitefield and the Construction of Intercolonial Revival, 1739-1745." *Church History* 60 (June 1991): 223-46.

———. "'Pedlar in Divinity': George Whitefield and the Great Awakening, 1737-1745." *Journal of American History* 77 (December 1990): 812-37.

Landsman, Ned C. "Revivalism and Nativism in the Middle Colonies: The Great Awakening in the Scots Community in East New Jersey." *American Quarterly* 34 (June 1982): 149-64.

———. *Scotland and Its First American Colony, 1683-1765.* Princeton: Princeton University Press, 1985.

Lodge, Martin E. "The Crises of the Churches in the Middle Colonies, 1720-1750." *Pennsylvania Magazine of History and Biography* 95 (April 1971): 195-220.

———. "The Great Awakening in the Middle Colonies." Ph.D. diss., University of California at Berkeley, 1964.

Loetscher, Frederick W. "The Adopting Act." *Journal of the Presbyterian Historical Society* 13 (December 1929): 337-55.

Lovejoy, David S. *Religious Enthusiasm and the Great Awakening.* Englewood Cliffs, N.J.: Prentice-Hall, 1969.

———. *Religious Enthusiasm in the New World: Heresy to Revolution.* Cambridge: Harvard University Press, 1985.

McCartney, Clarence Edward. "The Period of the General Synod." *Journal of the Presbyterian Historical Society* 15 (March 1932): 18-30.

McDermott, Gerald R. "Jonathan Edwards, the City on a Hill, and the Redeemer Nation: A Reappraisal." *American Presbyterians* 69 (spring 1991): 33-47.

McLachlan, James. *Princetonians, 1748-1768: A Biographical Dictionary.* Princeton: Princeton University Press, 1976.

MacLean, John. *History of the College of New Jersey, 1746-1854.* Philadelphia: J. B. Lippincott, 1887; reprint, New York: Arno Press, 1969.

McLoughlin, William G. *Isaac Backus and the American Pietistic Tradition.* Boston: Little, Brown, 1967.

———. *New England Dissent, 1630-1833: The Baptists and the Separation of Church and State.* Cambridge: Harvard University Press, 1971.

_____. *Revivals, Awakenings, and Reform.* Chicago: University of Chicago Press, 1978.

Manley, Kenneth Ross. "Origins of the Baptists: The Case for Development from Puritan Separatism." *Baptist History and Heritage* 22 (October 1987): 34-46.

Maring, Norman H. *Baptists in New Jersey: A Study in Transition.* Valley Forge, Penn.: Judson Press, 1964.

Marsden, George M. *Fundamentalism and American Culture: The Shaping of Twentieth-Century Evangelicalism, 1870-1925.* New York: Oxford University Press, 1980.

_____. *Religion and American Culture.* New York: Harcourt Brace Jovanovich, 1990.

Marty, Martin E. *Pilgrims in Their Own Land: 500 Years of Religion in America.* New York: Penguin Books, 1986.

_____. *Religion and the Republic: The American Circumstance.* Boston: Beacon Press, 1987.

Materials toward a History of the Baptists in New Jersey. New York: Robert Carter, 1865.

Maxson, Charles Hartshorn. *The Great Awakening in the Middle Colonies.* Gloucester, Mass.: Peter Smith, 1958.

May, Henry F. *The Enlightenment in America.* New York: Oxford University Press, 1976.

Mead, Sidney E. "From Coercion to Persuasion: Another Look at the Rise of Religious Liberty and the Emergence of Denominationalism." *Church History* 25 (September 1956): 317-37.

Miller, Howard. *The Revolutionary College: American Presbyterian Higher Education, 1707-1837.* New York: New York University Press, 1973.

Miller, Perry. *Errand into the Wilderness.* New York: Harper and Row, 1956.

_____. *Jonathan Edwards.* New York: William Sloane Associates, 1949.

_____. *The New England Mind: From Colony to Province.* Cambridge: Harvard University Press, 1953.

_____. *Orthodoxy in Massachusetts: 1630-1650.* Gloucester, Mass.: Peter Smith, 1965.

Mills, Frederick V. "The Society in Scotland for Propagating Christian Knowledge in British North America, 1730-1775." *Church History* 63 (March 1994): 15-30.

Minkema, Kenneth P. "The Great Awakening Conversion: The Relation of Samuel Belcher." *William and Mary Quarterly,* 3d ser., 44 (January 1987): 121-26.

Morgan, David T. "A Most Unlikely Friendship: Benjamin Franklin and George Whitefield." *Historian* 47 (February 1985): 208-18.

Murphey, Murray G. "The Psychodynamics of Puritan Conversion." *American Quarterly* 31 (summer 1979): 135-47.

Murphy, Thomas. *The Presbytery of the Log College.* Philadelphia: Presbyterian Board of Publication, 1889.

Murray, Nicholas. *Notes, Historical and Biographical, Concerning Elizabeth Town, Its Eminent Men, Churches, and Ministers.* Elizabeth Town, N.J.: E. Sanderson, 1844.

Nevin, Alfred. *History of the Presbytery of Philadelphia.* Philadelphia: W. S. Fortescue, 1888.

Newman, Albert H. *A History of the Baptist Churches in the United States.* New York: Scribner, 1915.

Newman, Robert C. *Baptists and the American Tradition.* Des Plaines, Ill.: Regular Baptist Press, 1976.

Nicholas, Robert. *Presbyterianism in New York State.* Philadelphia: Westminster Press, 1963.

Nichols, James Hastings. "Colonial Presbyterianism Adopts Its Standards." *Journal of the Presbyterian Historical Society* 34 (March 1956): 53-66.

———. "The First Synod of New York, 1745-1758, and Its Permanent Effects." *Church History* 14 (December 1945): 239-55.

Nissenbaum, Stephen, ed. *The Great Awakening at Yale College.* Belmont, Calif.: Wadsworth, 1972.

Noll, Mark A., ed. *Religion and American Politics: From the Colonial Period to the 1980s.* New York: Oxford University Press, 1990.

Nybakken, Elizabeth I. "New Light on the Old Side: Irish Influences on Colonial Presbyterianism." *Journal of American History* 68 (March 1982): 813-32.

O'Brien, Susan. "A Transatlantic Community of Saints: The Great Awakening and the First Evangelical Network, 1735-1755." *American Historical Review* 91 (October 1986): 811-32.

Olson, Alison B. "The Founding of Princeton University: Religion and Politics in Eighteenth-Century New Jersey." *New Jersey History* 87 (autumn 1969): 133-50.

Olson, Allison G. "The Eighteenth-Century Empire: The London Dissenters' Lobbies and the American Colonies." *Journal of American Studies* 26 (April 1992): 41-58.

Osgood, Charles G. *Lights in Nassau Hall: A Book of the Bicentennial, Princeton, 1746-1946.* Princeton: Princeton University Press, 1951.

Packer, James I. "Revival." *Evangelical Quarterly* 52 (January 1980): 2-16.

Pahl, Jon. *Paradox Lost: Free Will and Political Liberty in American Culture, 1630-1760.* Baltimore: Johns Hopkins University Press, 1992.

Pears, Thomas Clinton Jr. "Colonial Education among Presbyterians." *Journal of the Presbyterian Historical Society* 30 (June, September 1952): 115-26; 165-74.

Pears, Thomas Clinton, and Guy Klett. "Documentary History of William Tennent and the Log College." *Journal of the Presbyterian Historical Society* 28 (March; June; September 1950): 37-64; 105-28; 167-204.

Pettit, Norman, "Prelude to Mission: Brainerd's Expulsion from Yale." *New England Quarterly* 59 (March 1986): 28-50.

Pomfret, John E. *Colonial New Jersey: A History.* New York: Scribner, 1973.

Pope, Robert G. *The Half-way Covenant: Church Membership in Puritan New England.* Princeton: Princeton University Press, 1969.

The Princeton Book. Boston: Houghton, Osgood, 1879.

Purvis, Thomas L. *Proprietors, Patronage, and Paper Money: Legislative Politics in New Jersey, 1703-1776.* New Brunswick, N.J.: Rutgers University Press, 1986.

Rutman, Darrett B. *Great Awakening: Events and Exegesis.* New York: Wiley, 1970.

Ryden, George H. "The Relation of the Newark Academy of Delaware to the Presbyterian Church and to Higher Education in the American Colonies." In *Delaware Notes, 9th series.* Newark: University of Delaware Press, 1935.

Schafer, Thomas A. "The Beginnings of Confessional Subscription in the Presbyterian Church." *McCormick Quarterly* 19 (January 1966): 102-19.

Schmidt, Leigh Eric. *Holy Fairs: Scottish Communions and American Revivals in the Early Modern Period.* Princeton: Princeton University Press, 1989.

_____. "A Second and Glorious Reformation: The New Light Extremism of Andrew Croswell." *William and Mary Quarterly,* 3d ser., 43 (April 1986): 214-44.

Schmotter, James W. "The Irony of Clerical Professionalism: New England's Congregational Ministers and the Great Awakening." *American Quarterly* 31 (summer 1979): 148-68.

Scott, Donald M. *From Office to Profession: The New England Ministry, 1750-1850.* Philadelphia: University of Pennsylvania Press, 1978.

Seavey, Ormond. *Becoming Benjamin Franklin: The Autobiography and the Life.* University Park: Pennsylvania State University Press, 1988.

Sewall, Richard B. *The Life of Emily Dickinson.* New York: Farrar, Straus and Giroux, 1987.

Silverman, Kenneth. *The Life and Times of Cotton Mather.* New York: Harper and Row, 1984.

Sloan, Douglas. *The Great Awakening and American Education: A Documentary History.* New York: Teachers College Press, 1973.

_____. *The Scottish Enlightenment and the American College Ideal.* New York: Teachers College Press, 1971.

Smith, Elwyn. "The Doctrine of Imputation and the Presbyterian Schism of 1837-1838." *Journal of the Presbyterian Historical Society* 38 (September 1960): 129-51.

Sprague, William B., ed. *Annals of the American Pulpit.* 9 vols. New York: Robert Carter, 1857-1869.

Stearns, Jonathan. *Historical Discourses Relative to the Presbyterian Church in Newark.* Newark, N.J.: Daily Advertiser, 1853.

Stein, Stephen J., ed. *Jonathan Edwards, Apocalyptic Writings.* New Haven: Yale University Press, 1977.

Stokes, Anson Phelps. *Memorials of Eminent Yale Men.* New Haven: Yale University Press, 1914.

Stout, Harry S. *The New England Soul: Preaching and Religious Culture in Colonial New England.* New York: Oxford University Press, 1986.

Stout, Harry S. and Peter Onuf. "James Davenport and the Great Awakening in New London." *Journal of American History* 71 (December 1983): 556-78.

Tanner, Edwin P. "The Province of New Jersey, 1664-1778." Ph.D. diss., Columbia University, 1908.

Tewksbury, Donald G. *The Founding of American Colleges and Universities before the Civil War: With Particular Reference to the Religious Influences Bearing upon the College Movement.* New York: Archon Books, 1965.

Thayer, Theodore. *As We Were: The Story of Old Elizabethtown.* Elizabeth: Grassmann, 1964.

Thompson, Robert Ellis. *A History of the Presbyterian Churches in the United States.* New York: Christian Literature, 1895.

Tolles, Frederick B. "Quietism vs. Enthusiasm: the Philadelphia Quakers and the Great Awakening." *Pennsylvania Magazine of History and Biography* 69 (January 1945): 26-49.

Torbet, Robert G. *A History of the Baptists.* Philadelphia: Judson Press, 1950.

Tracy, Joseph. *The Great Awakening: A History of the Revival of Religion in the Times of Edwards and Whitefield.* New York: Arno Press, 1969.

Trinterud, Leonard J. *The Forming of an American Tradition: A Re-examination of Colonial Presbyterianism.* Freeport, N.Y.: Books for Libraries Press, 1949.

____. "The New England Contributions to Colonial American Presbyterianism." *Church History* 17 (March 1948): 32-43.

Van Doren, Carl. *Benjamin Franklin.* Westport, Conn.: Greenwood Press, 1973.

Van Rensselaer, Cornelius. "Biographical Sketch of Jonathan Dickinson." *Presbyterian Magazine* 2 (March 1852): 124-29.

____. "Biographical Sketch of Aaron Burr." *Presbyterian Magazine* 3 (January 1853): 33-57.

Vedder, Henry C. *A History of the Baptists in the Middle States.* Philadelphia: American Baptist Publication Society, 1898.

Wacker, Peter O. *Land and People: A Cultural Geography of Preindustrial New Jersey: Origins and Settlement Patterns.* New Brunswick, N.J.: Rutgers University Press, 1975.

Wadhams, Calvin. *History of the College of New Jersey.* Princeton: J. T. Robinson, 1844.

Walker, Williston. *The Creeds and Platforms of Congregationalism.* Boston: Pilgrim Press, 1969.

Warch, Richard. *School of the Prophets: Yale College, 1701-1740.* New Haven: Yale University Press, 1973.

____. "The Shepherd's Tent: Education and Enthusiasm in the Great Awakening." *American Quarterly* 30 (summer 1978): 177-98.

Watson, Patricia A. *The Angelical Conjunction: The Preacher-Physician of Colonial New England.* Knoxville: University of Tennessee Press, 1991.

Webster, Richard. *A History of the Presbyterian Church in America, from Its Origin until the Year 1760.* Philadelphia: Joseph M. Wilson, 1857.

Wertenbaker, Thomas Jefferson. "The College of New Jersey and the Presbyterians." *Journal of the Presbyterian Historical Society* 36 (December 1958): 209-16.

_____. *The Founding of American Civilization: The Middle Colonies*. New York: Scribner, 1938.

_____. *Princeton, 1746-1896*. Princeton: Princeton University Press, 1946.

Westerkamp, Marilyn J. *Triumph of the Laity: Scots-Irish Piety and the Great Awakening, 1625-1760*. New York: Oxford University Press, 1988.

Whicher, George Frisbie. *This Was a Poet: A Critical Biography of Emily Dickinson*. Amherst: Amherst College Press, 1992.

White, Barrie. "Early Baptist Arguments for Religious Freedom: Their Overlooked Agenda." *Baptist History and Heritage* 24 (October 1989): 3-10.

White, B. R. *The English Baptists of the Seventeenth Century*. London: Baptist Historical Society, 1983.

_____. *The English Separatist Tradition*. New York: Oxford University Press, 1971.

Wickes, Stephen. *History of Medicine in New Jersey and of Its Medical Men, from the Settlement of the Province to A.D. 1800* (Newark: Martin R. Dennis, 1879).

Williams, John R. "The Strange Case of Dr. Franklin and Mr. Whitefield." *Pennsylvania Magazine of History and Biography* 102 (October 1978): 399-421.

Woolverton, John Frederick. *Colonial Anglicanism in North America*. Detroit: Wayne State University Press, 1984.

Wright, Esmond. *Franklin of Philadelphia*. Cambridge, Mass.: Belknap Press, 1986.

Youngs, J. William T. Jr. "Congregational Clericalism: New England Ordination before the Great Awakening." *William and Mary Quarterly*, 3d ser., 31 (July 1974): 481-90.

INDEX

Crosswell, Andrew, 158-60
Cutler, Timothy, 68

Davenport, James, 132-34, 138,
158, 160
Davies, Samuel, 65
Deism. *See* Jonathan Dickinson on
Deism
Dickinson, Abigail Blackman, 6-7
Dickinson, Emily, 192 n 2
Dickinson, Hezekiah, 6-7
Dickinson, Joanna Melyen, 6, 11, 149
Dickinson, Jonathan, life: diary, 2;
youth, 6-7; higher education, 7-
11; family, 11, 13, 149, 187,
208-9 n 29; ordination, 11-12;
Elizabeth Town ministry, 12-13,
121-23; source of Presbyterianism,
15-16; enters Philadelphia
Presbytery and Synod, 17-18;
debates the Baptists, 4, 18, 23-26,
155-57; participation in the
subscription controversy, 27, 29-
44, 190; role in the Samuel
Hemphill affair, 3, 52-55, 59-63;
debates the Anglicans, 3, 17, 65,
68, 70-77, 79-84, 149-55, 190;
considered for post at Philadelphia church, 43; responds to the
Enlightenment, 86-103; wel-
comes and defends the (moderate) Great Awakening, 4, 104-5,
108-23, 130-64, 190; trip to New
England, 134-36; proposed trip
to Virginia, 202 n 4; helps form
the New York Synod, 146-49;
becomes a founder and first
president of the College of New
Jersey, 172, 174, 176-86;
intervenes in the David Brainerd
affair, 170-71; involvement in the
New Jersey land riots, 175-76;
death, 183, 187-88
–Ideas: on freedom of conscience

(within the Presbyterian Church),
27-28, 32-33, 36-38, 43-44, 53,
59-60, 63; on religious freedom
(and the state), 63, 65, 71, 77-80,
83-84; on Deism, 54-55, 87-88,
93, 95, 97, 100; on Arminianism,
100, 105, 116, 140, 158; on
Antinomianism, 96, 101, 140-43,
158-60, 164; on the conversation
experience (justification, sanctification, assurance, and regeneration), 98-103, 114-21, 139-41,
143, 149-51, 153-54, 160-62.
–Works: *Observations on that
Terrible Disease Vulgarly Called the
Throat Distemper*, 9; *Remarks
upon Mr. Gale's Reflections on Mr.
Wall's History of Infant Baptism*,
18, 23; *A Sermon Preached at the
Opening of the Synod at Philadelphia, September 19, 1722*, 31-32;
*Remarks upon . . .. An Overture
Presented to the Reverend Synod . . .
in 1728*, 36; *A Vindication of the
. . . Synod*, 52-55; *Remarks upon
. . . A Letter to a Friend in the
Country*, 59-60; [Obadiah
Jenkins] *Remarks upon the Defense
of . . . Hemphill's Observations*, 61;
*A Defense of Presbyterian Ordina-
tion*, 70-73; *Remarks upon . . . the
Defense of . . . A Modest Proof*, 74-
75; *The Scripture Bishop*, 76-77;
The Scripture Bishop Vindicated,
79-80; *The Vanity of Human
Institutions*, 81-82; *A Defense of . . .
the Vanity of Human Institutions*,
205 n 39; *The Reasonableness of
Nonconformity*, 205 n 39; *A Brief
Discourse upon . . . the Gospel
Ministry*, 205 n 39; *The Reason-
ableness of Christianity*, 88-95;
Familiar Letters to a Gentleman,
95-103; *The Danger of Schisms*,